I0762425

WEIRD BUILDINGS

***Hoxton Mini Press** is a small independent publisher based in east London. We are committed to making beautiful but affordable books that don't screw up the planet. We offset all our printing, and we hope that the trees we do use will continue their life as books that you'll pass on to your grandchildren.*

(Front cover) Cleveland Clinic Lou Ruvo Center for Brain Health, Las Vegas, USA. *Architect: Frank Gehry, 2010*

WEIRD BUILDINGS

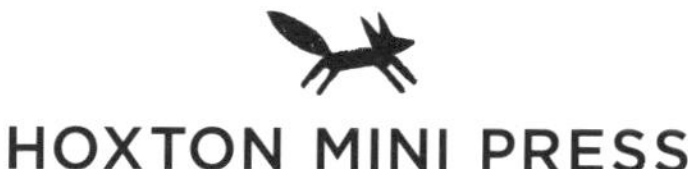

HOXTON MINI PRESS

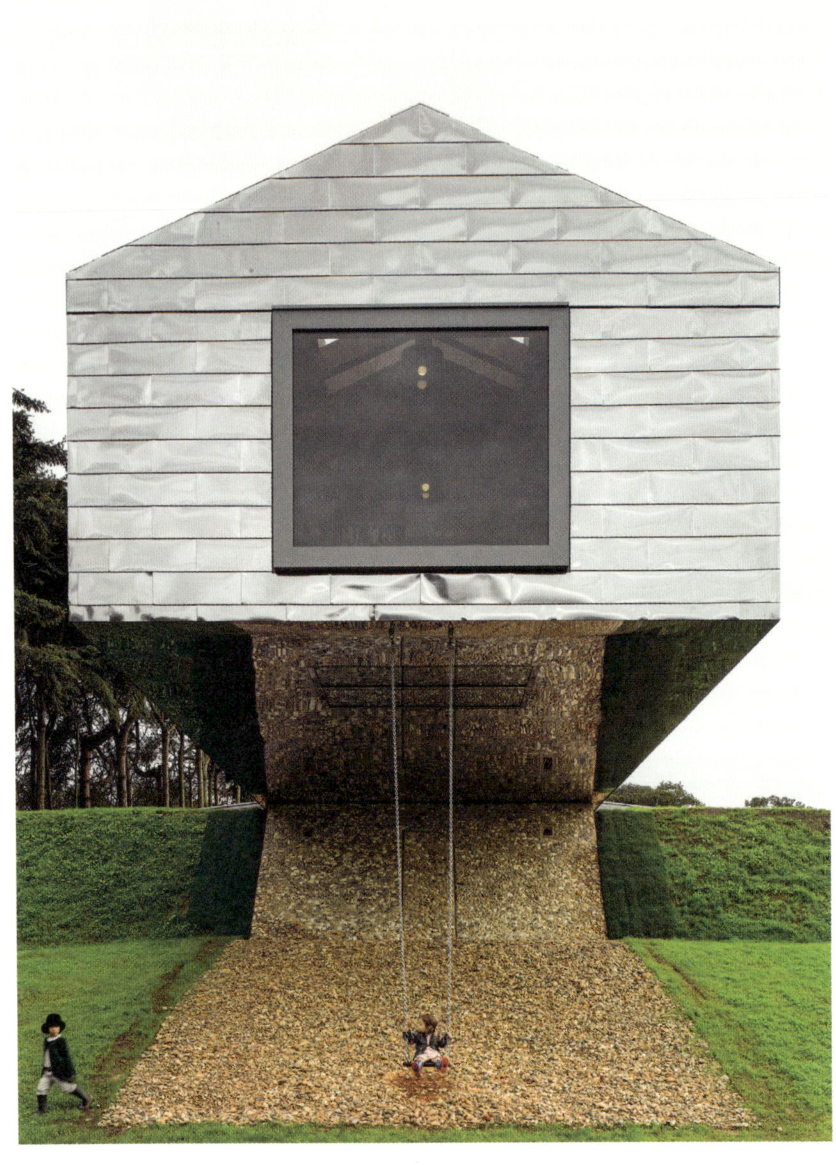

(Above) The Balancing Barn, Suffolk, England, p.24
(Opposite) Inntel Hotel, Zaandam, Netherlands, p.14

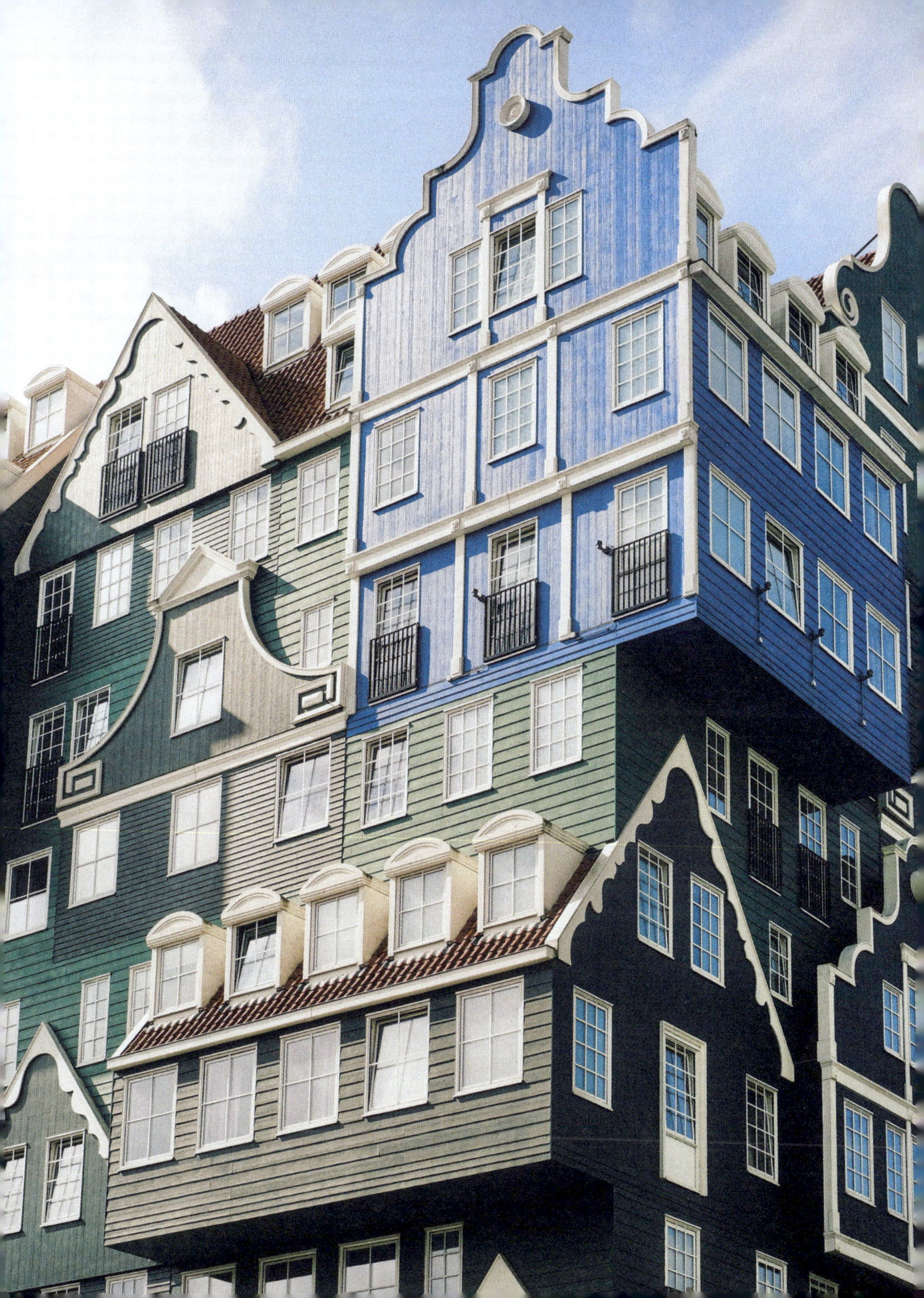

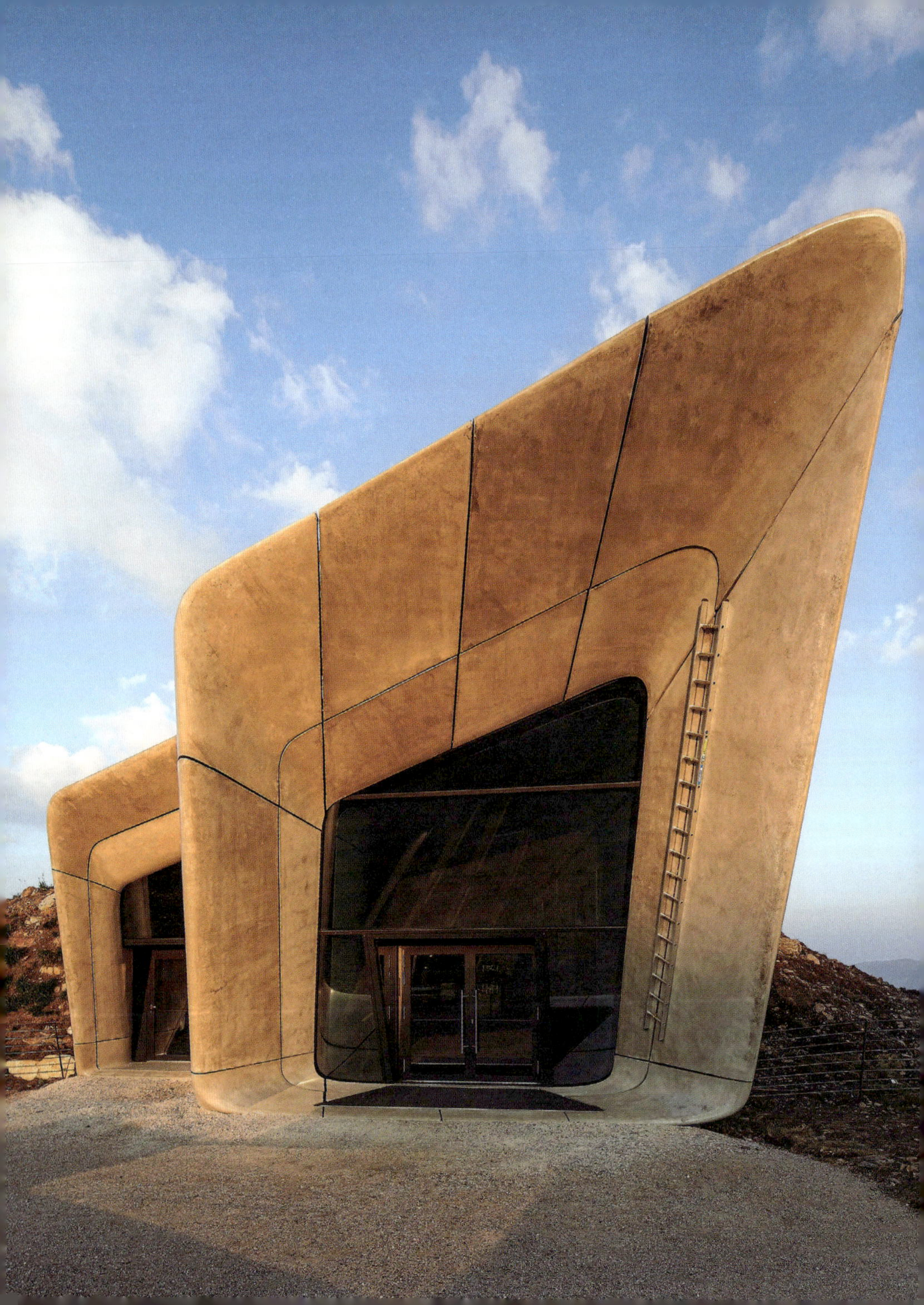

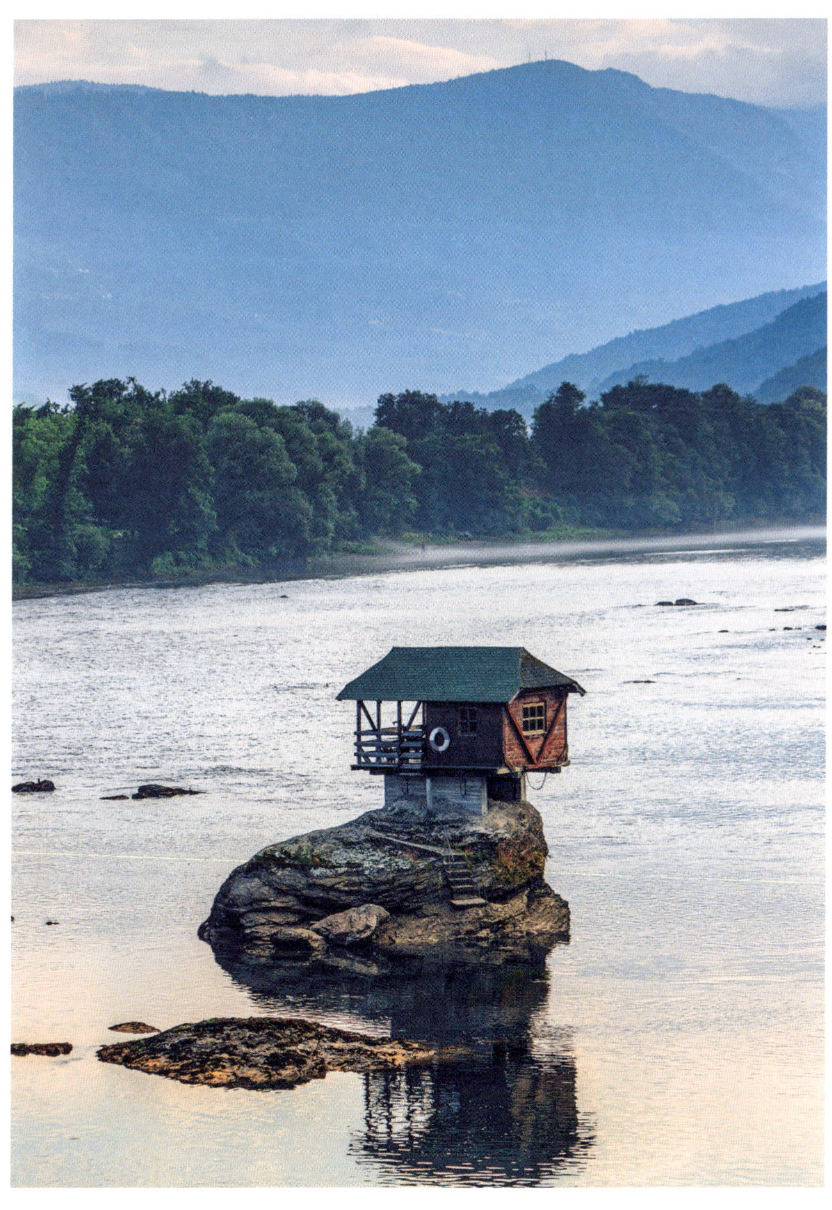

(Above) Drina River House, Bajina Bašta, Serbia, p.48
(Opposite) Messner Mountain Museum Corones, Italy, p.228

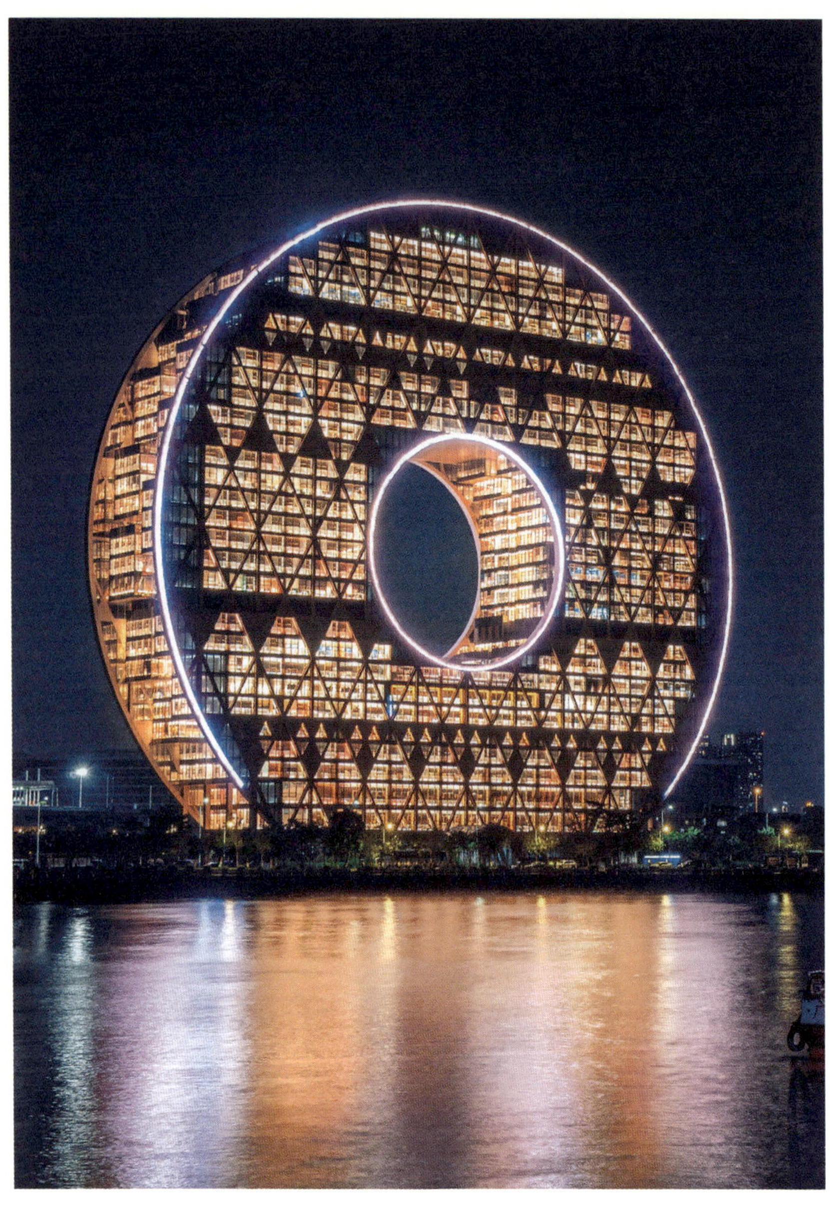

(Above) Guangzhou Circle, Guangzhou, China, p.190
(Opposite) The Twist, Jevnaker, Norway, p.186

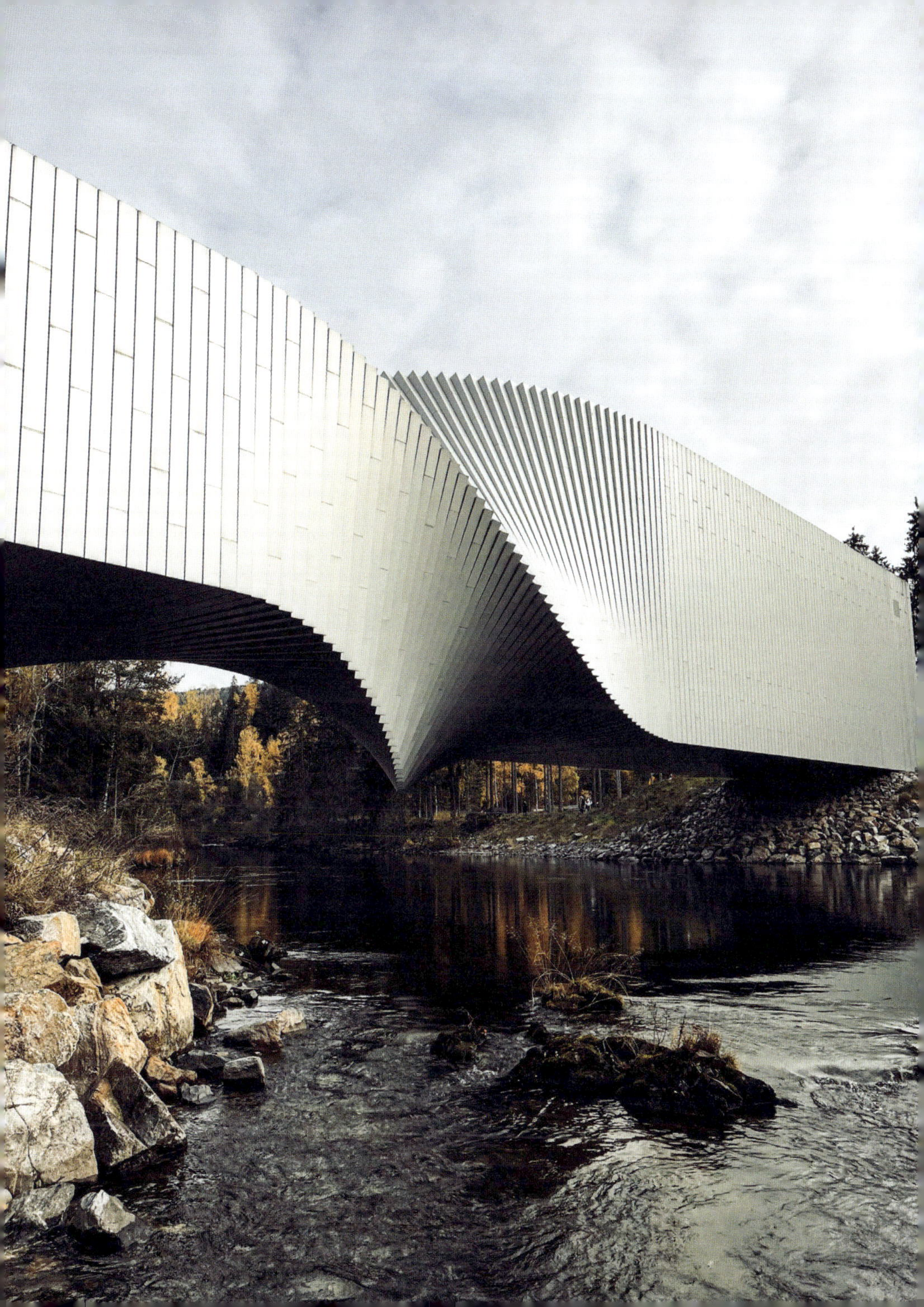

WEIRD IS WONDERFUL

IMOGEN FORTES

'Weirdness' has always offered a peculiar fascination. As humans, we are innately drawn to the offbeat, the unusual and the things that don't quite fit. Weirdness catches our eye; it invites curiosity and lingers in the imagination long after the ordinary has faded. And in a world increasingly shaped by automation and engineered for speed, simplicity and sameness – a world in which algorithms serve us what we already like, and cities grow ever more homogenous – weird offers friction. It makes us pause, ask questions and see things from another perspective. It's a crack in the surface, reminding us that difference is not only valuable but vital to the human experience.

This book is a celebration of weirdness as it appears in one very particular and public form: architecture. So, what makes a building 'weird'? Is it a matter of shape, scale or surprise? Is it the way it challenges gravity, dares to confront our expectations or simply refuses to follow accepted norms and rules?

At first glance, many of the buildings in this book might seem like architectural jokes: oversized sculptures or the results of fanciful experimentation. And certainly, some were conceived purely to stop onlookers in their tracks – as a means of promoting a business or to make a political or social point, while some serve no practical purpose at all beyond delighting their creators, owners or those who encounter them. But behind these unusual facades often lies a deeper ambition. There are structures that aren't simply trying to stand out – they're asking us to reimagine what buildings can be. Some question how we occupy spaces and how space, in turn, shapes our lives. Others invite us to reconsider our relationship with the built environment, asking: what if a museum wasn't simply a white box? Why shouldn't a palace resemble a cluster of pink bubbles? What if a library were designed to encourage interaction and exchange? What if architecture could be both functional and fantastical? And how can buildings further humanitarian progress by helping to halt the decline of the natural environment and better our world for the future?

Architects have long sought to push boundaries – to bend, twist and warp their creations into forms that defy the ordinary. The buildings featured in this book ignore the conventional architectural script; many rebel against the rigid logic of right angles, rectangles and the restrained. Instead, they stretch and curve, bulge and tilt. Many feel sculptural and more like living organic organisms than static objects, and are as much about form as function.

Over the past century, some of the world's most celebrated architects have embraced the weird not as a gimmick but as a form of innovation. Frank Gehry's iconoclastic body of work, which includes the dynamic Dancing House in Prague (p.156) and his trailblazing Guggenheim Museum in Bilbao (p.86), tore up the rulebook, replacing grids and order with curves, chaos and movement. Zaha Hadid pushed fluidity to its limits, designing buildings that seem to melt and flow. Before them, Antoni Gaudí, sculpted Barcelona with whimsical, nature-inspired forms. And today, the Danish collective BIG (Bjarke Ingels Group) carries that spirit forward with sustainable, resourceful designs that embody its desire to promote 'hedonistic sustainability' – buildings that espouse boldness and prioritise fun and enjoyment but also offer pragmatism and a means of addressing social concerns, such as the CopenHill power plant (p.208), which is topped with a ski slope.

These architects demonstrate that when we let go of rigid constraints, we don't descend into disorder; we create new forms of beauty. Beauty that is dynamic, democratic and delightfully unexpected.

In the pages that follow, you'll find everything from homes to religious buildings, libraries and museums to apartment blocks and artworks – all daring to be different. Some are famous, others obscure, but each one challenges the limits of design and invites us to rethink the relationship between people and the shared spaces they occupy.

These buildings were conjured by architects willing to experiment, to have fun and to provoke. They reject the trend towards uniformity and mass production and speak instead to individuality, eccentricity and imagination. They remind us that architecture is not just about shelter or utility; it's about expression, emotion and enjoyment. In an age when so much of our world feels standardised and streamlined, weird buildings remind us of the joy of divergence. And perhaps most importantly, they encourage us to approach the everyday with curiosity and a willingness to live just a little more playfully.

A House for Essex

Wrabness, England
Architect: Charles Holland and artist Grayson Perry, 2015

This kitsch fairytale structure is a collaboration between two homegrown Essex boys wanting to celebrate their county. It's an eccentric fusion of art and architecture that references English Baroque style, with its gold roof and extravagant sculptures, and the folk tradition of wayside pilgrimage chapels.

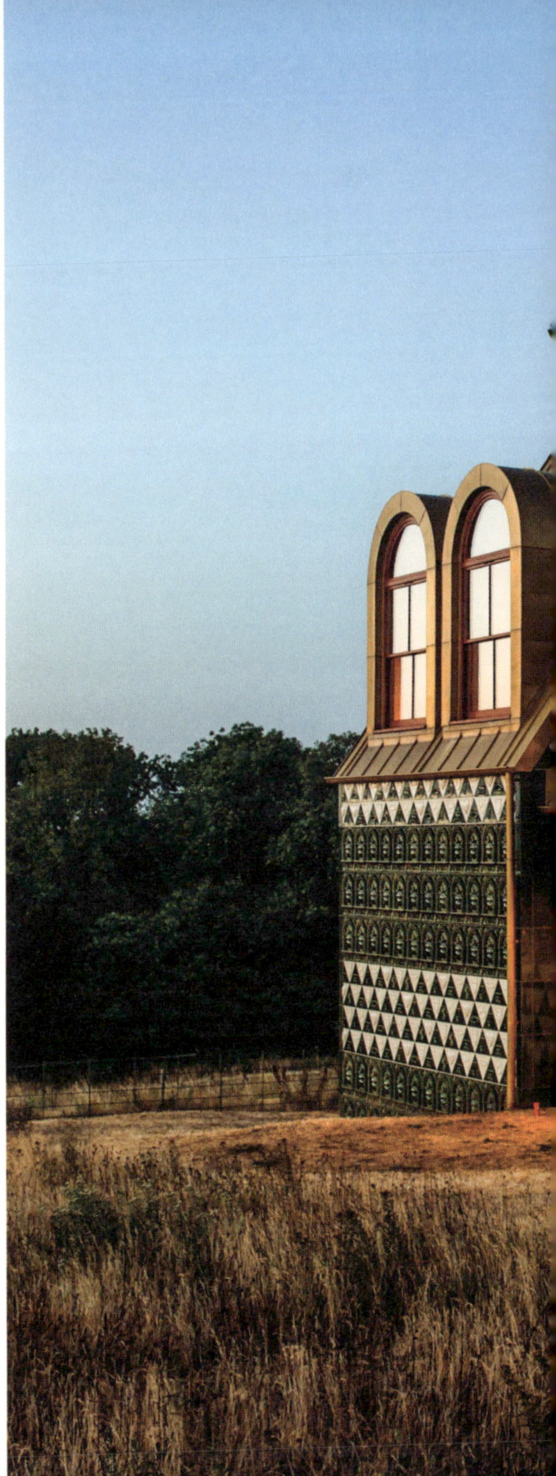

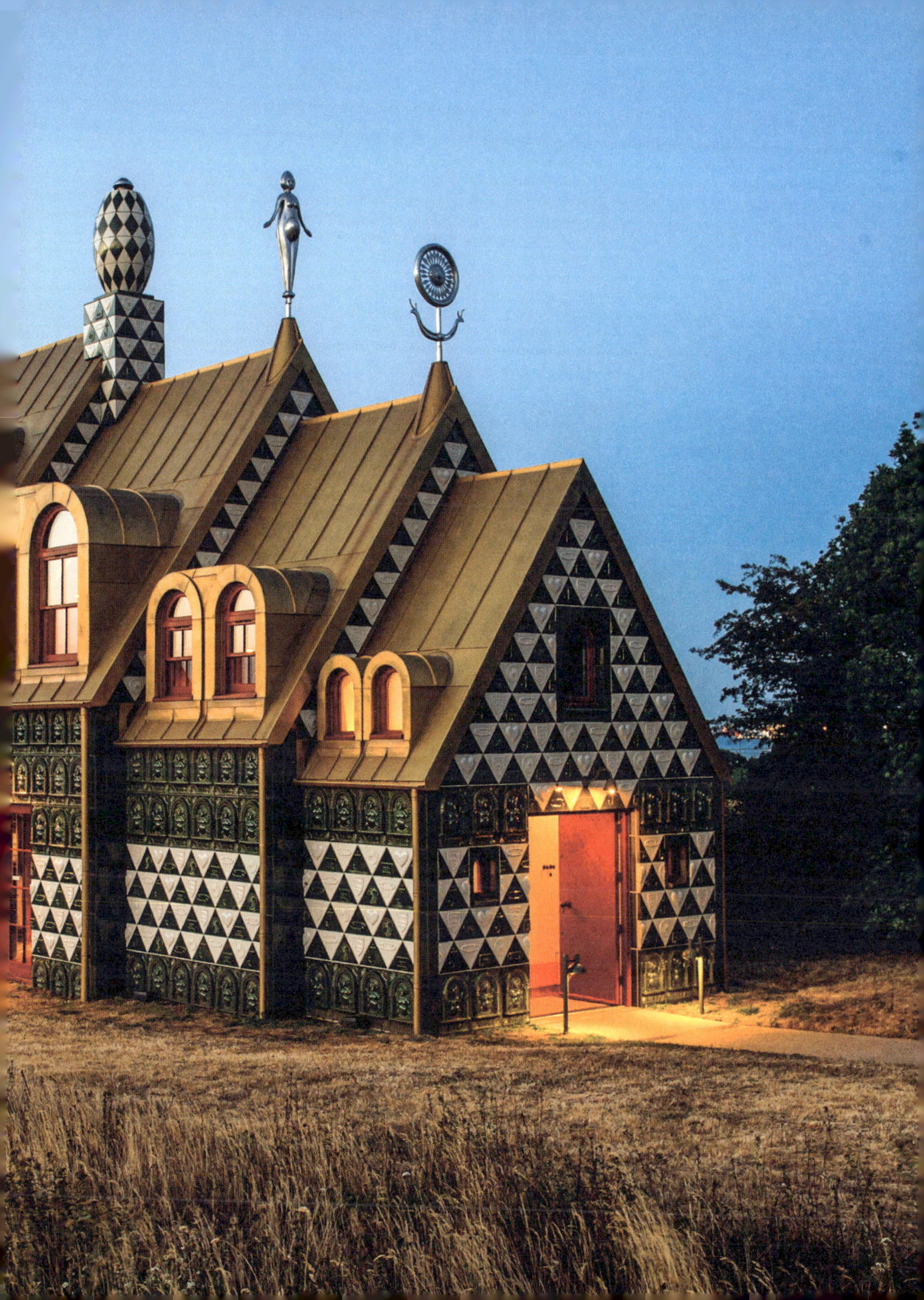

Inntel Hotel
Zaandam, Netherlands
Architect: WAM Architecten, 2010

This madcap 12-storey hotel looks like an exploded fairy tale. It stacks interpretations of the traditional wooden houses from the Zaan region, with styles ranging from a notary's dwelling to workers' cottages. The blue house was inspired by a work painted by Claude Monet during a visit to Zaandam.

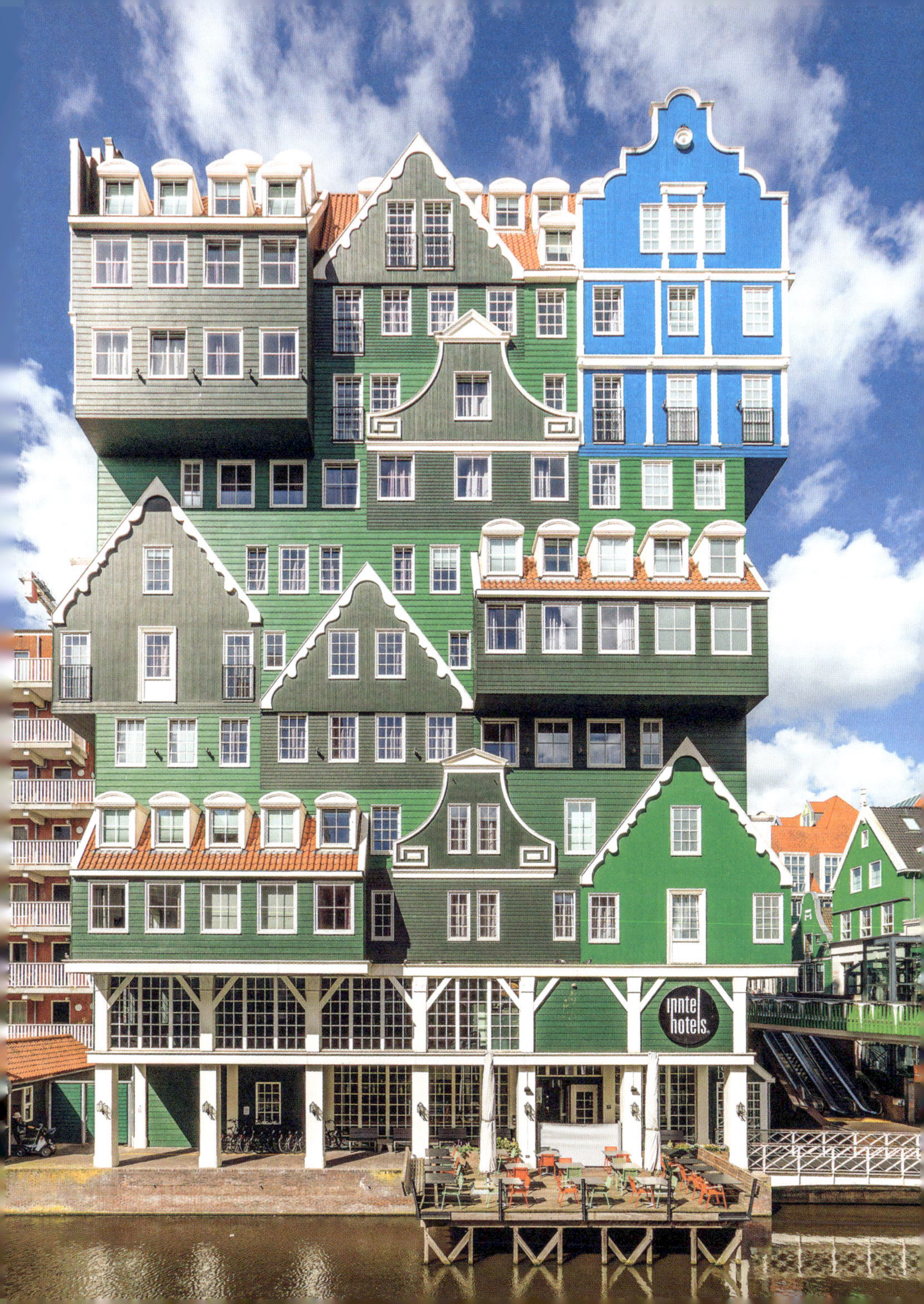
inntel
hotels

Casa do Penedo
Fafe, Portugal
1974

Squished between four enormous boulders, from which it takes its name (*do penedo* means 'of stone'), this house was built by a local family as a rural retreat. Blending architecture and nature, it was designed to immerse its occupants in their surroundings. Now only used by its owners for holidays, a stream of curious visitors arrives throughout the year for guided tours.

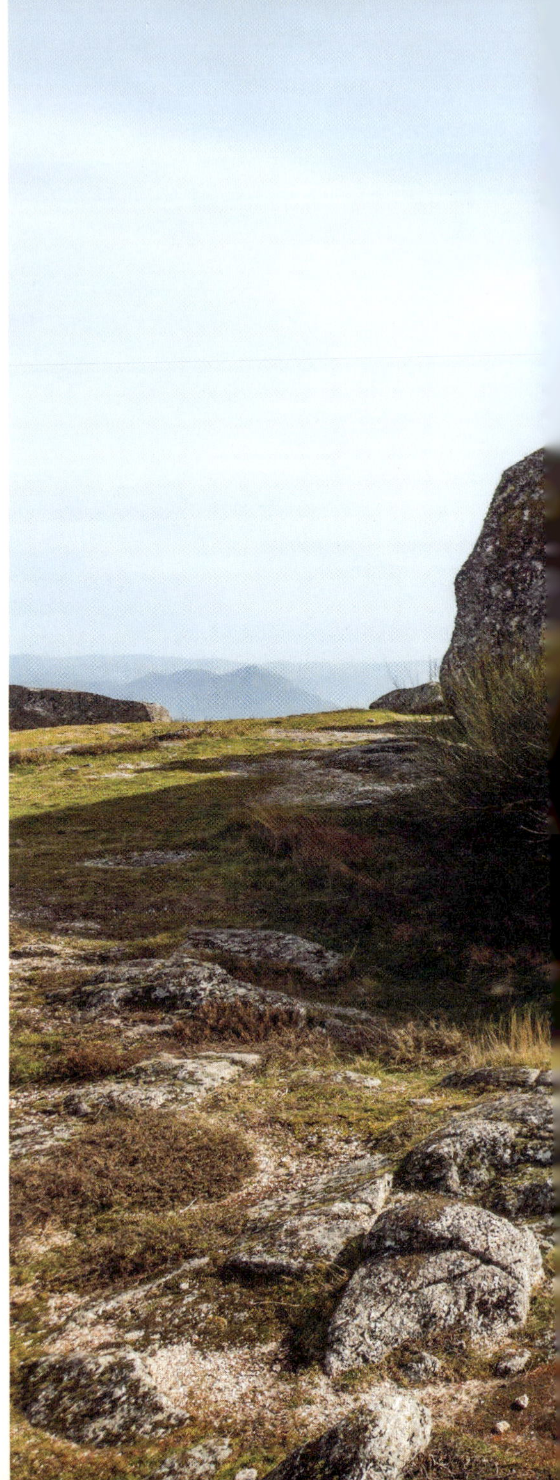

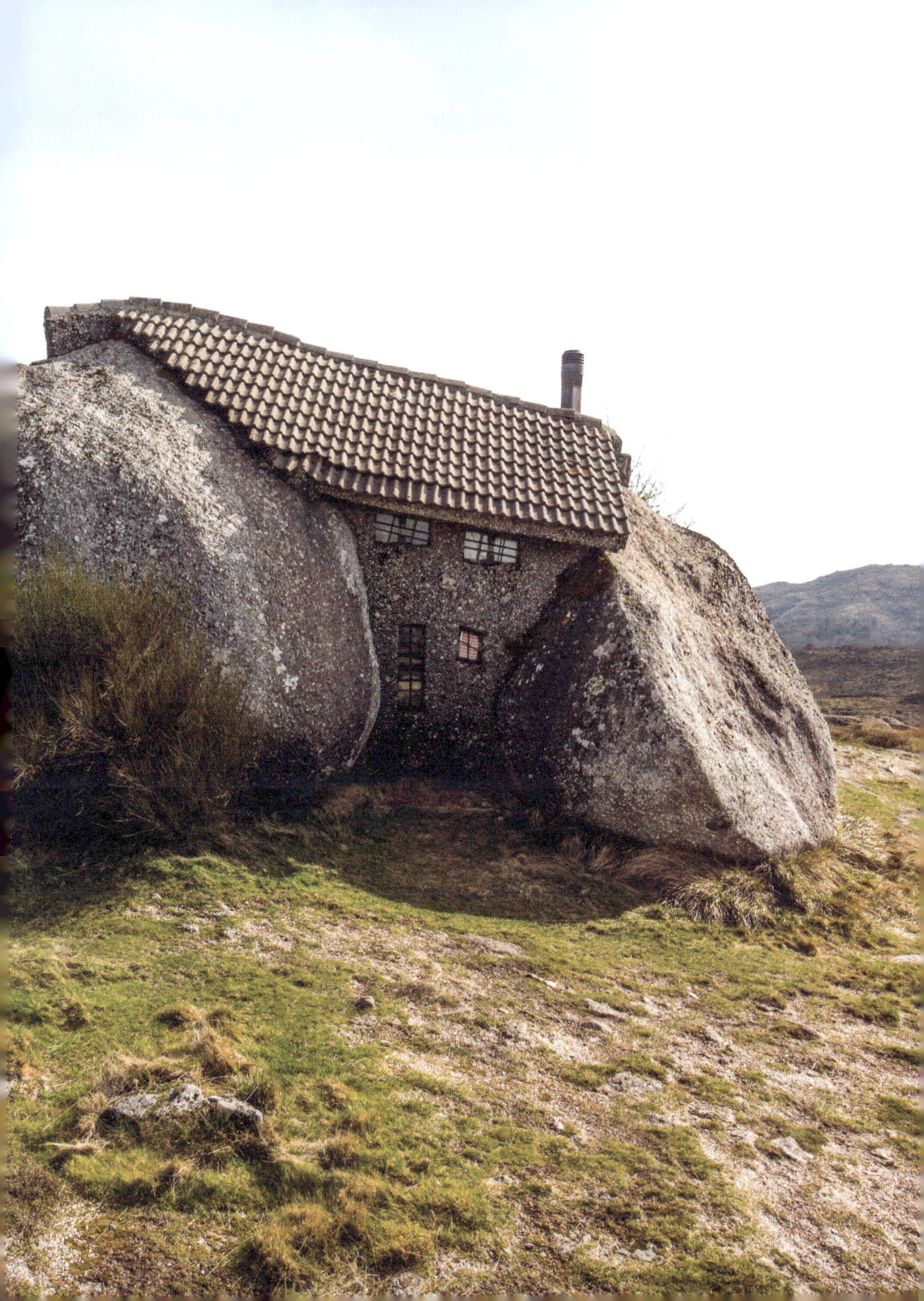

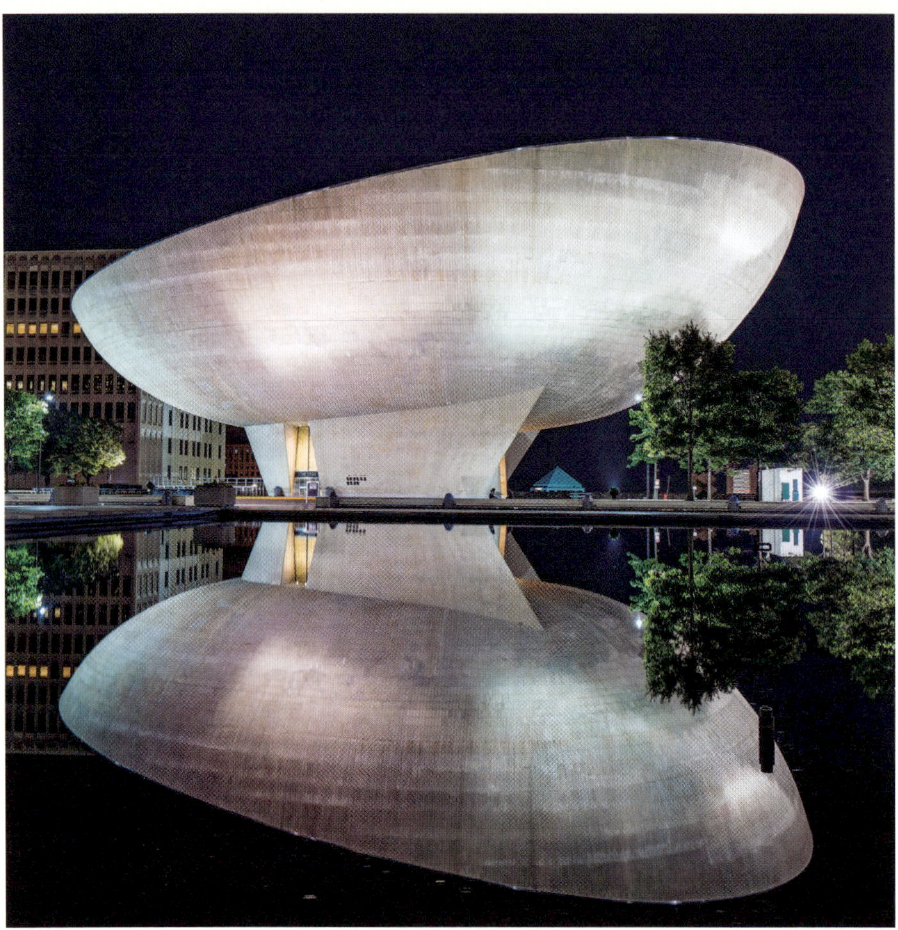

The Egg
Albany, New York, USA
Architect: Harrison & Abramovitz, 1978

Taking 12 years to build, this performing arts centre is a feat of Brutalist architecture that scrambles expectations with its avant-garde design and structural ingenuity. From the outside, the reinforced concrete shell's distinctive form appears precariously balanced on top of its pedestal, while the interior features an acoustically state-of-the-art auditorium.

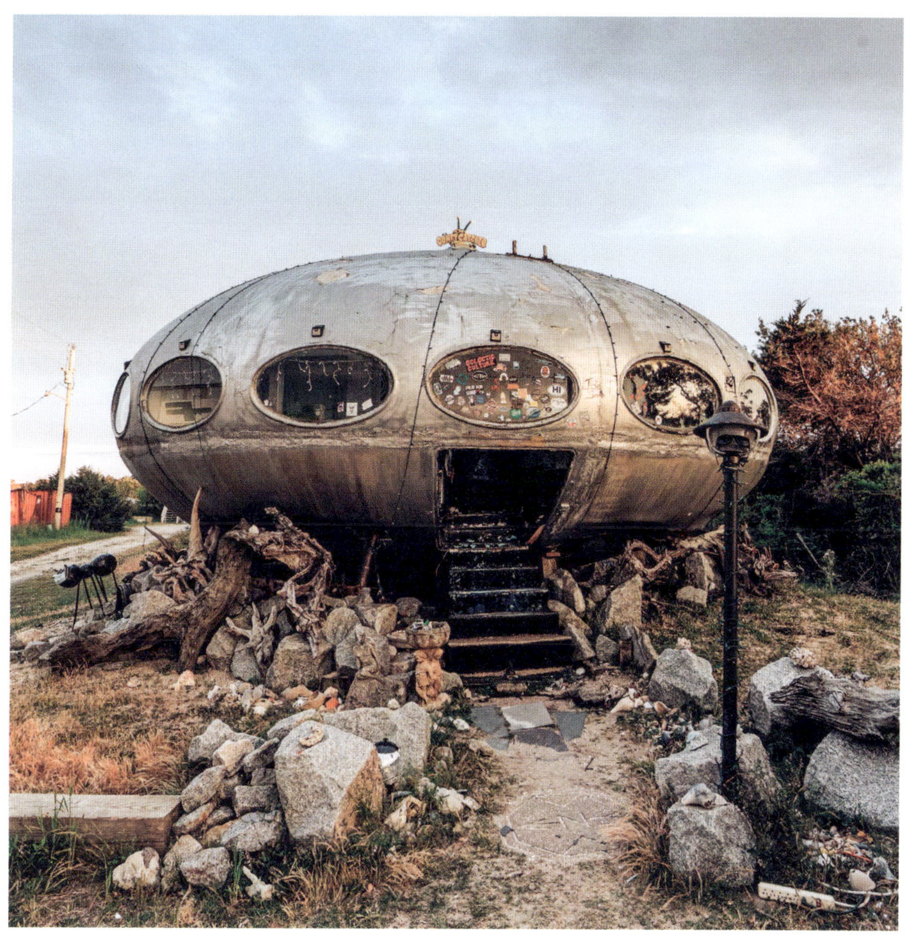

Futuro House
68 known Futuro houses worldwide
Architect: Matti Suuronen, 1968

Originally designed as a portable ski chalet, Futuro houses were later marketed as prefabricated plastic homes that could be constructed on any terrain. Despite making headlines, they never achieved commercial success, with only around 100 built in the late 1960s to mid-70s. In the 1990s, their space-age design sparked renewed interest among the arts community.

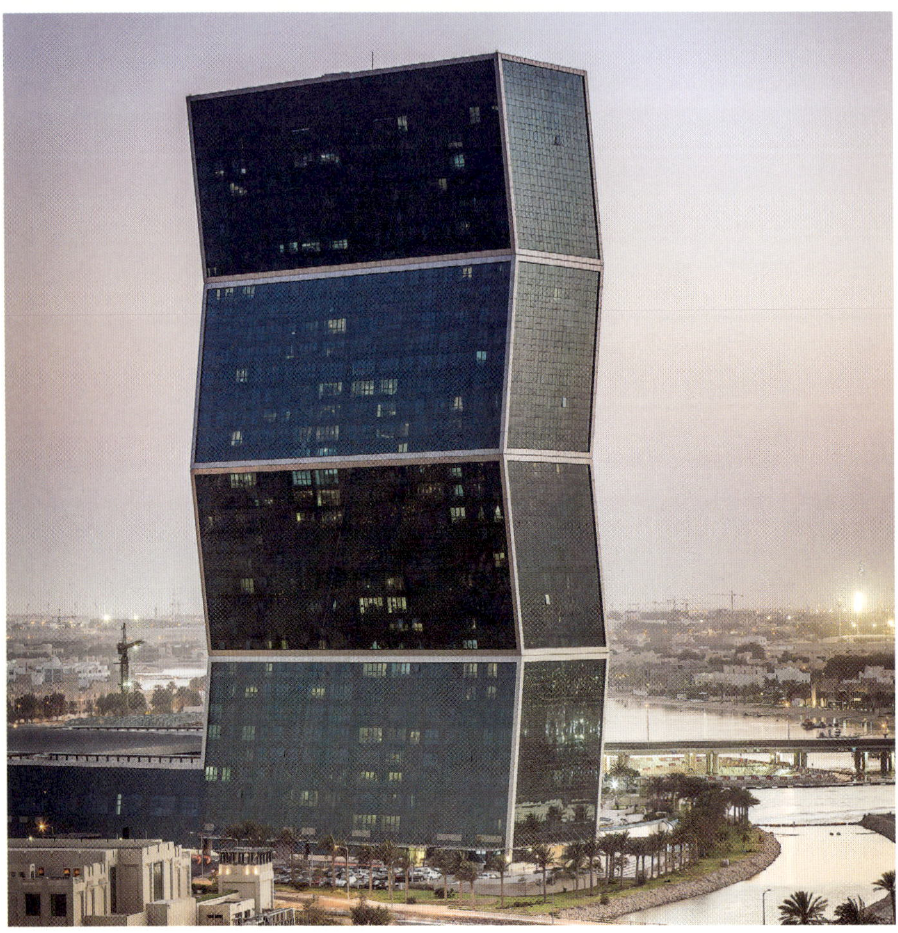

Zig Zag Towers
Doha, Qatar
Architect: MZ & Partners, 2009

This tower, and its neighbouring twin, leans in defiance of gravity, its zigzagging form mirroring the waves in the Gulf below. Bold and rock-solid, despite looking as though they may topple at any moment, the 143-metre-high blocks house upscale apartments and transform the skyline into a futuristic dreamscape.

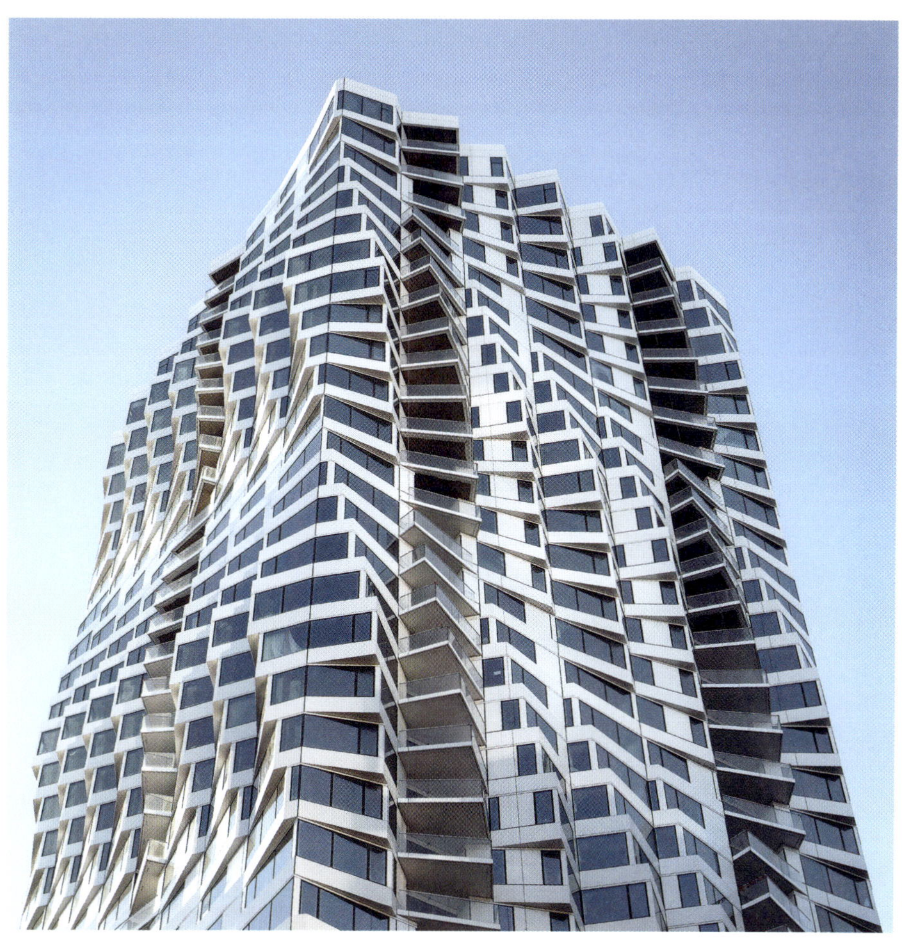

MIRA
San Francisco, California, USA
Architect: Studio Gang, 2020

The fanned bay windows of this residential block's twisting facade pay homage to San Francisco's historic architecture and love of standout features, reinterpreting them within a futuristic high-rise context. The 120-metre-tall building provides a new angle on living in the city, with almost every residence offering expansive 180° views.

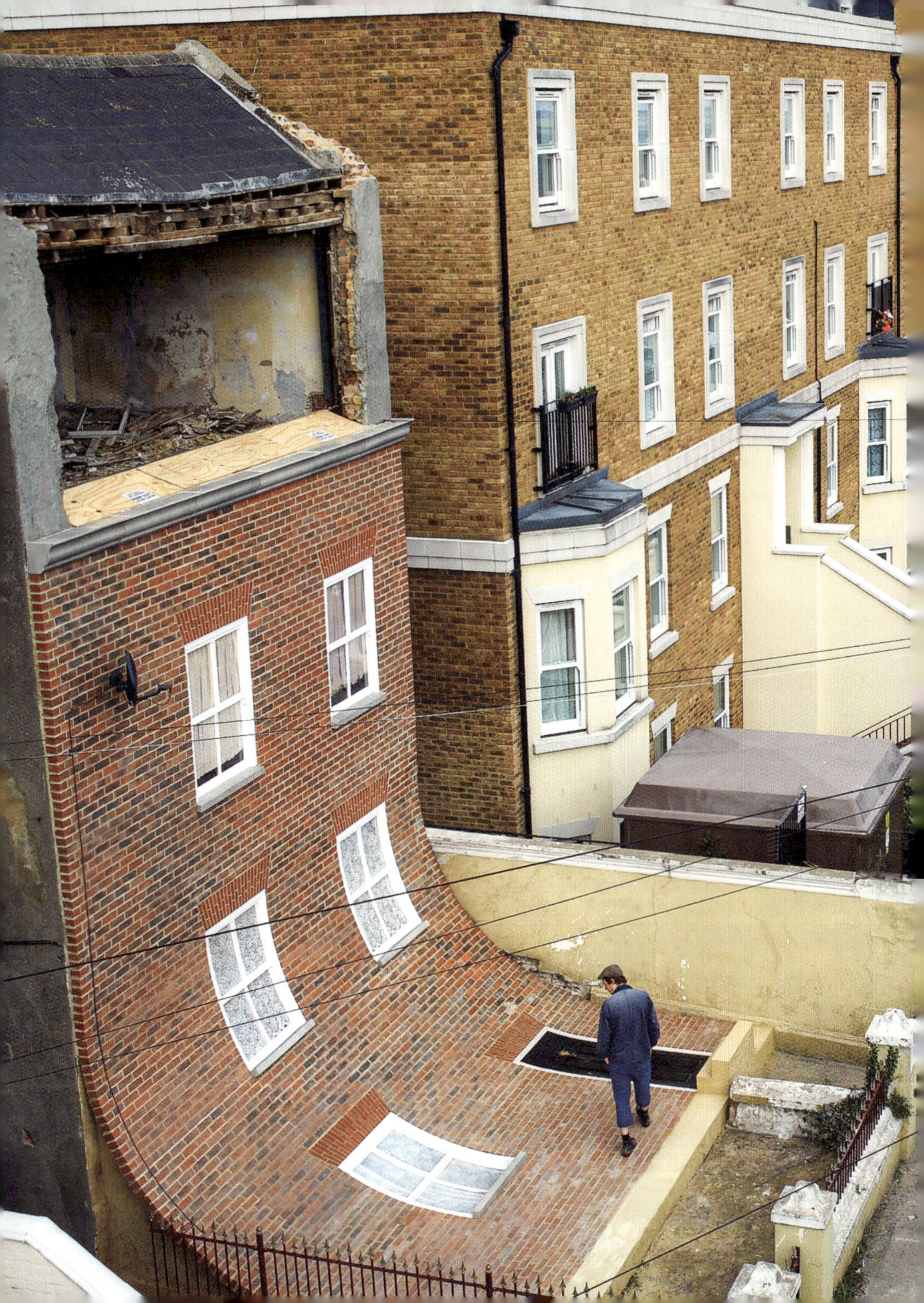

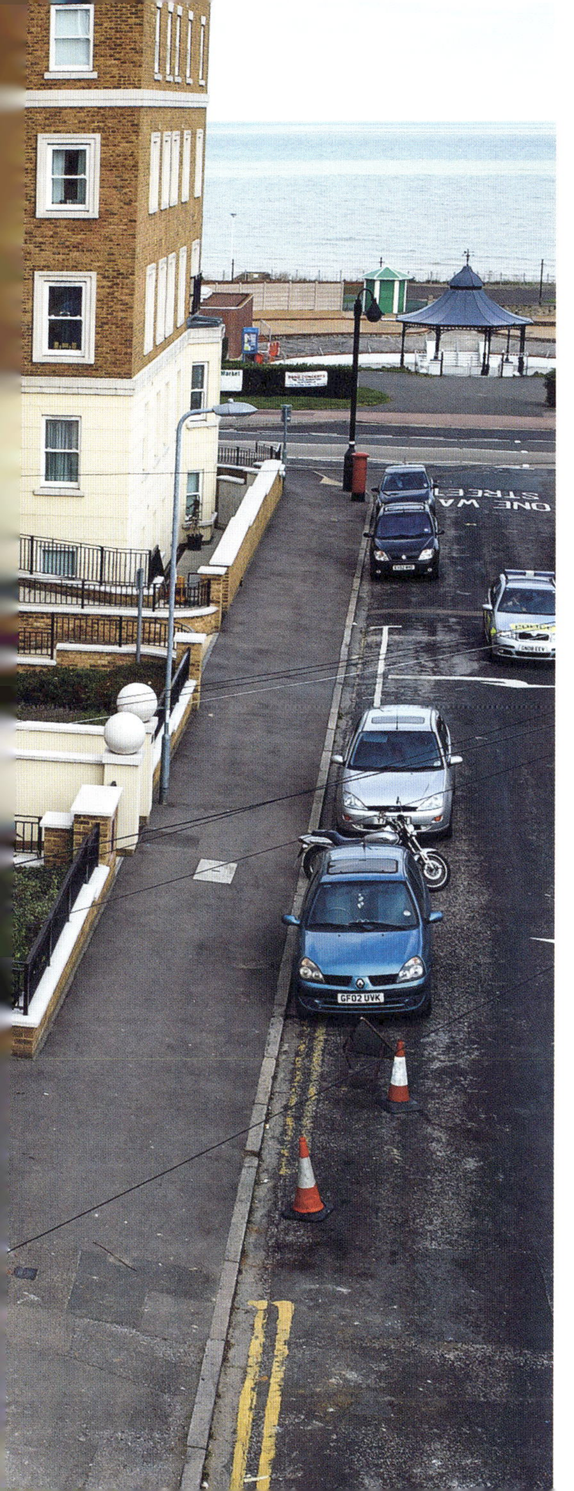

From the Knees of my Nose to the Belly of my Toes
Margate, England
Artist: Alex Chinneck, 2013

The artist removed the facade of this house, left derelict for 11 years, and replaced it with a curving frontage to create the illusion that the fascia is sliding into the street. A weird but wonderful expression of his humour, it also spoke of urban decay and the gaping social divisions within the popular seaside town.

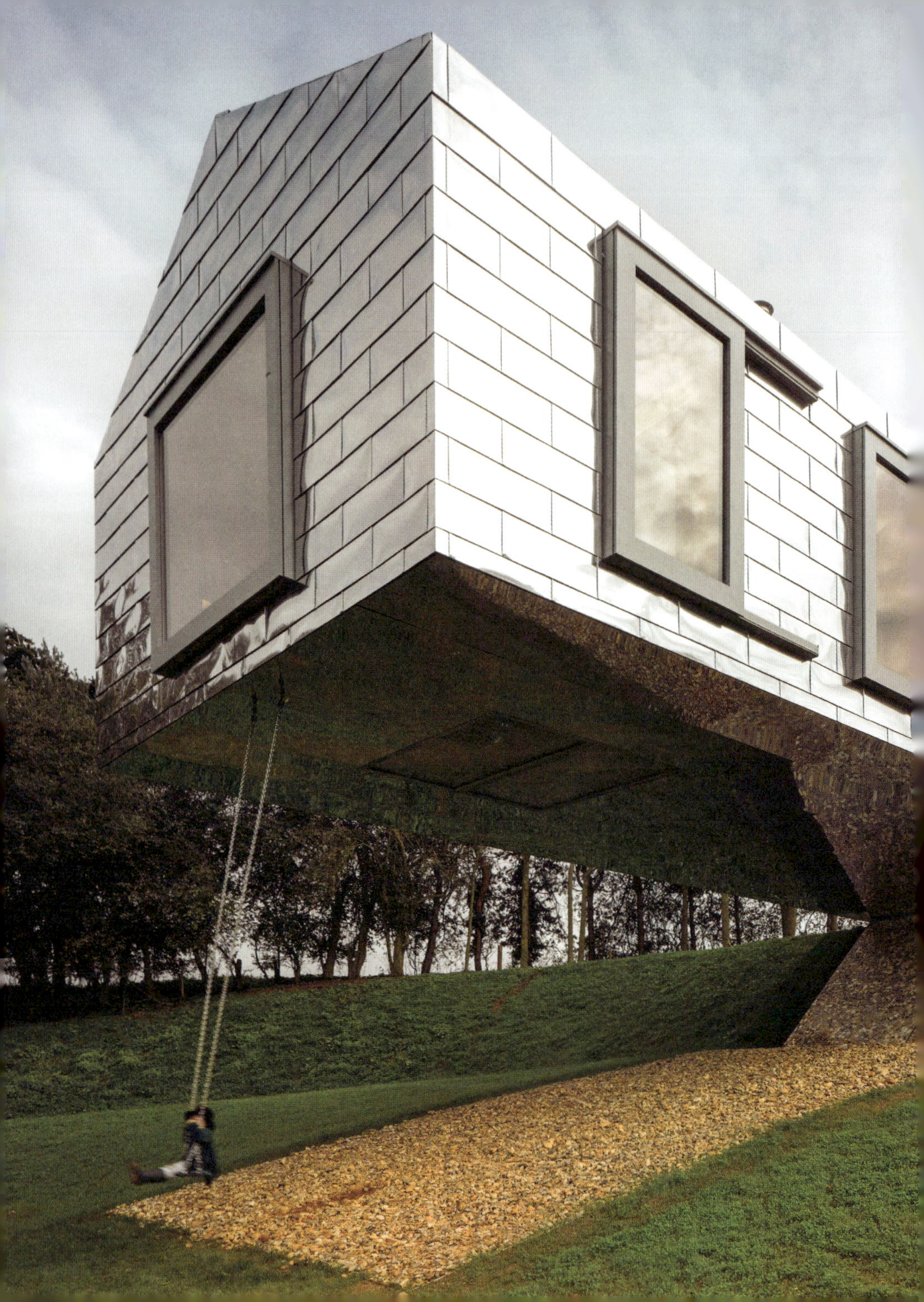

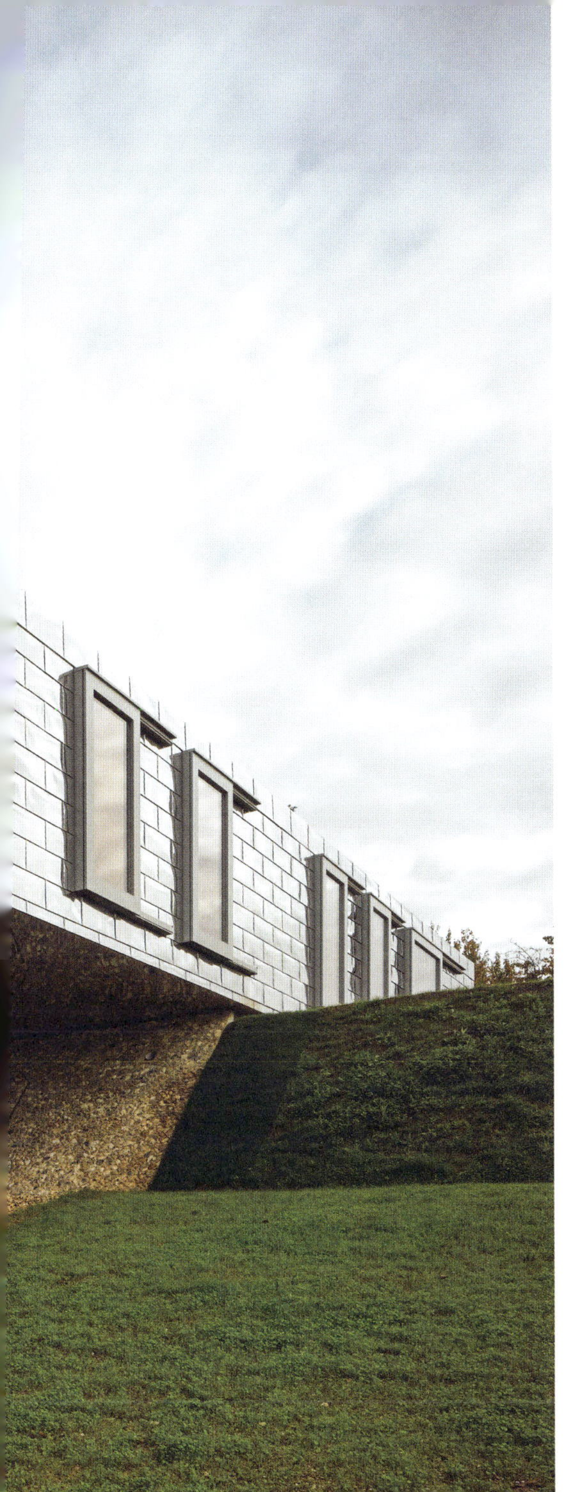

The Balancing Barn
Suffolk, England
Architect: MVRDV, 2010

Part house, part optical illusion, this seesaw structure is poised dramatically above the countryside. Modelled on the old farm buildings once prevalent in this rural region, reflective steel tiles have replaced traditional weatherboarding. The adventurous Dutch architects designed the barn to encourage people to re-evaluate their relationship with nature and engage with modern architecture.

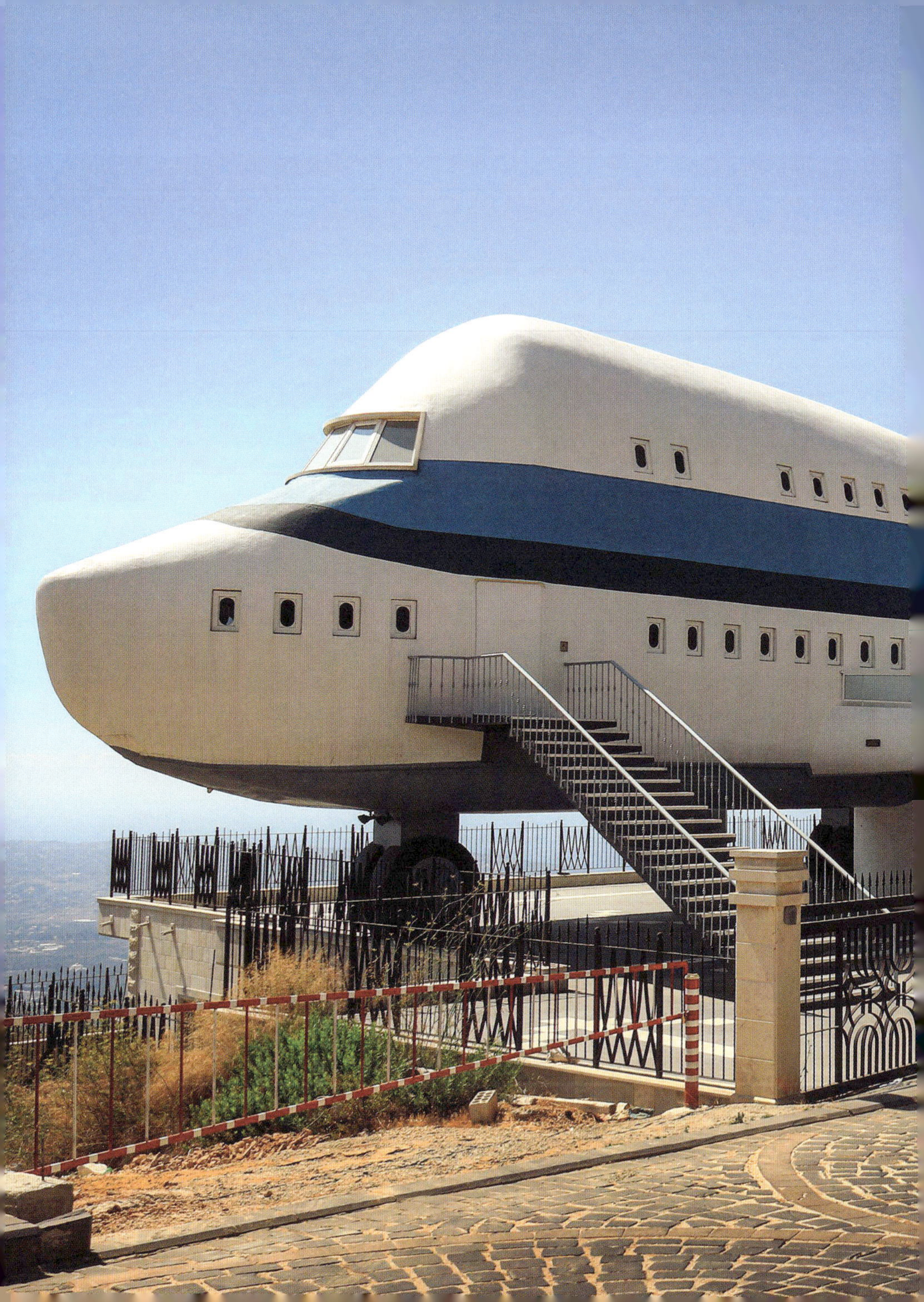

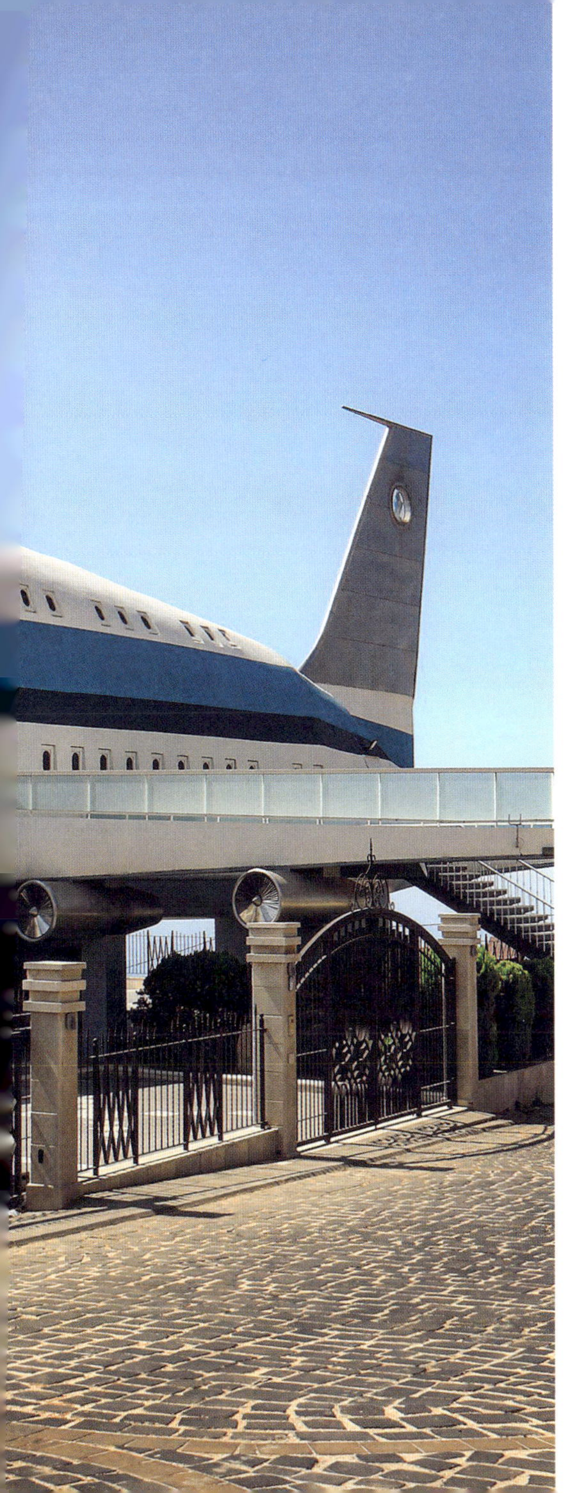

The Airplane House

Miziara, Lebanon

Architect: Michael Suleiman, 1975

The village of Miziara boasts a collection of creative and characterful residences, but this is one of its most flamboyant and iconic. A local businessman built this detailed copy of an Airbus A380, and the two-storey home includes 30 portholes on each side, a short nose cone and balconies on both wings.

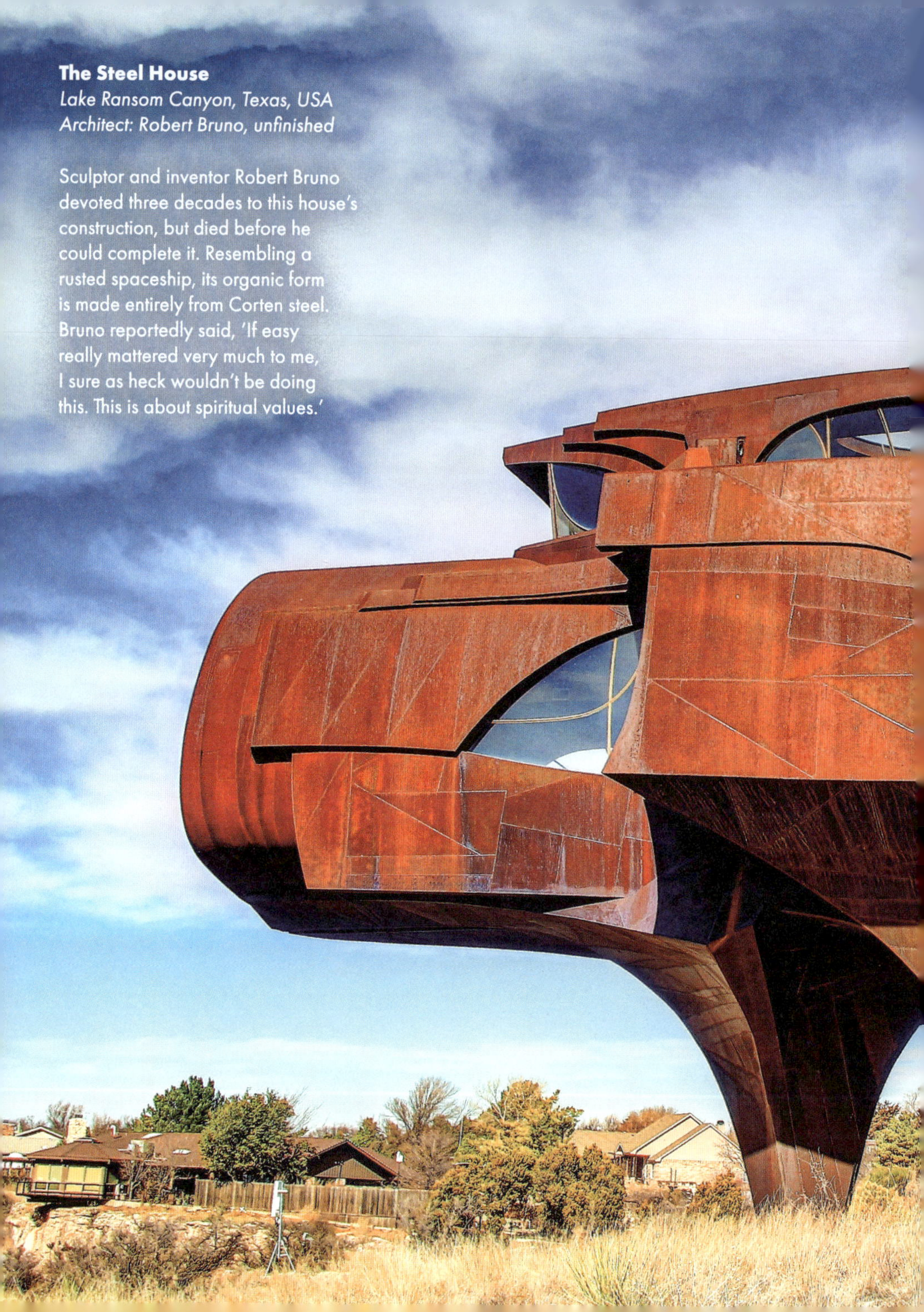

The Steel House
Lake Ransom Canyon, Texas, USA
Architect: Robert Bruno, unfinished

Sculptor and inventor Robert Bruno devoted three decades to this house's construction, but died before he could complete it. Resembling a rusted spaceship, its organic form is made entirely from Corten steel. Bruno reportedly said, 'If easy really mattered very much to me, I sure as heck wouldn't be doing this. This is about spiritual values.'

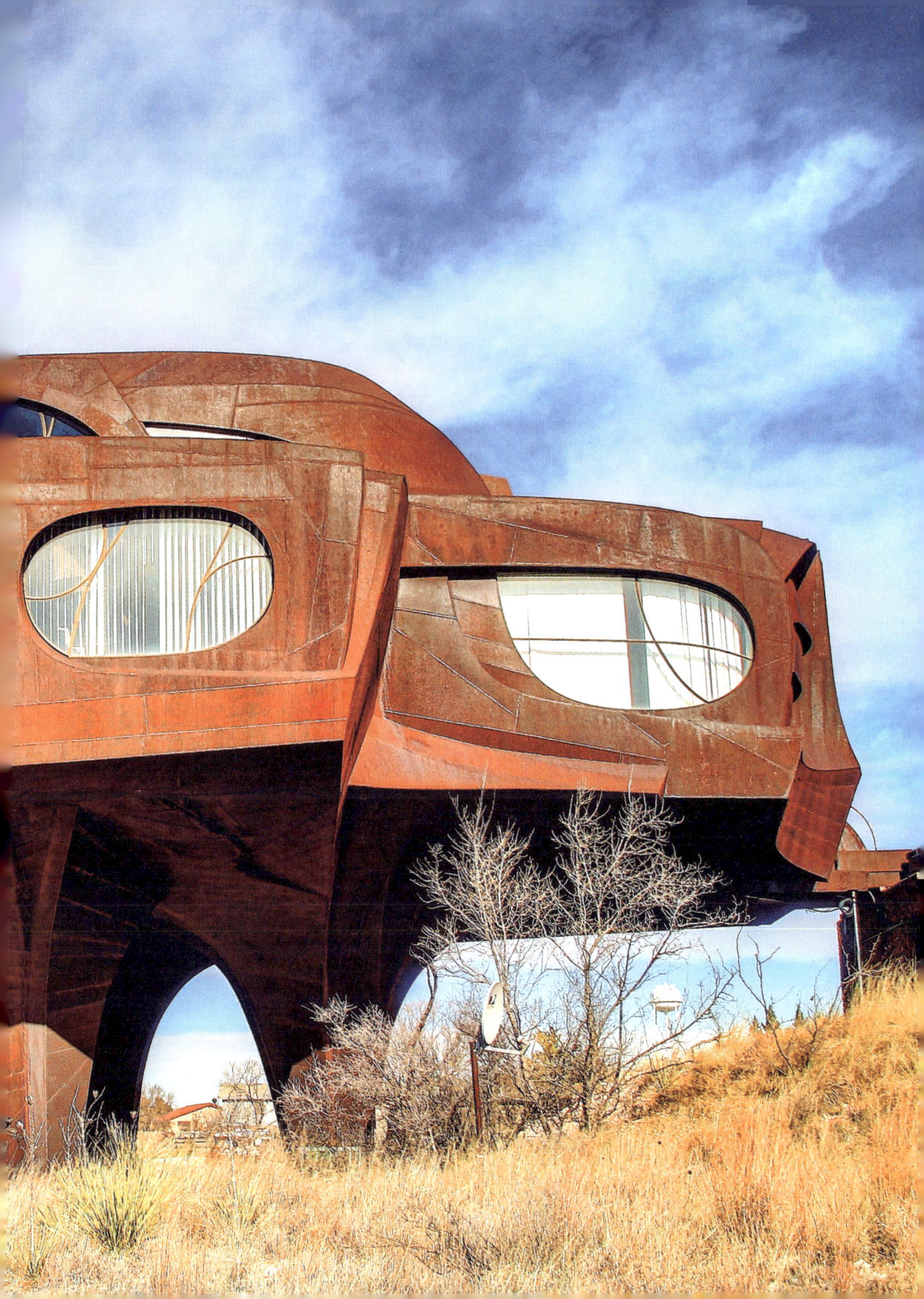

Malator House

Pembrokeshire, Wales
Architect: Future Systems, 1998

Carved out of the hillside in a protected Welsh National Park, this 'earth house' offers panoramic views of the coastline while remaining hidden from public view. The architects had to follow strict guidelines to avoid impacting the landscape, and the resulting home demonstrates how modern structures can cohabit with nature.

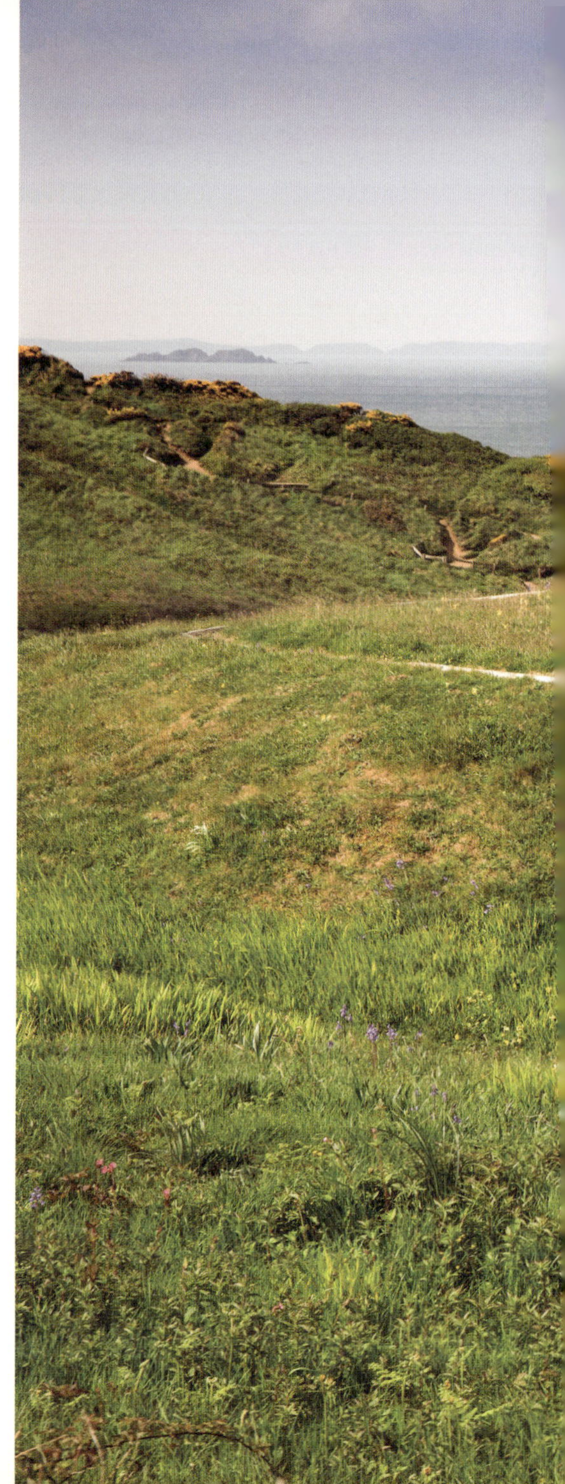

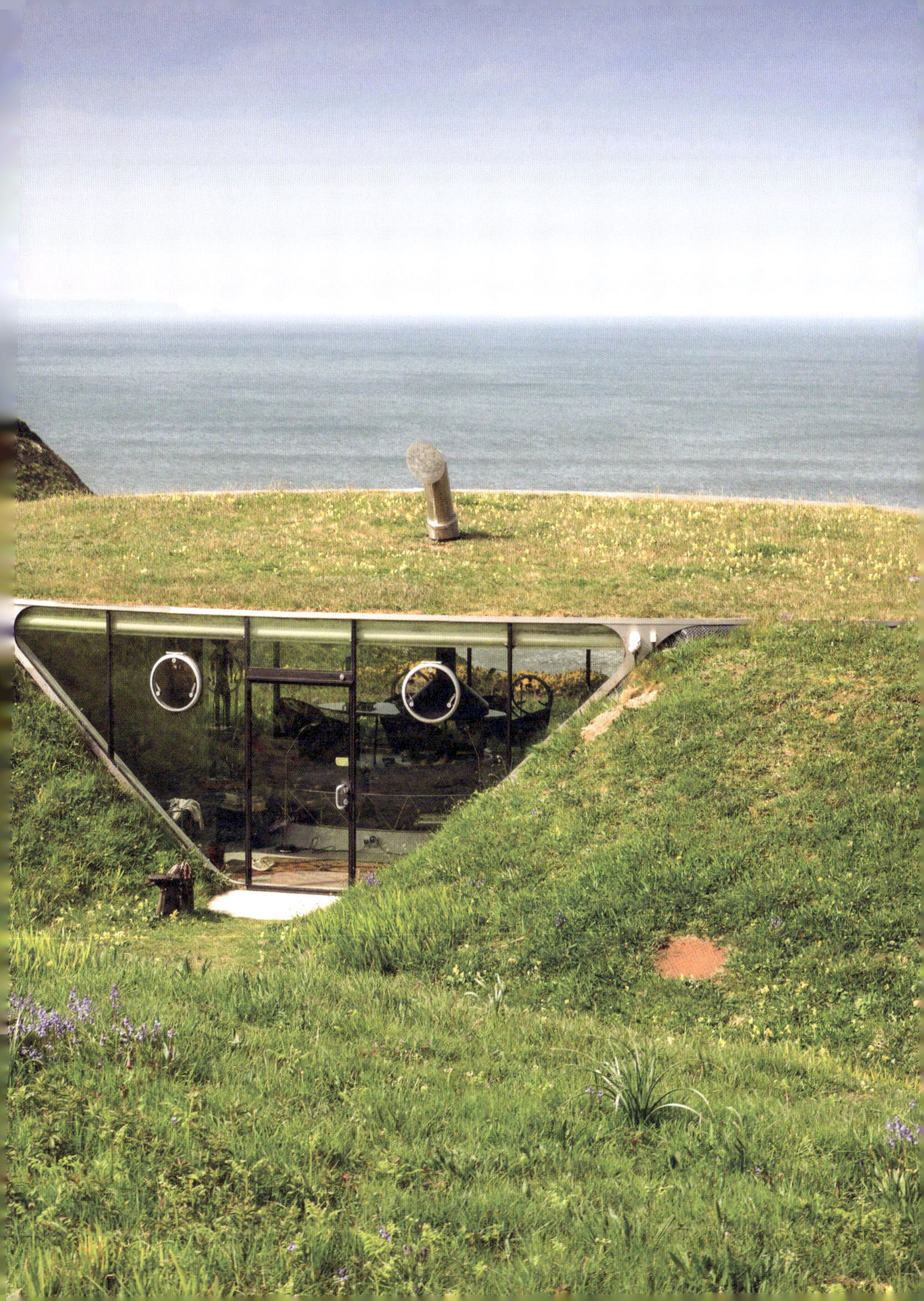

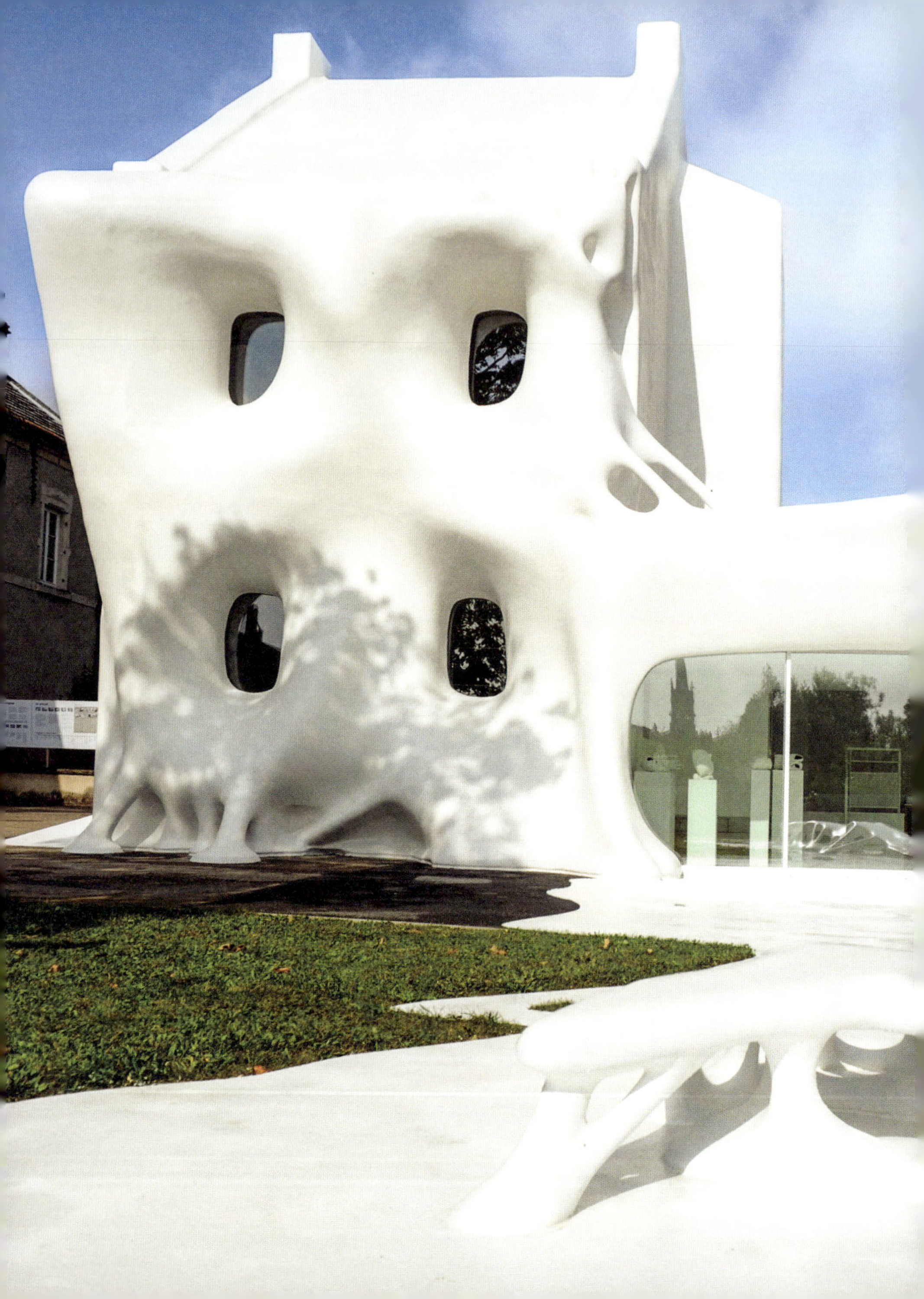

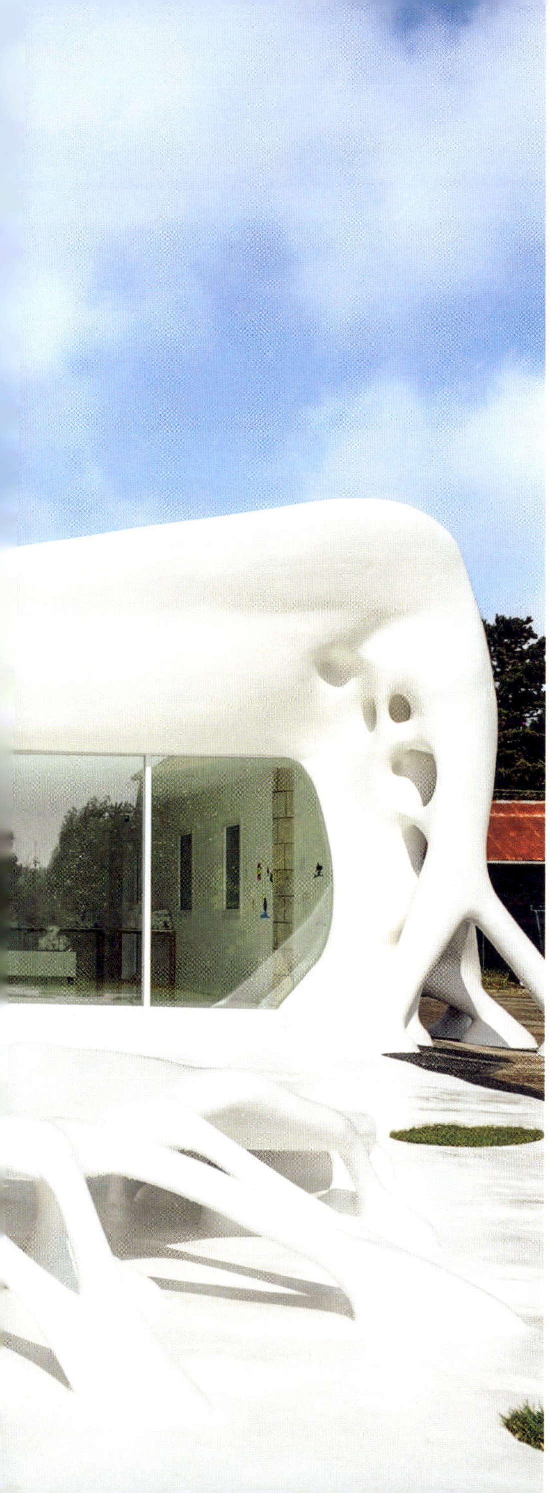

Gue(ho)st House
Delme, France
Architects: Christophe Berdaguer and Marie Péjus, 2012

Artists Christophe Berdaguer and Marie Péjus transformed a funeral home into this visitor centre for a contemporary arts organisation by giving it a 'ghostly' cloak of polystyrene, resin and paint. The name alludes to the building's former identity and borrows from Marcel Duchamp's wordplay: A Guest + A Host = A Ghost.

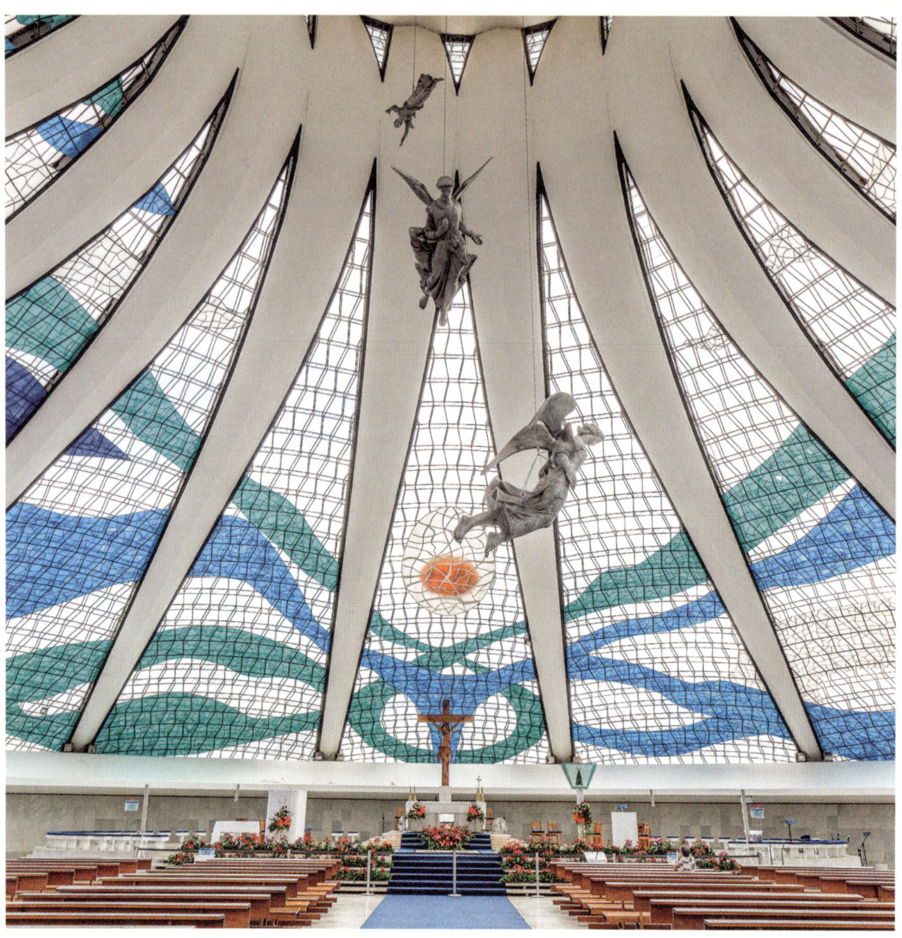

Brasília Cathedral

Brasília, Brazil

Architect: Oscar Niemeyer, 1970

Oscar Niemeyer was himself an atheist, but believed that buildings should reflect beliefs and wanted his cathedral for Brazil's capital to be a deep expression of faith. The divine design incorporates 16 concrete columns, rising as though hands reaching heavenward. Inside, a brightly lit nave with triangular stained-glass windows is ethereal within the columns' embrace.

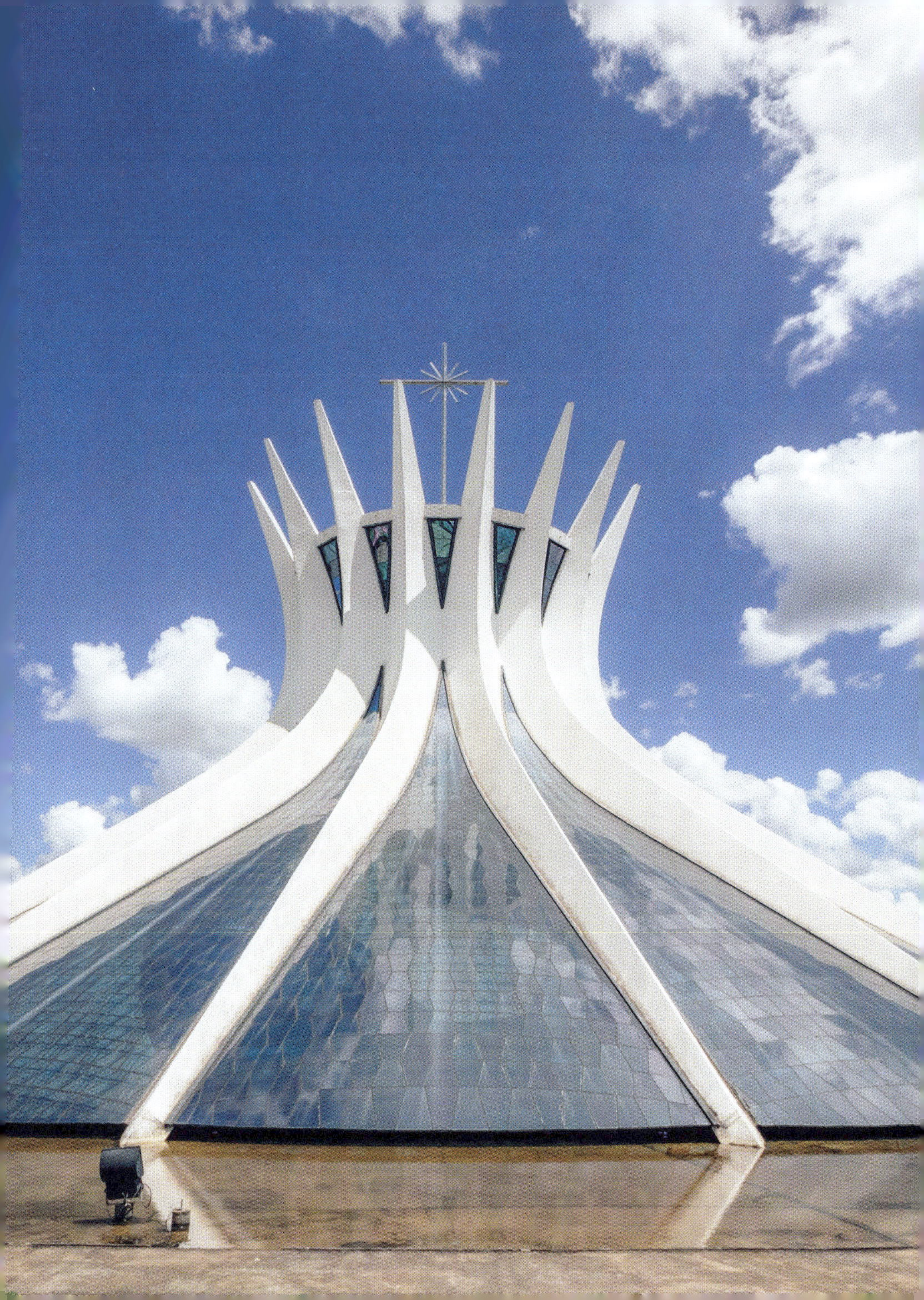

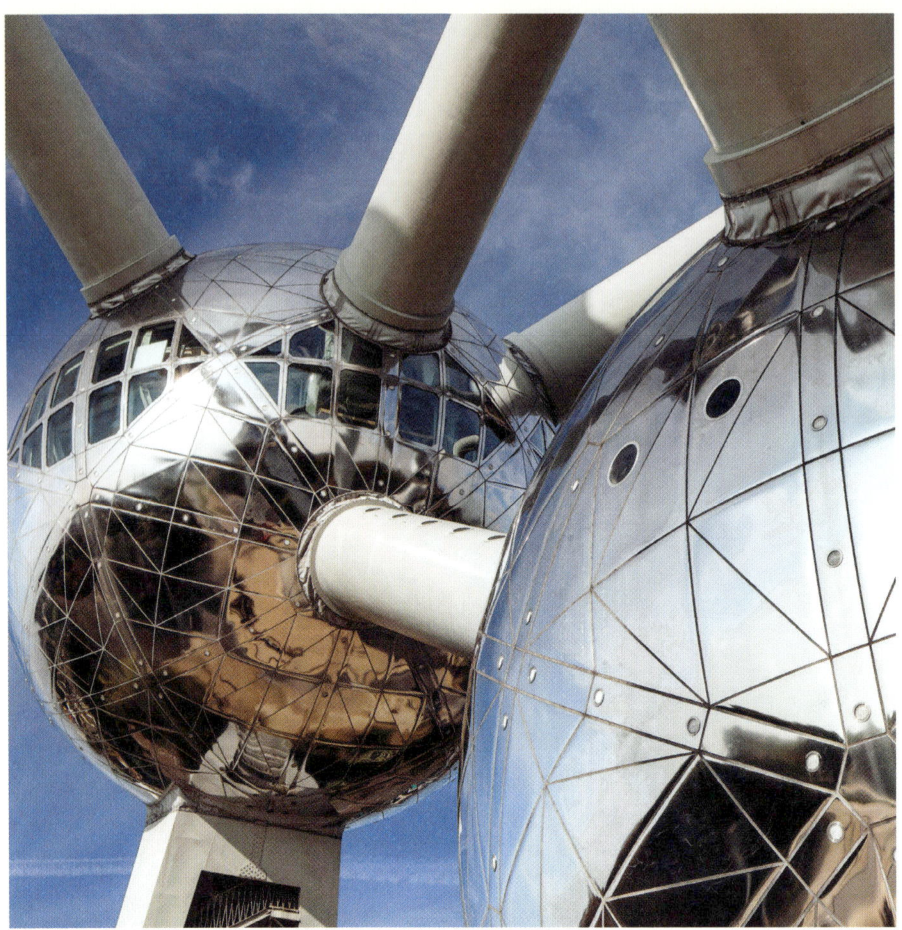

The Atomium

Brussels, Belgium
Architects: André and Jean Polak, 1958

Resembling a gigantic atomic disco ball, the Atomium was designed for the 1958 Brussels World Fair as a tribute to scientific progress. The stainless steel spheres, each spanning 18 metres, represent the nine atoms in an iron cell magnified 165 billion times. Iron was chosen as its atoms are organised in a regular cubic structure, which could be scaled and reproduced as a building.

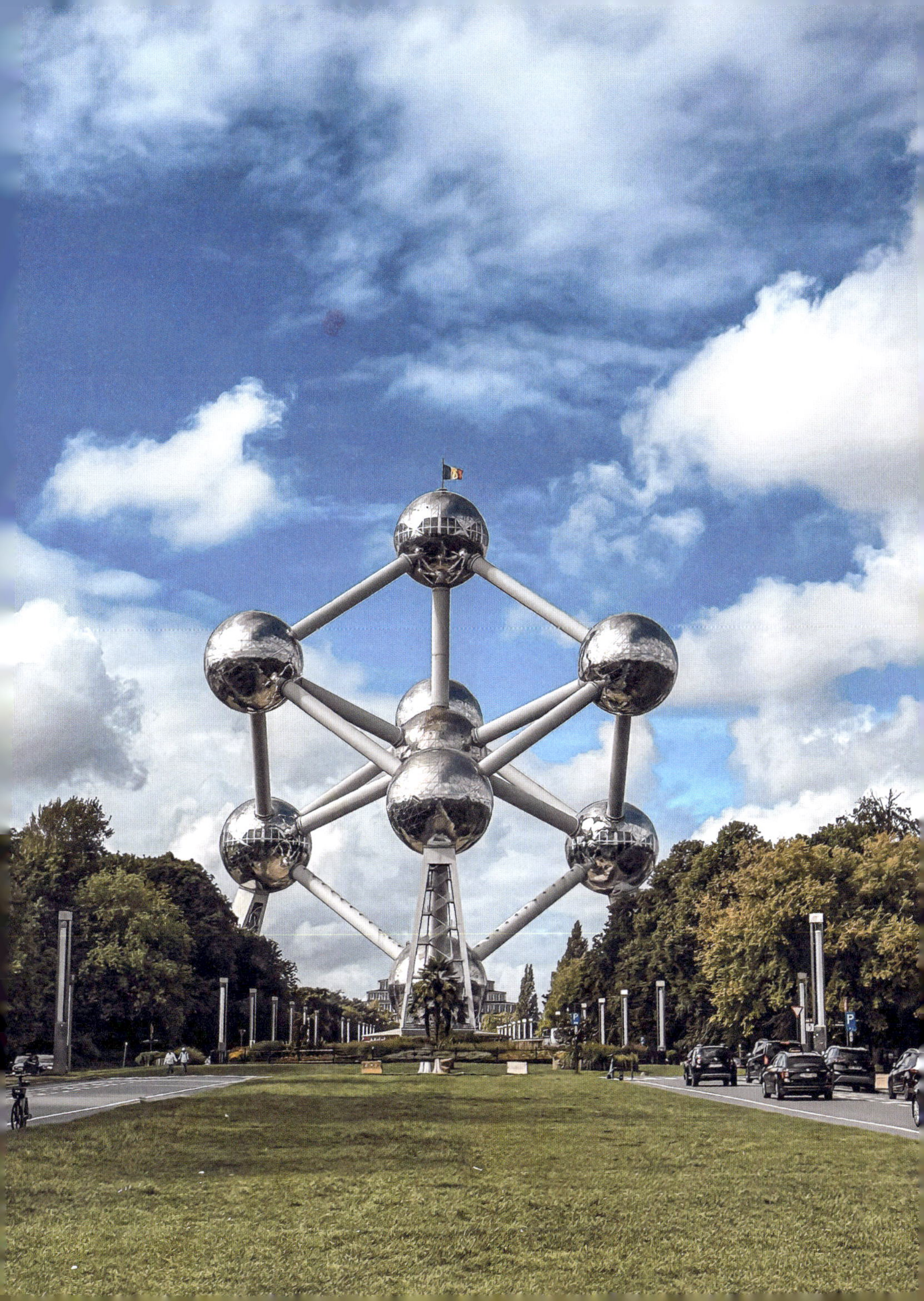

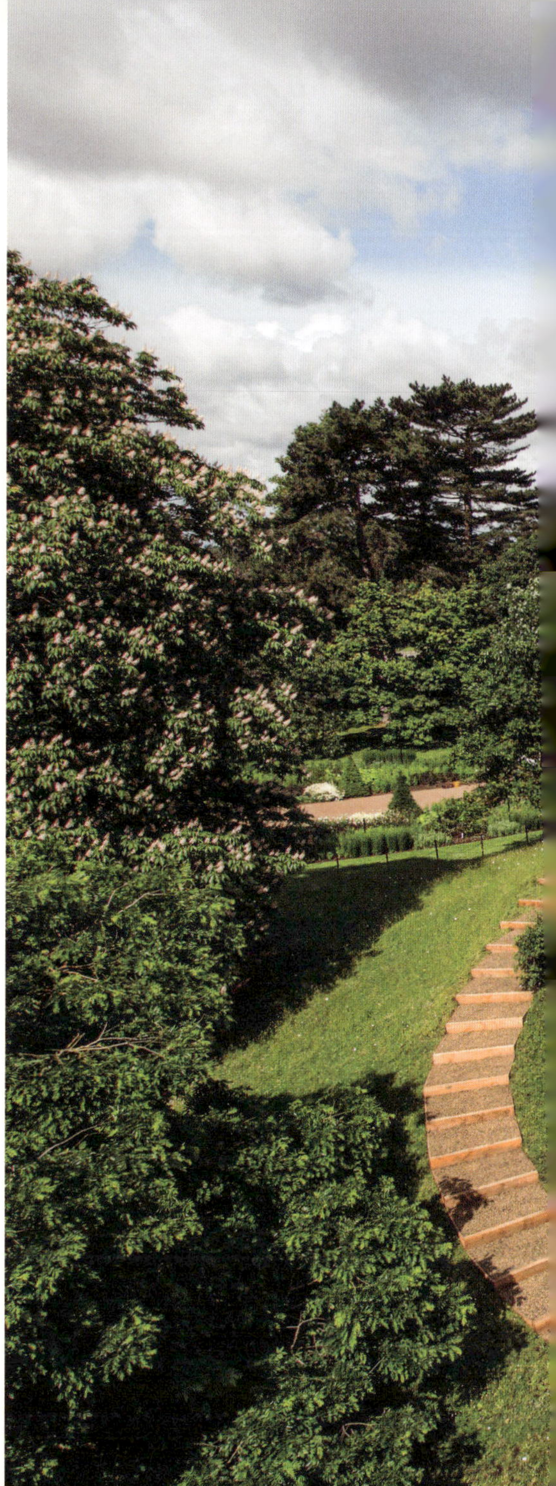

The Hive at Kew Gardens
London, England
Architect: Wolfgang Buttress, 2015

Mimicking a giant mesh beehive, this immersive installation is designed to give visitors an insight into the life of a worker bee and highlight the importance of these vital pollinators. The vibrations of honeybees in a nearby hive cause 1,000 LED lights to glow and a soundscape of low humming is generated in response to their activity.

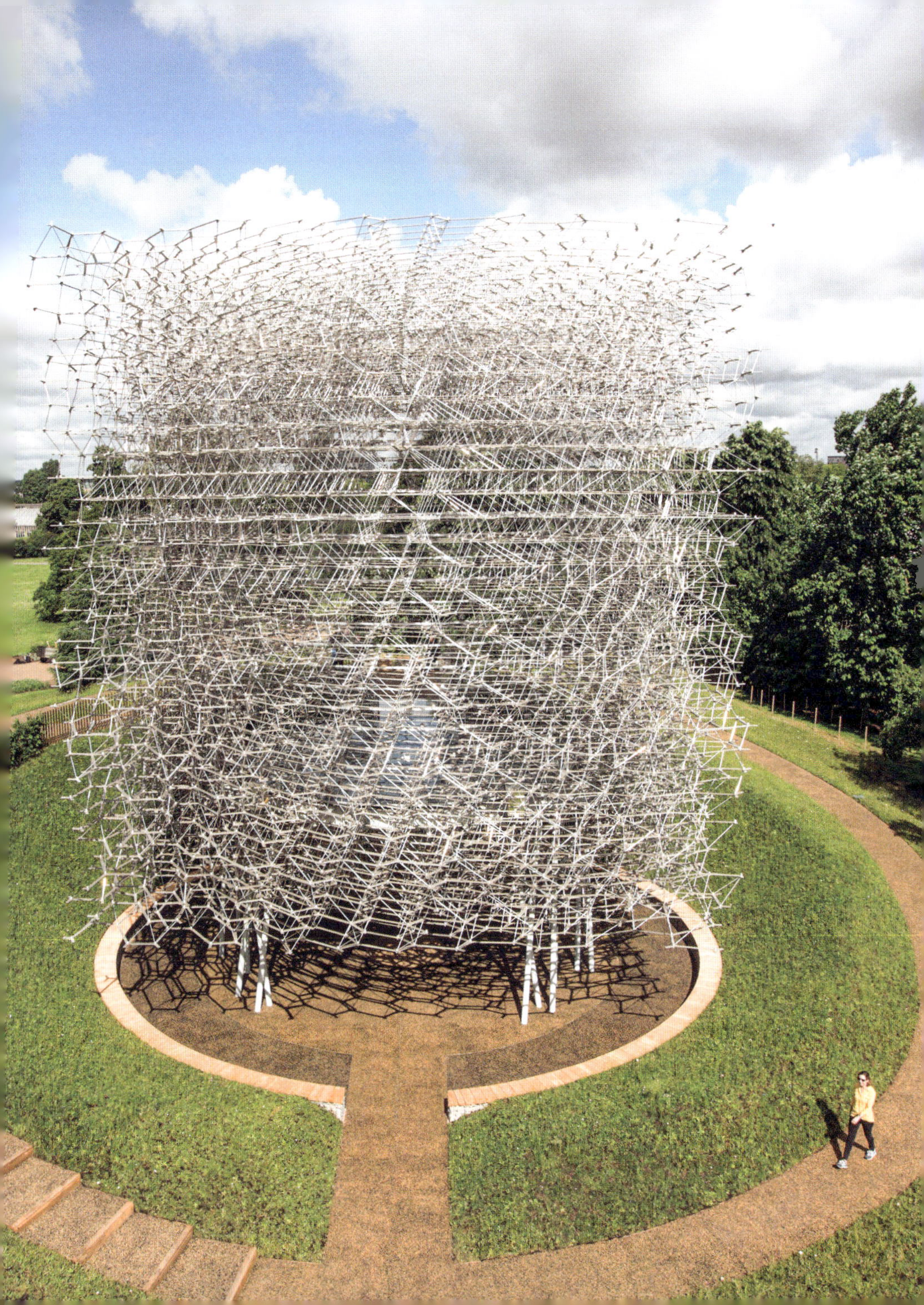

The Louvre Abu Dhabi
Abu Dhabi, UAE
Architect: Jean Nouvel, 2017

Designed to emulate a traditional Arabic walled city, the first of the famous French museum's outposts consists of 55 buildings loosely assembled around stone-paved courtyards and deep reflecting pools. An intricate metal dome, inspired by the curved roofs and geometric motifs of traditional Islamic architecture, provides refuge from the desert sun.

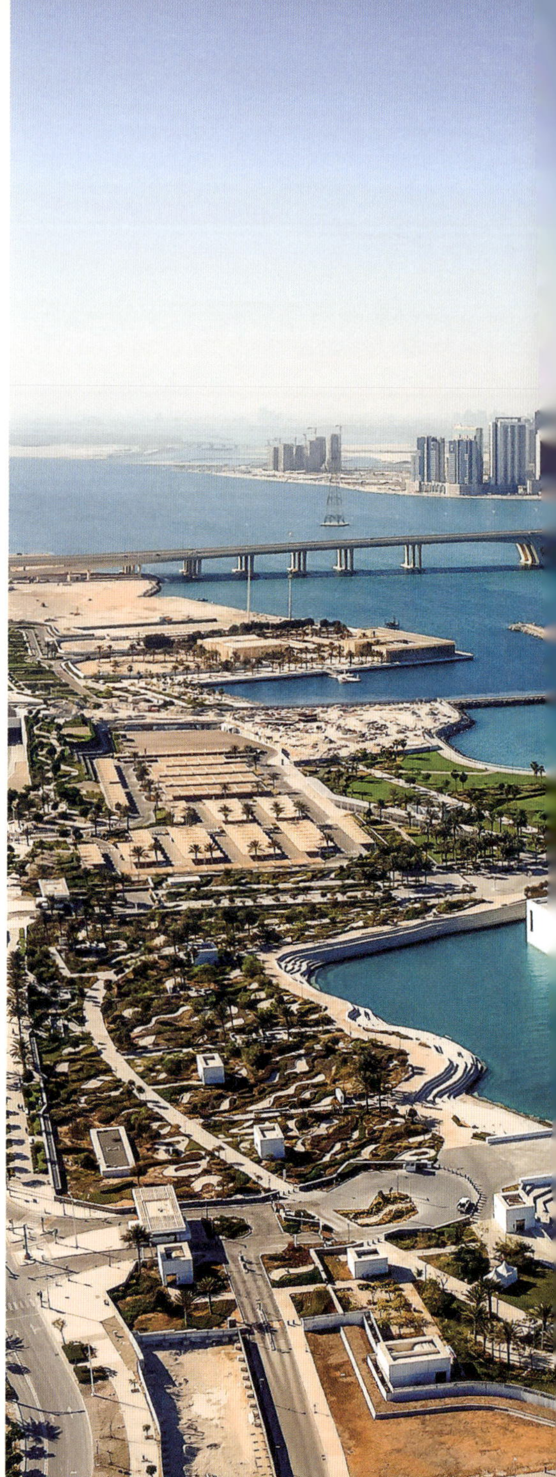

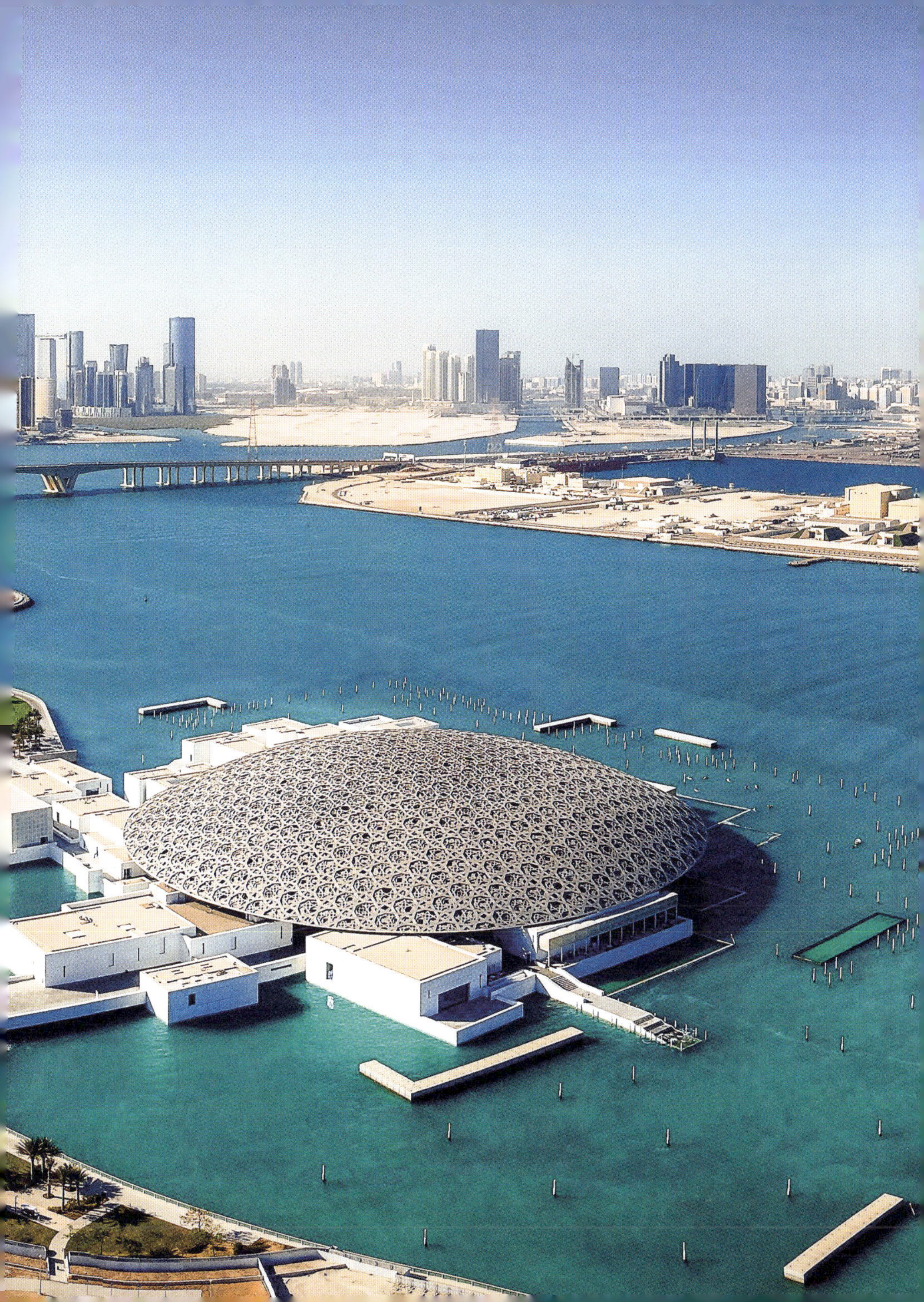

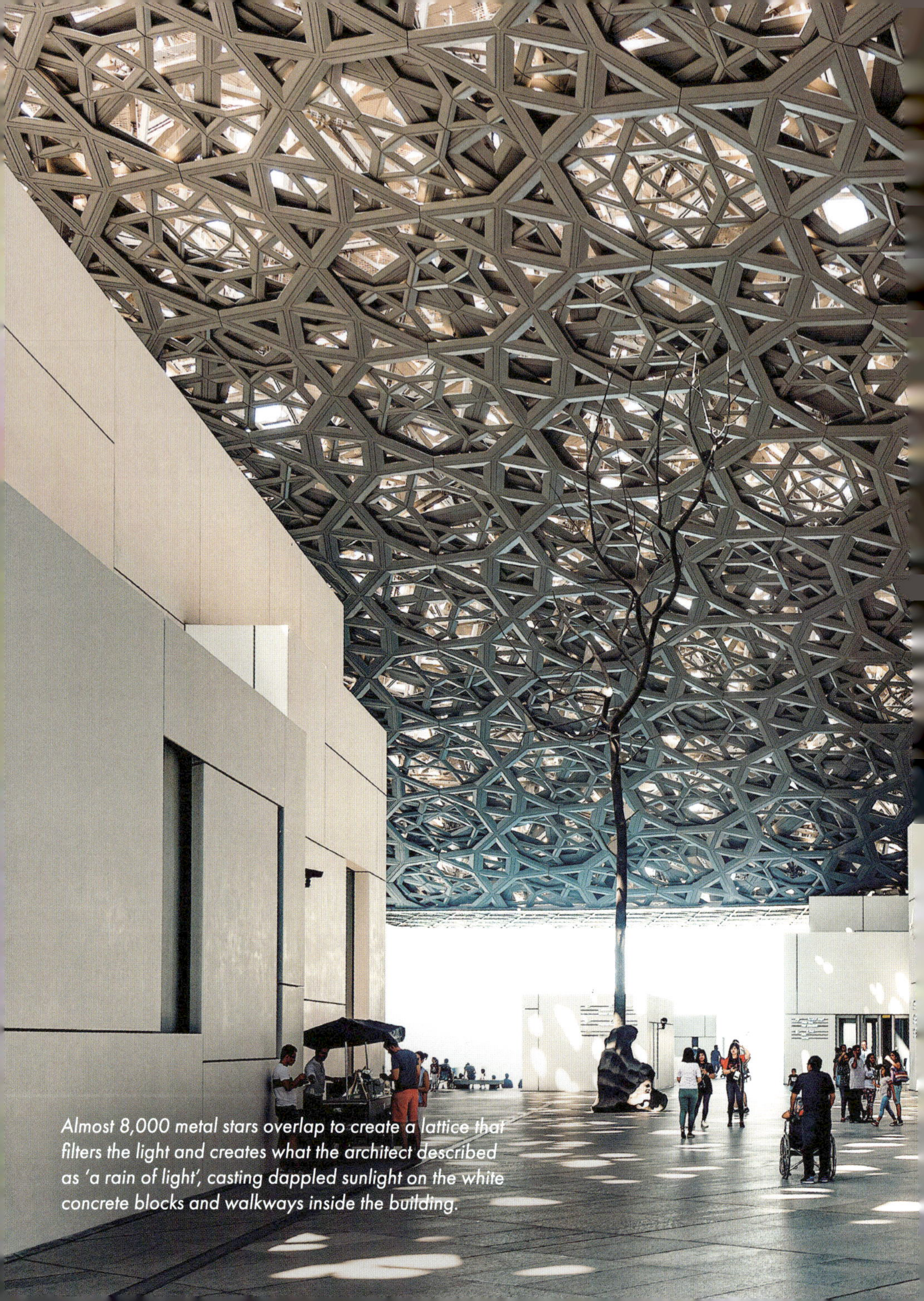

Almost 8,000 metal stars overlap to create a lattice that filters the light and creates what the architect described as 'a rain of light', casting dappled sunlight on the white concrete blocks and walkways inside the building.

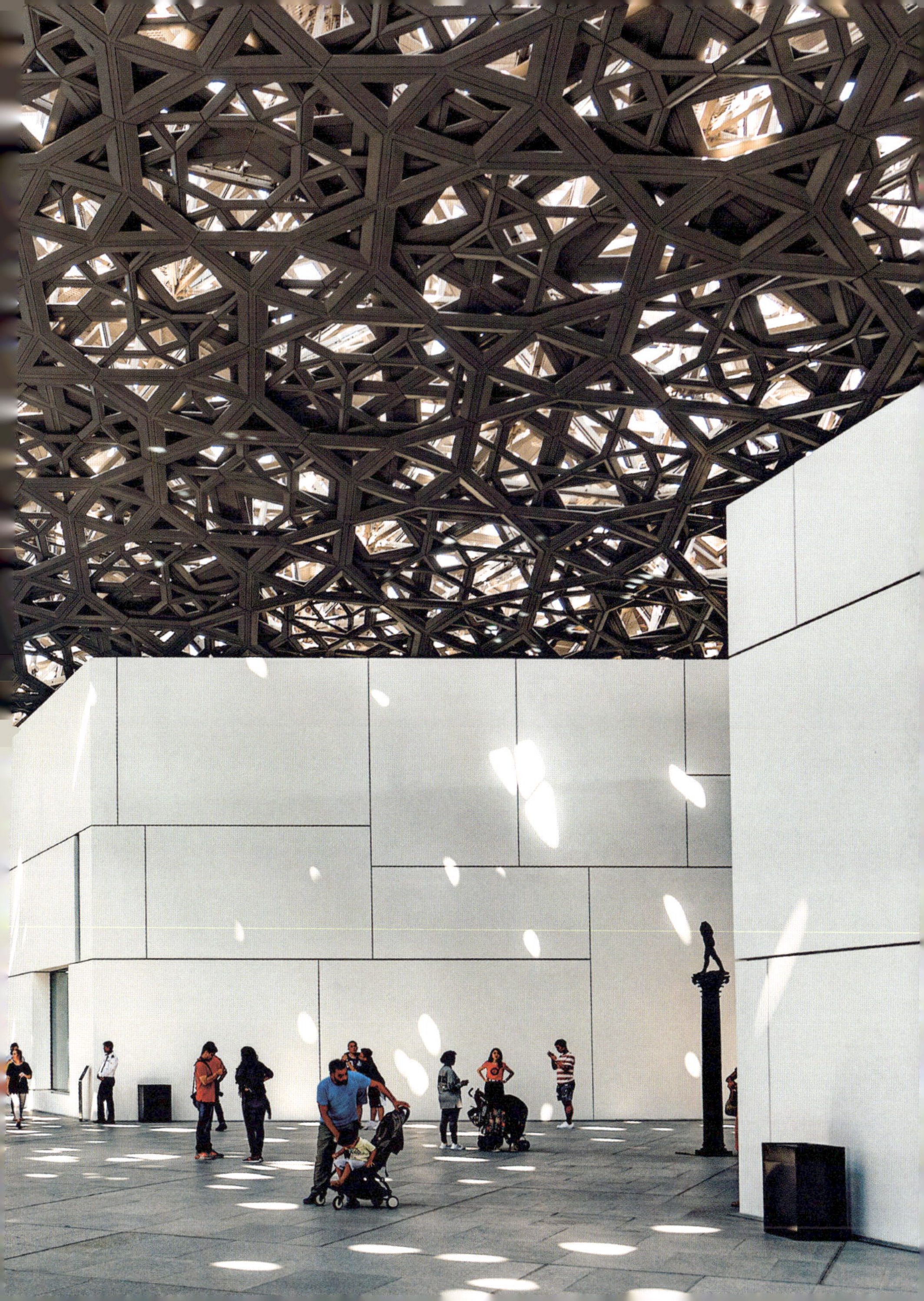

Under
Lindesnes, Norway
Architect: Snøhetta, 2019

Europe's first underwater restaurant is designed to resemble a sunken periscope and offers a unique dining experience. It also has a dual environmental function: the rough finish of the concrete tube acts like an artificial reef, attracting algae, limpets and molluscs and supporting local biodiversity, while the building is also a research centre for marine biologists.

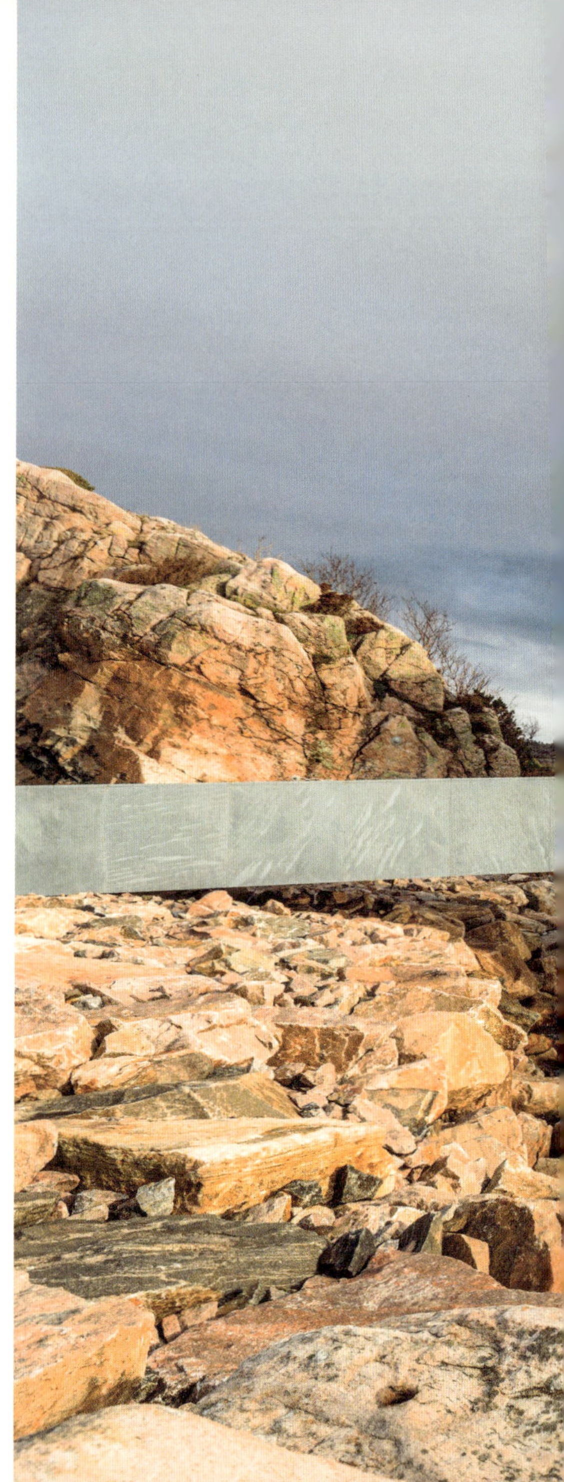

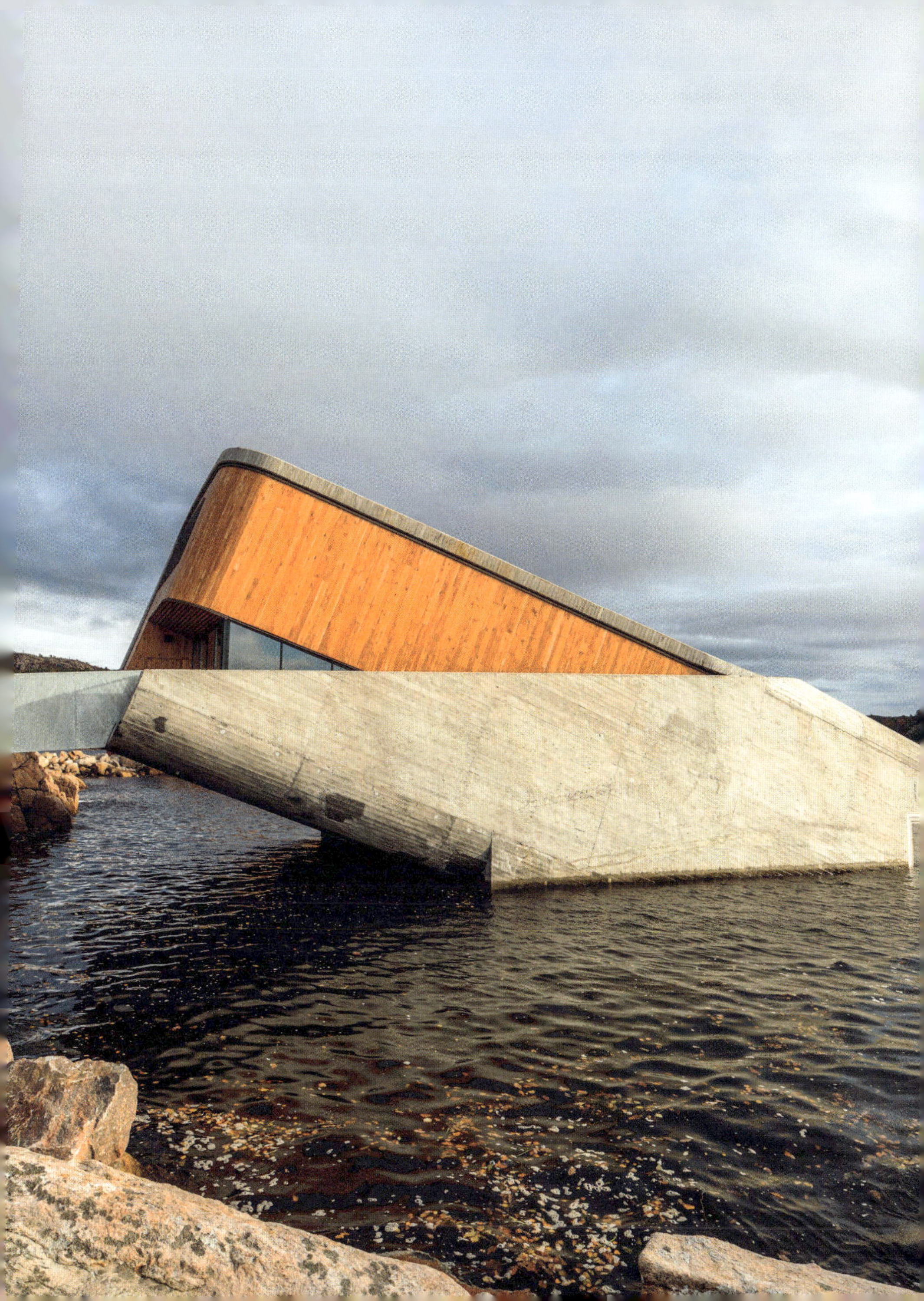

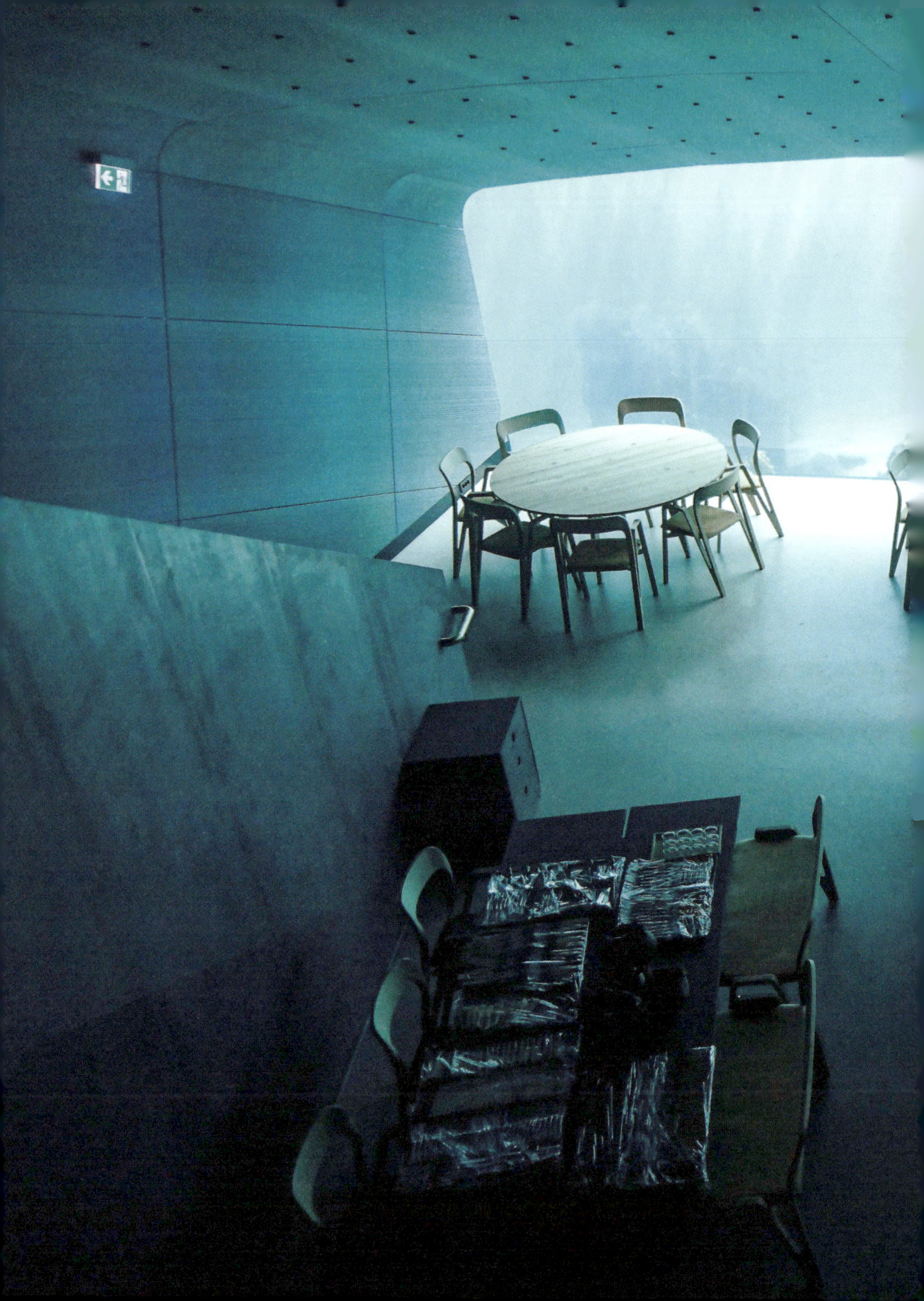

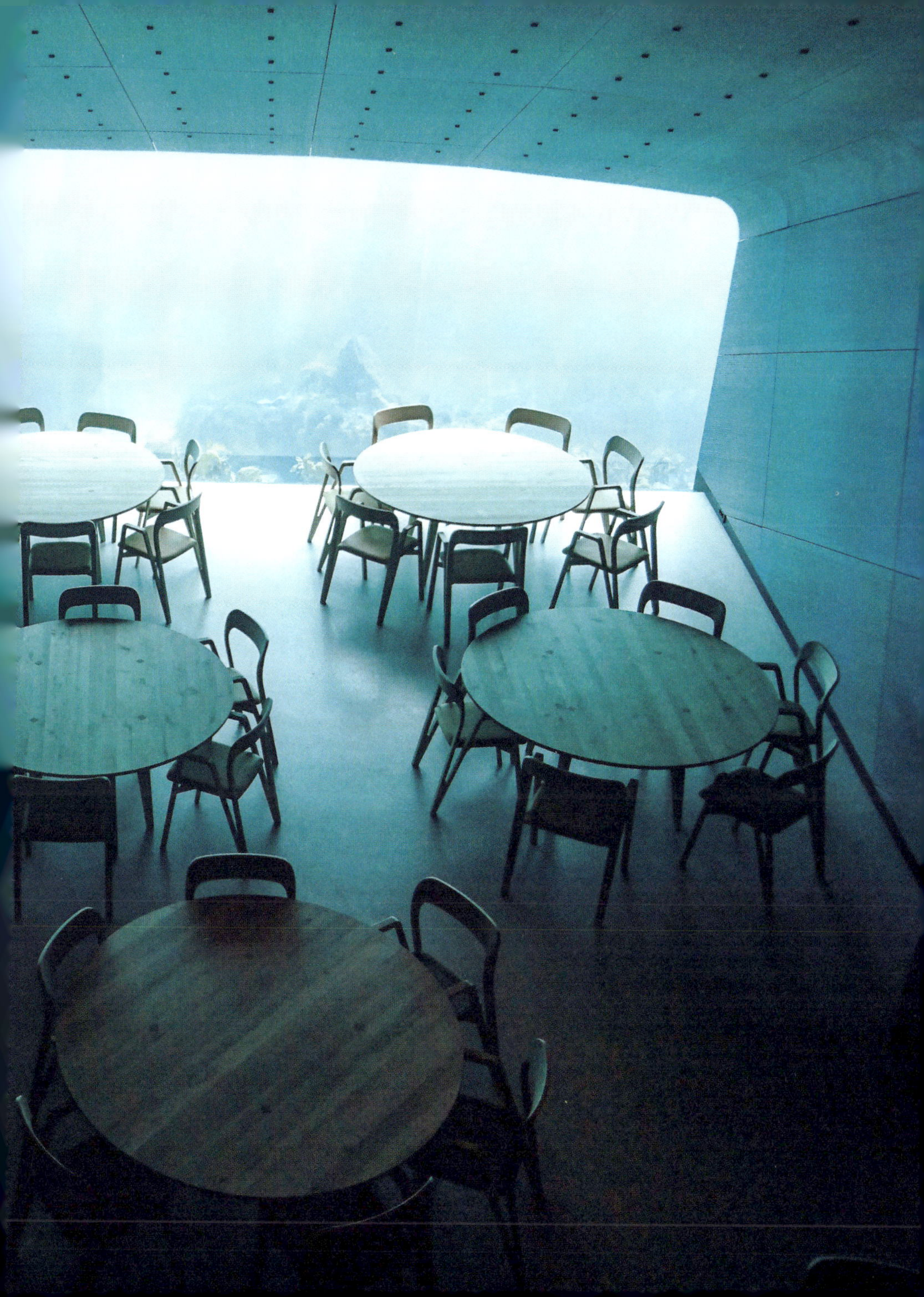

Drina River House
Bajina Bašta, Serbia
Architects: Milija and Milan Mandić and local community, 1968

Appearing as if in a dream, perched atop a jagged rock, this extraordinary house was originally built by teenage brothers as a place to shelter from the mighty Drina's strong currents after a swim. It has since been reconstructed several times by locals and is a resilient symbol of creativity and community.

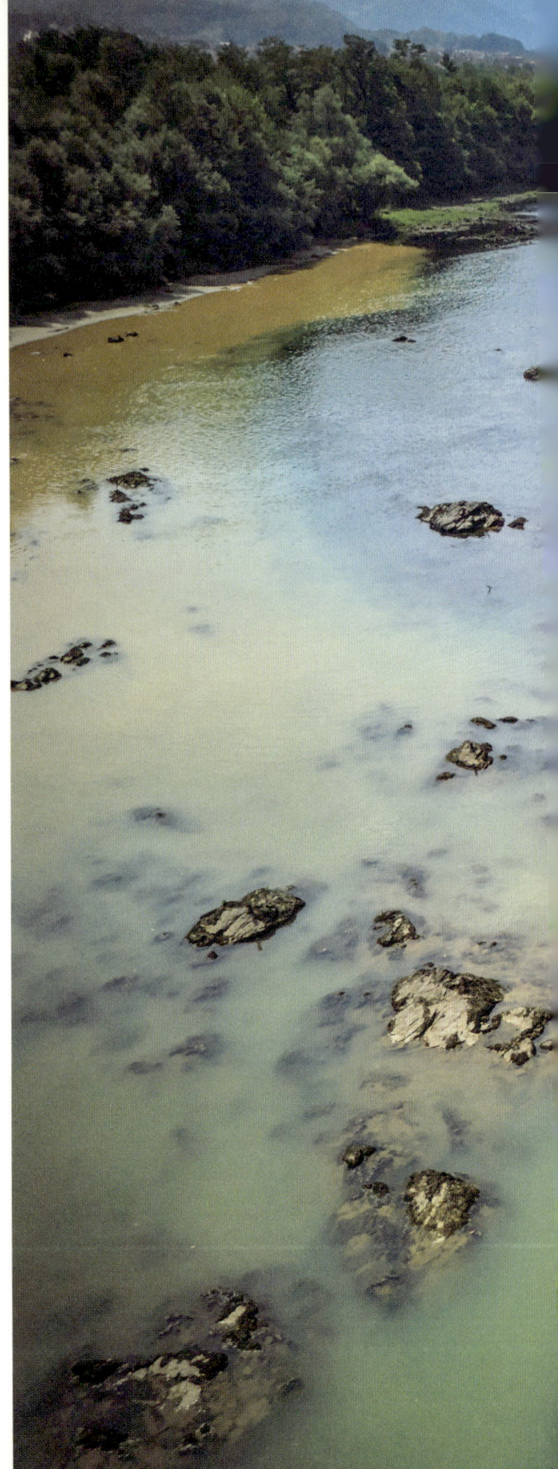

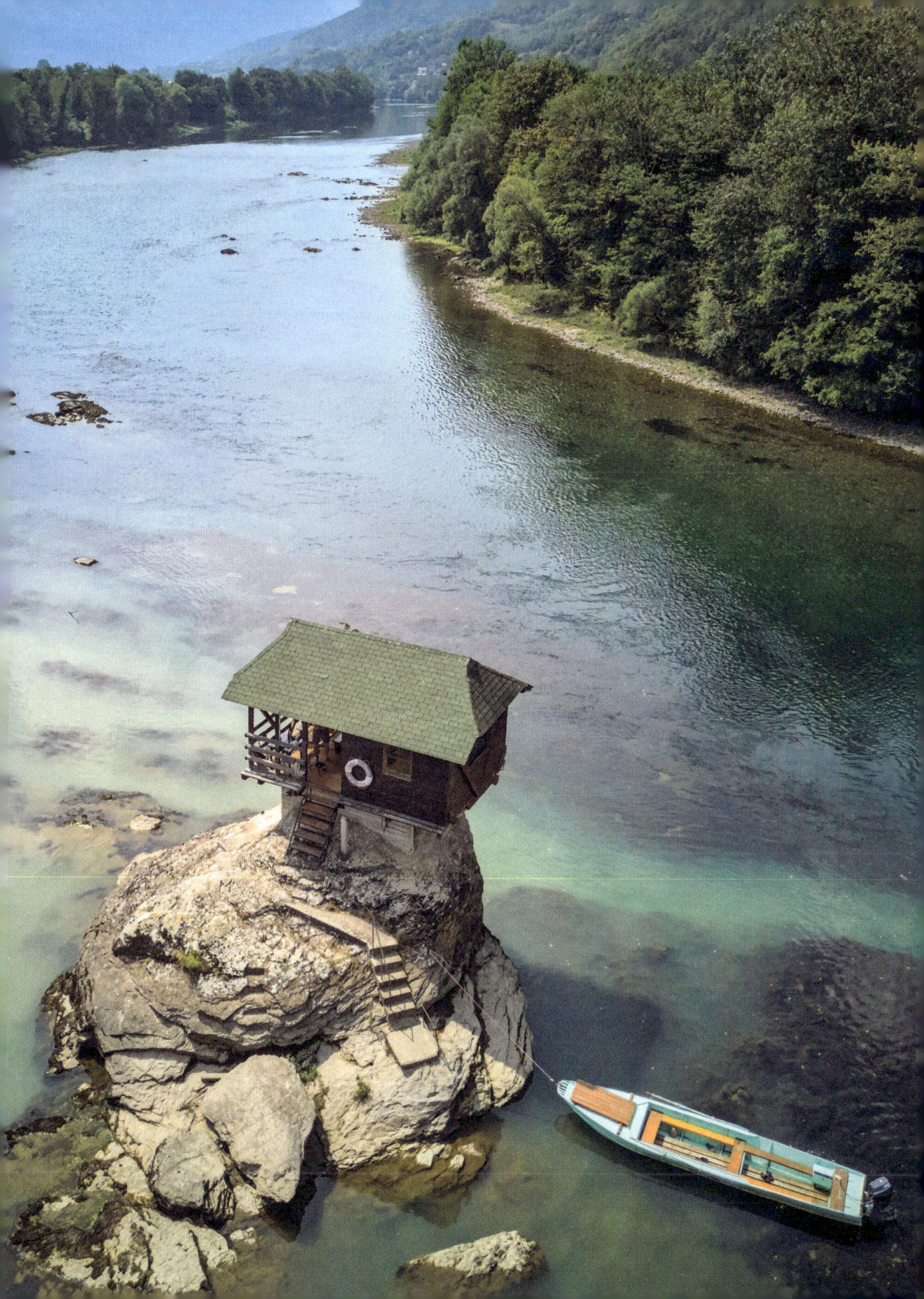

Montreal Biosphere
Montreal, Canada
Architect: Buckminster Fuller, 1967

The legendary architect's famous geodesic dome was originally created for Canada's World Fair, Expo 67. Emphasising the economical and efficient use of materials, it comprises hundreds of cylindrical steel tubes fashioned into a strong, lightweight structure. It now houses a museum dedicated to raising environmental awareness, reflecting the sustainable principles behind its architecture.

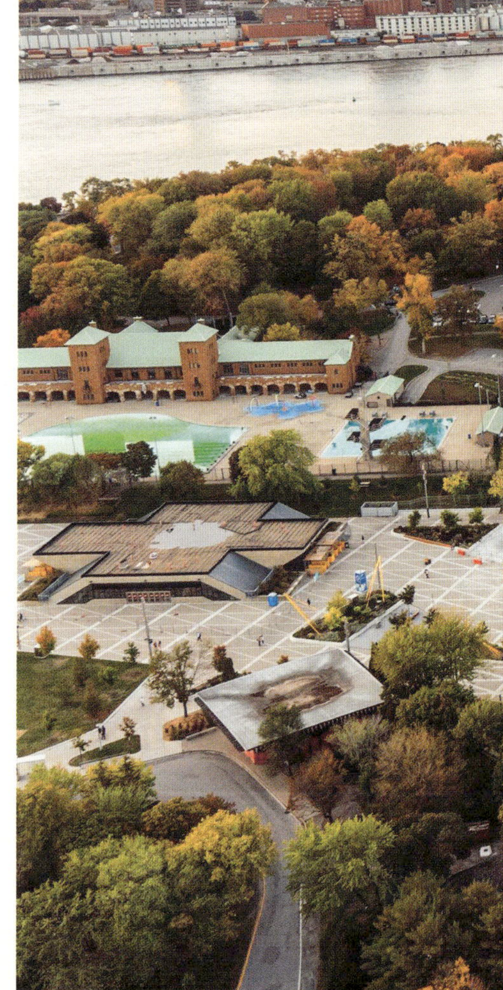

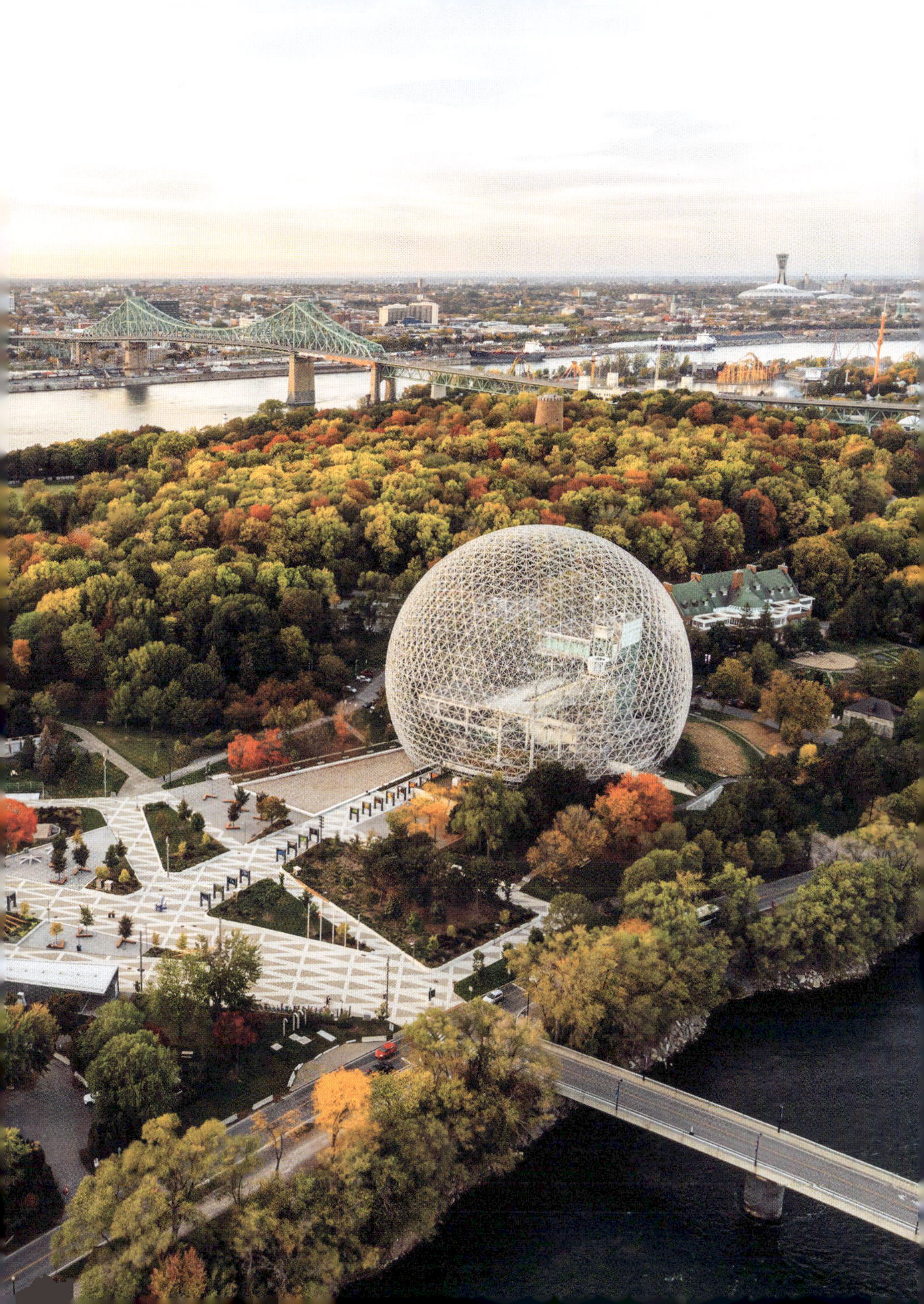

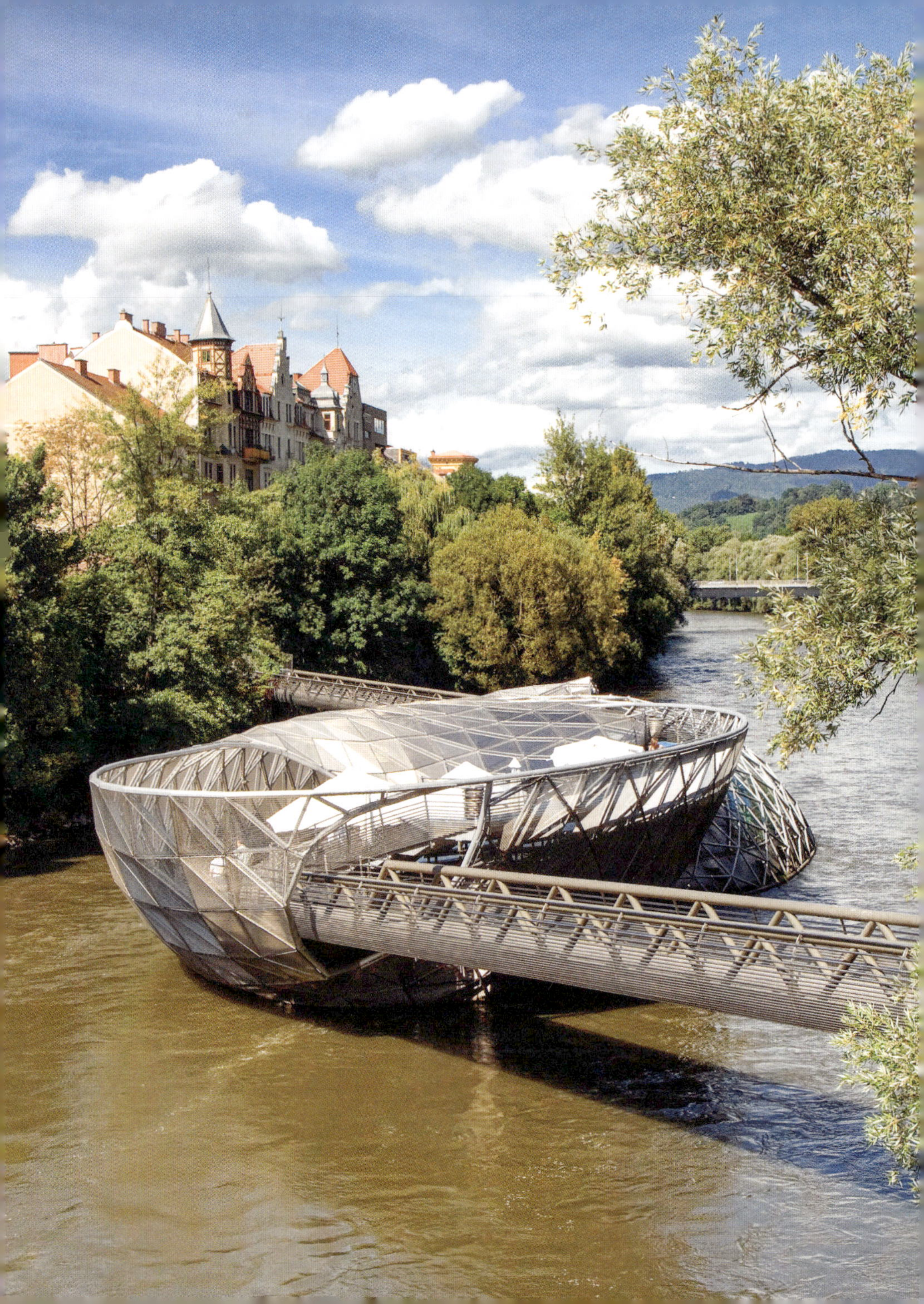

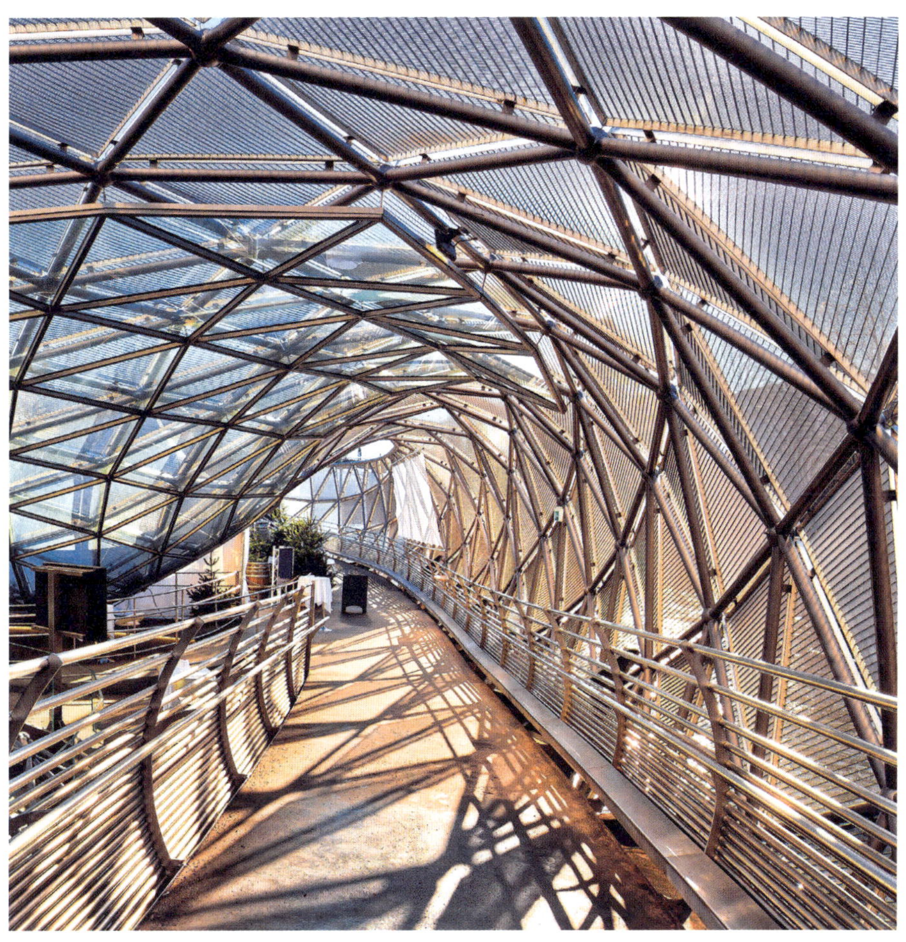

The Murinsel

Graz, Austria

Architect: Vito Acconci, 2003

Part bridge, part cafe and venue, the twisted form of the central structure was constructed in the shape of a giant seashell. Commissioned to celebrate Graz's role as Europe's Capital of Culture in 2003, the Murinsel (meaning island of the Mur) was designed as a physical and metaphorical bridge for the city.

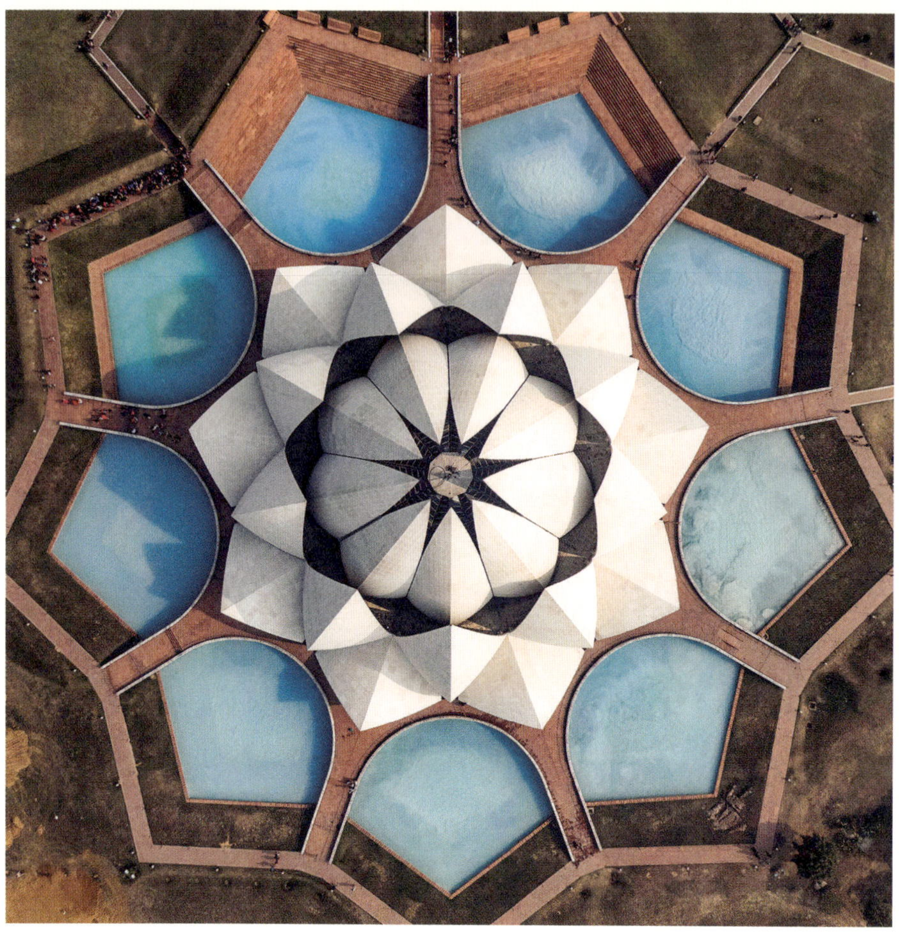

Lotus Temple
New Delhi, India
Architect: Fariborz Sahba, 1986

Blooming in the centre of the city, this is one of 14 Bahá'í Houses of Worship around the world. Like all Bahá'í temples, its form is inspired by the lotus flower, with 27 white marble 'petals' clustered to create the structure. The nine-sided shape is surrounded by nine tranquillity pools, this number having symbolic significance in the Bahá'í Faith.

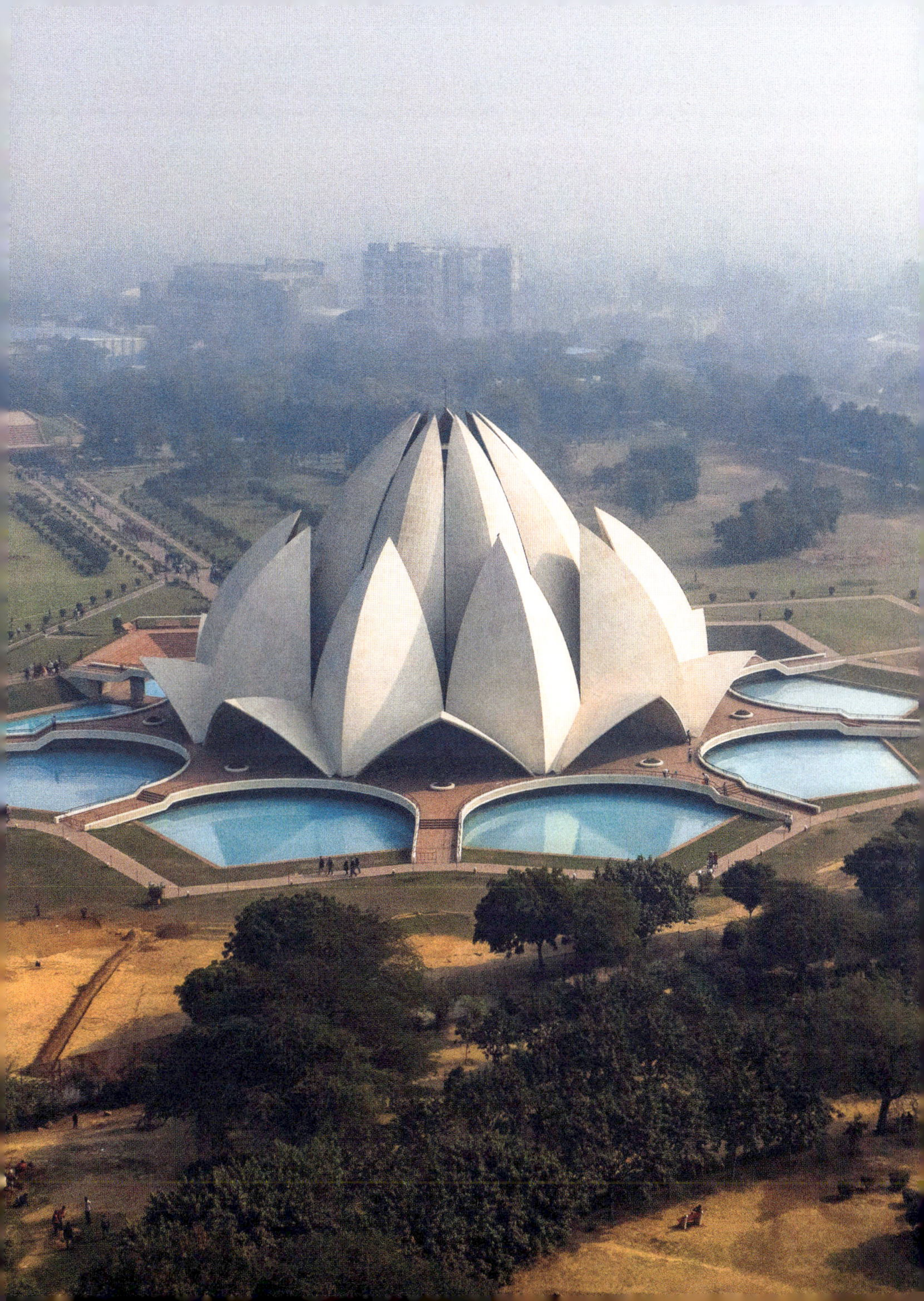

The Hive Learning Hub
Nanyang Technological University, Singapore
Architect: Heatherwick Studio, 2015

Resembling a cluster of papery beehives or piled dim sum boxes, this building was conceived to reimagine the higher educational environment. Twelve towers with circular tutorial rooms – and therefore no obvious front or back of the class – are stacked on top of each other. The open plan fosters collaboration and maximises natural light and ventilation.

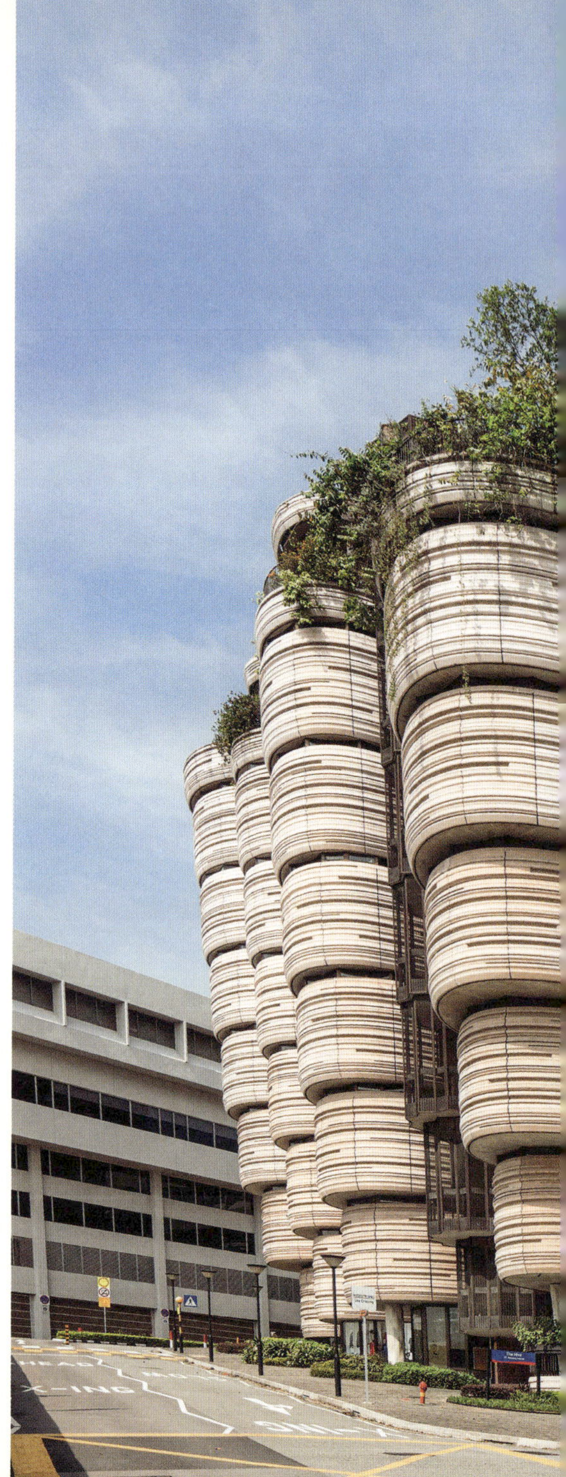

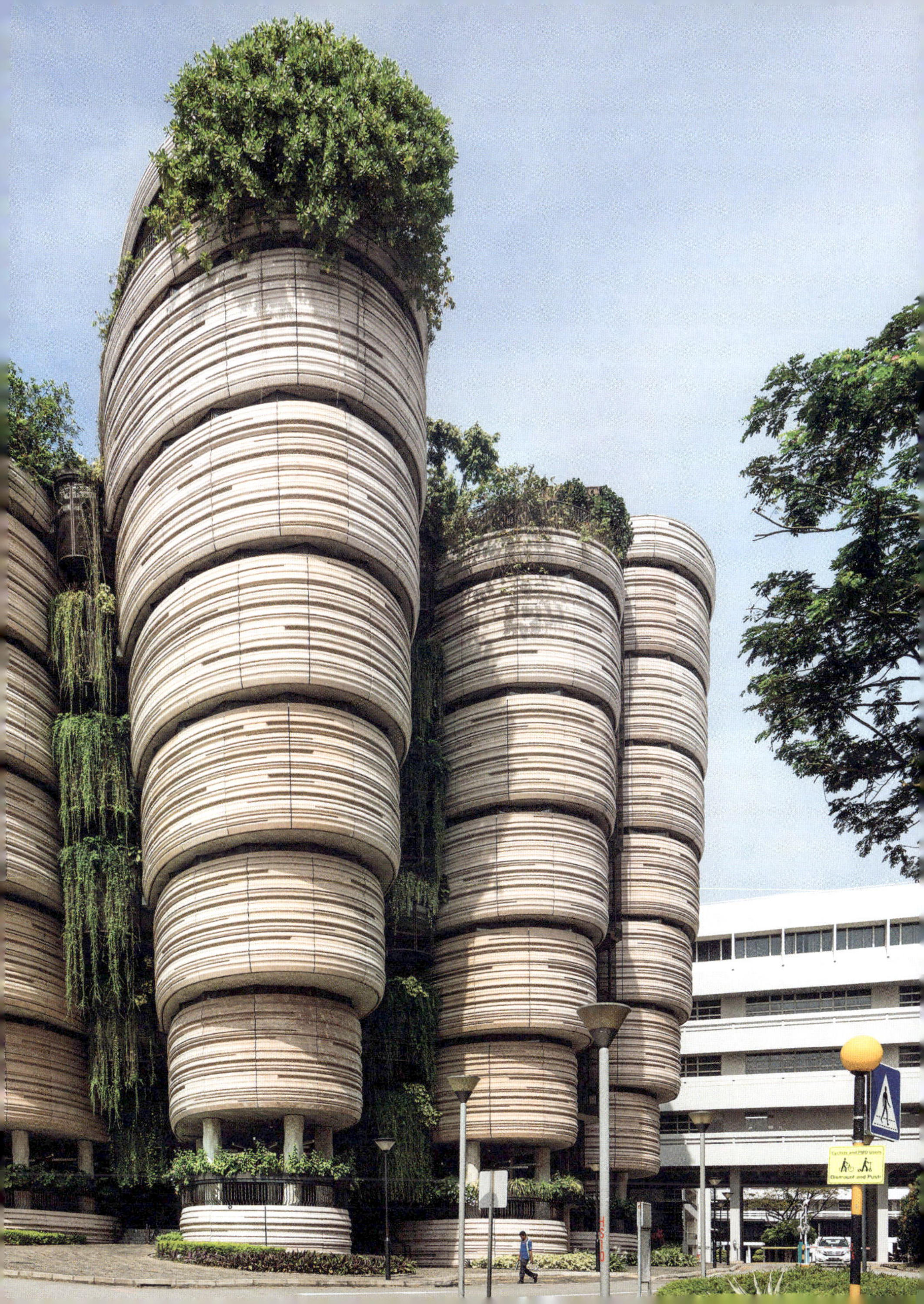
Dismount and Push

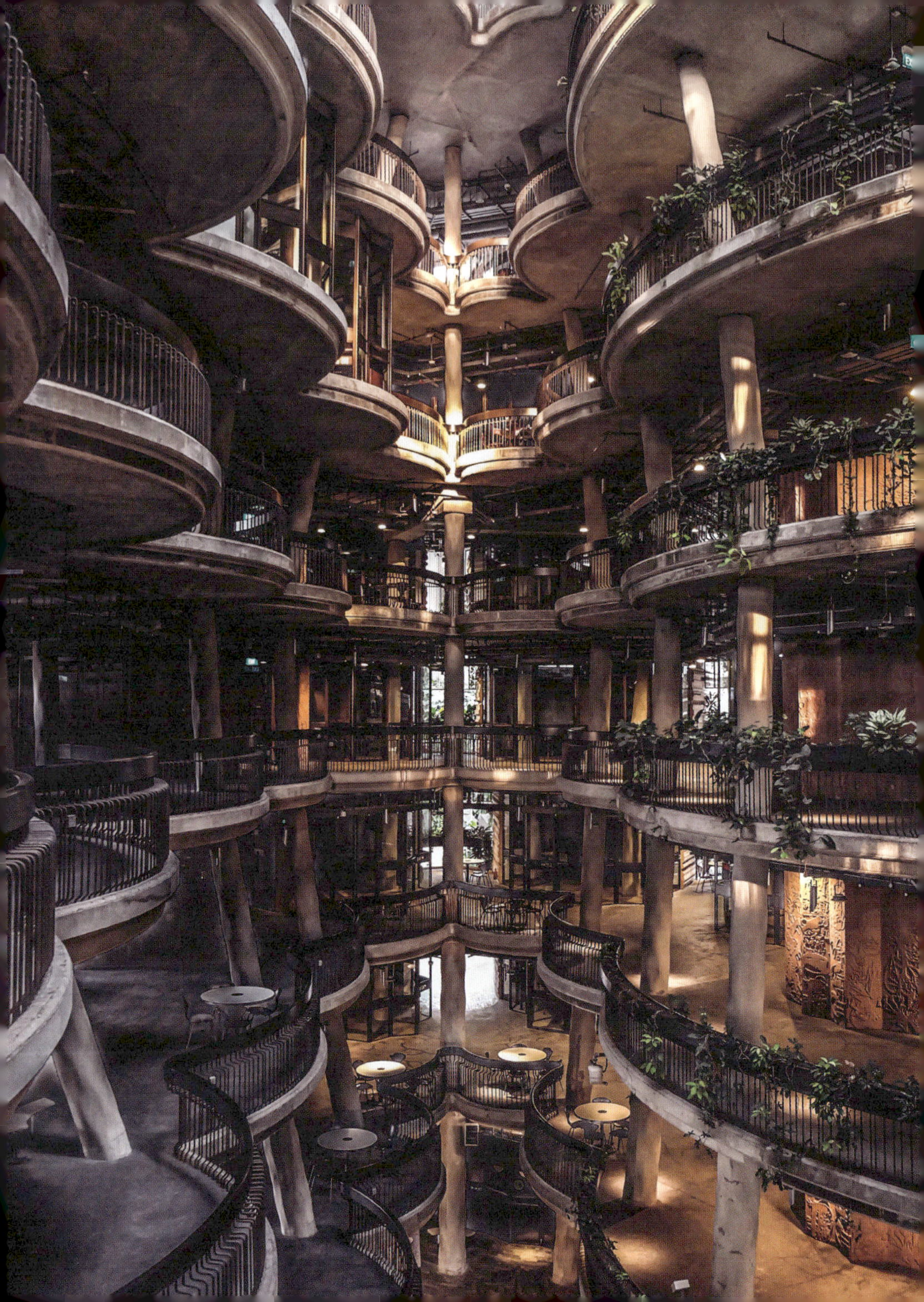

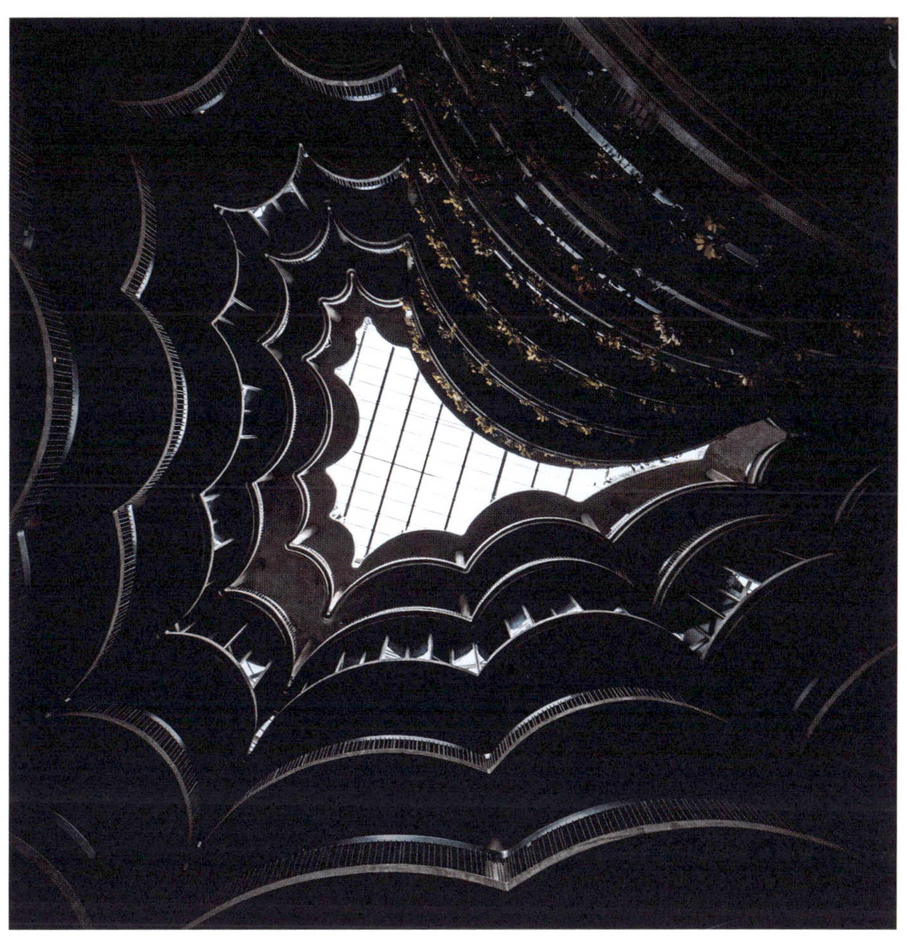

There are no corridors, and social and learning spaces are interwoven to create a dynamic setting that encourages students and teachers to interact. Between the classrooms are garden balconies – calming places to linger and reflect.

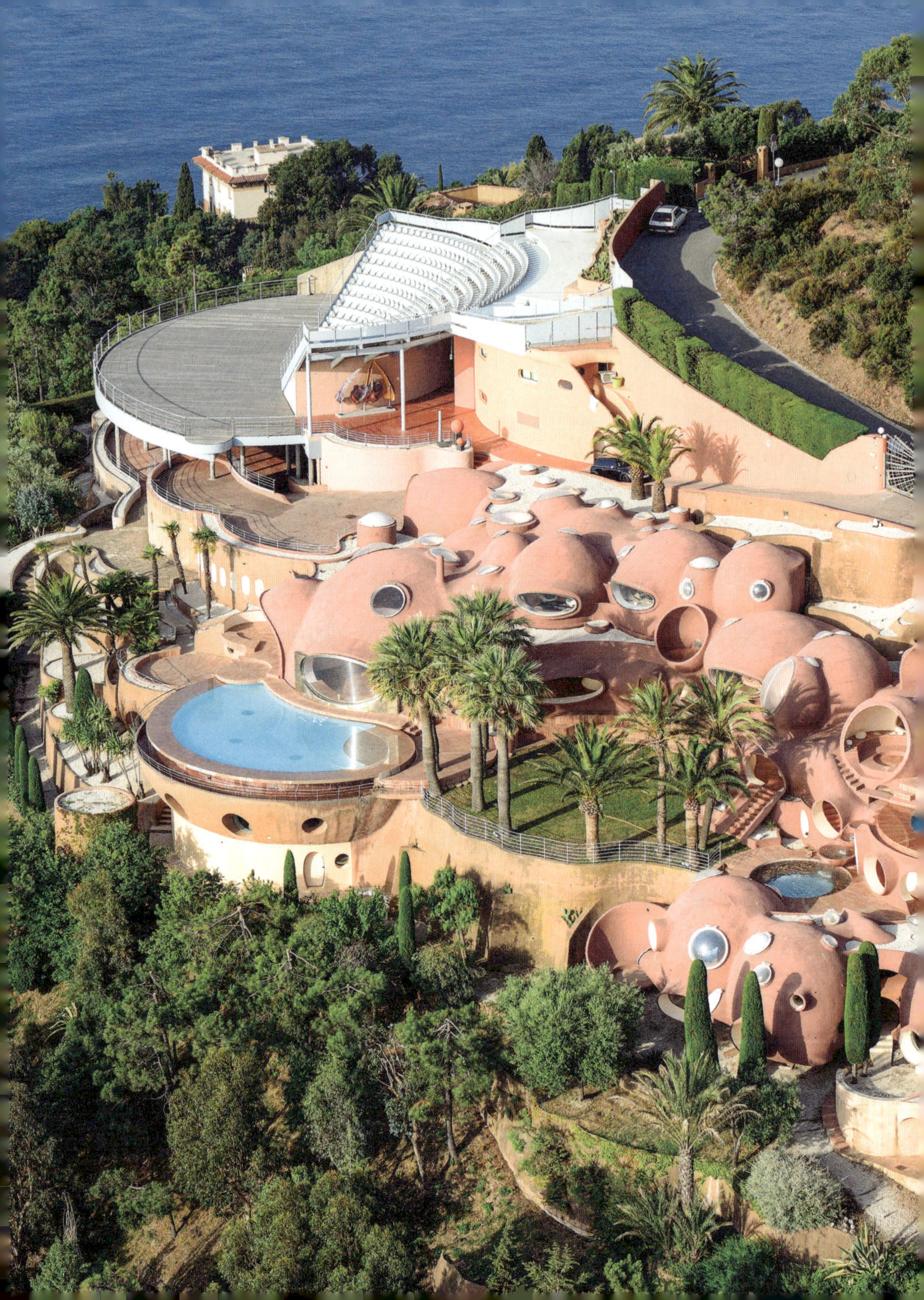

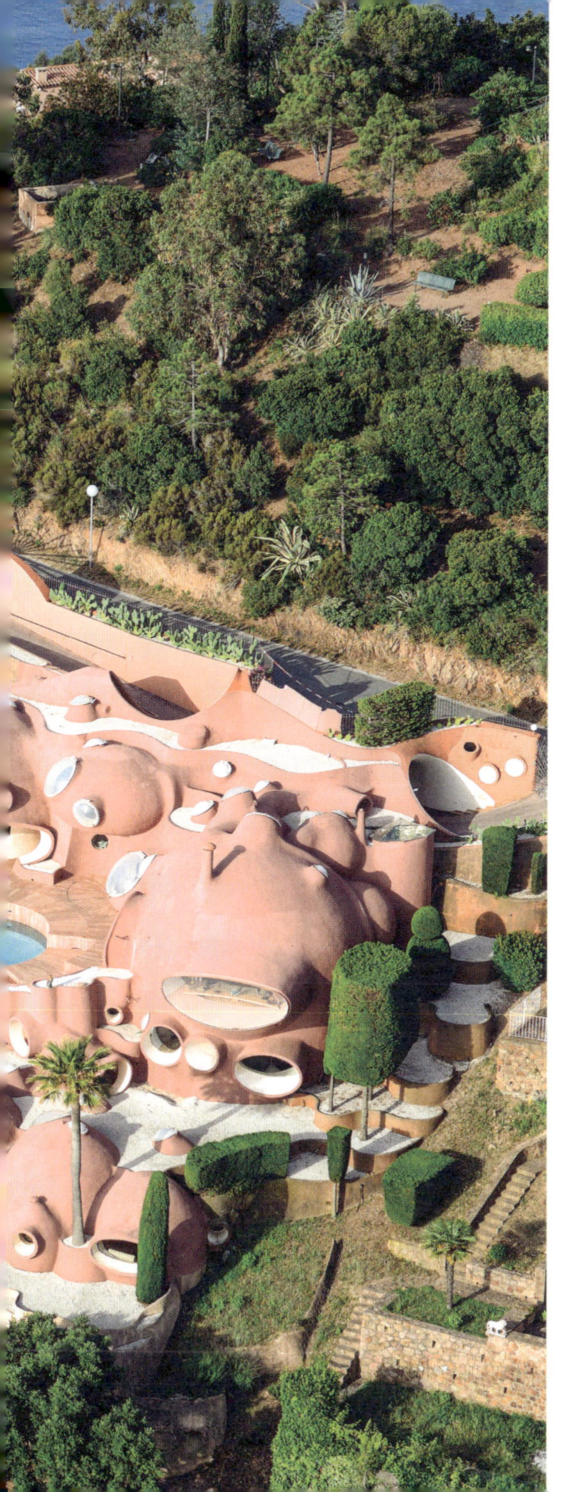

Bubble Palace
Théoule-sur-Mer, France
Architect: Antti Lovag, 1989

Fourteen years in the making, this fantastical residential complex looks like a Mars colony. The architect was interested in how humans interact with spaces and felt that the softness of spheres and curves was better suited to how we occupy buildings, and that the harsh lines of cubes were an 'aggression against nature'.

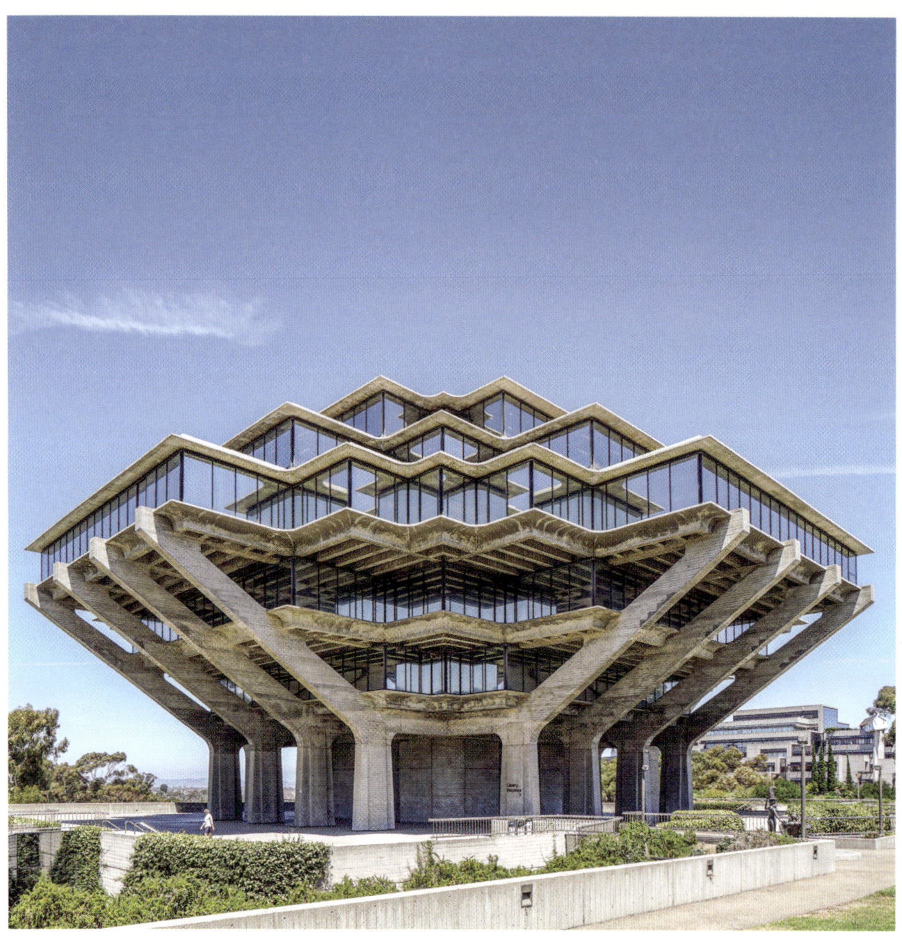

Geisel Library at UCSD
San Diego, California, USA
Architect: William Pereira, 1970

The main library at the University of California is renowned for its distinctive futuristic form. Built when Brutalism was at its zenith, the architect's use of reinforced concrete and sculptural elements made the building a groundbreaking feature of the 1960s architectural landscape, reflecting the era's fascination with space exploration and technological advancement.

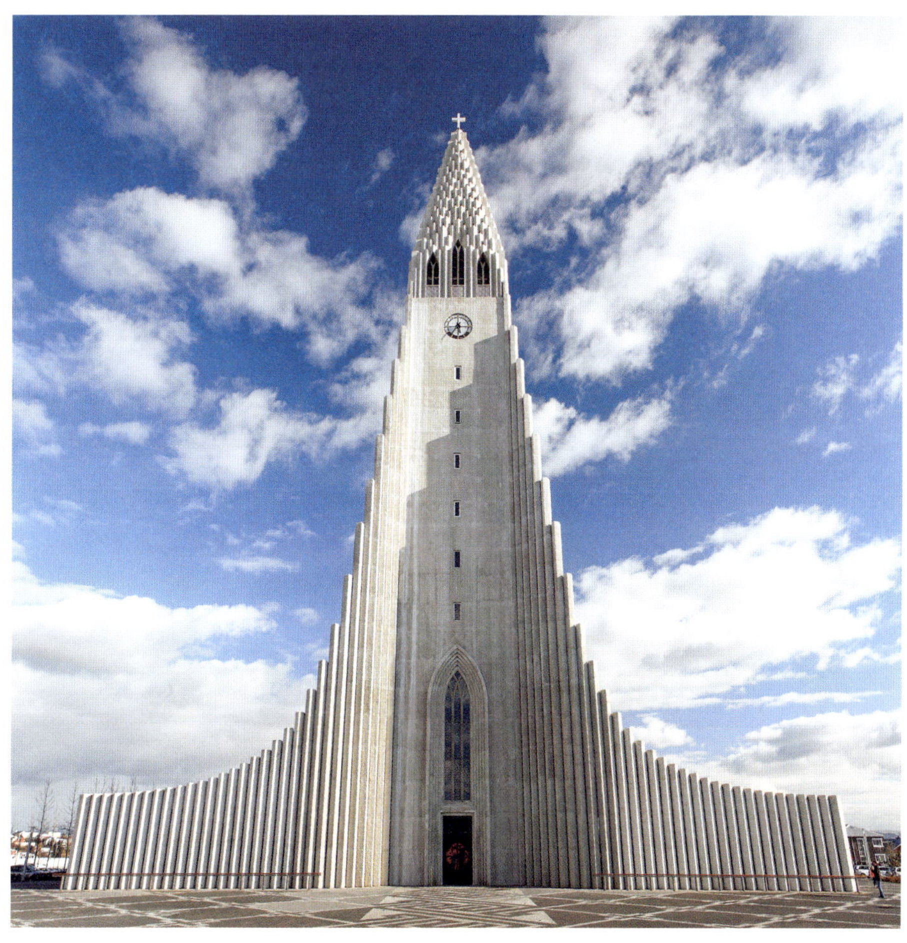

Hallgrímskirkja Church
Reykjavík, Iceland
Architect: Guðjón Samúelsson, 1986

Resembling a rocket ship ready to ascend the heavens, this is a minimalist monument to Icelandic cool. State architect Guðjón Samúelsson's arresting white stone design drew inspiration from Iceland's volcanic landscapes, particularly its distinctive basalt columns, which are formed as lava cools and contracts.

CCTV Headquarters
Beijing, China
Architect: OMA, 2012

Nicknamed 'big pants' due to its distinctive shape, this gravity-defying icon of Deconstructivism is the headquarters for state-owned China Central Television. Two leaning towers connect to create the bizarre effect of a hollow centre to the building. Their construction posed enormous challenges due to Beijing's extreme temperature swings, causing expansion and contraction of the structure.

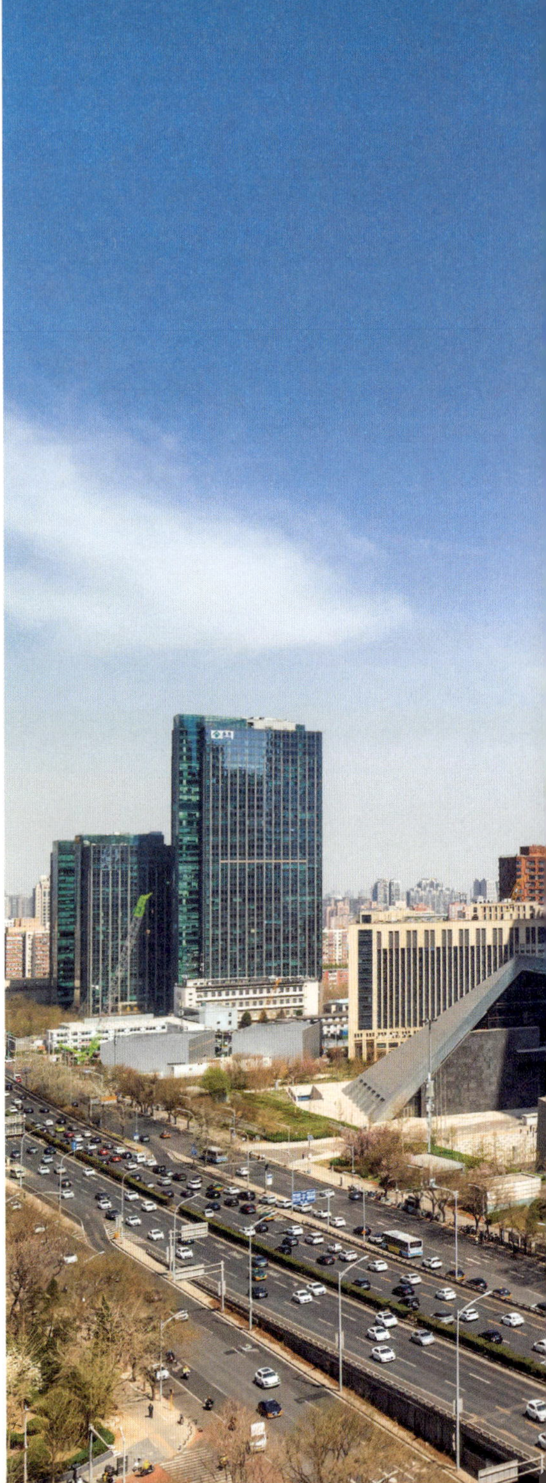

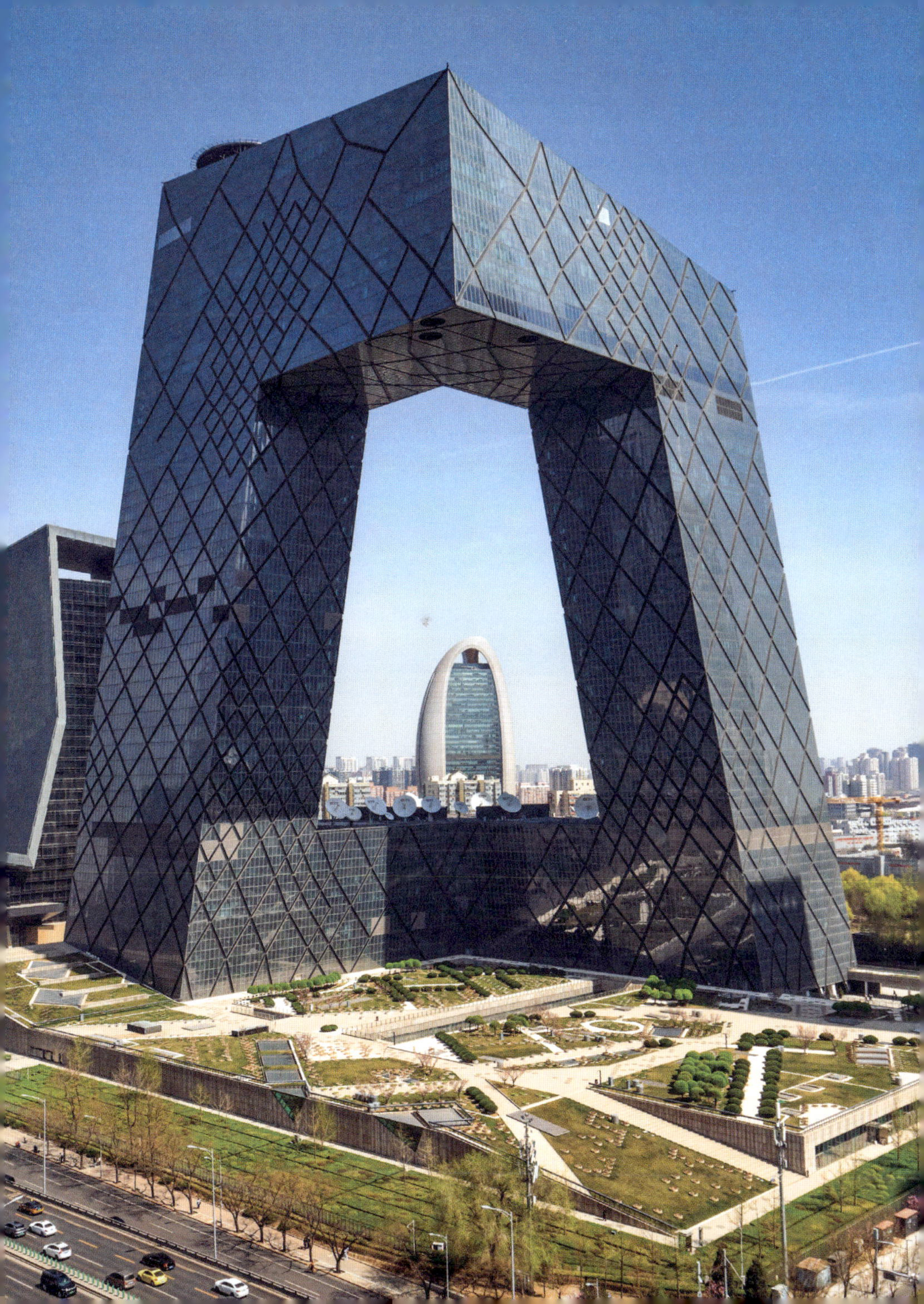

The Robot Building

Bangkok, Thailand

Architect: Sumet Jumsai, 1986

This playful sci-fi tower was designed as headquarters for the Bank of Asia (now UOB), inspired by the architect's son's robot toys. It was conceived to reflect the institution's pioneering embrace of technology – it was the first Asian bank to fully computerise. Currently under renovation, the building's new facade has yet to be revealed.

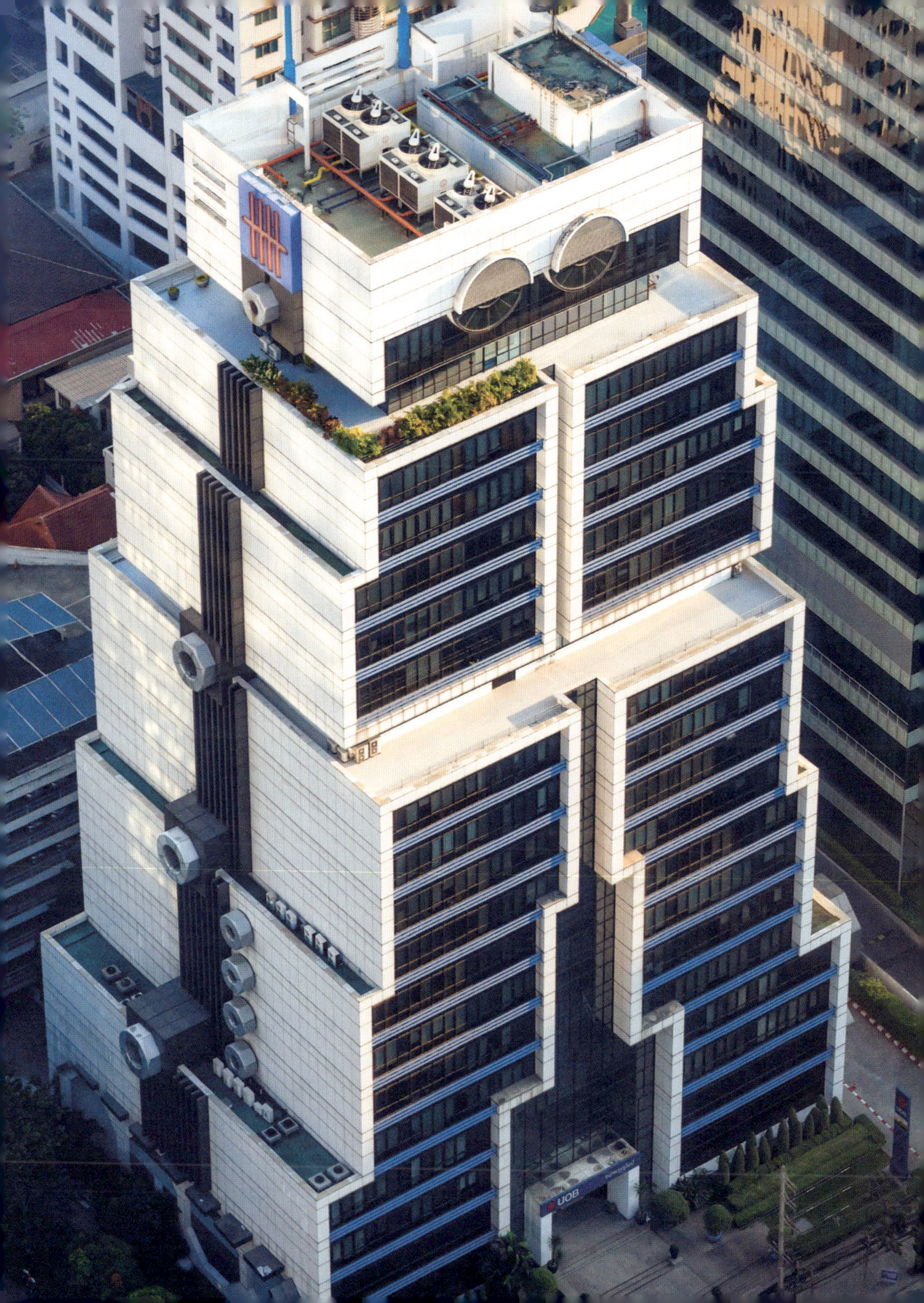
UOB

The Flatiron

New York City, New York, USA
Architect: Daniel Burnham, 1902

Officially 175 Fifth Avenue, but known as the Flatiron because of its resemblance to the clothing irons used at the turn of the 20th century, this striking triangular-shaped building has always captured public imagination. An iconic symbol of the city, it often cameos in films – famously in the *Spider-Man* franchise as the headquarters of the newspaper where Peter Parker worked.

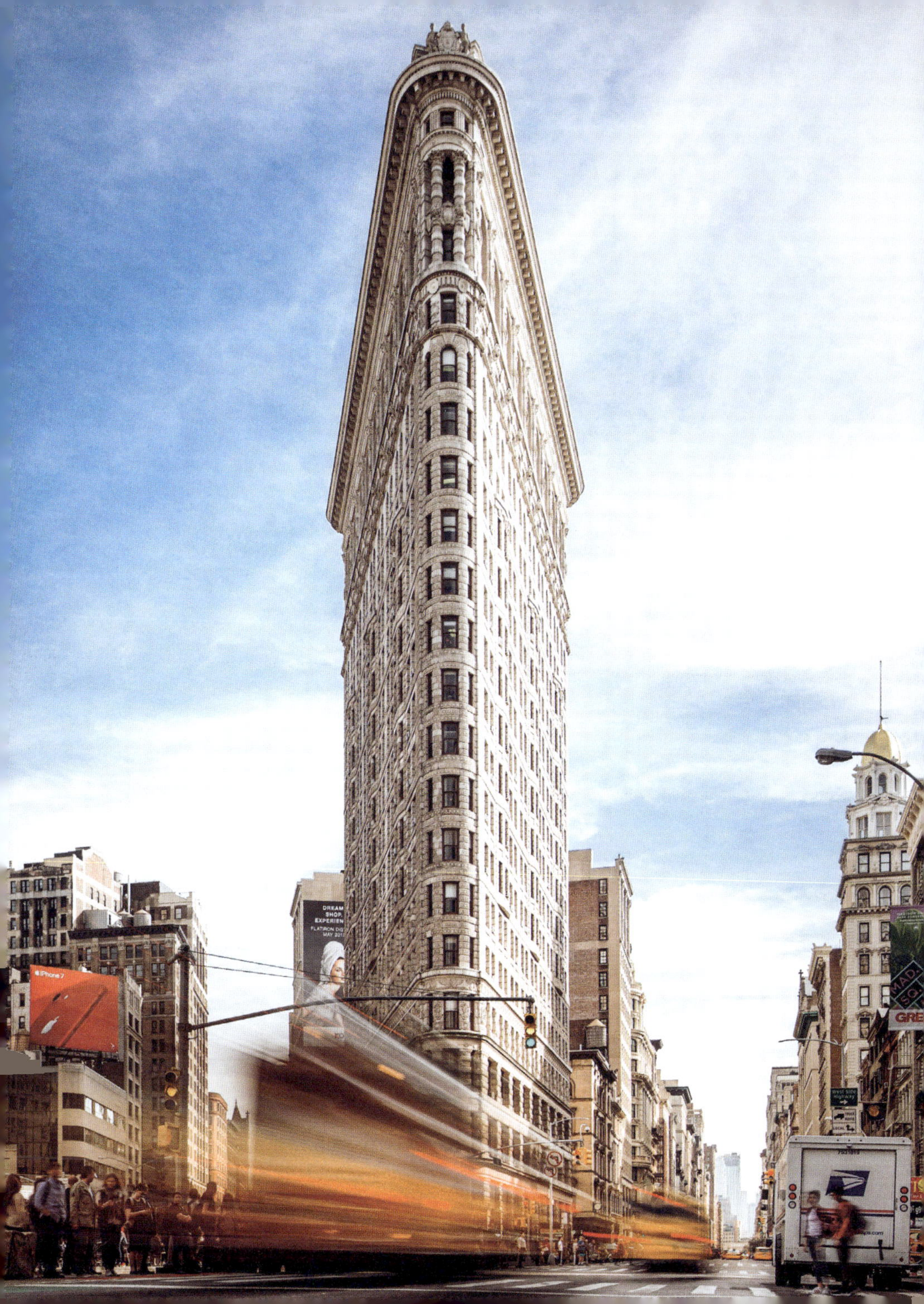
iPhone 7
DREAM
SHOP

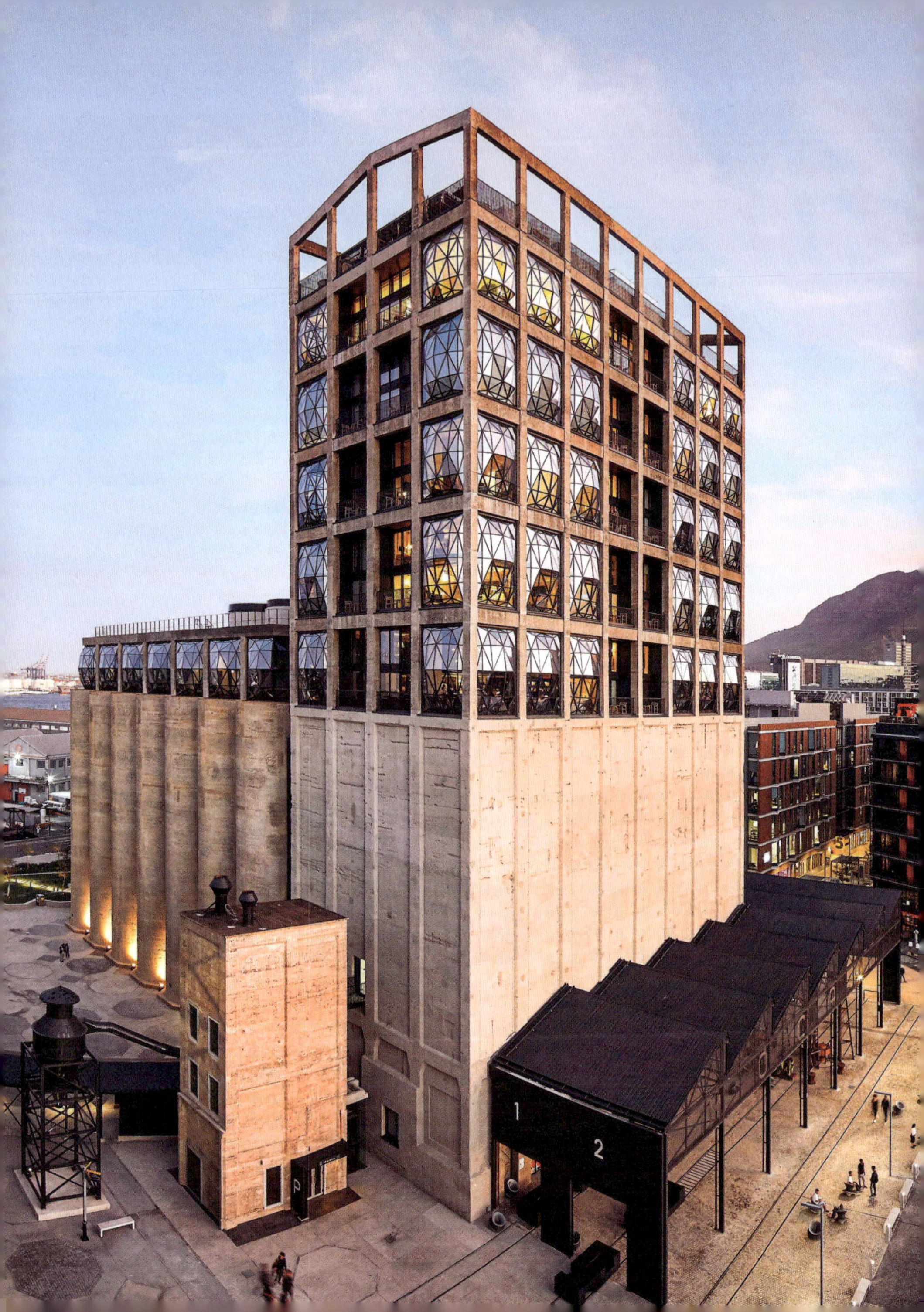

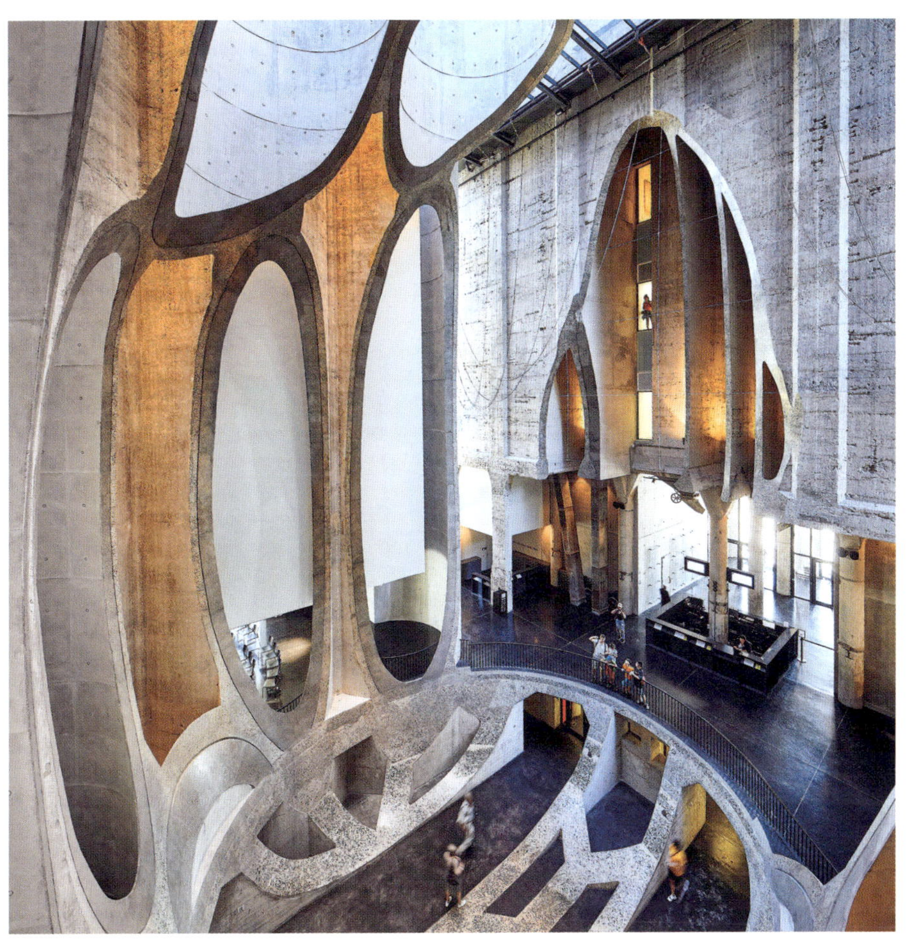

Zeitz MOCAA

Cape Town, South Africa

Architect: Heatherwick Studio, 2017

The world's largest museum dedicated to contemporary art from Africa and its diaspora is situated on Cape Town's bustling waterfront. It was created by hollowing out a historic grain silo built in the 1920s, and the interior is now a jaw-dropping concrete honeycomb of curves and light.

Crooked House

Sopot, Poland

Architects: Szotyńscy & Zaleski, 2004

Inspired by Polish fairy tale illustrations, this multi-use commercial building replicates the visual effect of a funhouse mirror. The unique design makes it appear warped, creating a disorienting and, for some, vertigo-inducing facade. It's like stepping into a wonky storybook world.

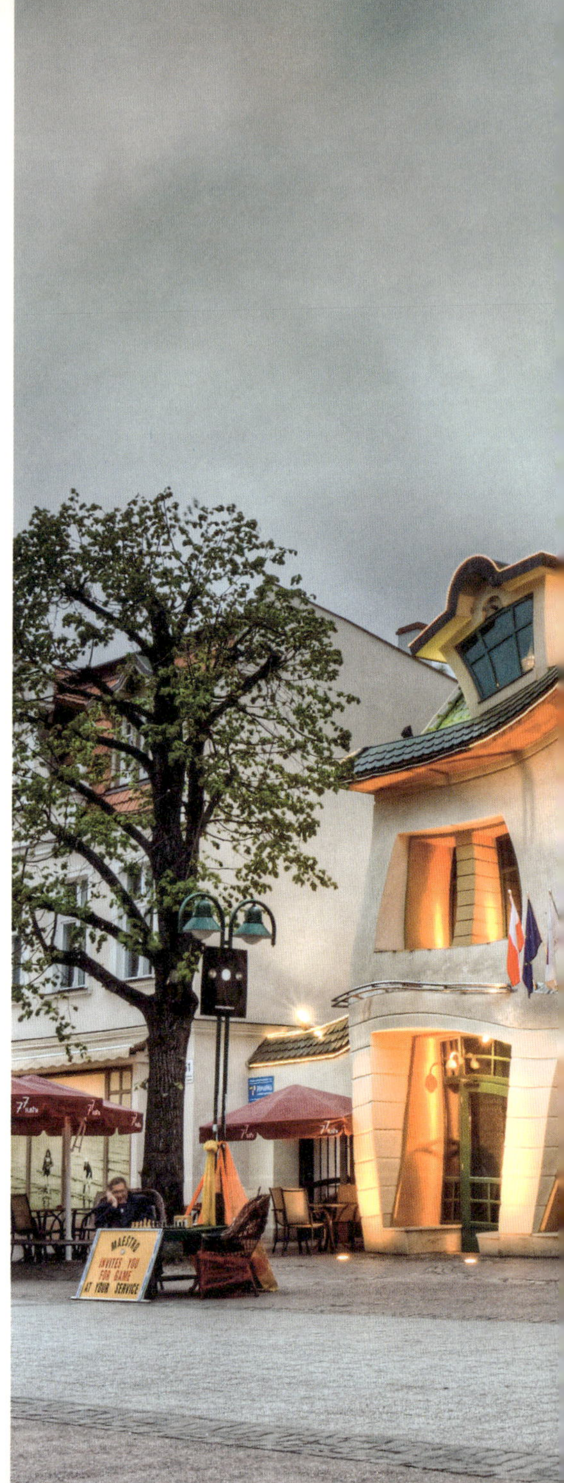

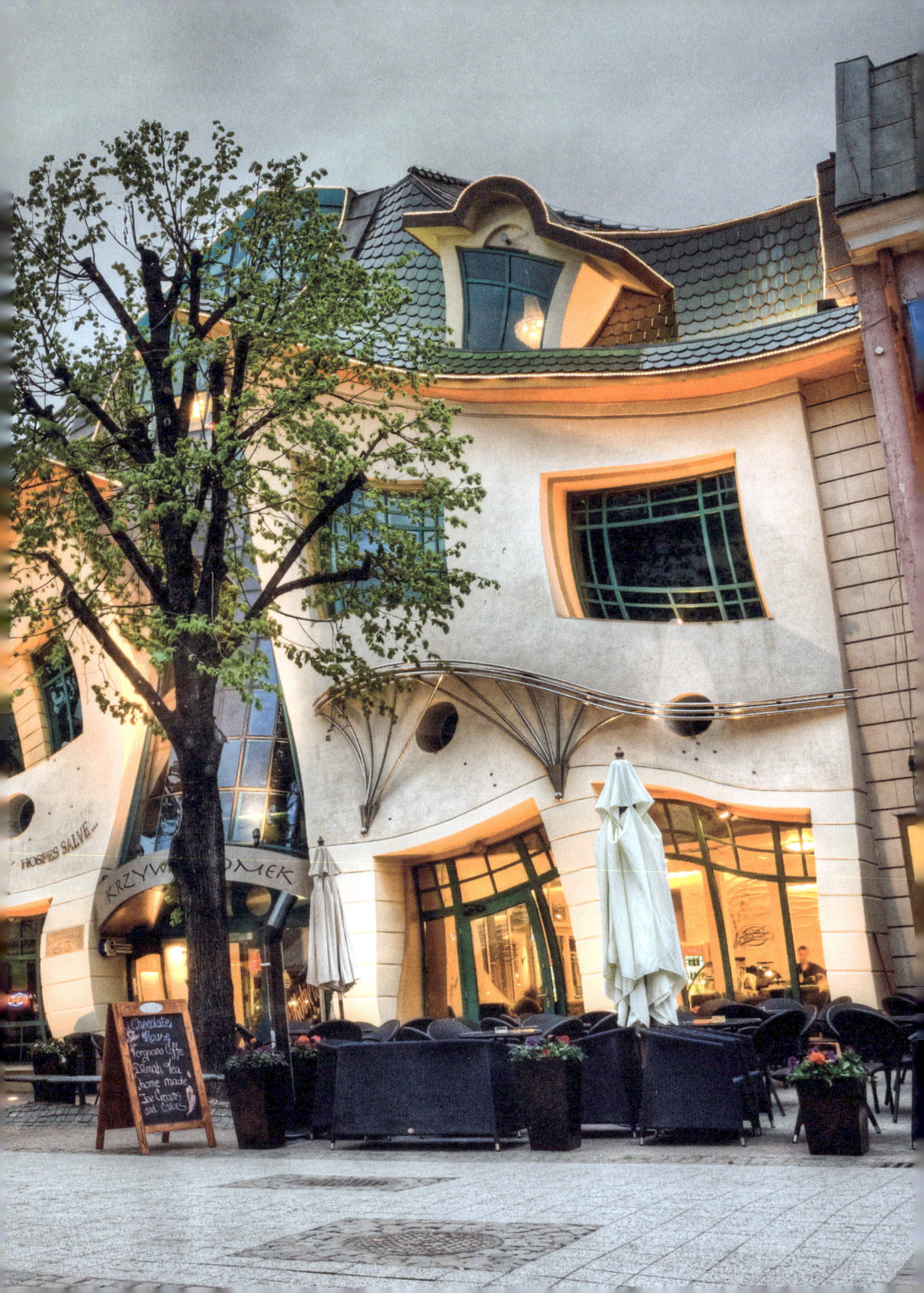
HOSPES SALVE...
KRZYW
OMEK
Chocolate House
Vergnano Coffe
Dilmah Tea
home made
Ice Creams
and Cakes

Capital Gate

Abu Dhabi, UAE

Architect: RMJM, 2011

Twisting up into the clouds like a high-tech tornado, this steel and glass tower is recognised as the world's farthest leaning manmade structure by Guinness World Records. The 160-metre-tall tower inclines at an angle of 18° – more than four times that of Pisa's famous landmark.

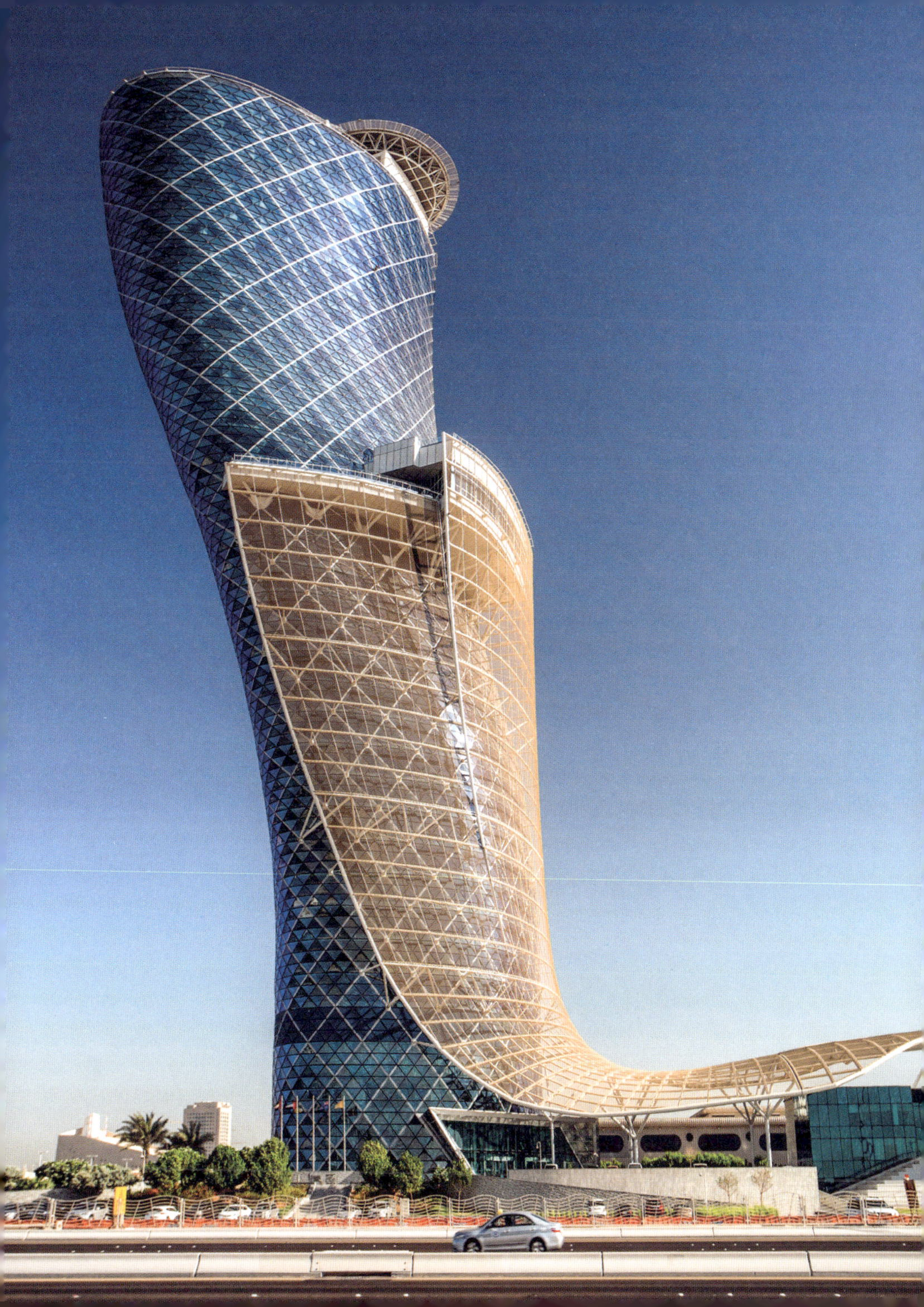

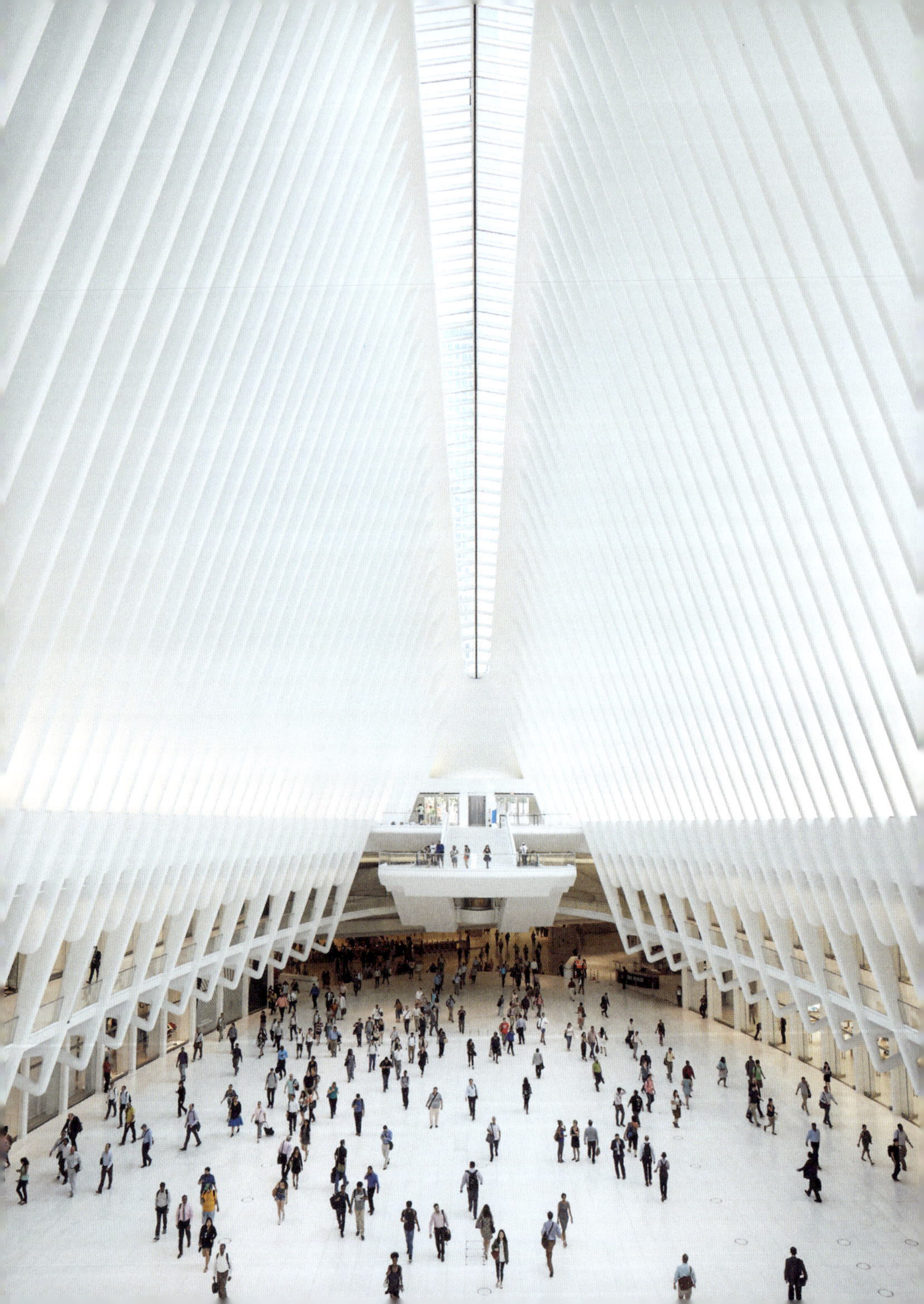

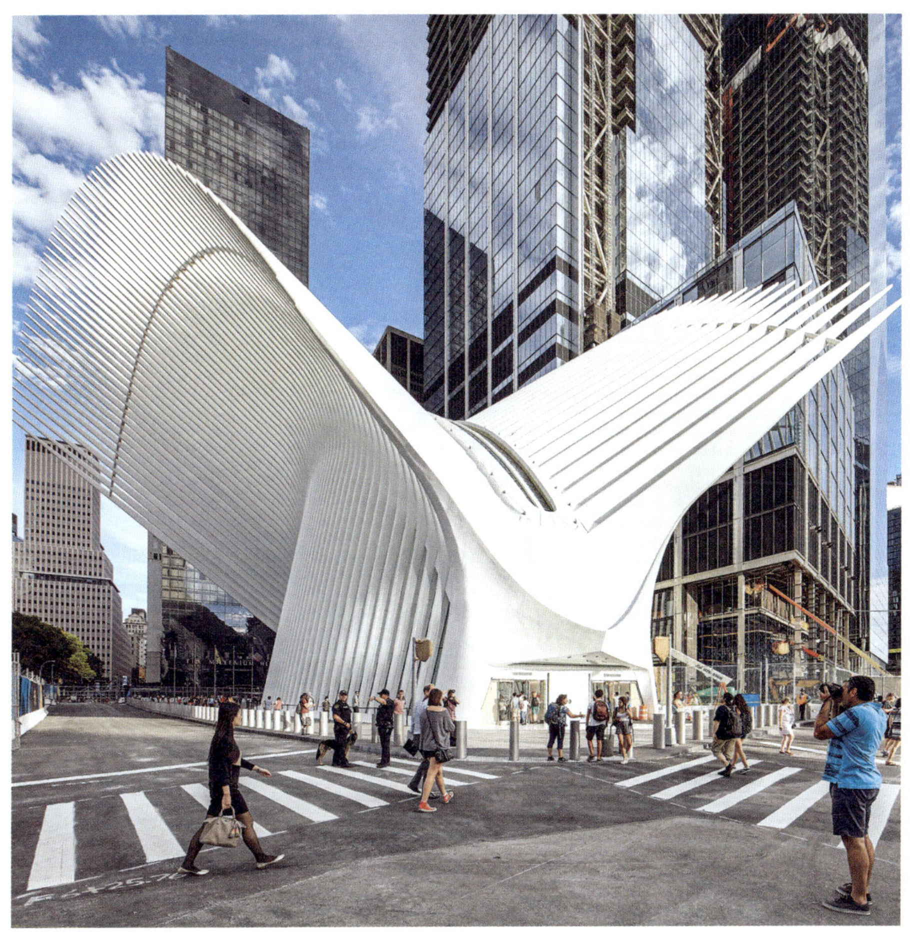

The Oculus
New York City, New York, USA
Architect: Santiago Calatrava, 2016

Built on the World Trade Center complex, The Oculus is a transit hub whose orientation is aligned with the sun's angles on 9/11 from the time of the first plane's impact until the second tower collapsed. White steel ribs reach skyward, representing a bird being released – a symbol of peace, hope and resilience.

Elbphilharmonie
Hamburg, Germany
Architects: Herzog & de Meuron, 2016

Built above a former warehouse, this concert hall's rippling glass facade and wave-inspired roofline echo the flow of the Elbe River. Renowned for its exceptional acoustics, with the interior featuring specially sculpted panels, the building is a hub for the arts and a spectacular sparkling crown atop the city's skyline.

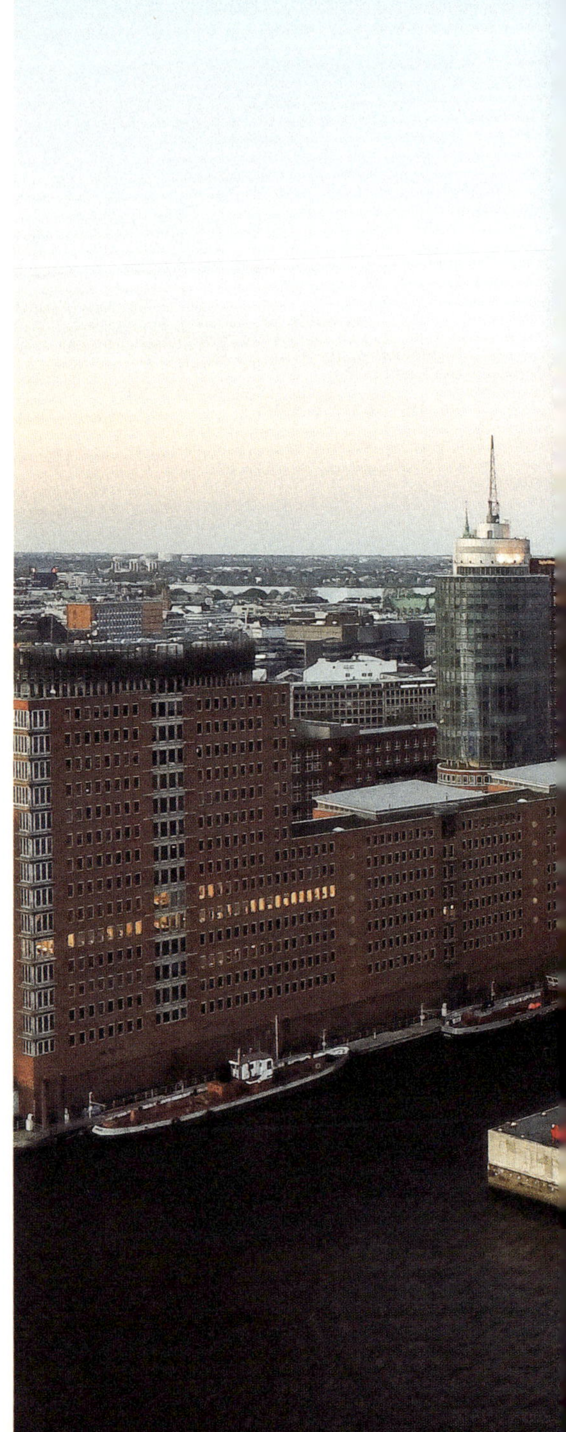

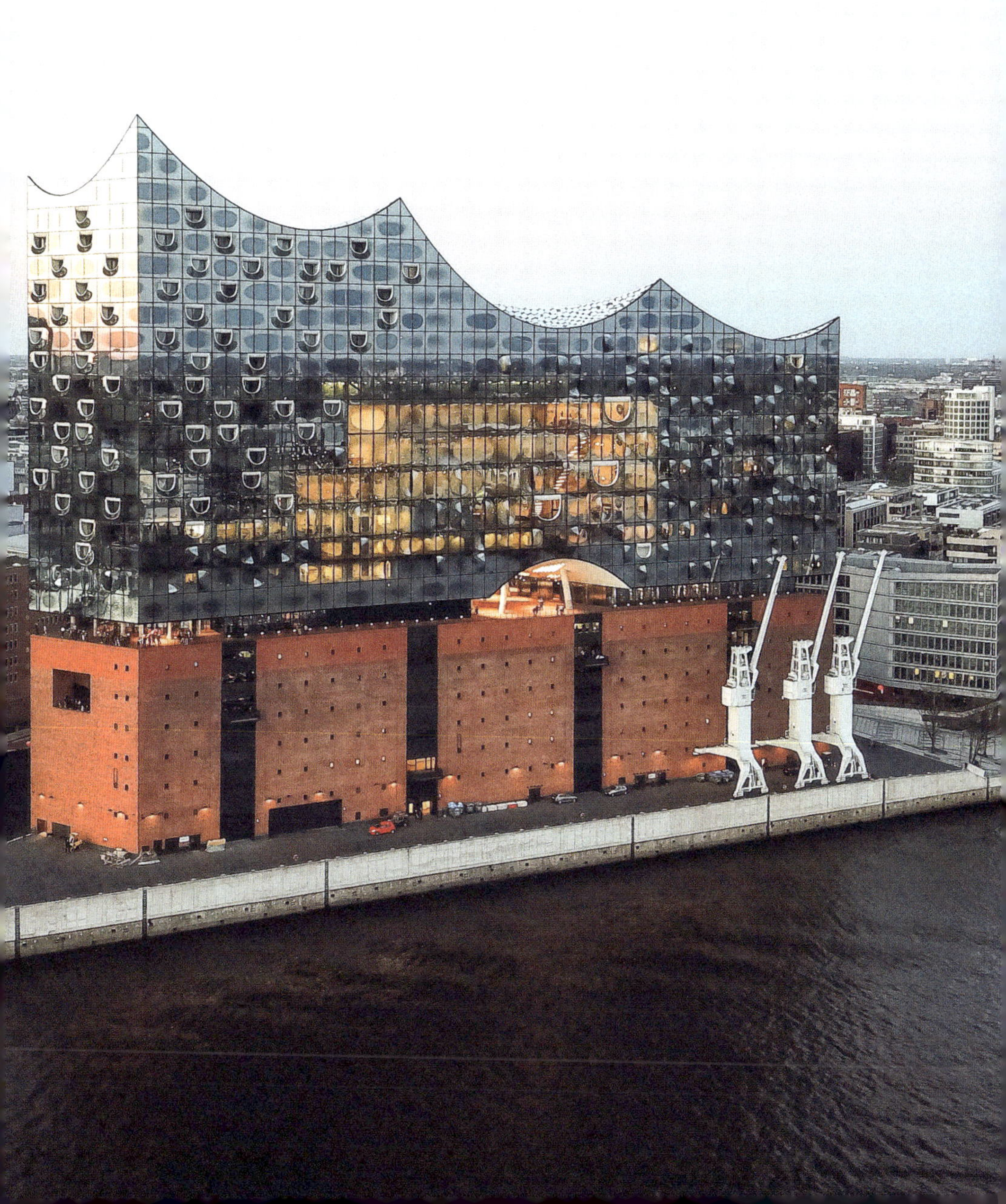

The Elephant Building
Bangkok, Thailand
Architect: Ong-ard Satrabhandhu, 1997

This mammoth building takes the city's love of elephants to new heights – literally. Part office, part apartment block, and all zoomorphic charm, it resembles a child's wooden toy with its eyes, tusks and blocky legs and stands proudly above Bangkok's concrete jungle.

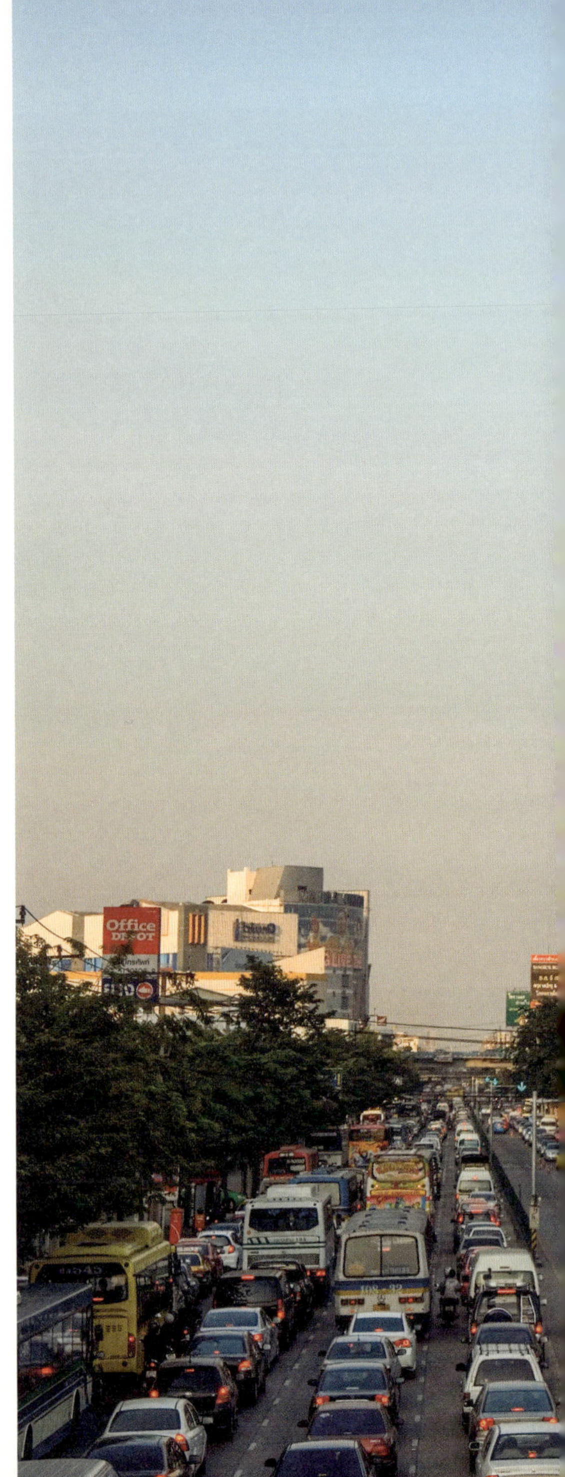

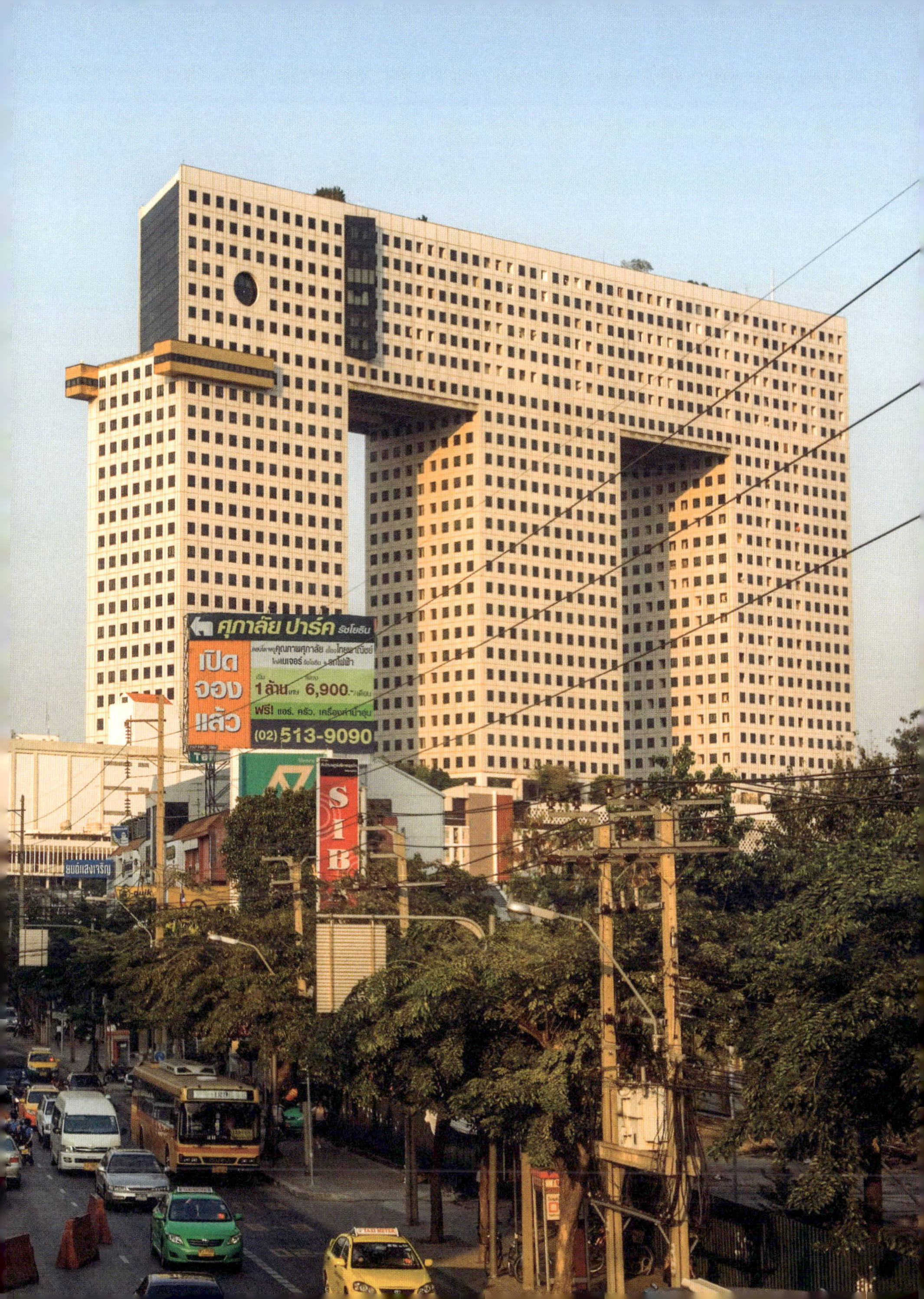
ศุภาลัย ปาร์ค รัชโยธิน
เปิด จอง แล้ว
1 ล้าน
6,900.-
(02) 513-9090
SIB

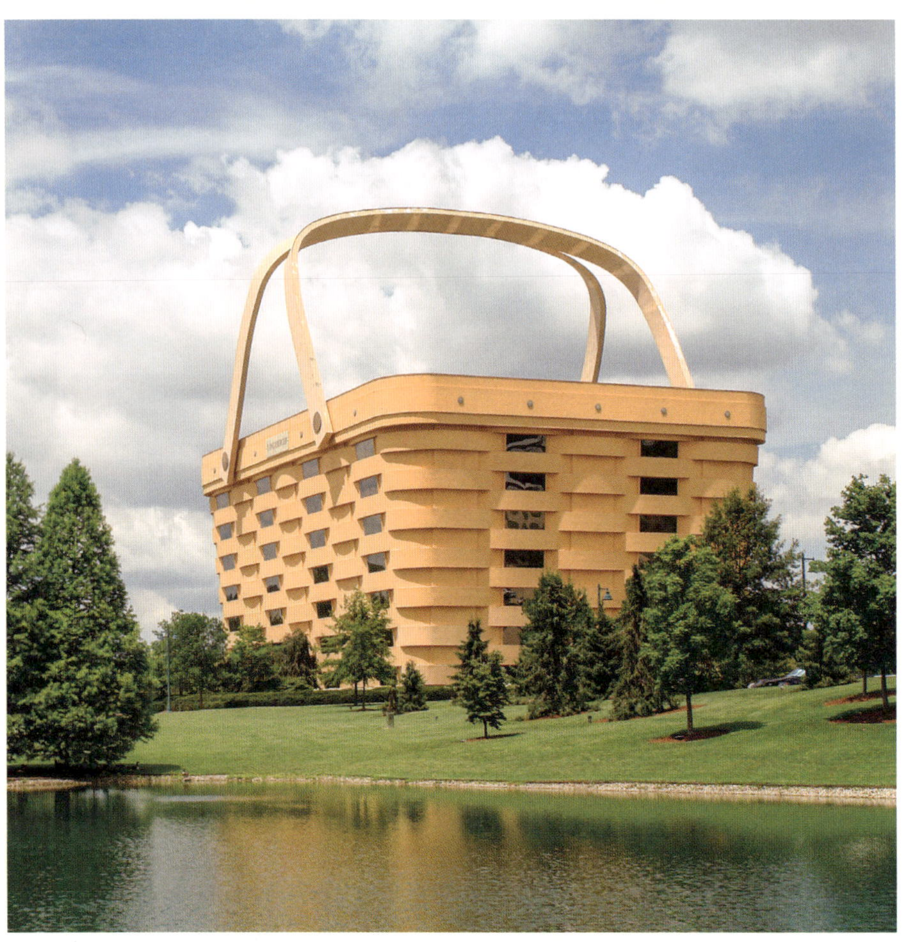

The Basket Building
Newark, Ohio, USA
Architects: Bohm-NBBJ, Inc, 1997

This seven-storey structure, formerly the headquarters of the Longaberger Company, was designed to resemble its best-selling product, the Medium Market Basket. The whimsical woven wonder features windows tucked among the weaves and steel handles that are heated to prevent them from icing over. It is a true monument to branding.

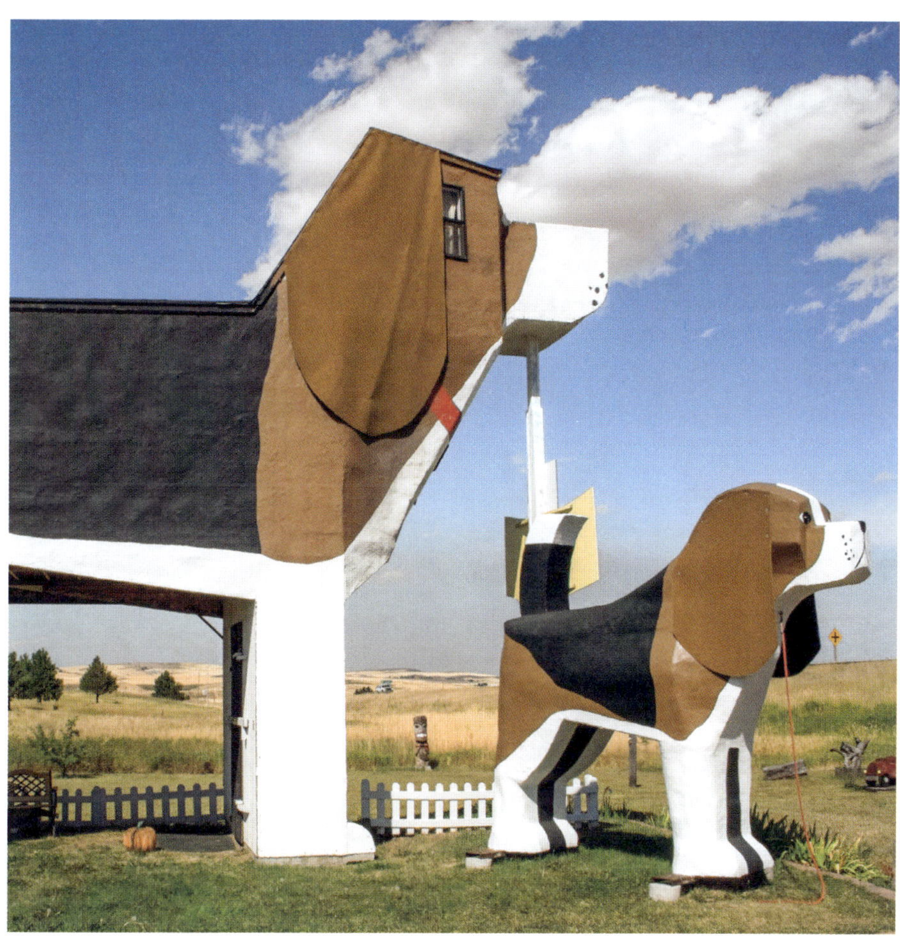

The Dog Bark Park Inn
Cottonwood, Idaho, USA
Architects: Dennis Sullivan and Frances Conklin, 2003

Continuing a rich tradition of American roadside whimsies, this much-loved guesthouse was created by husband-and-wife folk artists who carved wooden dogs. Inside the nine-metre-tall beagle, guests could marvel at handcrafted doggy decor and enjoy pooch-themed books, games and puzzles. Sadly, the inn has been closed since its owners retired in 2024.

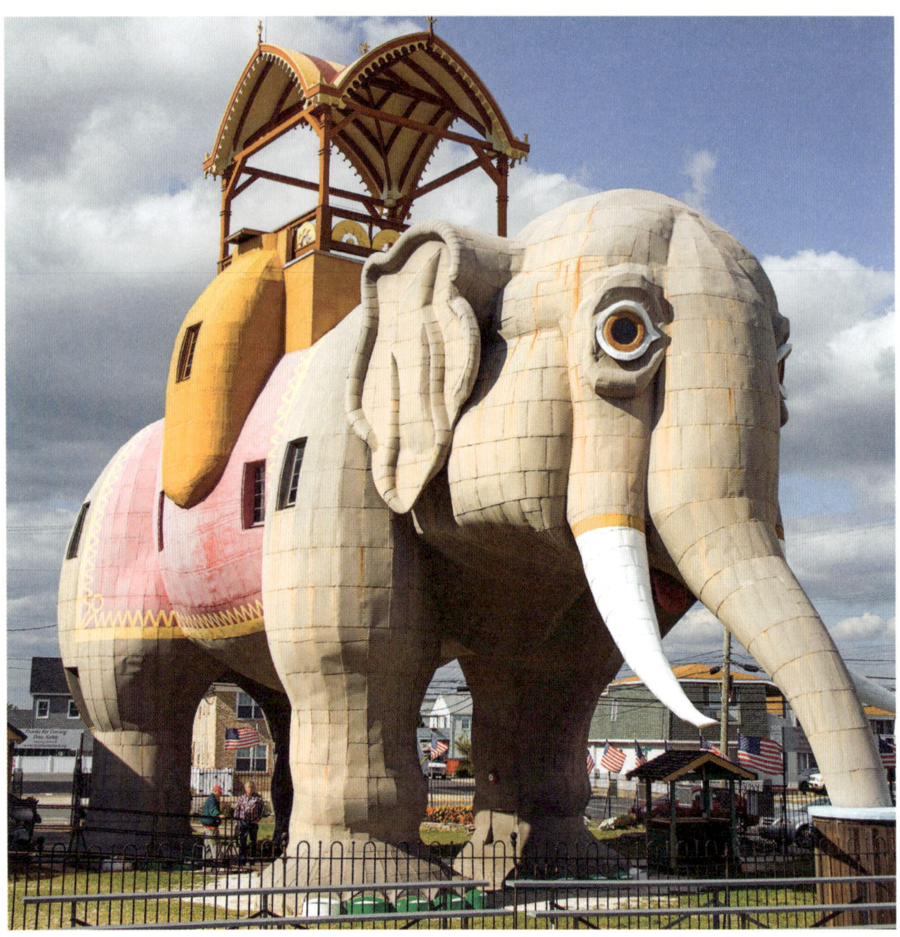

Lucy the Elephant
Margate, New Jersey, USA
Architect: James V. Lafferty, 1881

America's oldest roadside attraction was designed to attract property buyers to the area. Visitors could ascend the six-storey wooden structure and survey available land from her seat. Lucy has since been a restaurant, offices, a home and a tavern, and in 1976 joined the Statue of Liberty and the Hollywood Sign as a National Historic Landmark.

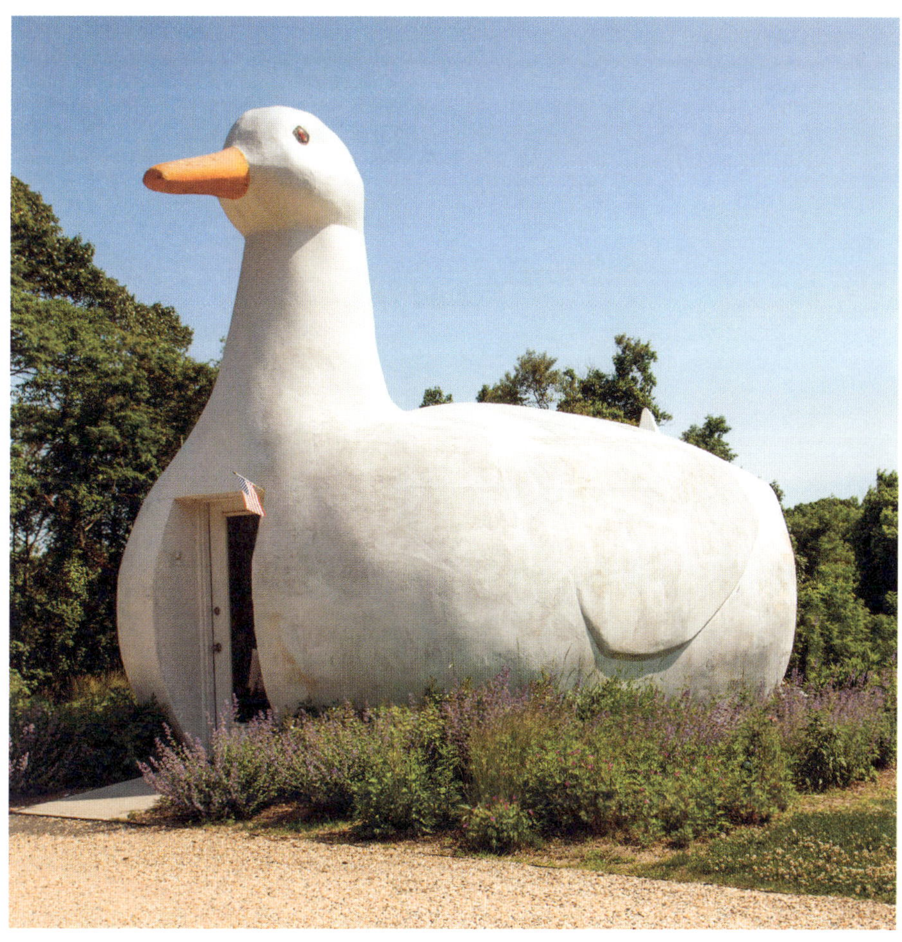

The Big Duck
Flanders, New York, USA
Architects: Martin Maurer, George Reeve, William and Samuel Collins, 1931

This duck-shaped structure inspired the term 'duck architecture', used to describe buildings that resemble what they represent. Commissioned by poultry farmer Martin Maurer to sell his produce in a roadside store, it is now a Long Island landmark with more quack appeal than ever, attracting historians, architecture buffs and duck lovers alike.

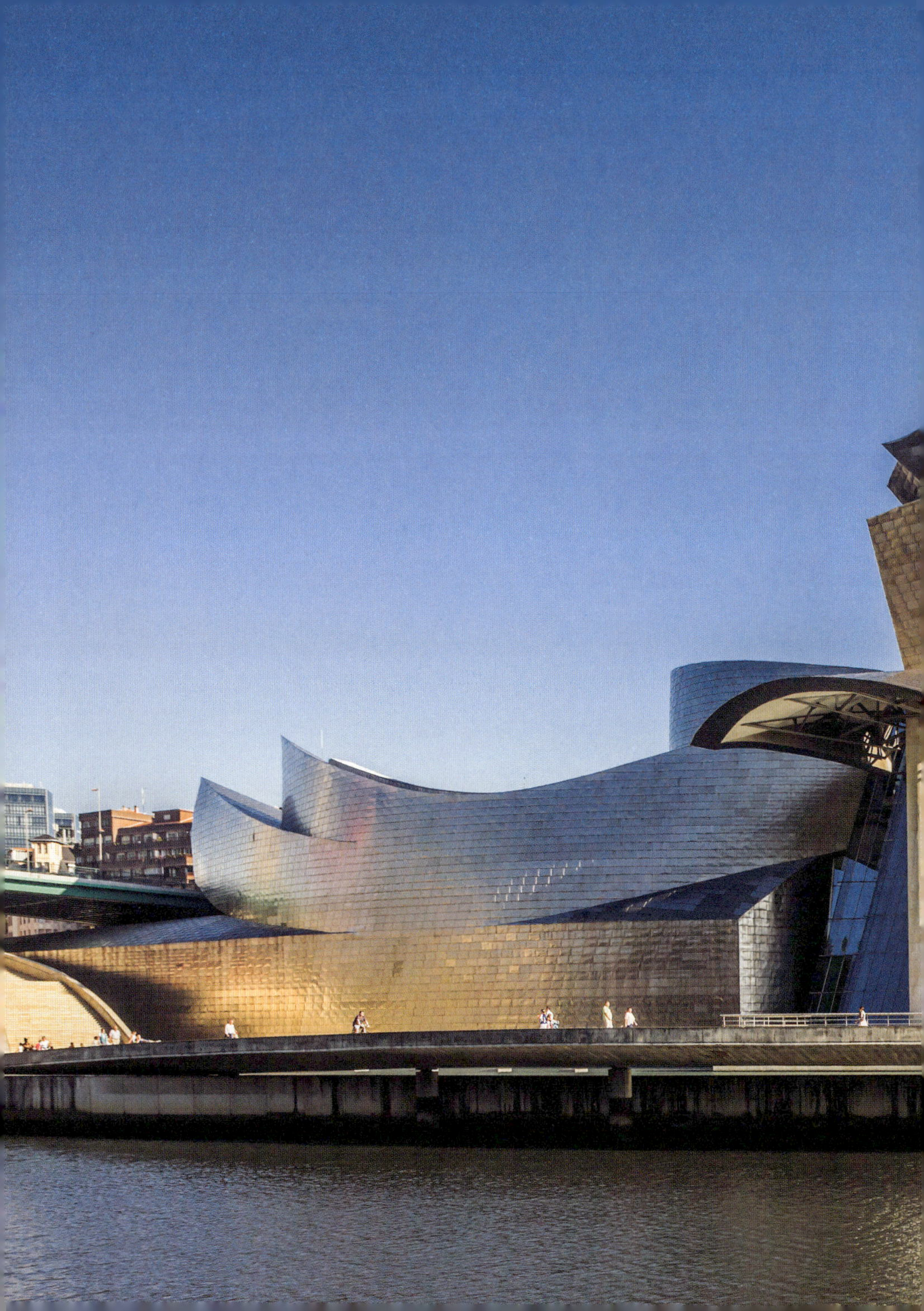

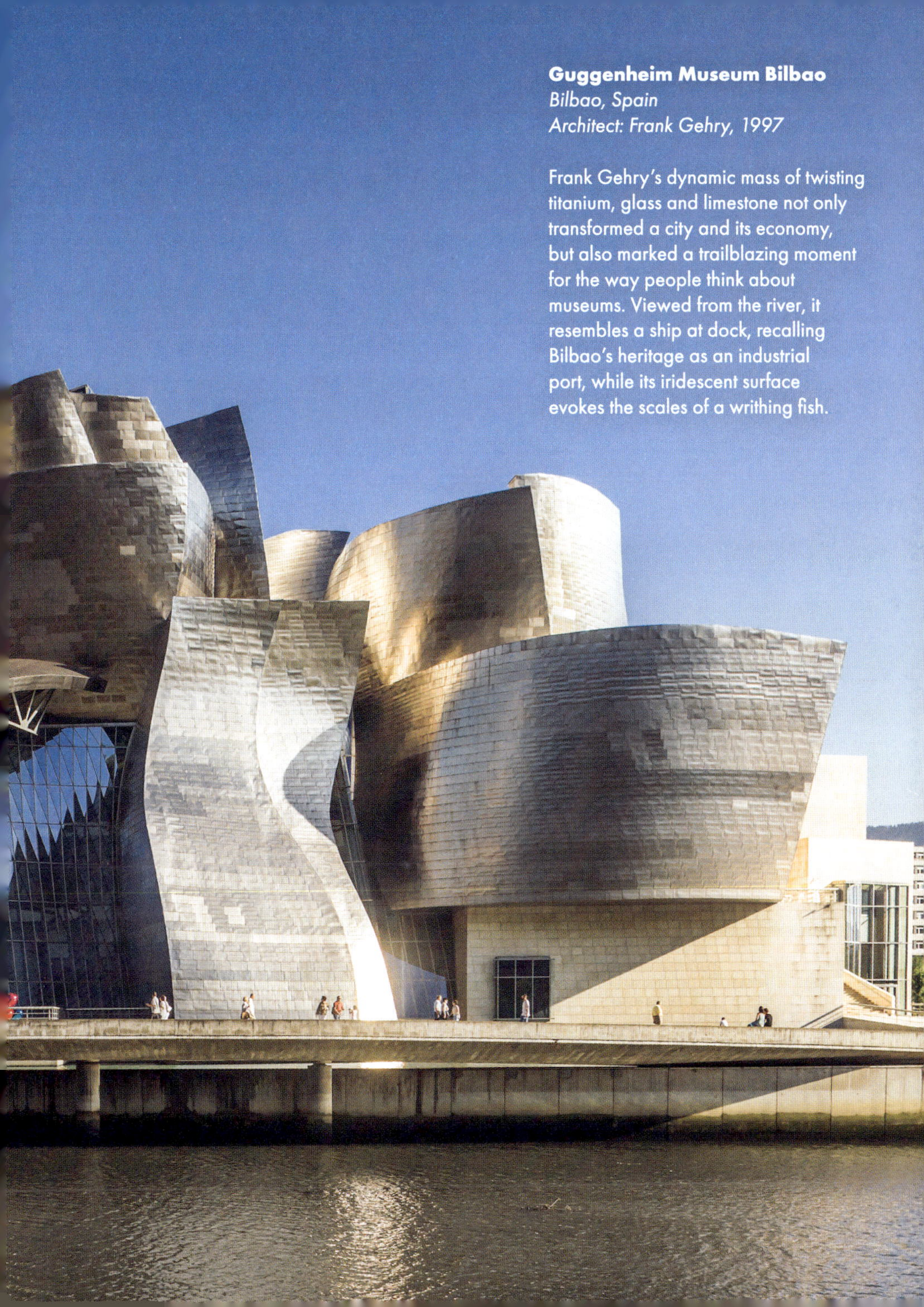

Guggenheim Museum Bilbao
Bilbao, Spain
Architect: Frank Gehry, 1997

Frank Gehry's dynamic mass of twisting titanium, glass and limestone not only transformed a city and its economy, but also marked a trailblazing moment for the way people think about museums. Viewed from the river, it resembles a ship at dock, recalling Bilbao's heritage as an industrial port, while its iridescent surface evokes the scales of a writhing fish.

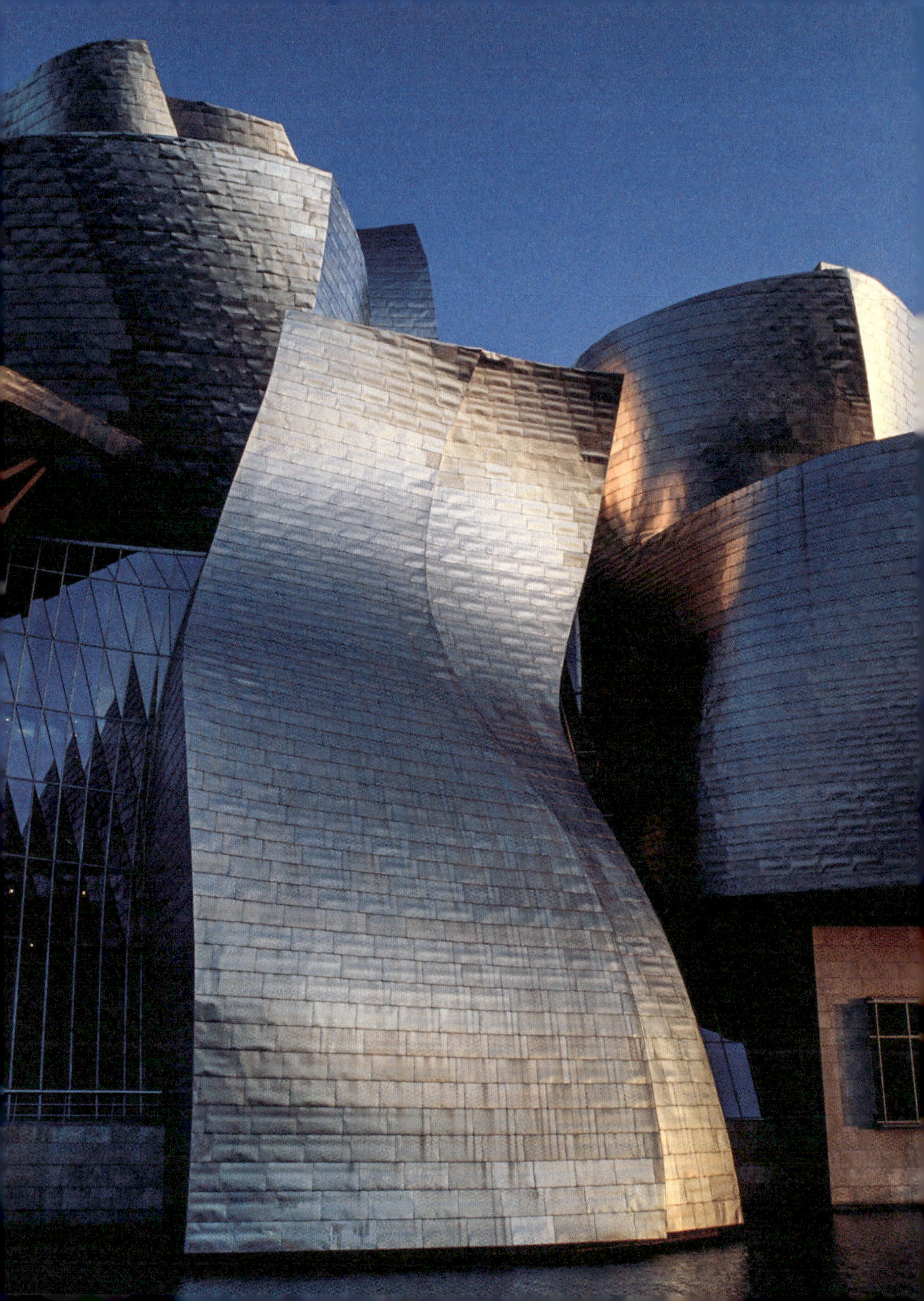

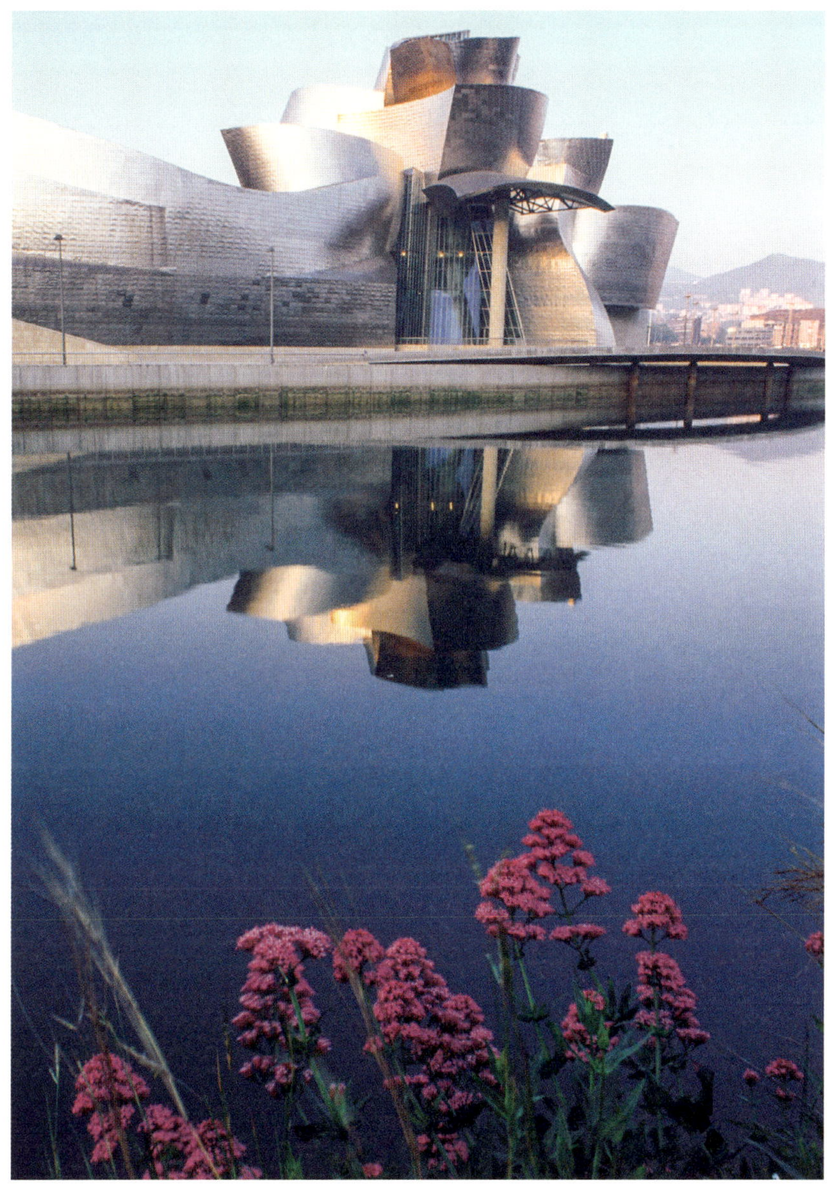

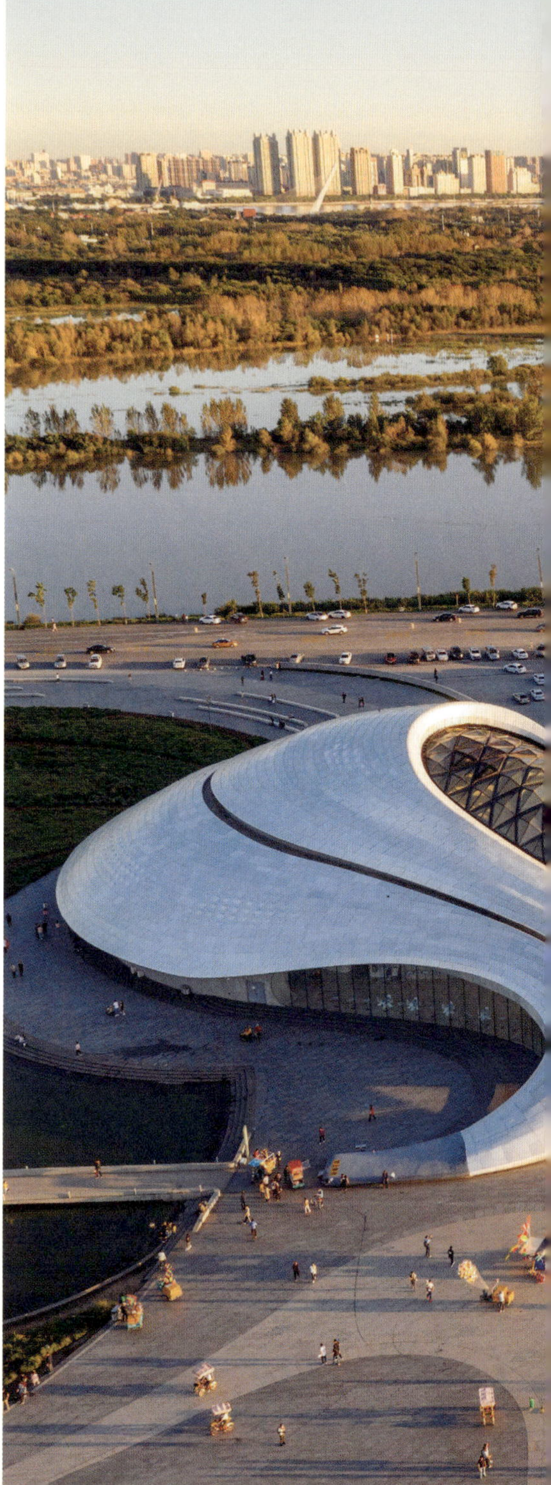

Harbin Opera House
Harbin, China
Architect: MAD Architects, 2015

Flowing like a shimmering wave alongside the wetlands of the Songhua River, this sinuous concert hall is part of an enormous arts complex. Made of smooth white aluminium panels and glass, its sculptural form is designed to mirror the graceful curves of the neighbouring marsh landscape.

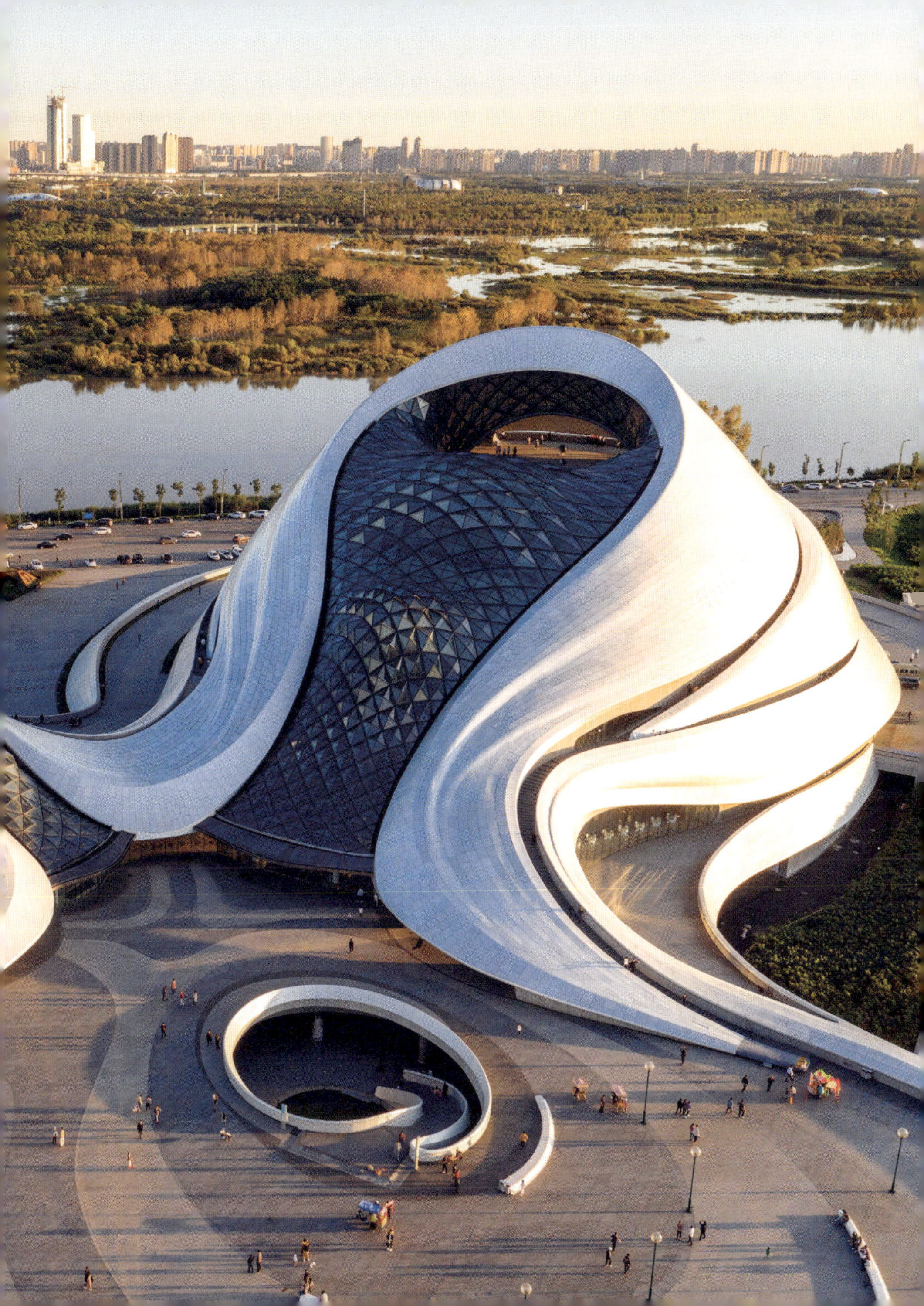

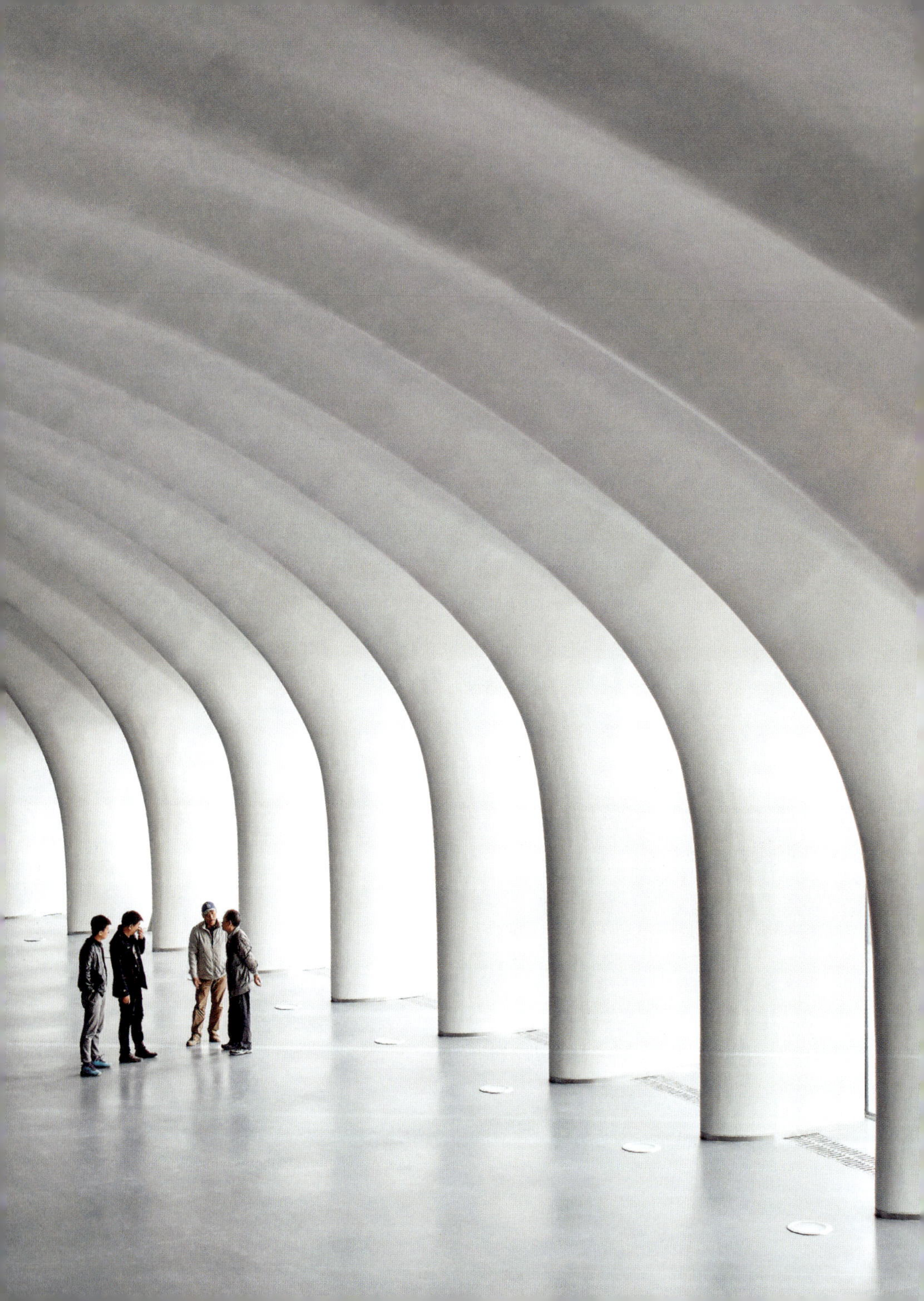

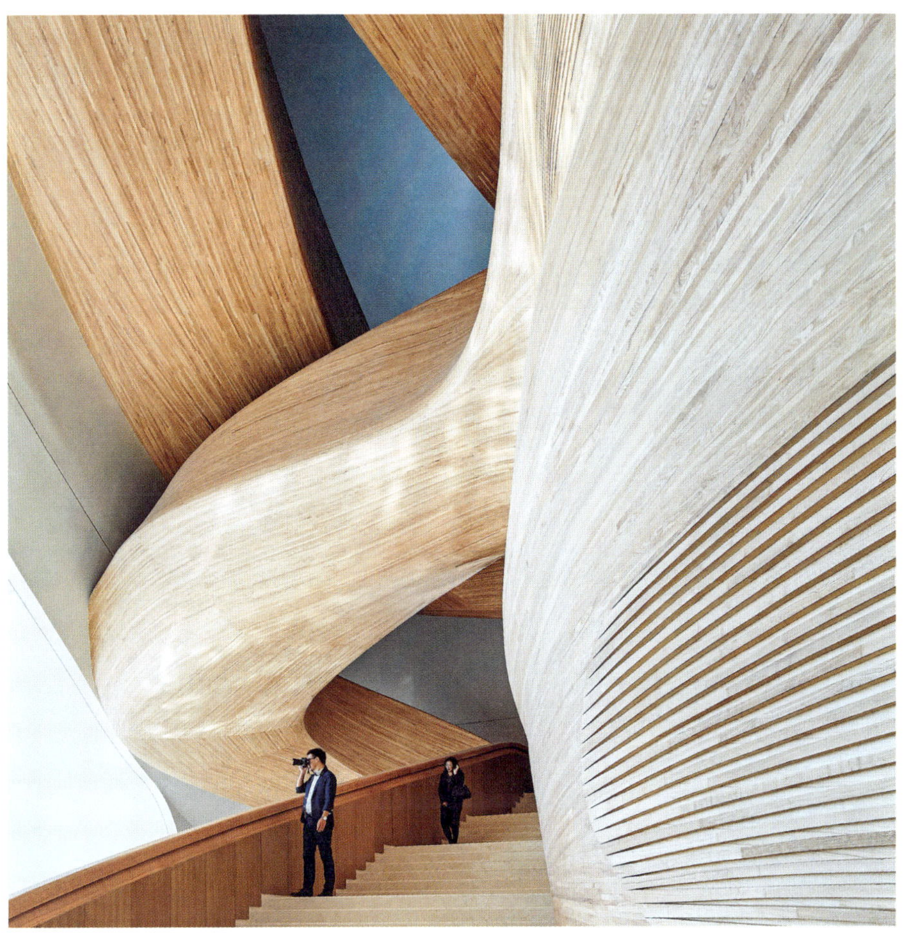

Inside are two theatres and a vast foyer, where large transparent glass walls echo the cool, clean design of the building's exterior. Arising from the atrium, a sculptural wooden mass carved out of Manchurian ash – also used in the Grand Theatre within– incorporates a curved stair, allowing visitors to ascend to the top of the building.

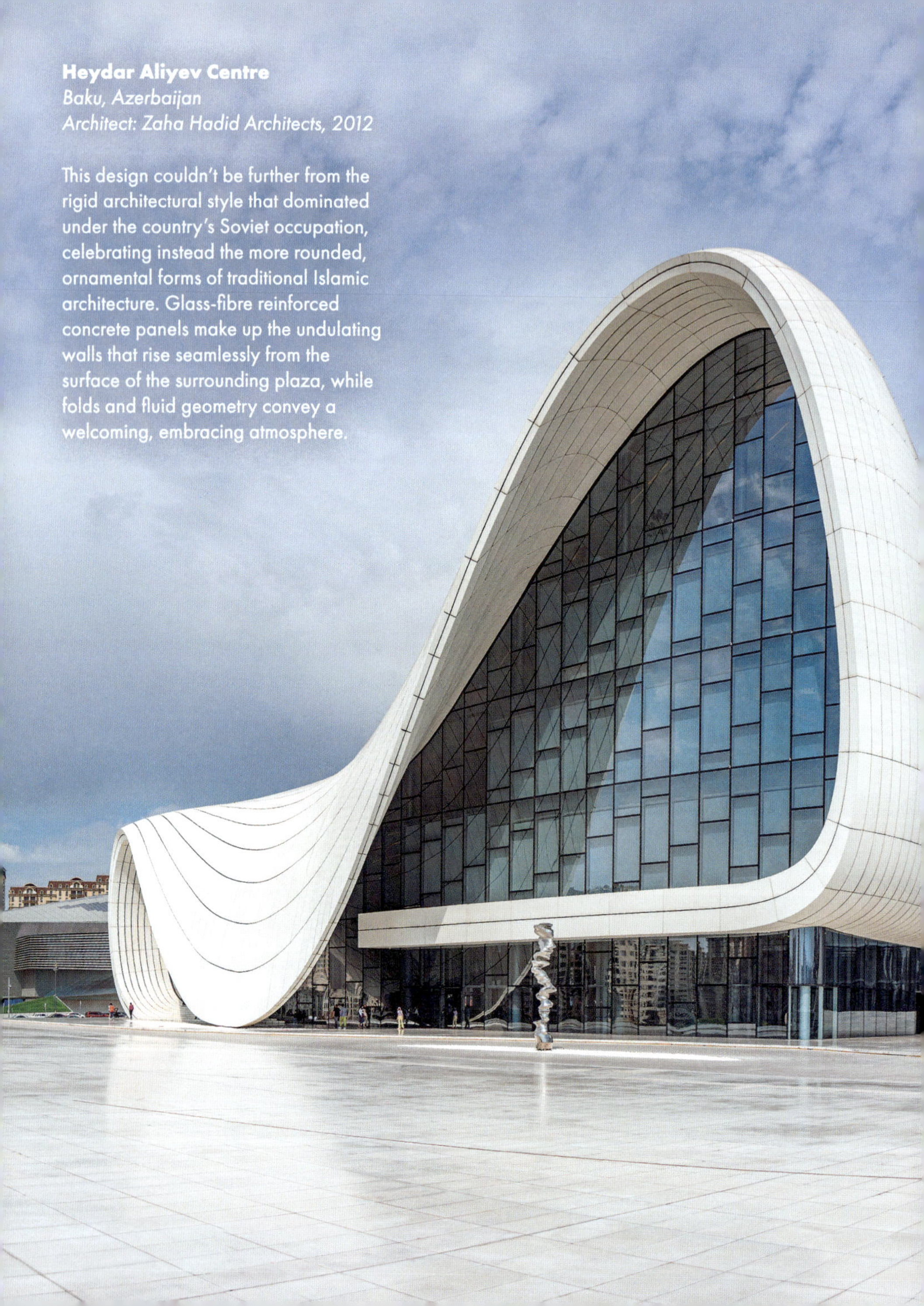

Heydar Aliyev Centre
Baku, Azerbaijan
Architect: Zaha Hadid Architects, 2012

This design couldn't be further from the rigid architectural style that dominated under the country's Soviet occupation, celebrating instead the more rounded, ornamental forms of traditional Islamic architecture. Glass-fibre reinforced concrete panels make up the undulating walls that rise seamlessly from the surface of the surrounding plaza, while folds and fluid geometry convey a welcoming, embracing atmosphere.

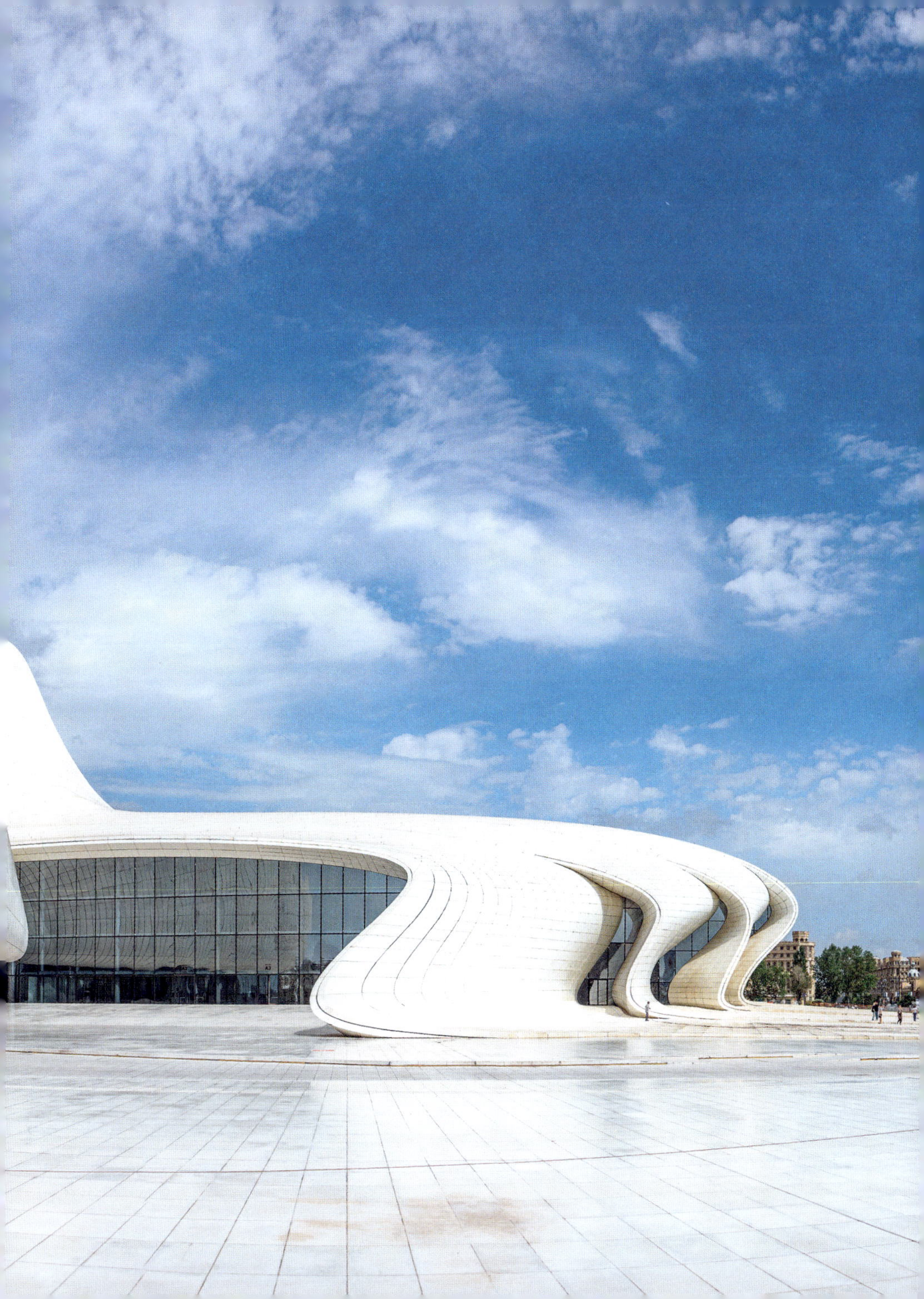

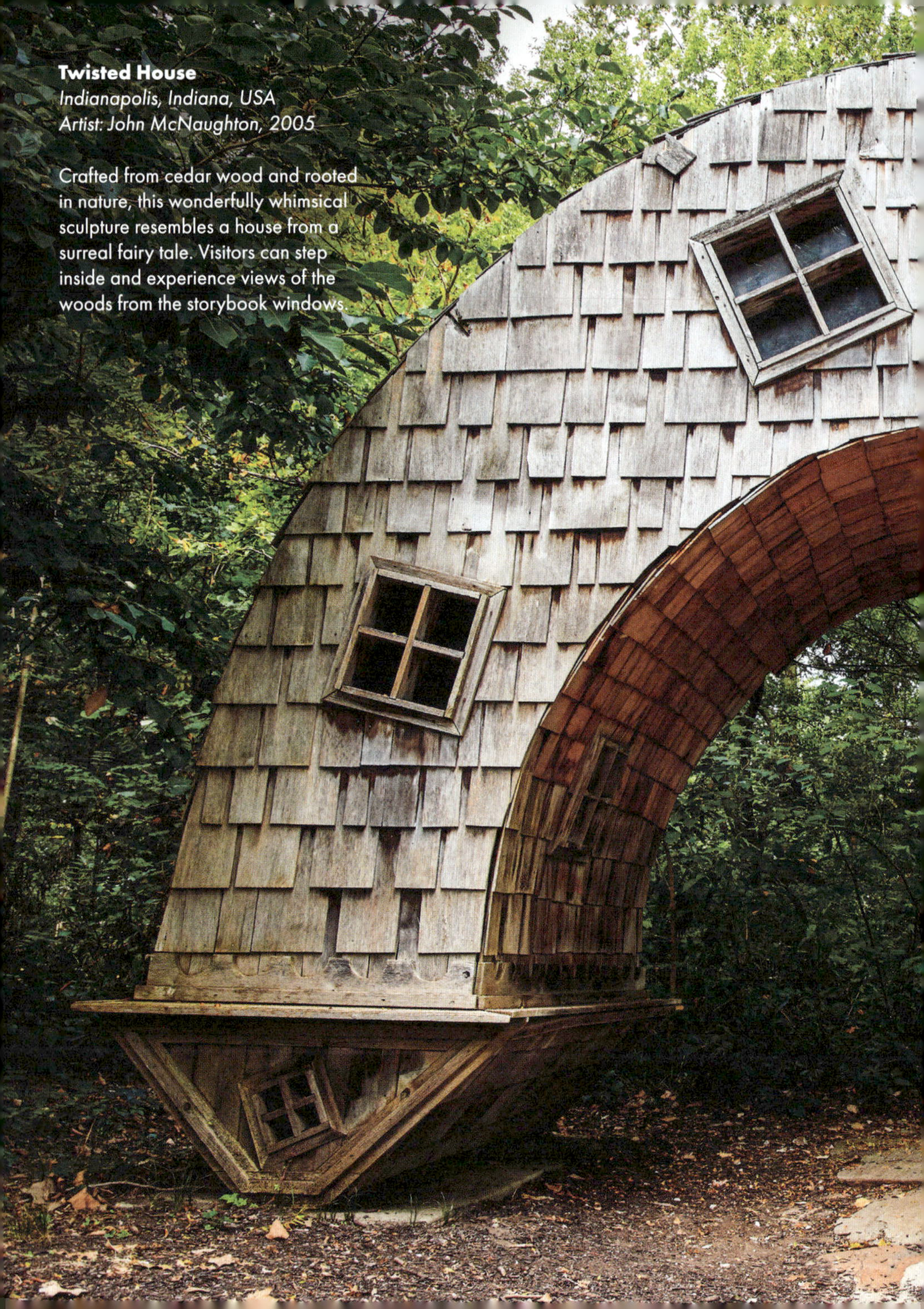

Twisted House
Indianapolis, Indiana, USA
Artist: John McNaughton, 2005

Crafted from cedar wood and rooted in nature, this wonderfully whimsical sculpture resembles a house from a surreal fairy tale. Visitors can step inside and experience views of the woods from the storybook windows.

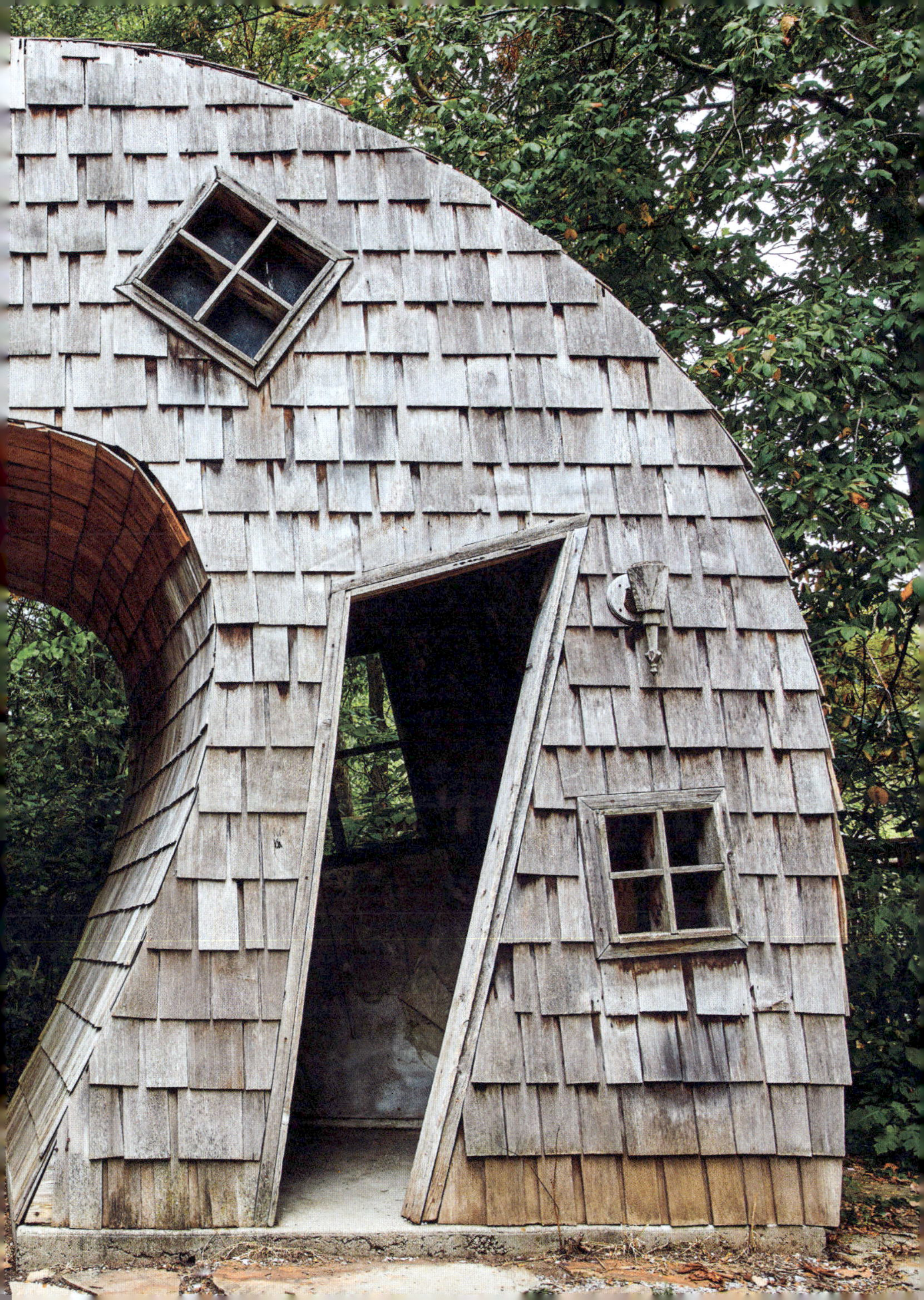

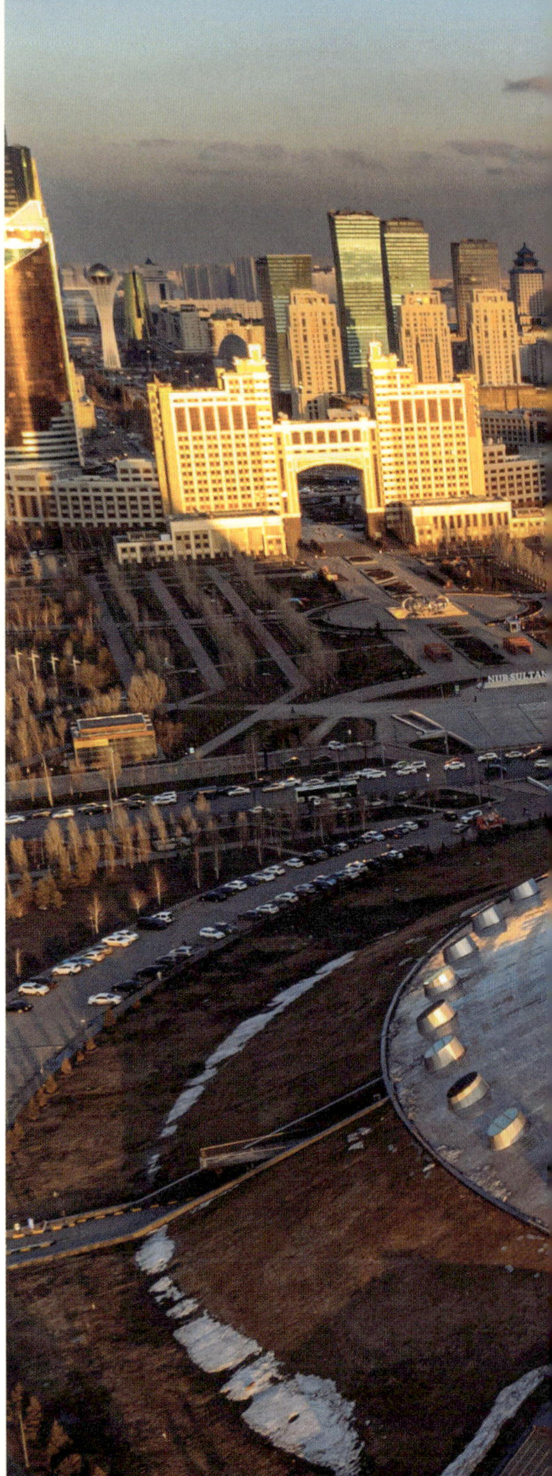

Khan Shatyr Entertainment Centre
Astana, Kazakhstan
Architect: Foster + Partners, 2010

Rising from the Kazakh capital like a futuristic circus top, the tent-like structure of this civic centre was designed to shelter visitors from weather extremes, where temperatures can climb to 35°C in summer and fall to -35°C in winter. It features a three-layered climatic envelope, and the translucent structure allows daylight to flood the interior.

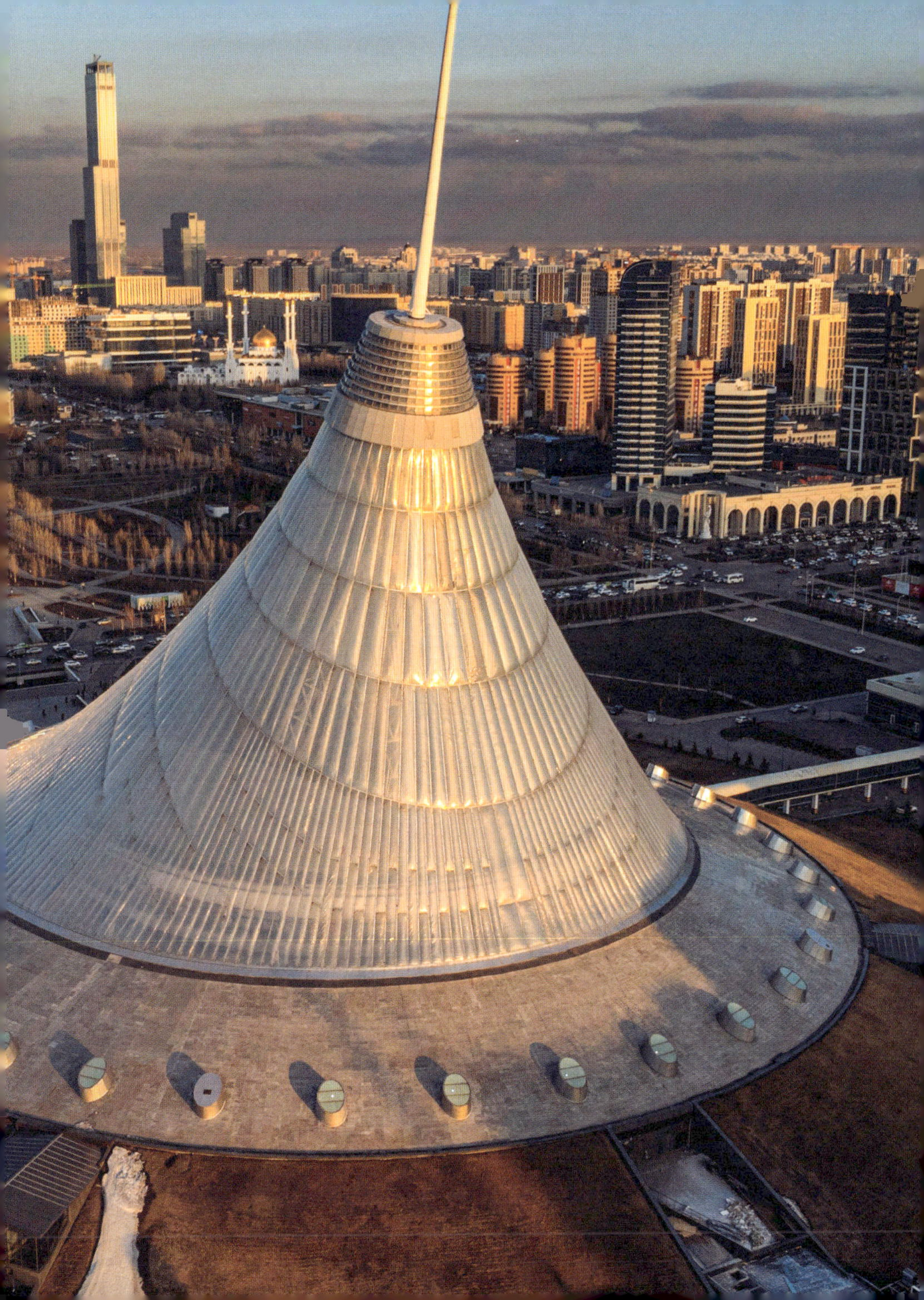

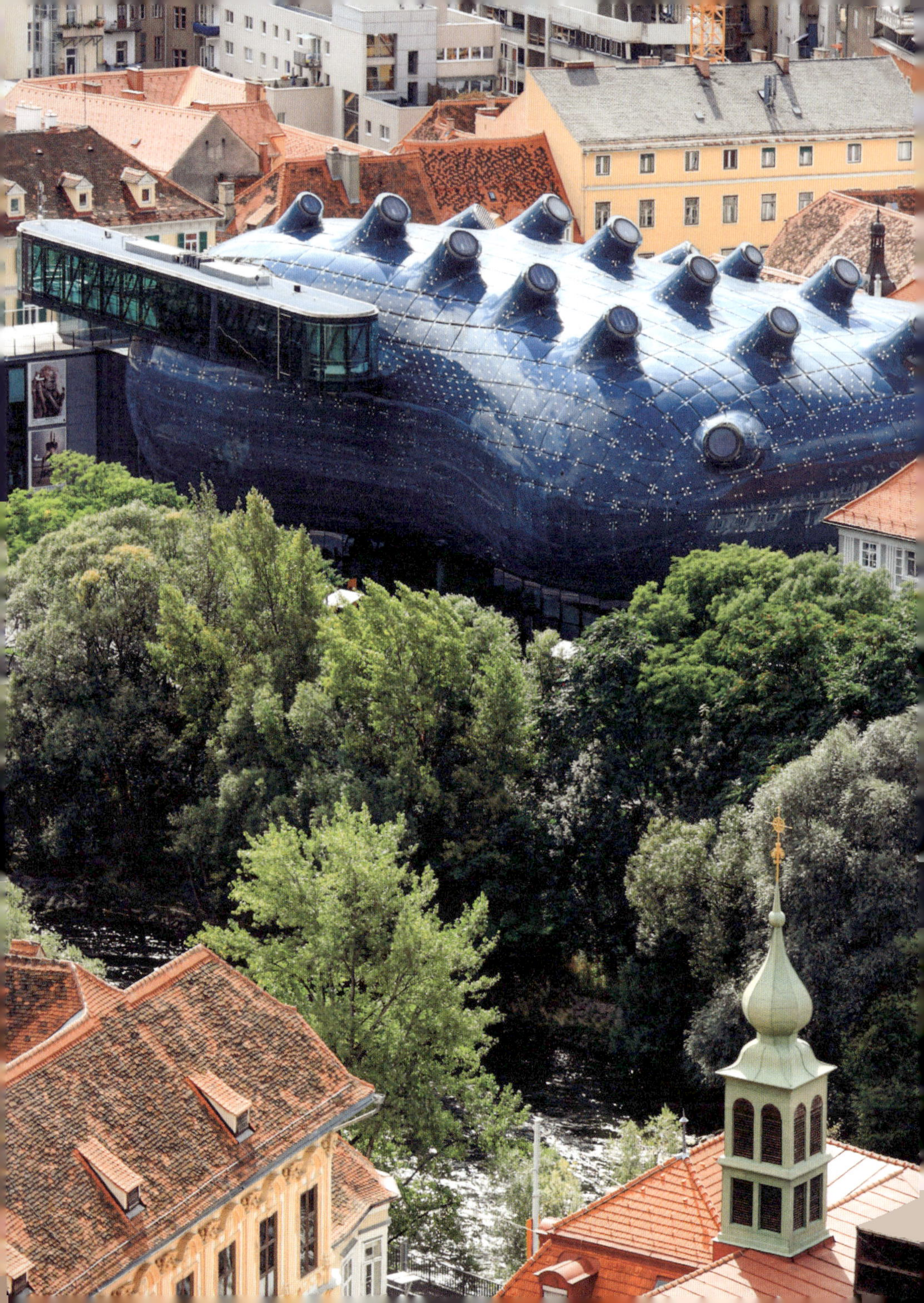

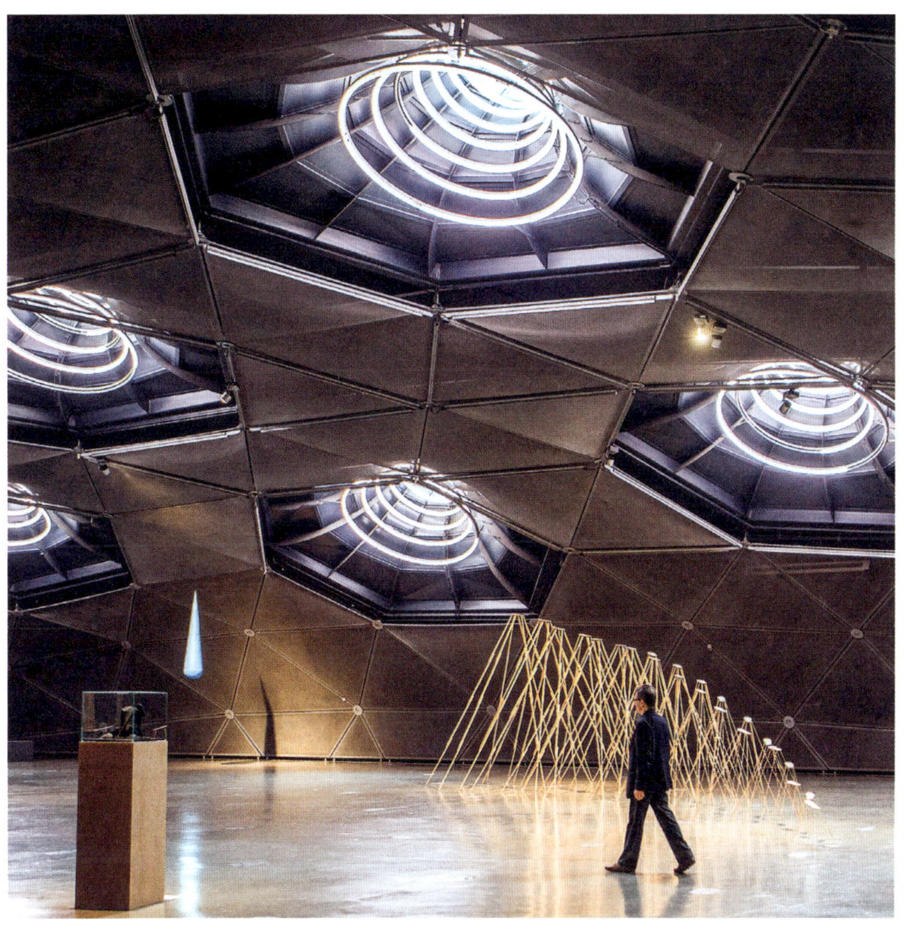

Kunsthaus
Graz, Austria
Architects: Peter Cook and Colin Fournier, 2003

Nestled among the red clay-tiled roofs of its Baroque neighbours, Graz's contemporary art museum provides a striking contrast to its historic surroundings. The building's unusual biomorphic shape, resembling an amoeba or a sea creature with suckers, is an example of 'blobitecture', a term coined to define buildings inspired by fluid, organic forms.

Svalbard Global Seed Vault

Svalbard, Norway

Architect: Peter W. Søderman, 2008

Jutting out of a mountainside on the remote Arctic island of Spitsbergen, and looking rather like a Bond villain's bunker, this vault stores 1.2 million duplicates of seeds from around the world. It was set up to provide security for the world's food supply by preventing the permanent loss of seeds through global catastrophe.

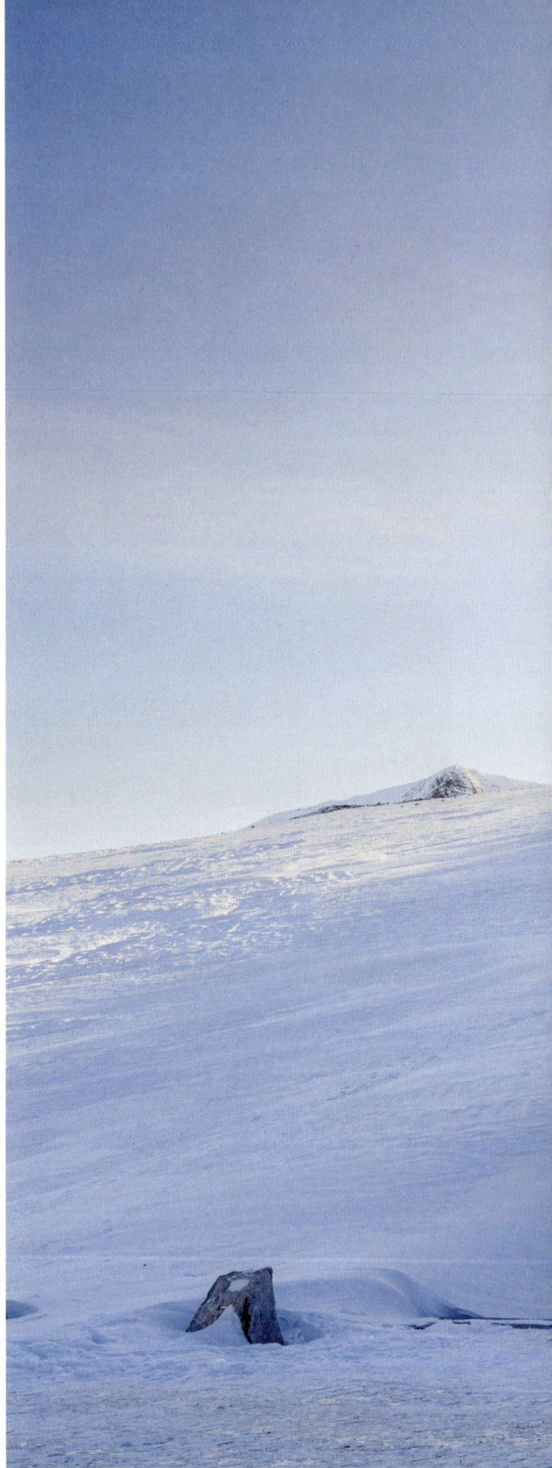

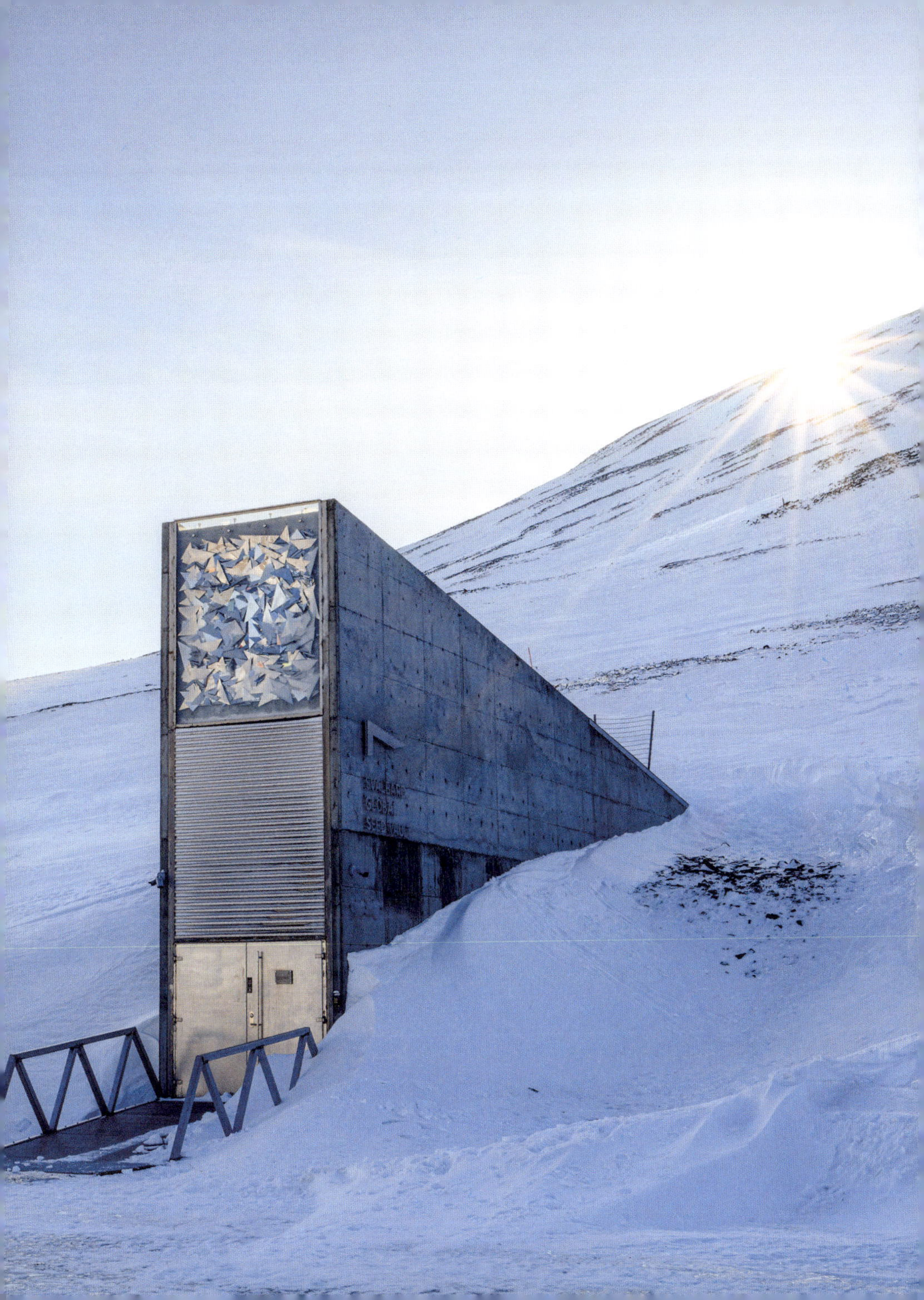

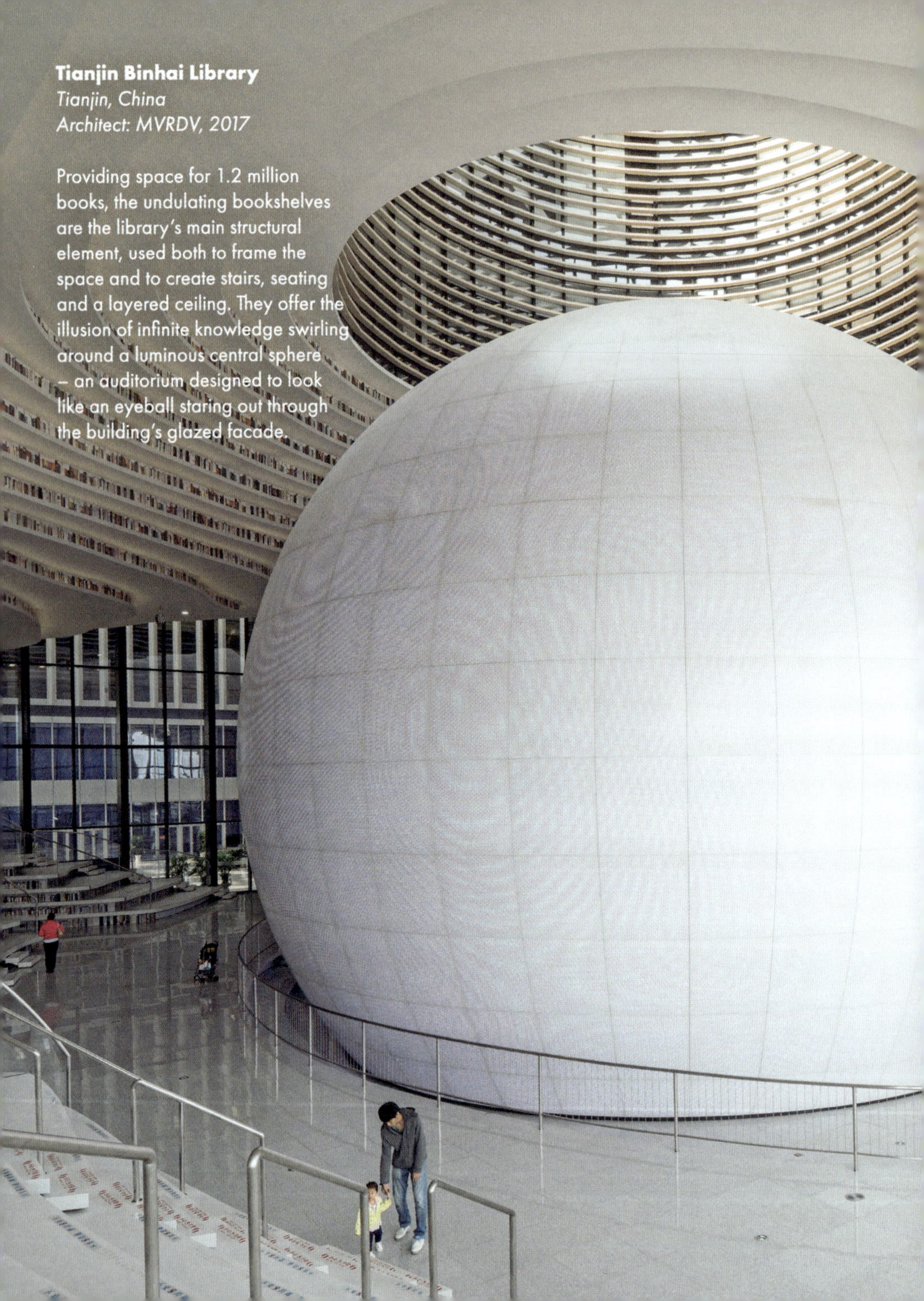

Tianjin Binhai Library
Tianjin, China
Architect: MVRDV, 2017

Providing space for 1.2 million books, the undulating bookshelves are the library's main structural element, used both to frame the space and to create stairs, seating and a layered ceiling. They offer the illusion of infinite knowledge swirling around a luminous central sphere – an auditorium designed to look like an eyeball staring out through the building's glazed facade.

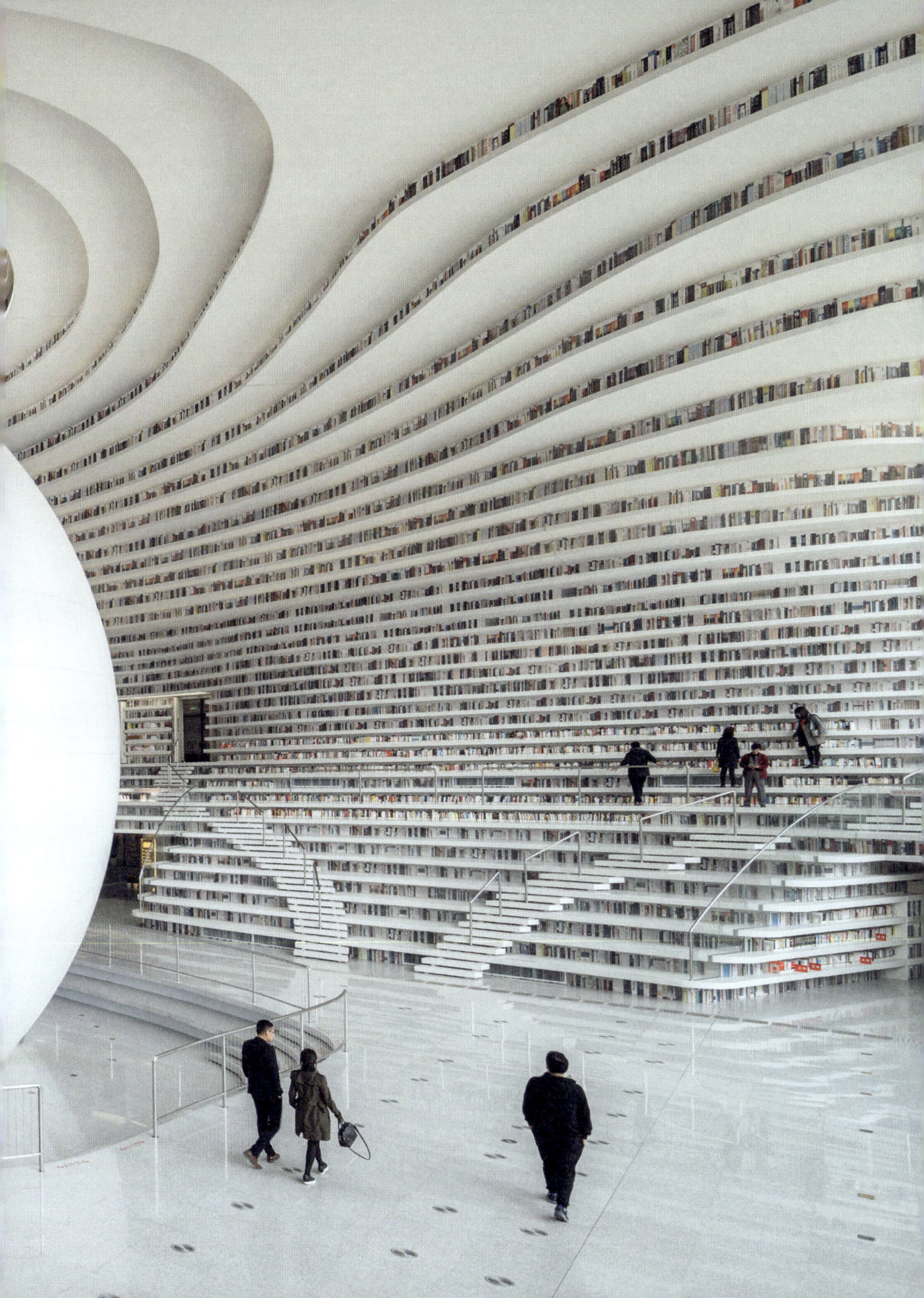

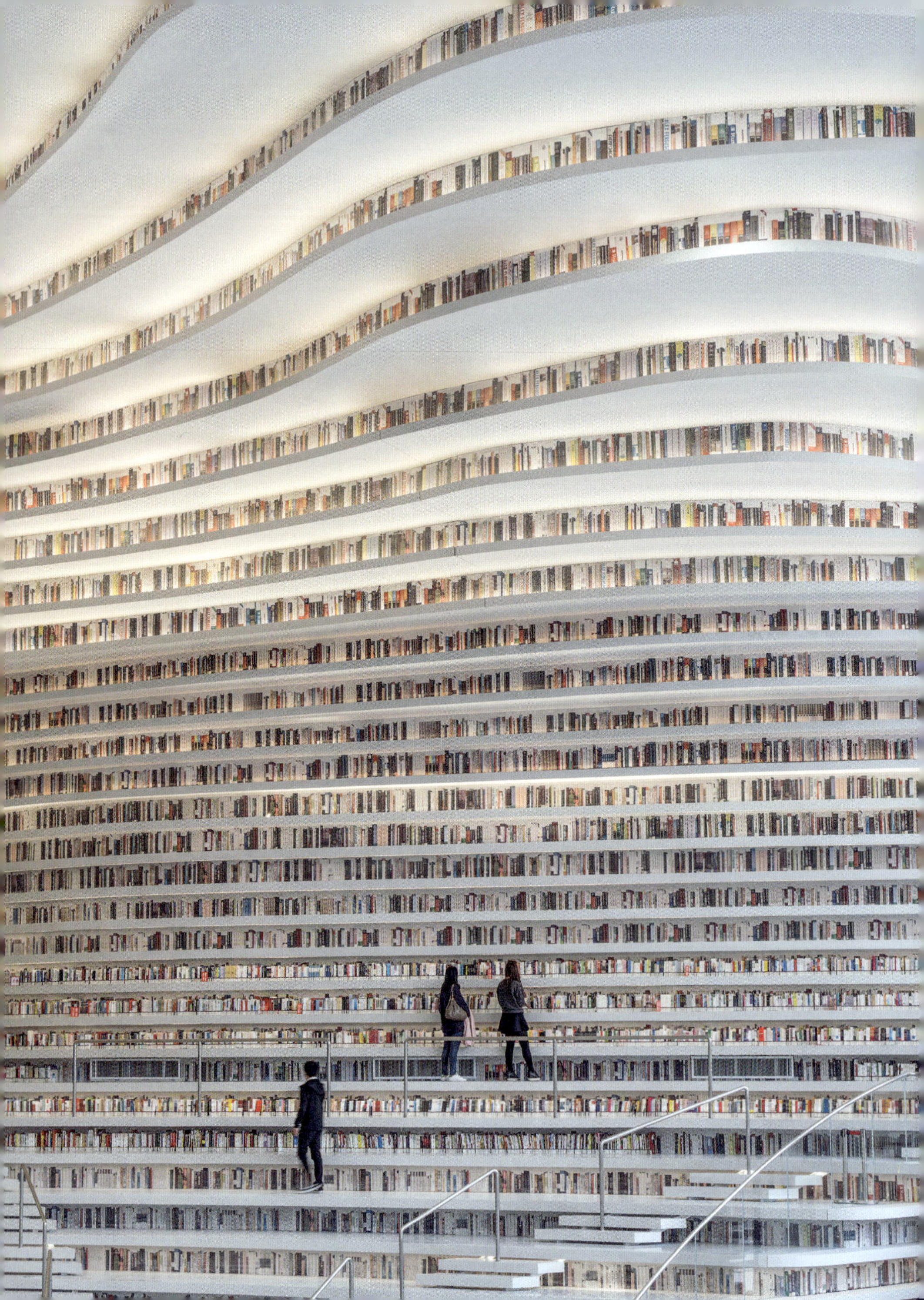

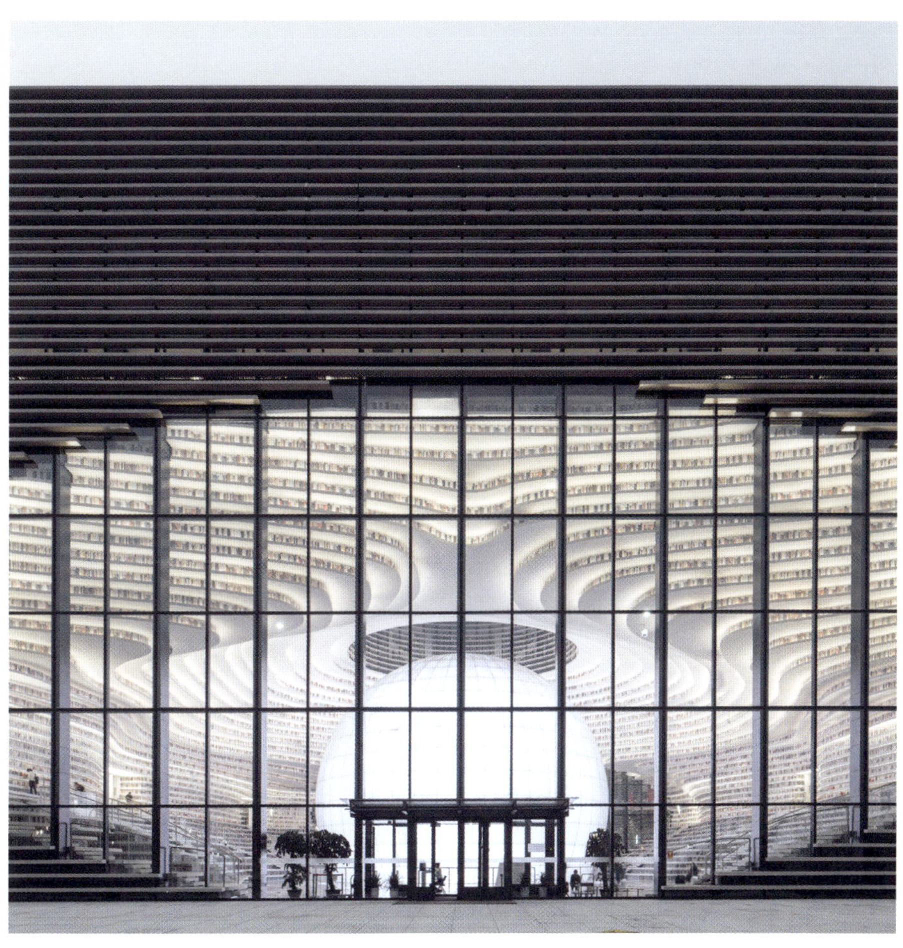

Books ripple like waves through the cavernous interior. The angles and curves of the bookshelves are designed to encourage different uses of the space, such as reading, walking, meeting and discussion.

The Imprint
Incheon, South Korea
Architect: MVRDV, 2018

This nightclub facade gives the impression of a golden curtain being raised for entrance. The entertainment complex houses the nightclub in one building and a theme park in another, and both needed a design with no windows that would still blend in with the surroundings. This was achieved by printing the facades of neighbouring buildings onto them using individually moulded panels.

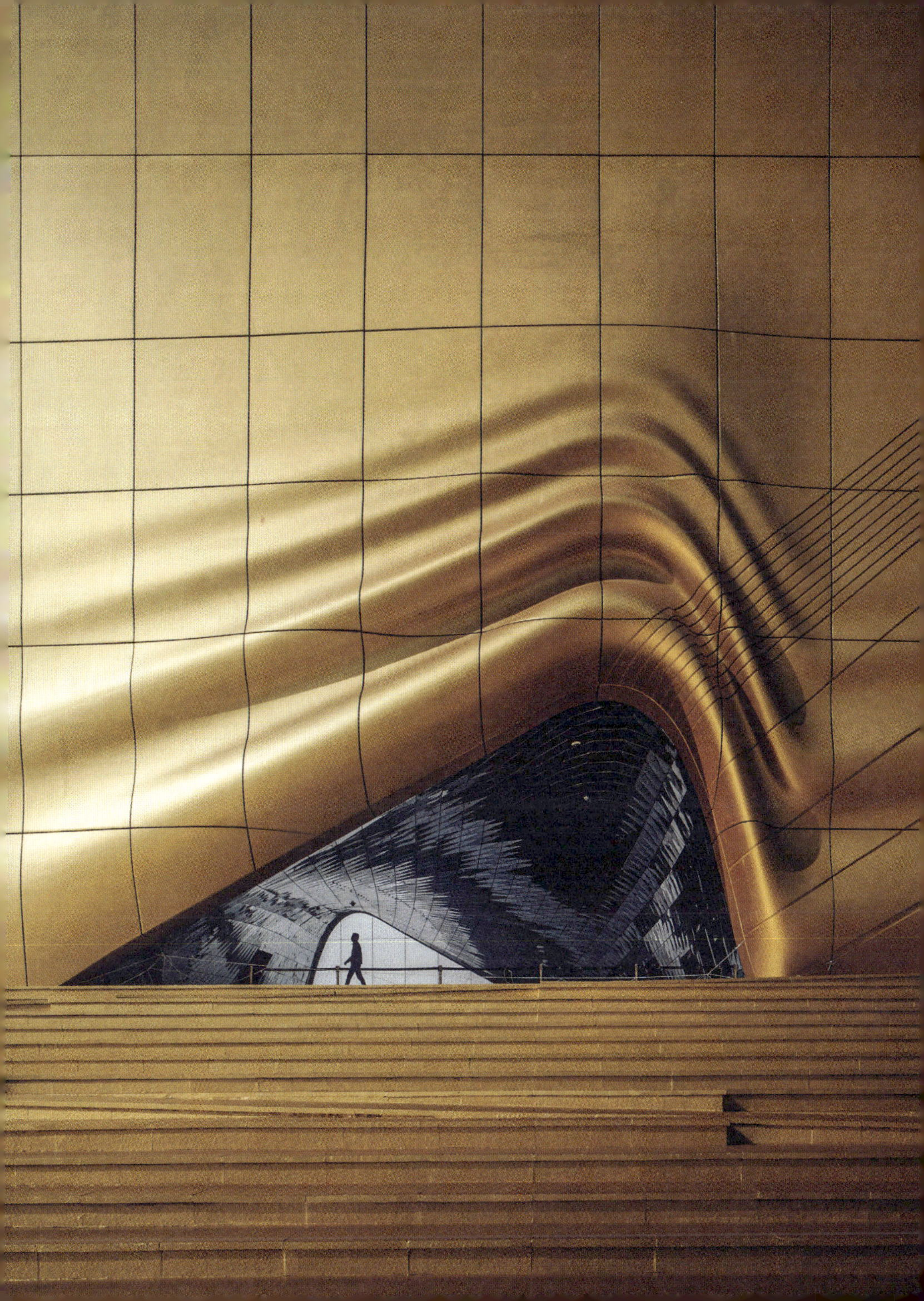

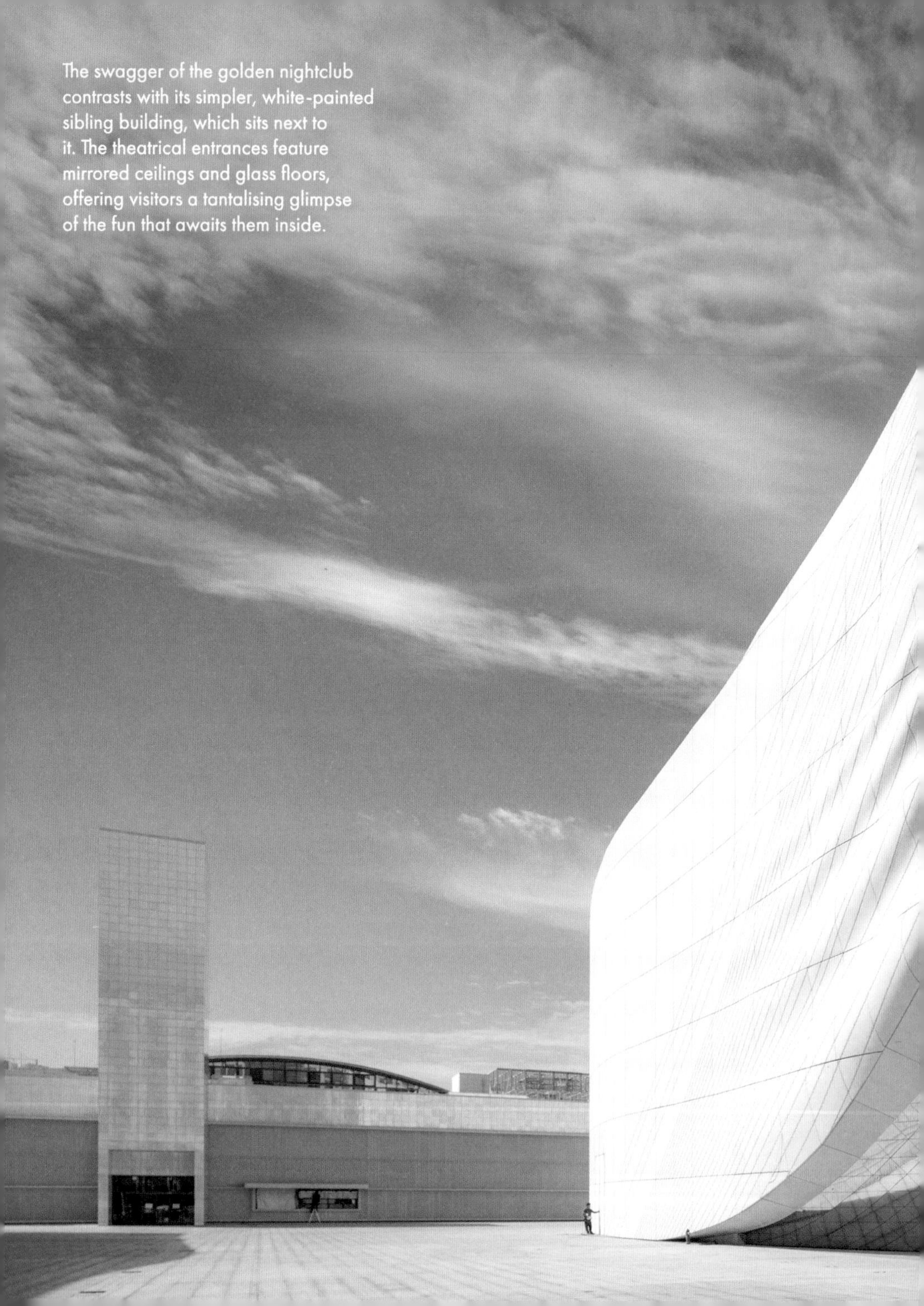

The swagger of the golden nightclub contrasts with its simpler, white-painted sibling building, which sits next to it. The theatrical entrances feature mirrored ceilings and glass floors, offering visitors a tantalising glimpse of the fun that awaits them inside.

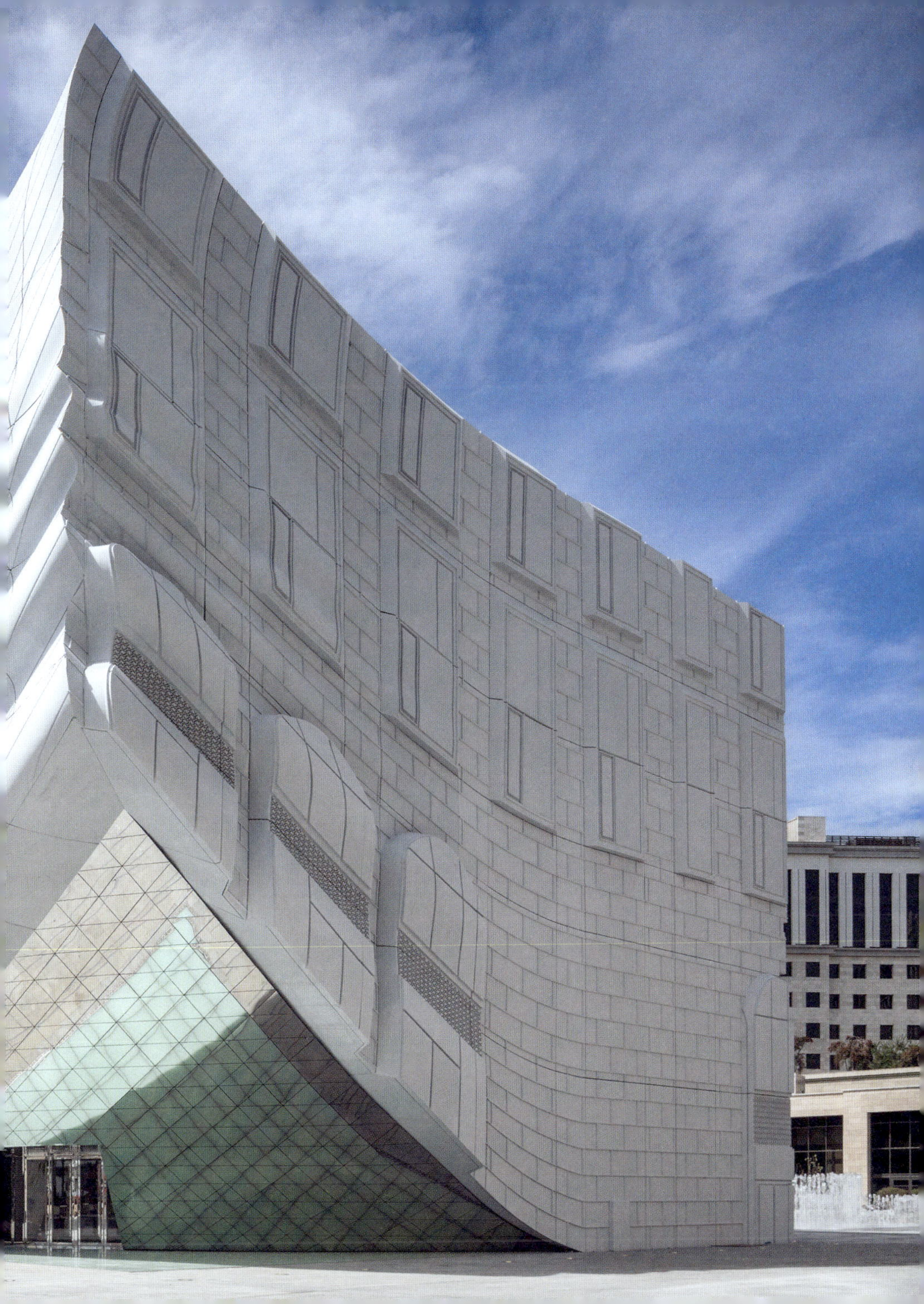

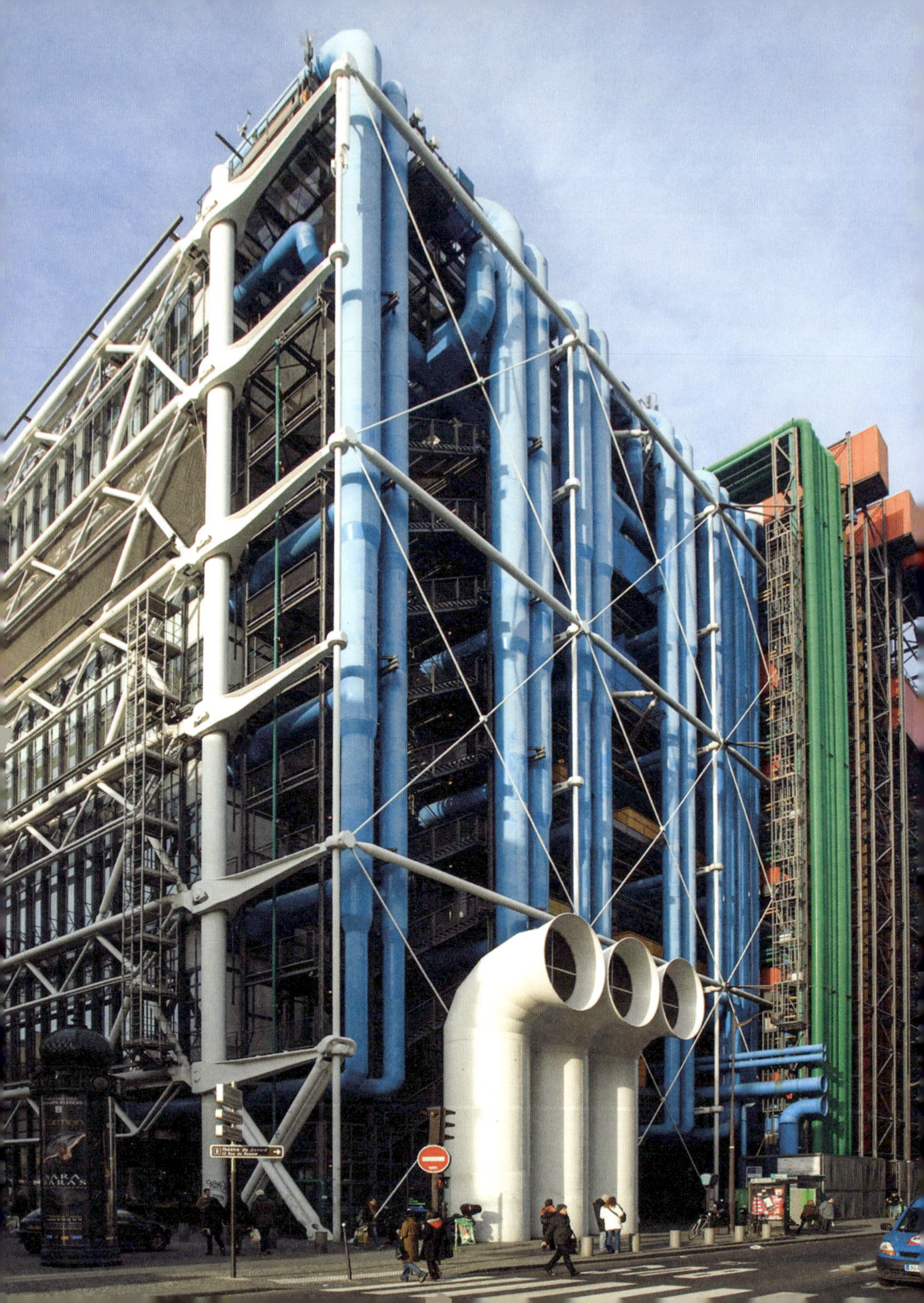
SARA
BARAS

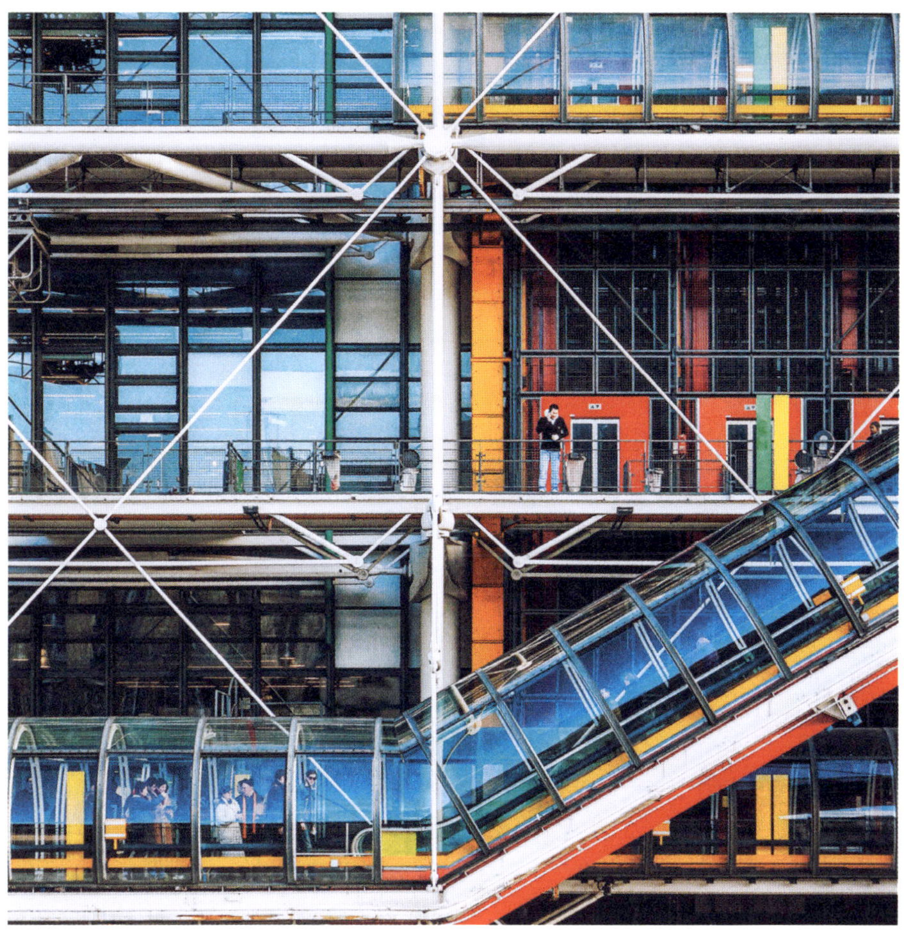

Centre Pompidou
Paris, France
Architects: Renzo Piano and Richard Rogers, 1977

Resembling a giant Meccano set, the Centre Pompidou is known for its 'inside-out' design, whereby structural and service elements are situated on the building's exterior, each function assigned a different colour by the architects. The visual signature of the building is the giant diagonal escalator, which serves as a zigzagging outdoor path and creates an ever-changing facade.

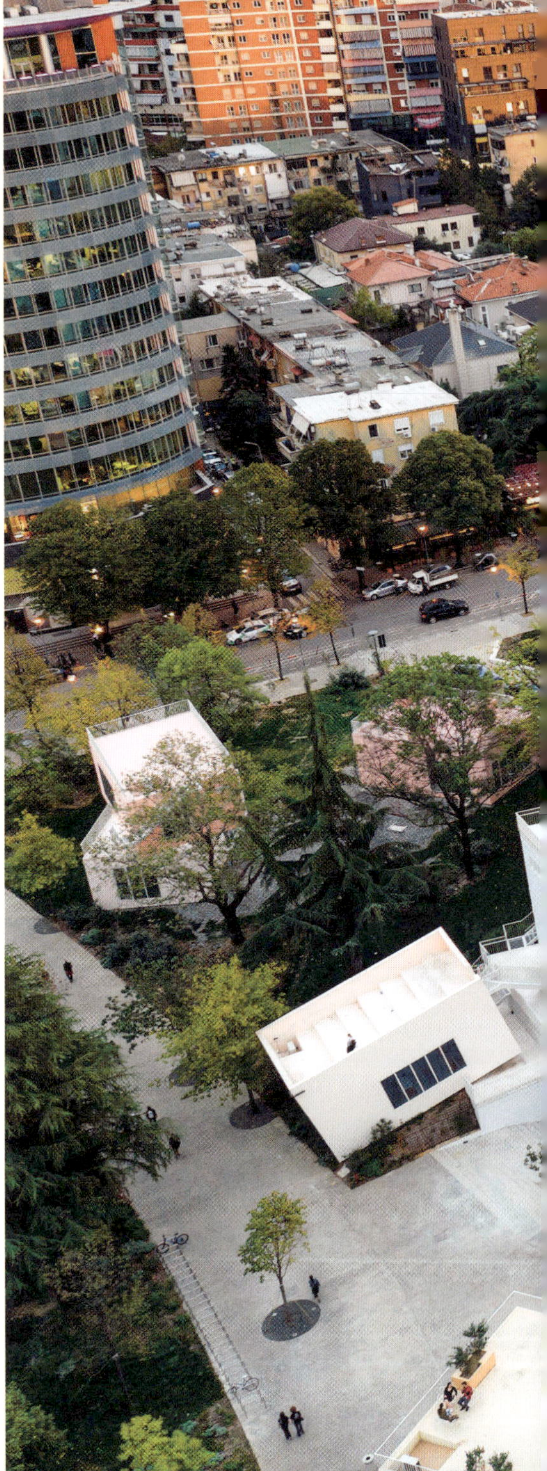

Pyramid of Tirana
Tirana, Albania
Architect: MVRDV, 2023

This concrete cone was once a museum dedicated to former communist leader Enver Hoxha during a dark period in the country's history, now reimagined as a cultural hub. The architects opened up the structure, added stairs to enable visitors to clamber all over it and scattered joyful coloured boxes around the site containing rooms for education and events.

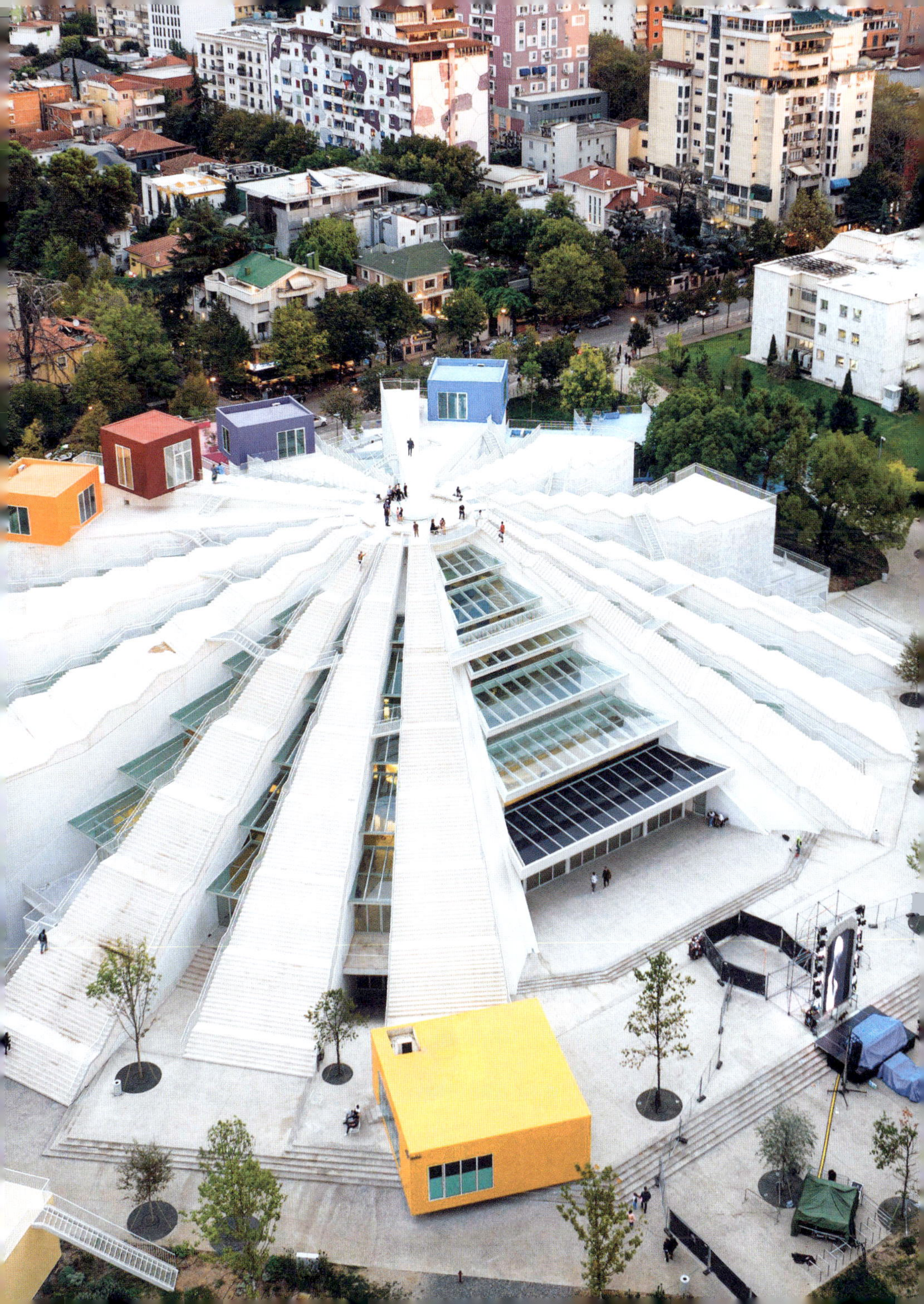

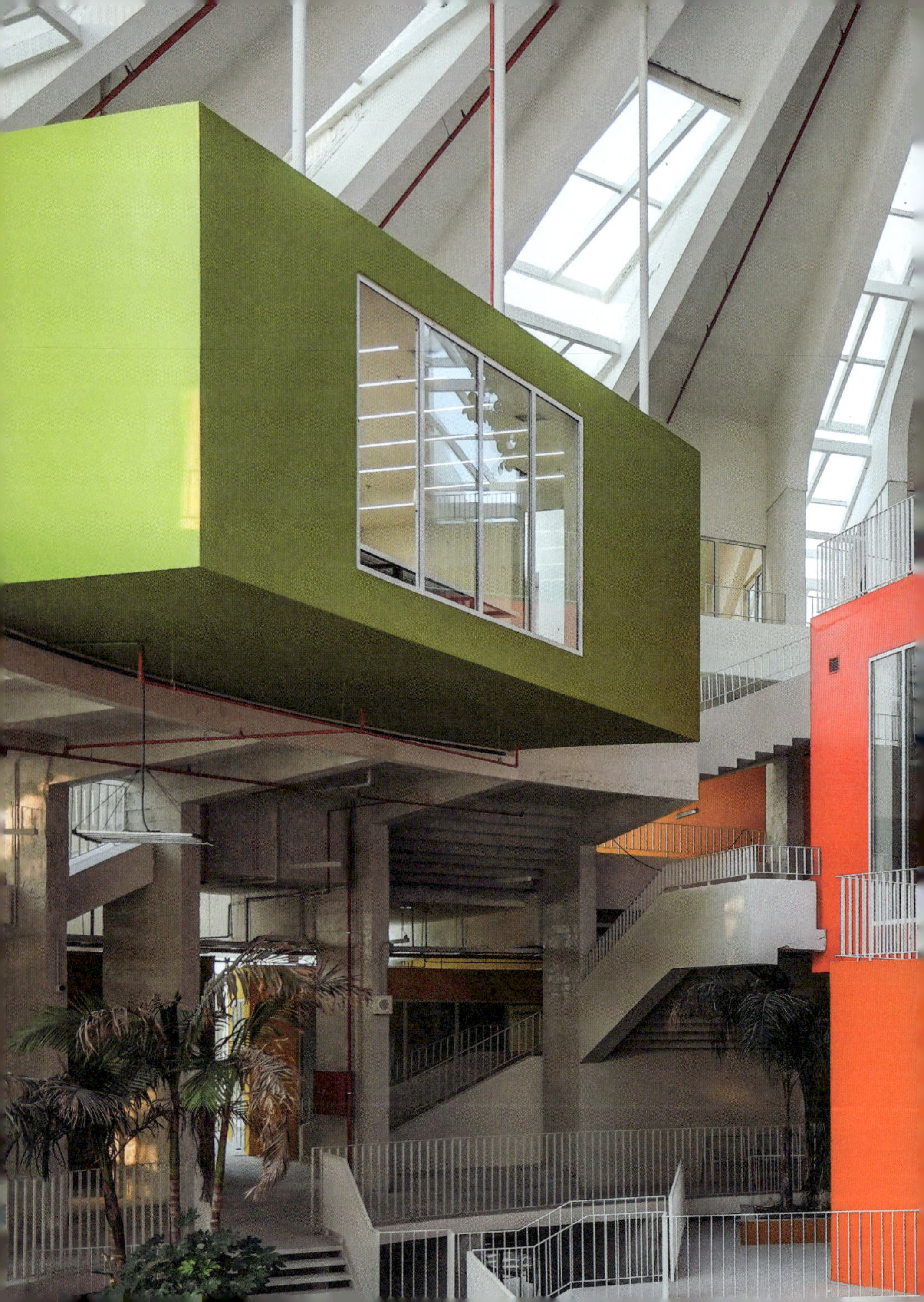

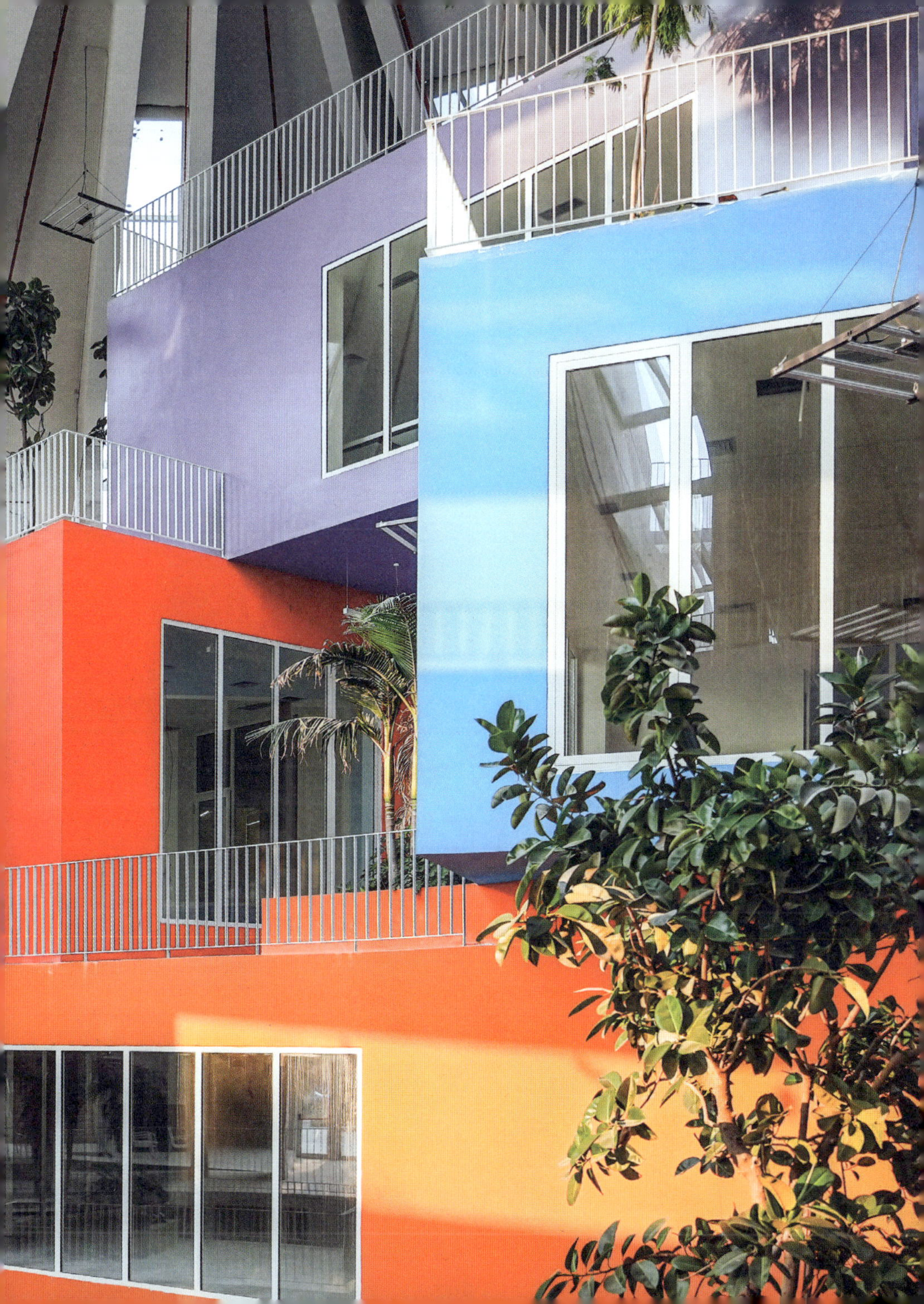

Habitat 67

Montreal, Canada
Architect: Moshe Safdie, 1967

Resembling a life-size Lego village, Habitat 67 was originally conceived as the architect's university thesis, until his supervisor invited him to submit it for Canada's Expo 67, where it became the pavilion exhibit. An experimental solution for urban housing as an alternative to high-rise blocks, each apartment has a roof garden, a flow of fresh air and abundant natural light.

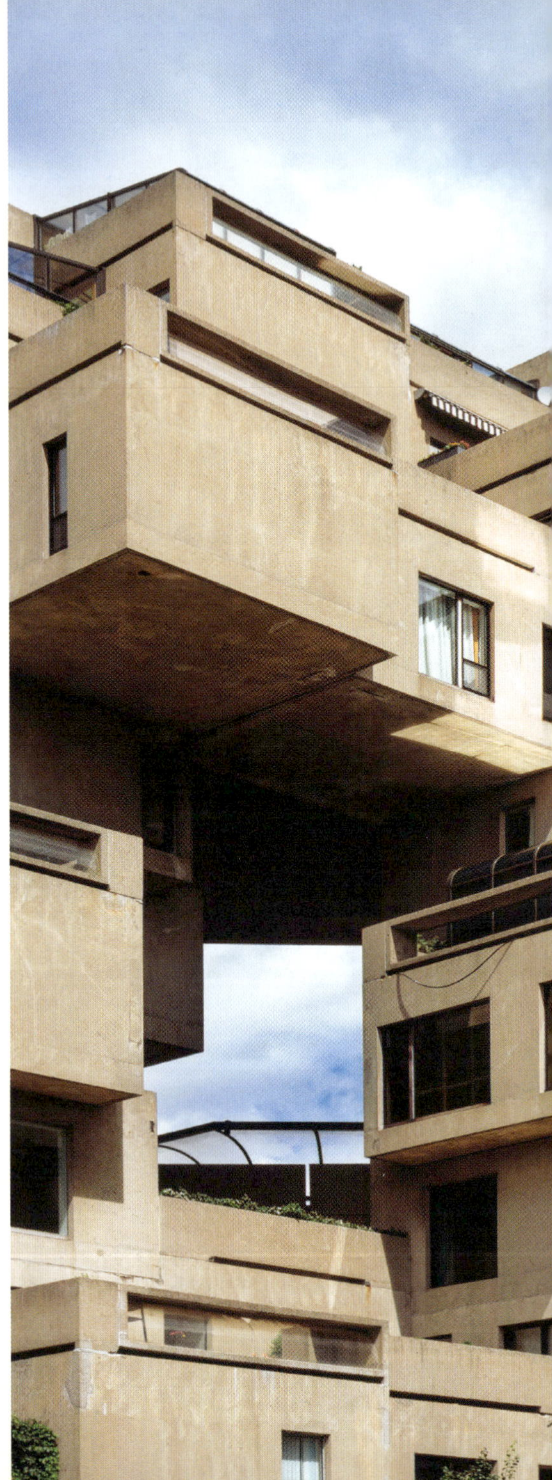

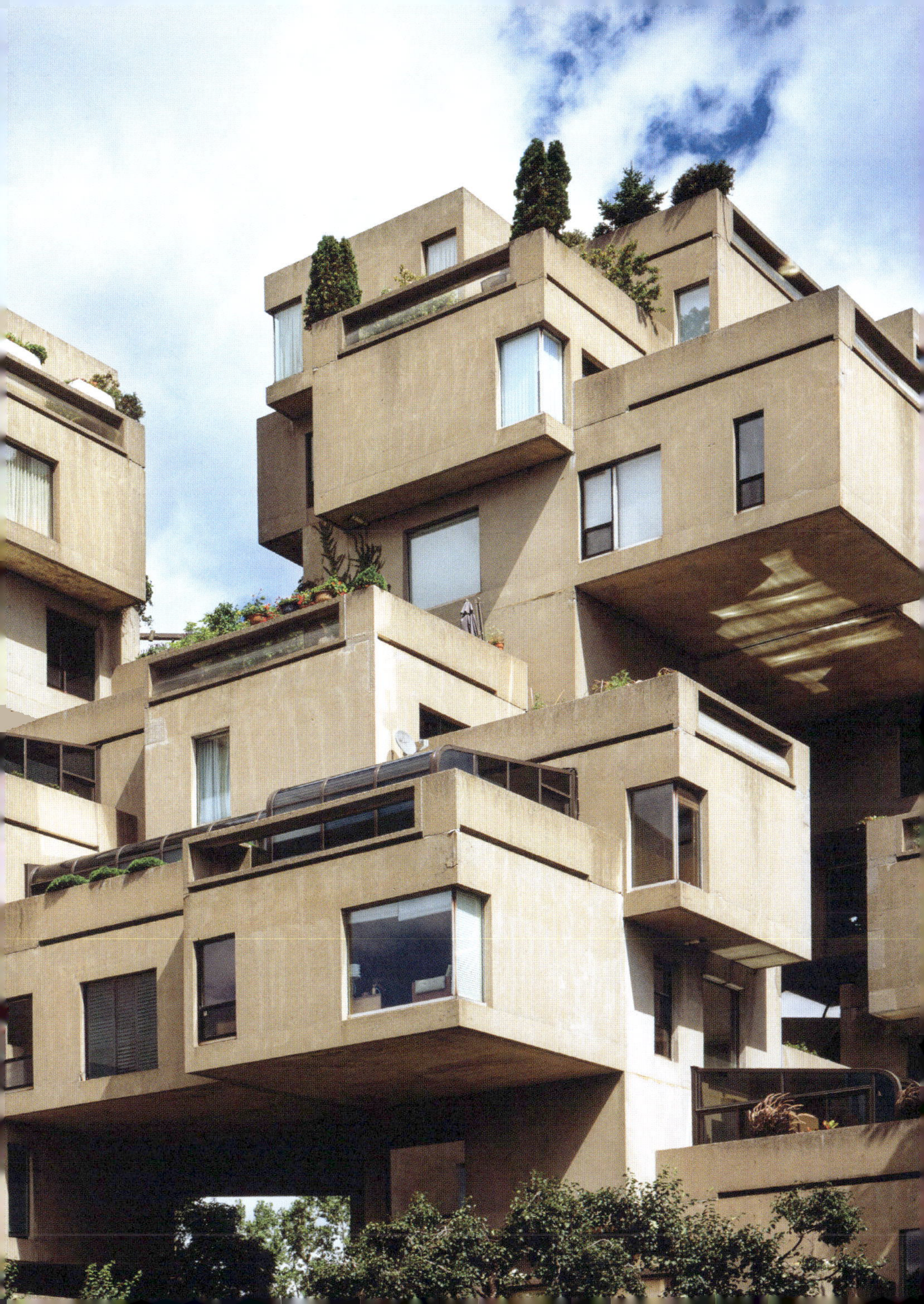

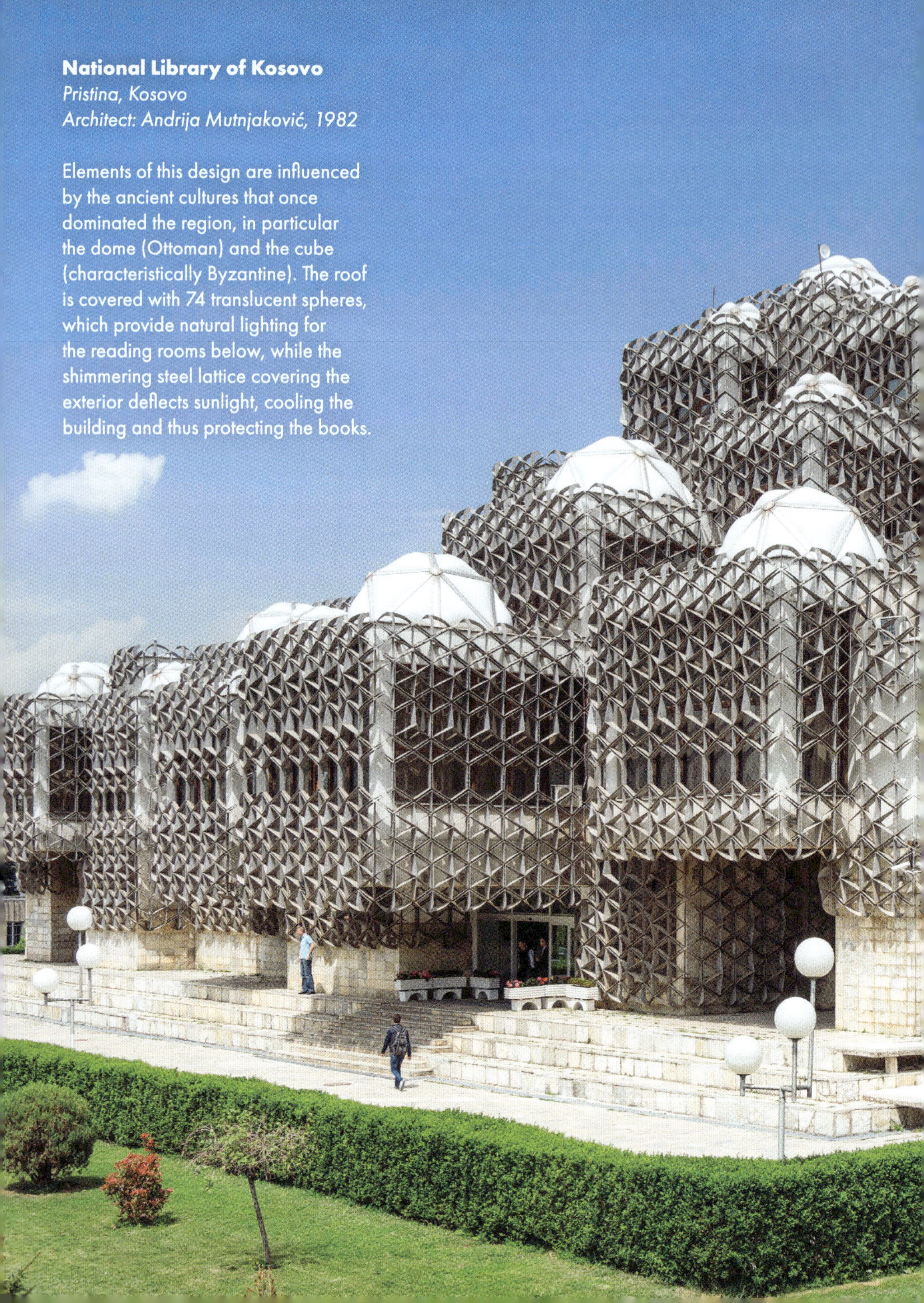

National Library of Kosovo
Pristina, Kosovo
Architect: Andrija Mutnjaković, 1982

Elements of this design are influenced by the ancient cultures that once dominated the region, in particular the dome (Ottoman) and the cube (characteristically Byzantine). The roof is covered with 74 translucent spheres, which provide natural lighting for the reading rooms below, while the shimmering steel lattice covering the exterior deflects sunlight, cooling the building and thus protecting the books.

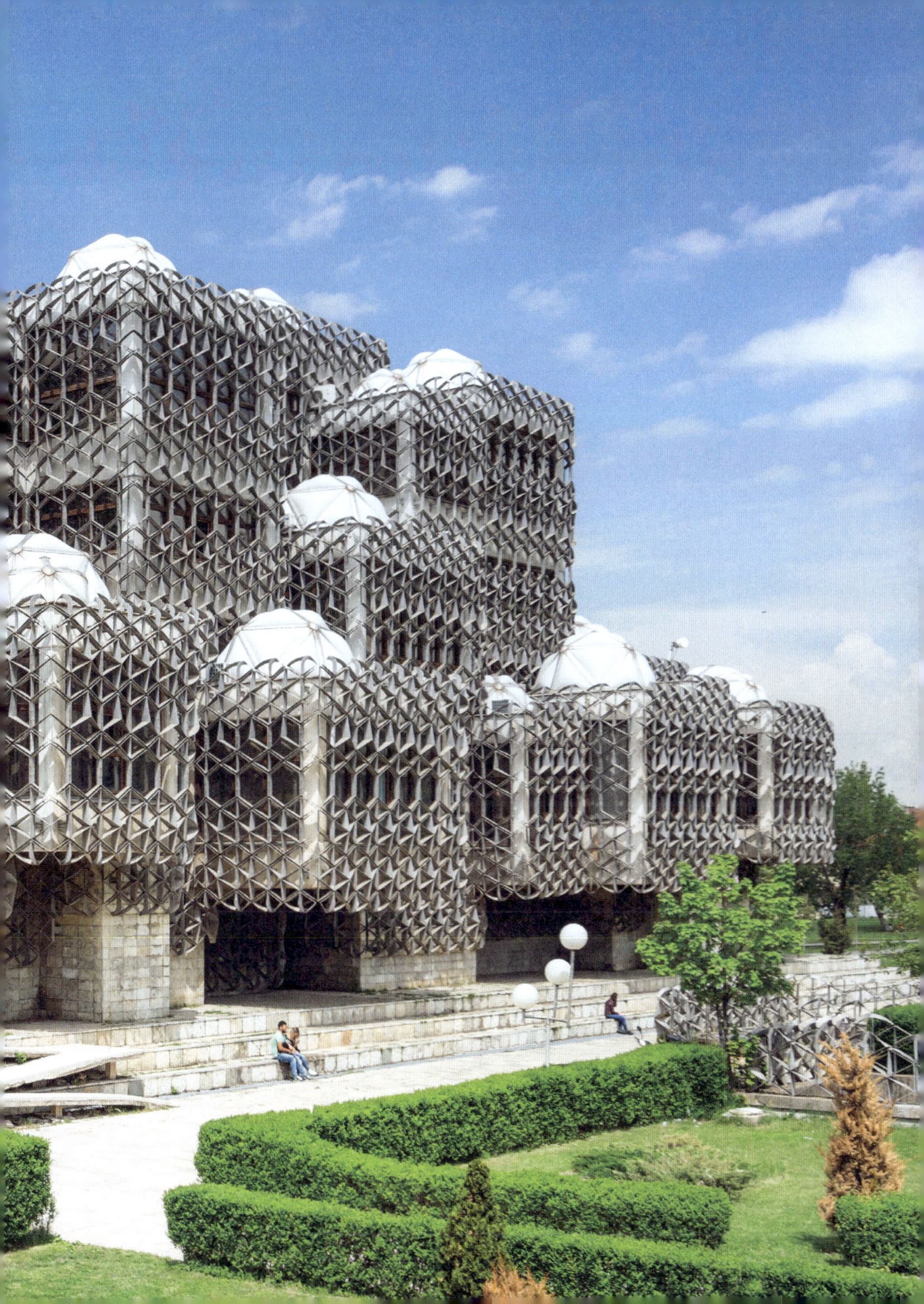

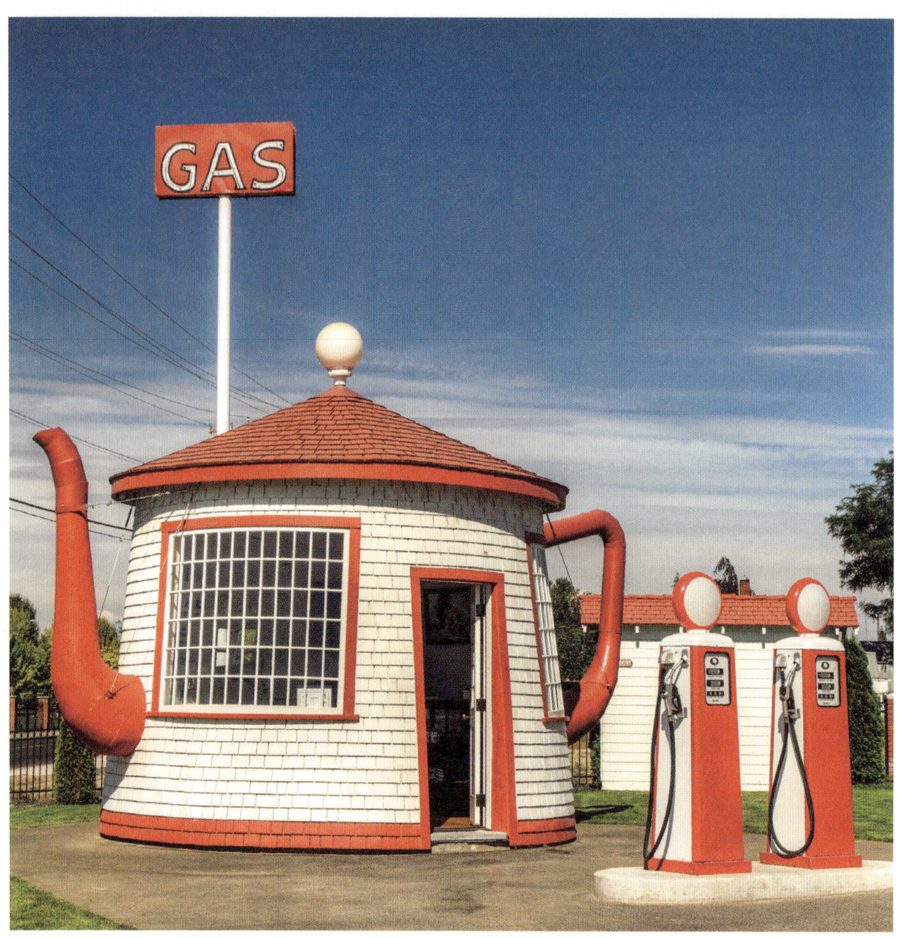

Teapot Dome Service Station
Zillah, Washington, USA
Architect: Jack Ainsworth, 1922

Not just another charming piece of roadside Americana, this petrol station was inspired by a notorious political scandal of the 1920s. A former US senator was secretly leasing American oil from the Teapot Dome reserves in Wyoming to private oil companies, and the service station was created by a local entrepreneur as a humorous nod to the national controversy.

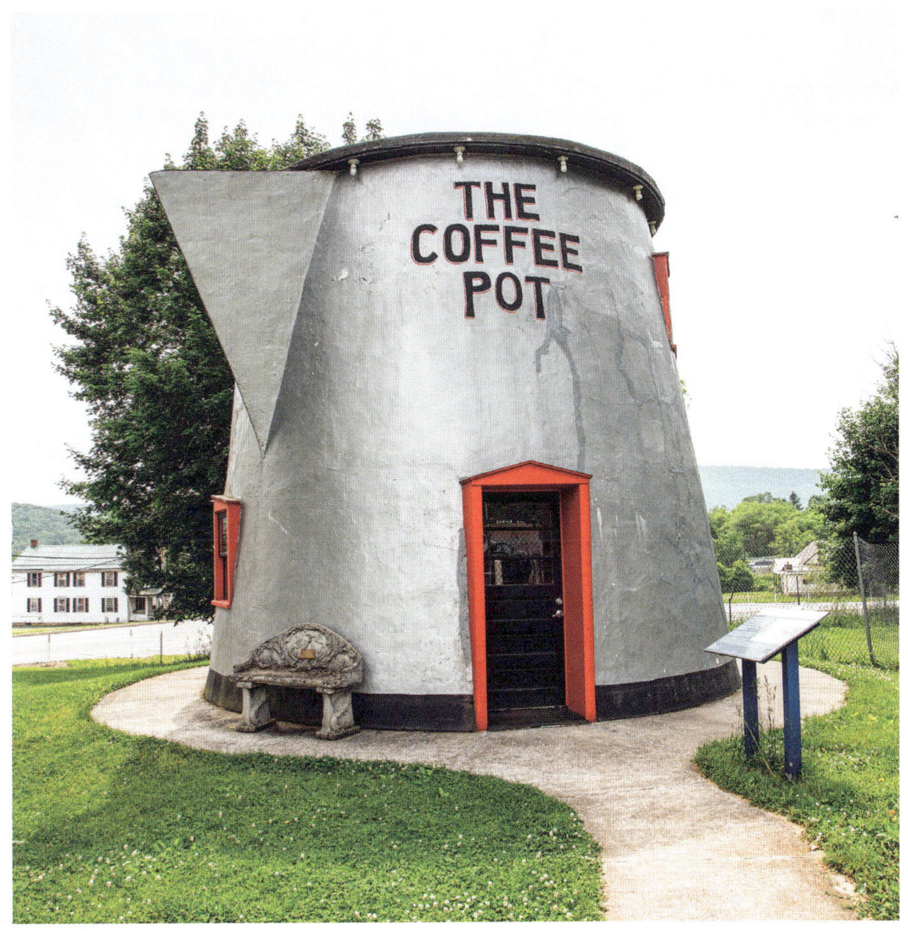

The Coffee Pot
Bedford, Pennsylvania, USA
Architect: David Koontz, 1927

A wonderfully kitsch landmark and example of mimetic architecture, where buildings mimic their function or purpose, this super-sized coffee pot was built next to its owner's service station to attract customers. Recognising its historical and cultural significance, preservationists bought the structure for one dollar in 2004 and restored it, and it now stands as a testament to America's roadside architectural heritage.

Museu de Arte Contemporânea de Niterói
Rio de Janeiro, Brazil
Architect: Oscar Niemeyer, 1996

Resembling a recently landed UFO, this sci-fi, saucer-shaped structure sits atop a cliffside overlooking Rio de Janeiro's Guanabara Bay. Built to house the João Sattamini collection of modern art, this futuristic landmark is surrounded by a reflective pool, mirroring its concrete curves, and a red, snake-like ramp circling up to its entrance. Once inside, black-framed vertical windows offer a striking contrast and panoramic views of the rocky coastline below.

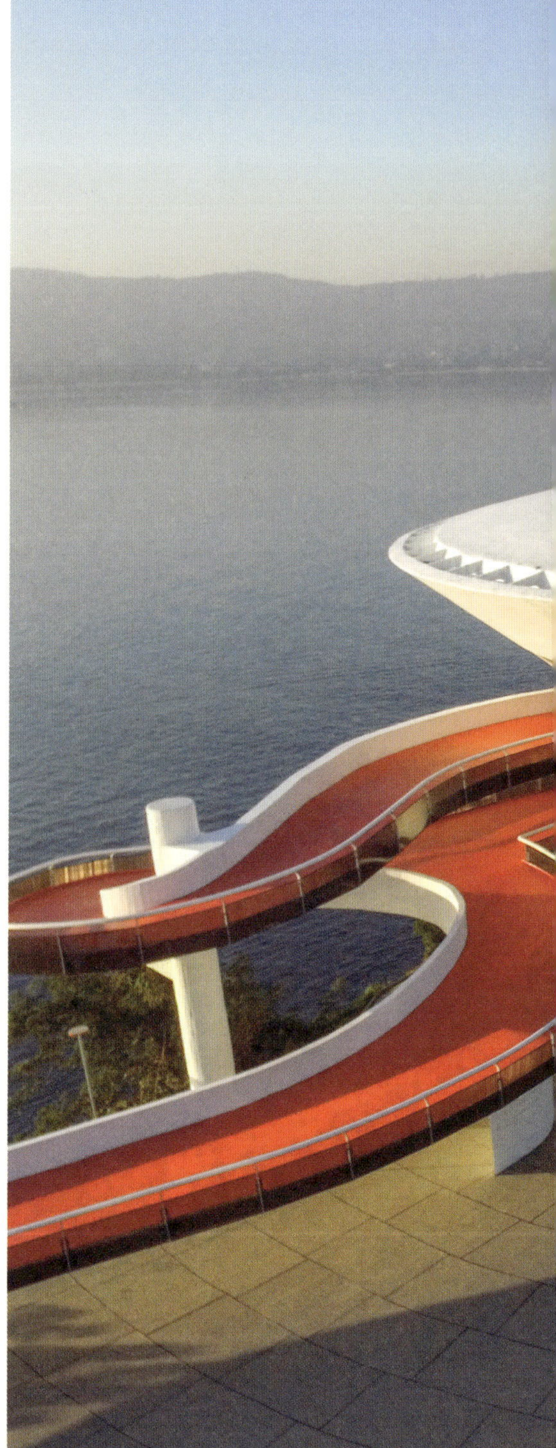

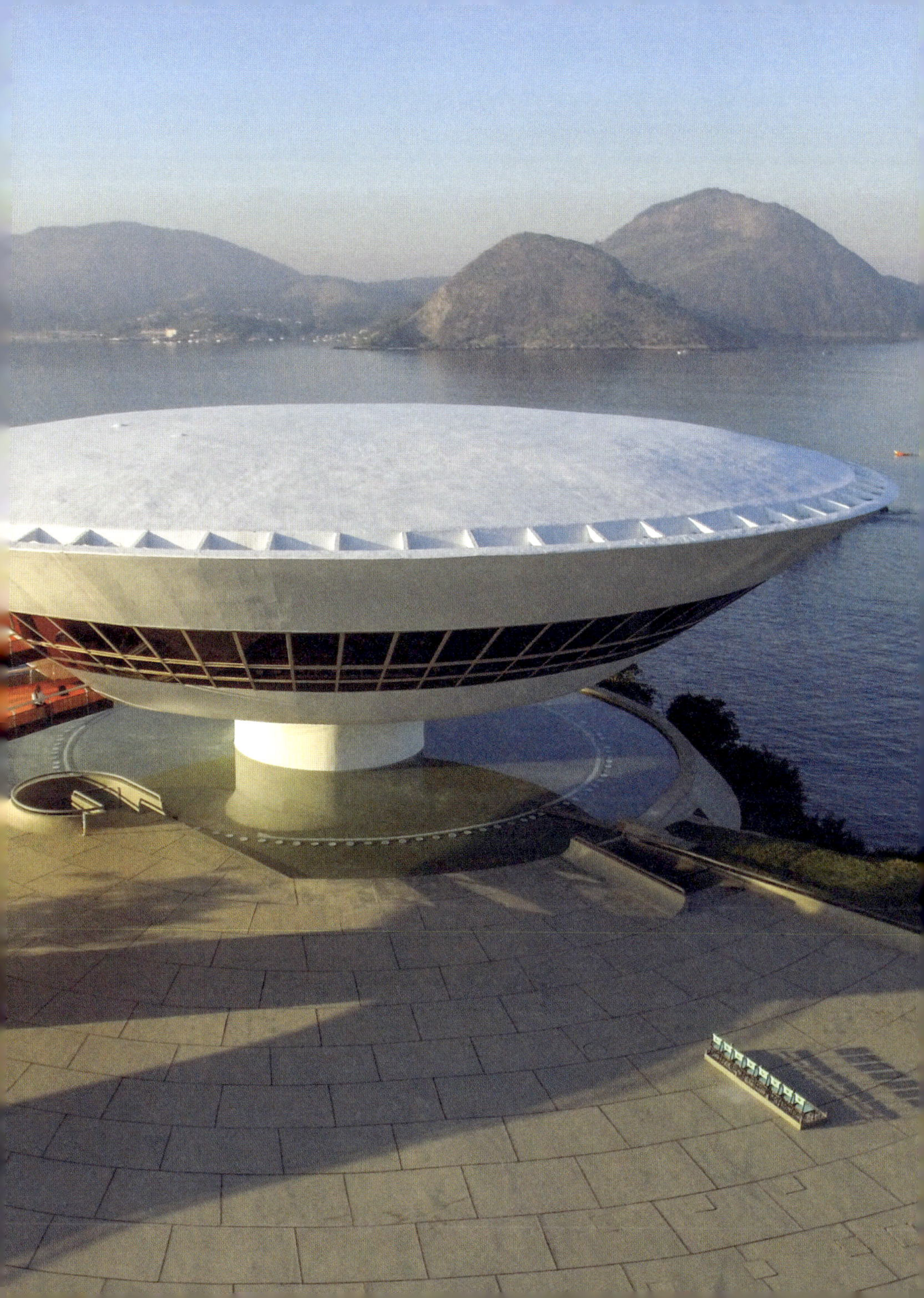

Nakagin Capsule Tower
Tokyo, Japan
Architect: Kisho Kurokawa, 1972

This 14-storey sci-fi tower, a stack of 140 capsules, was an early example of Metabolism, an architectural movement that believes structures could evolve. Created to house commuters working in central Tokyo during the week, the architect had intended for the capsules to be replaced every 25 years, but this became impracticable and the building was eventually dismantled in 2021.

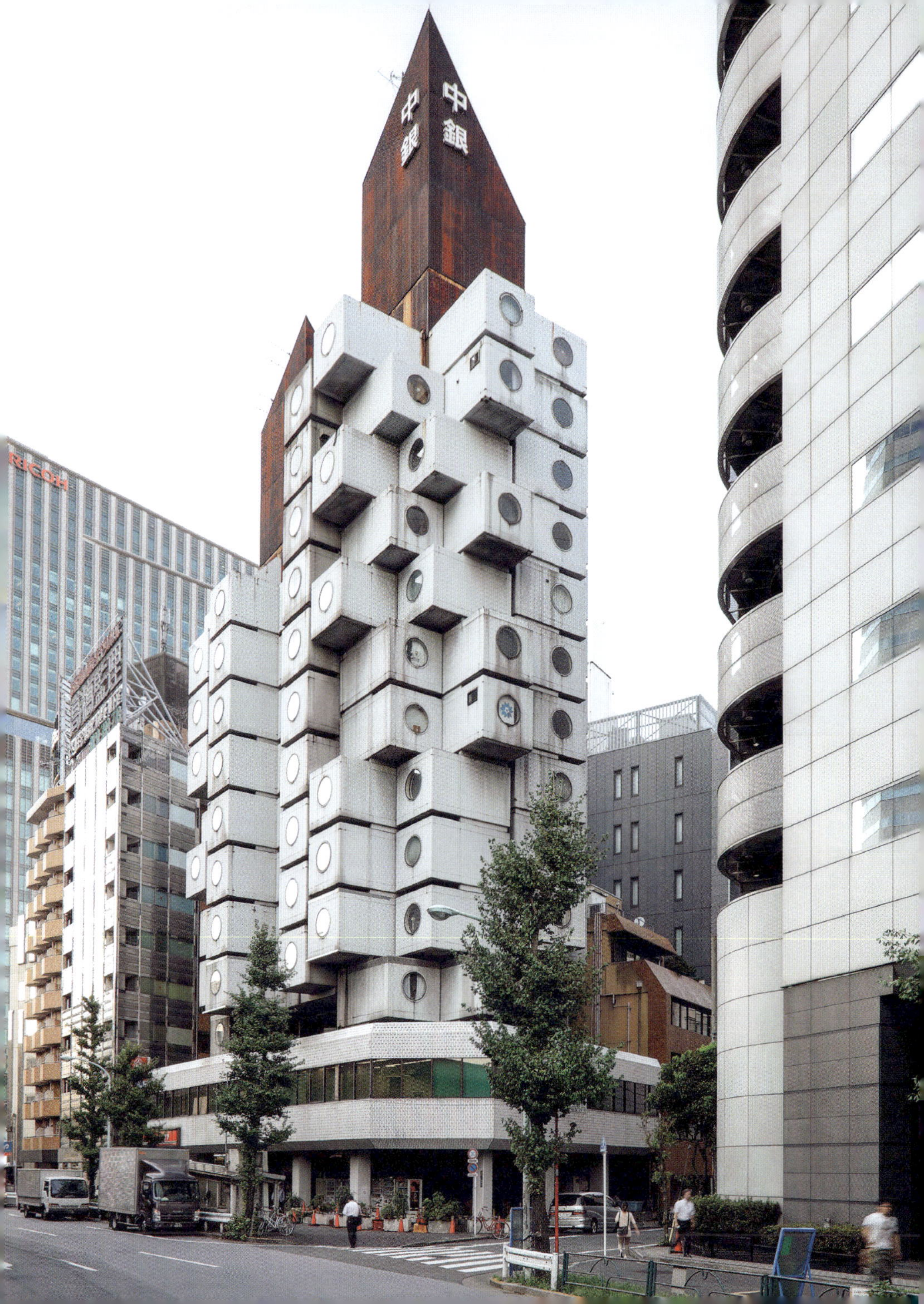
中銀
中銀
RICOH

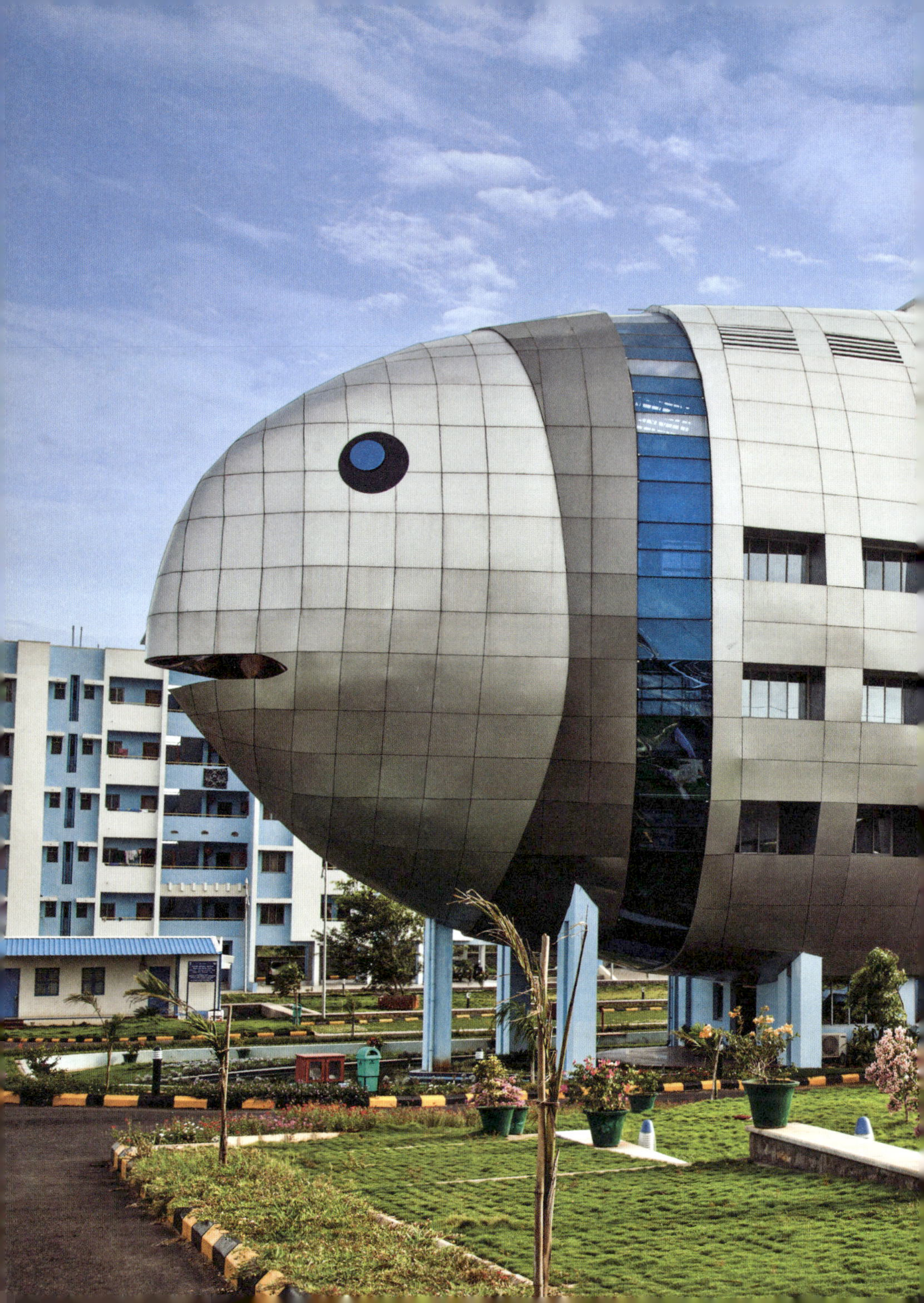

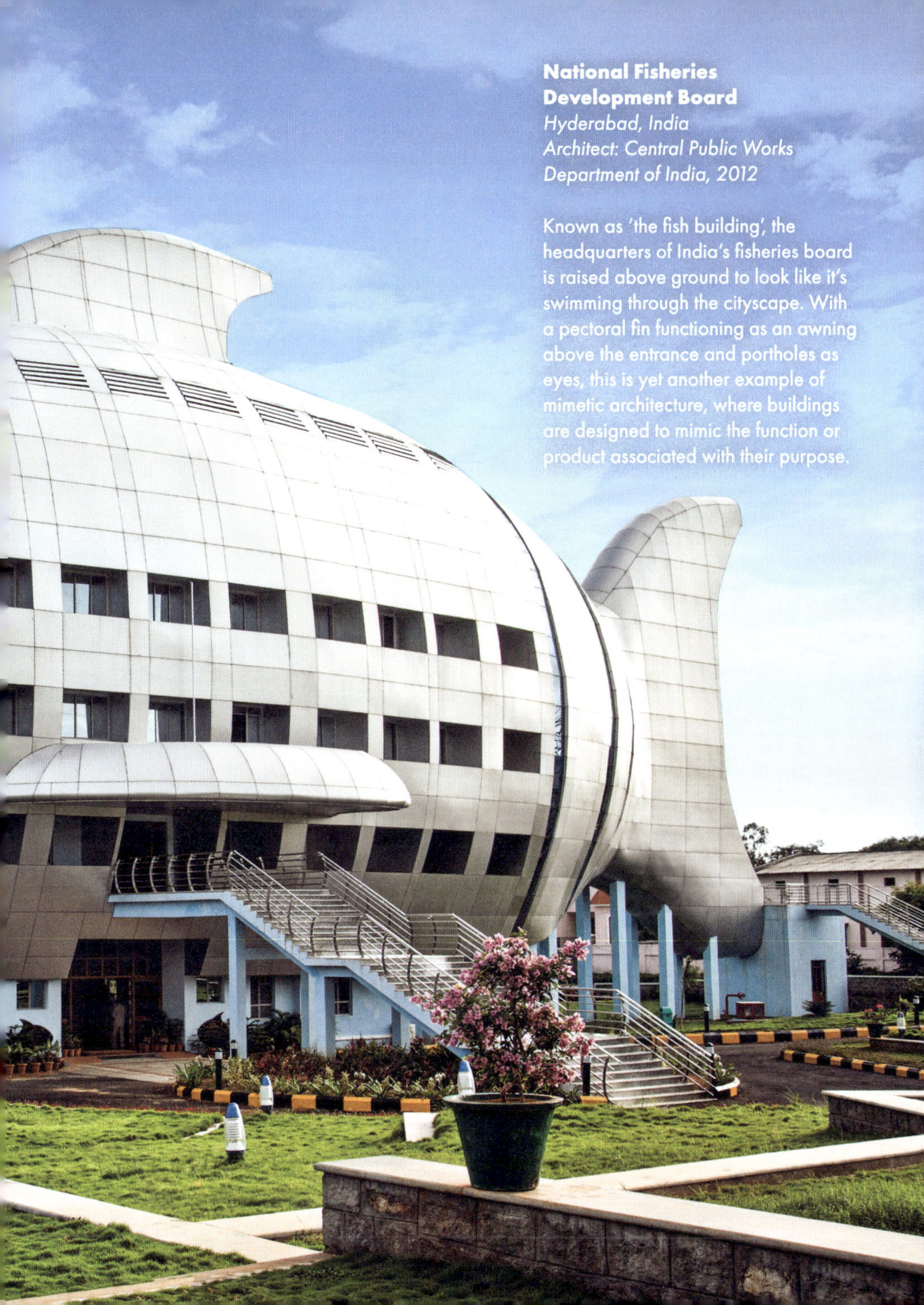

National Fisheries Development Board
Hyderabad, India
Architect: Central Public Works Department of India, 2012

Known as 'the fish building', the headquarters of India's fisheries board is raised above ground to look like it's swimming through the cityscape. With a pectoral fin functioning as an awning above the entrance and portholes as eyes, this is yet another example of mimetic architecture, where buildings are designed to mimic the function or product associated with their purpose.

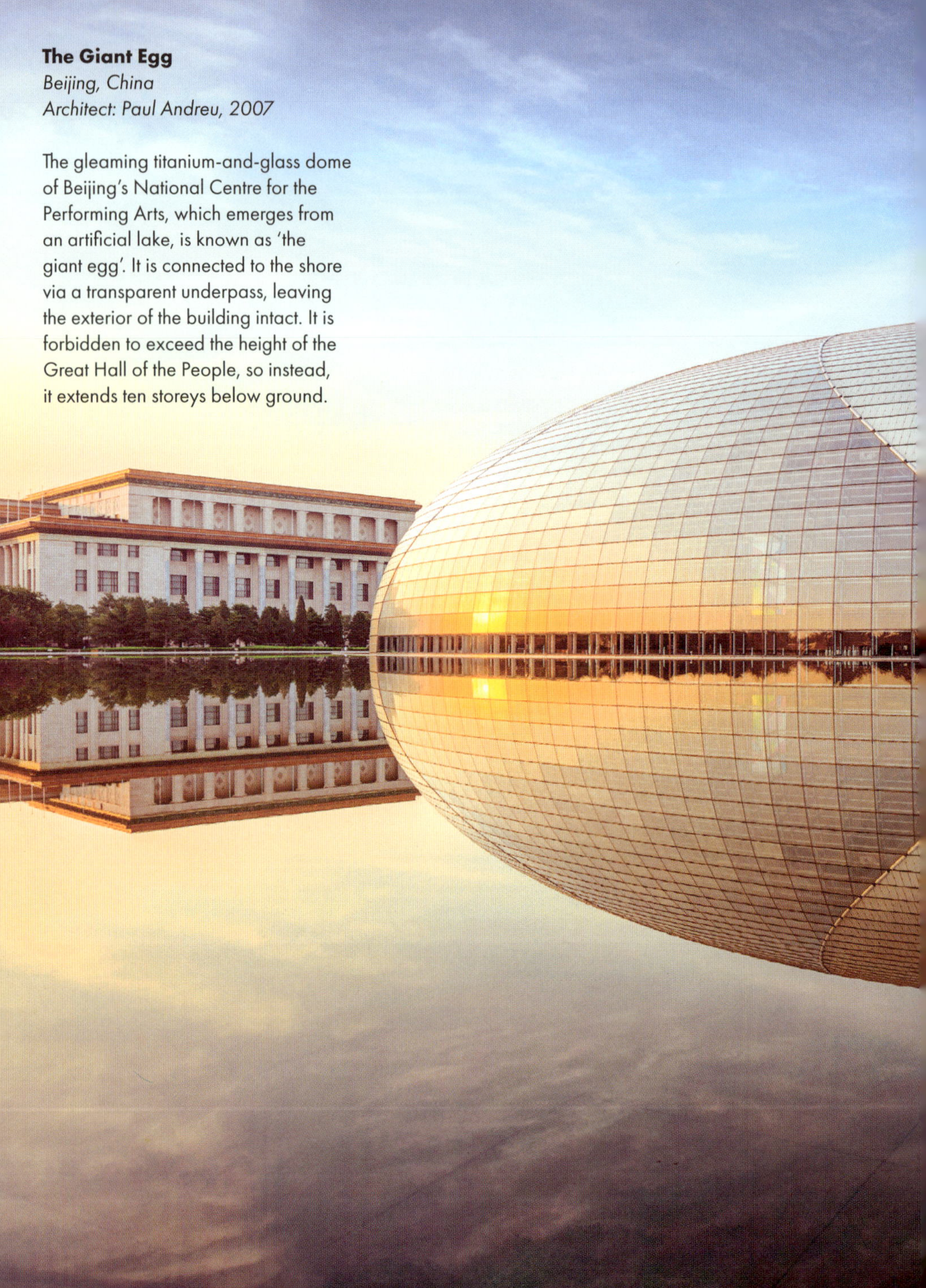

The Giant Egg
Beijing, China
Architect: Paul Andreu, 2007

The gleaming titanium-and-glass dome of Beijing's National Centre for the Performing Arts, which emerges from an artificial lake, is known as 'the giant egg'. It is connected to the shore via a transparent underpass, leaving the exterior of the building intact. It is forbidden to exceed the height of the Great Hall of the People, so instead, it extends ten storeys below ground.

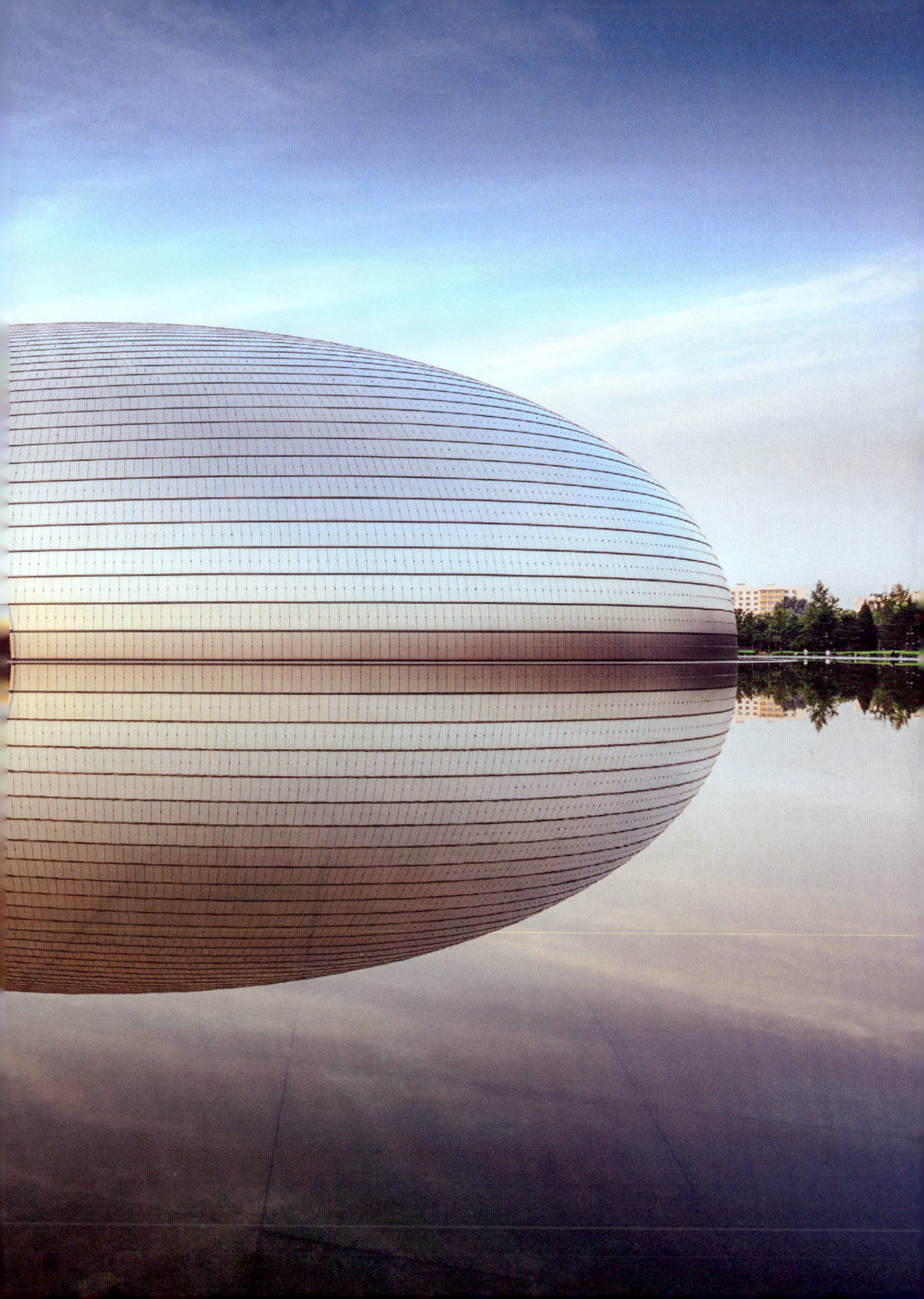

M by Montcalm Hotel
London, England
Architect: Squire and Partners, 2015

The dizzying, slanted facade of this sleek Shoreditch hotel was inspired by Op Art pioneer Bridget Riley's geometric paintings, in particular the rhythmic repetition of her diagonally striped *Nataraja*. The building's design also reflects its proximity to the famous Moorfields Eye Hospital, playing with optical effects and visual perception.

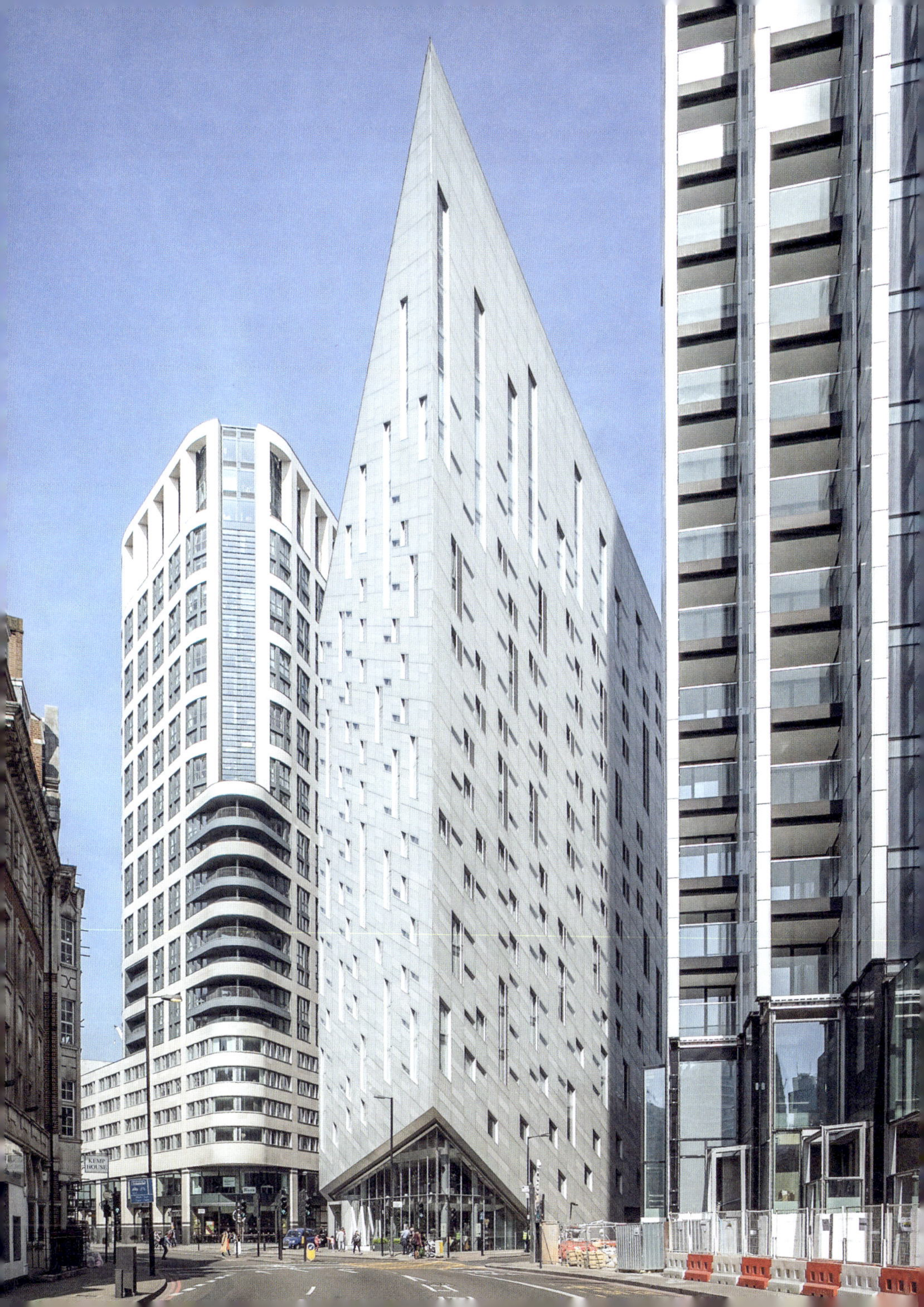
KEMP
HOUSE

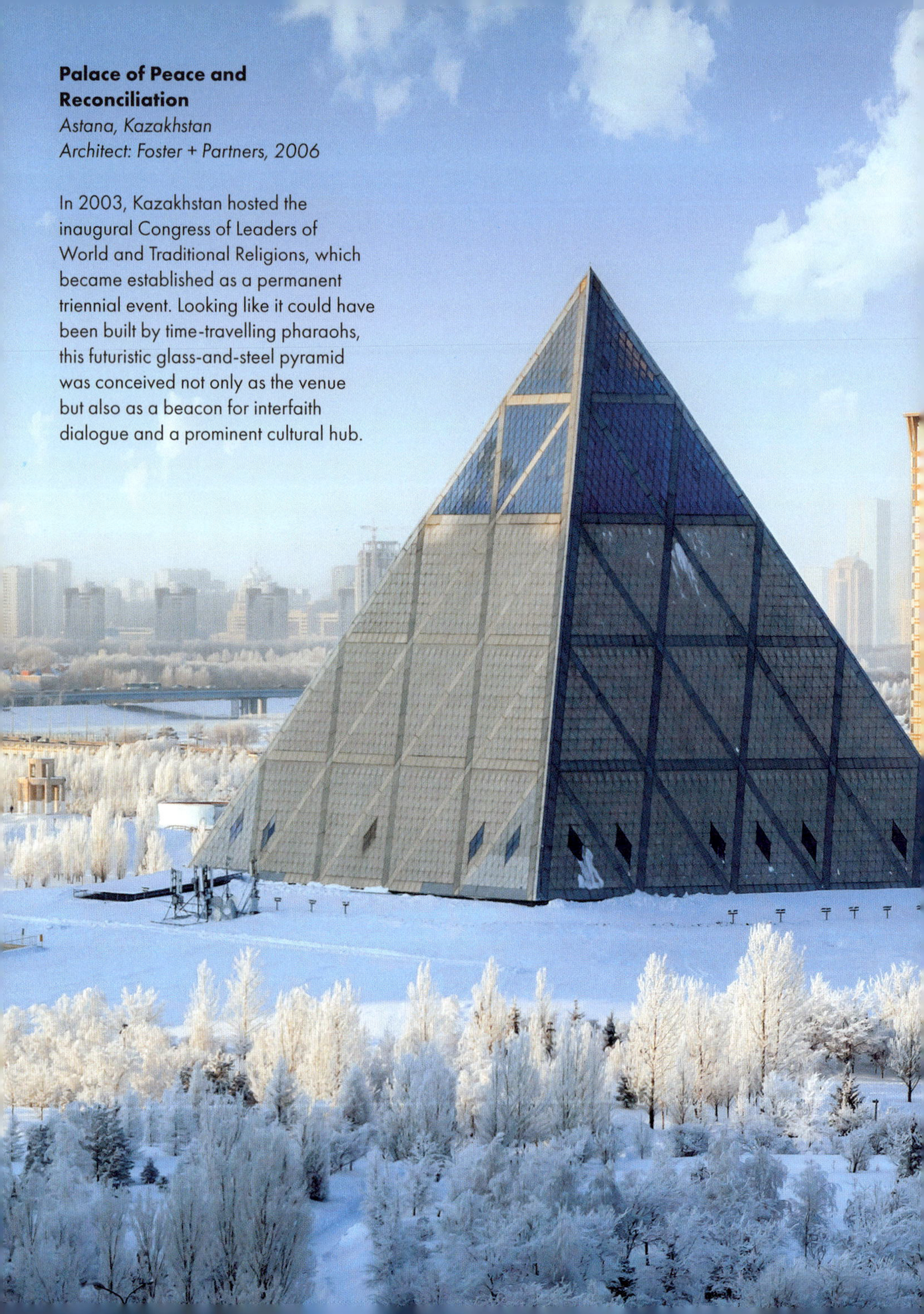

Palace of Peace and Reconciliation
Astana, Kazakhstan
Architect: Foster + Partners, 2006

In 2003, Kazakhstan hosted the inaugural Congress of Leaders of World and Traditional Religions, which became established as a permanent triennial event. Looking like it could have been built by time-travelling pharaohs, this futuristic glass-and-steel pyramid was conceived not only as the venue but also as a beacon for interfaith dialogue and a prominent cultural hub.

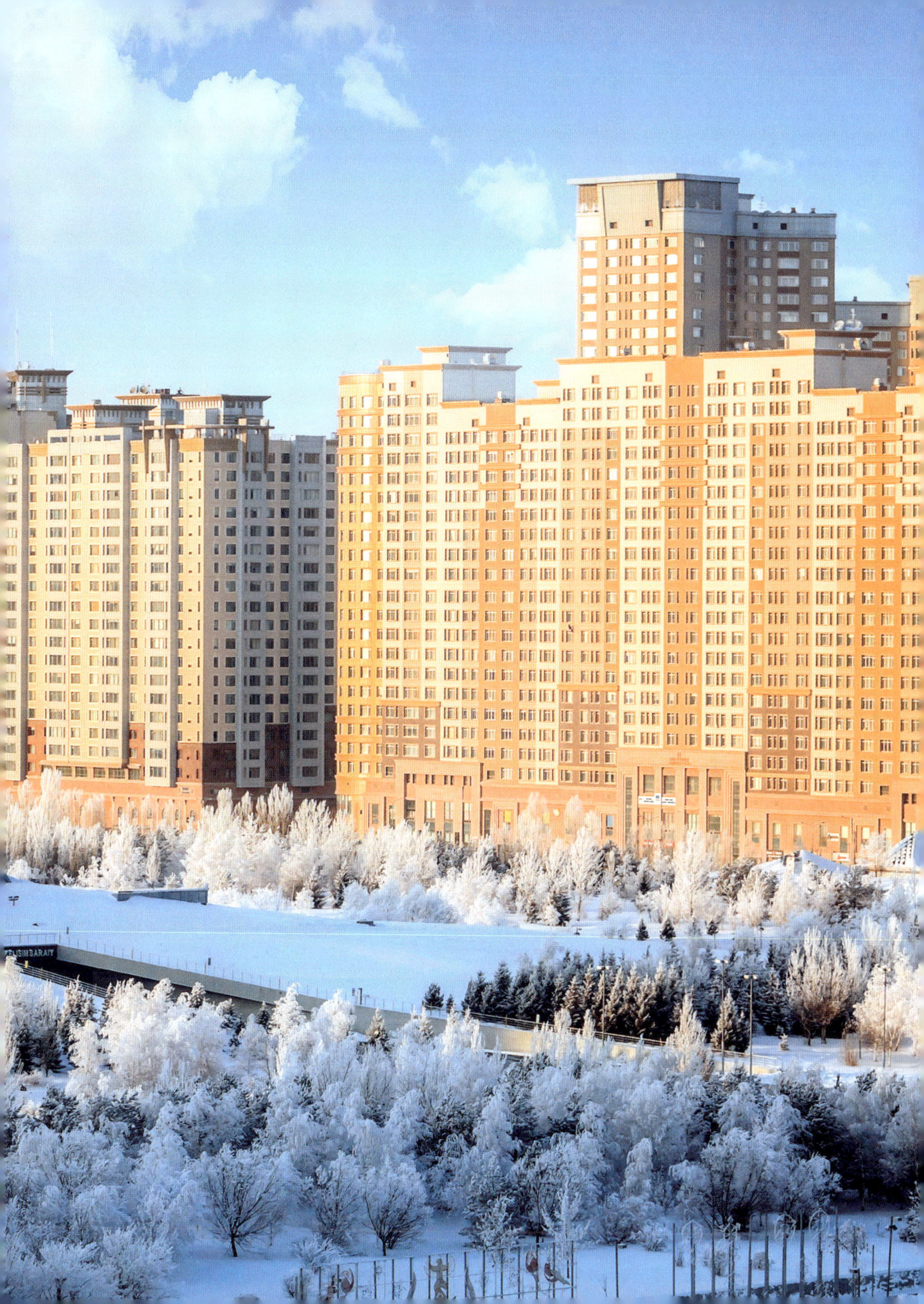
SARAIY

Centre Pompidou Málaga
Málaga, Spain
Architects: Javier Pérez de la Fuente and Juan Antonio Marín Malavé, 2013

A vibrant splash of modern art on the waterfront, the Centre Pompidou's first satellite venture was originally established in this historic city for five years. Located in a subterranean building beneath French artist Daniel Buren's brightly coloured glass cube, the success of this Spanish outpost prompted the licence to be renewed until 2034.

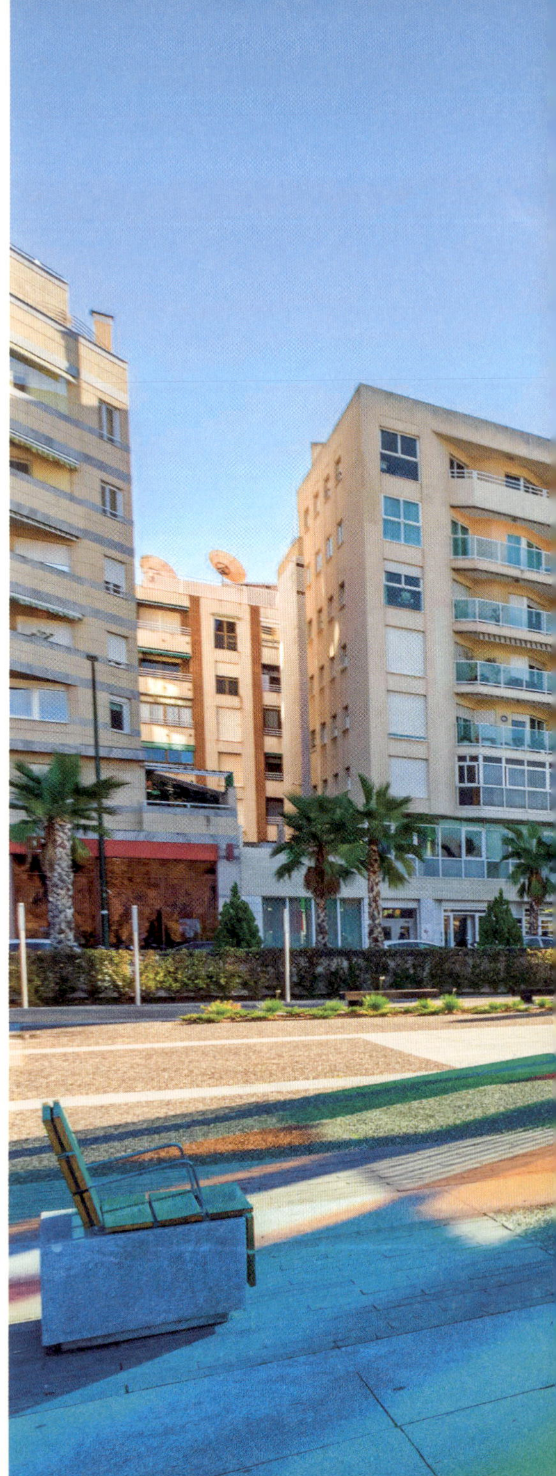

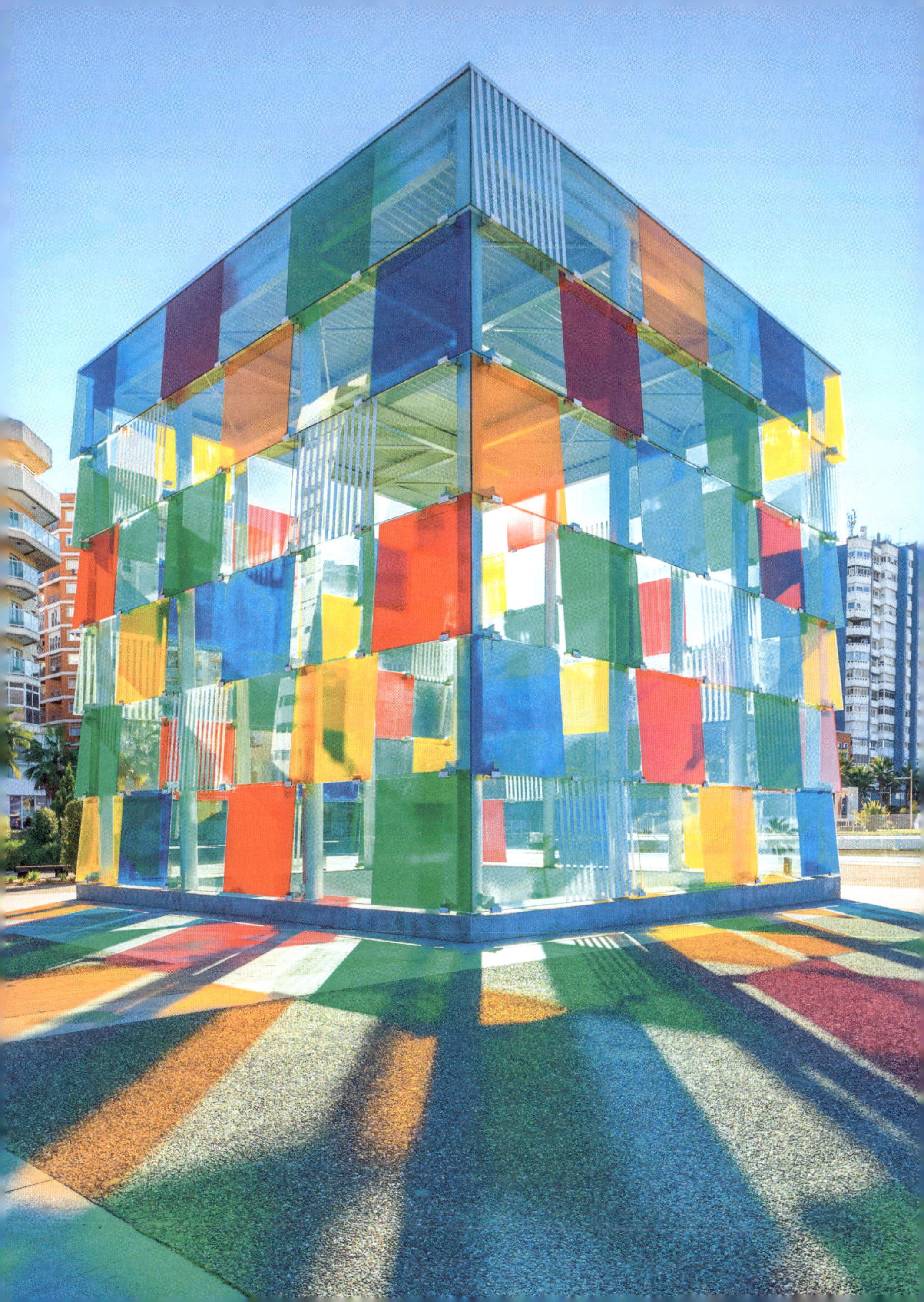

Holiday Home
Folkestone, England
Artist: Richard Woods, 2017

These two tiny houses were part of an art installation highlighting the UK housing crisis, where some own more than one property while others are homeless. Six differently coloured but otherwise identical houses, one-third of the size of a normal home, were placed in unlikely locations to encourage proprietors to consider the social impact of multiple-home ownership.

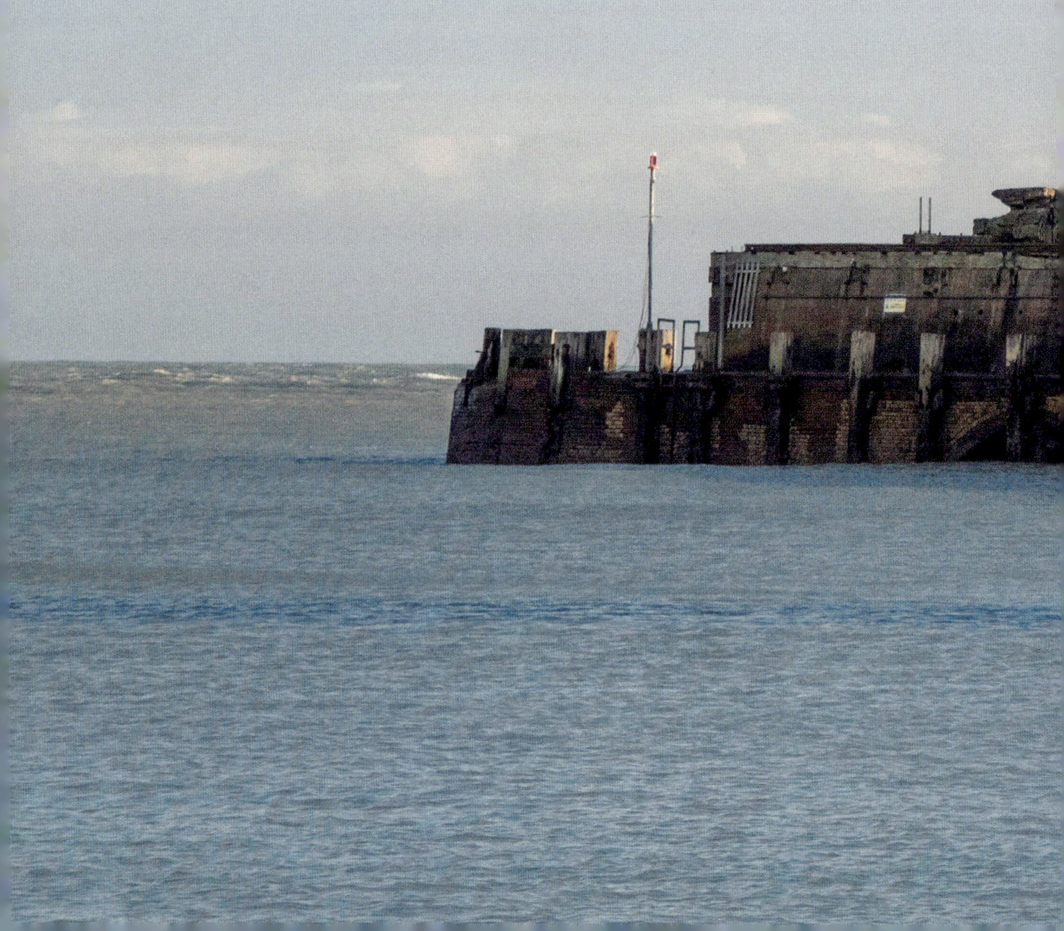

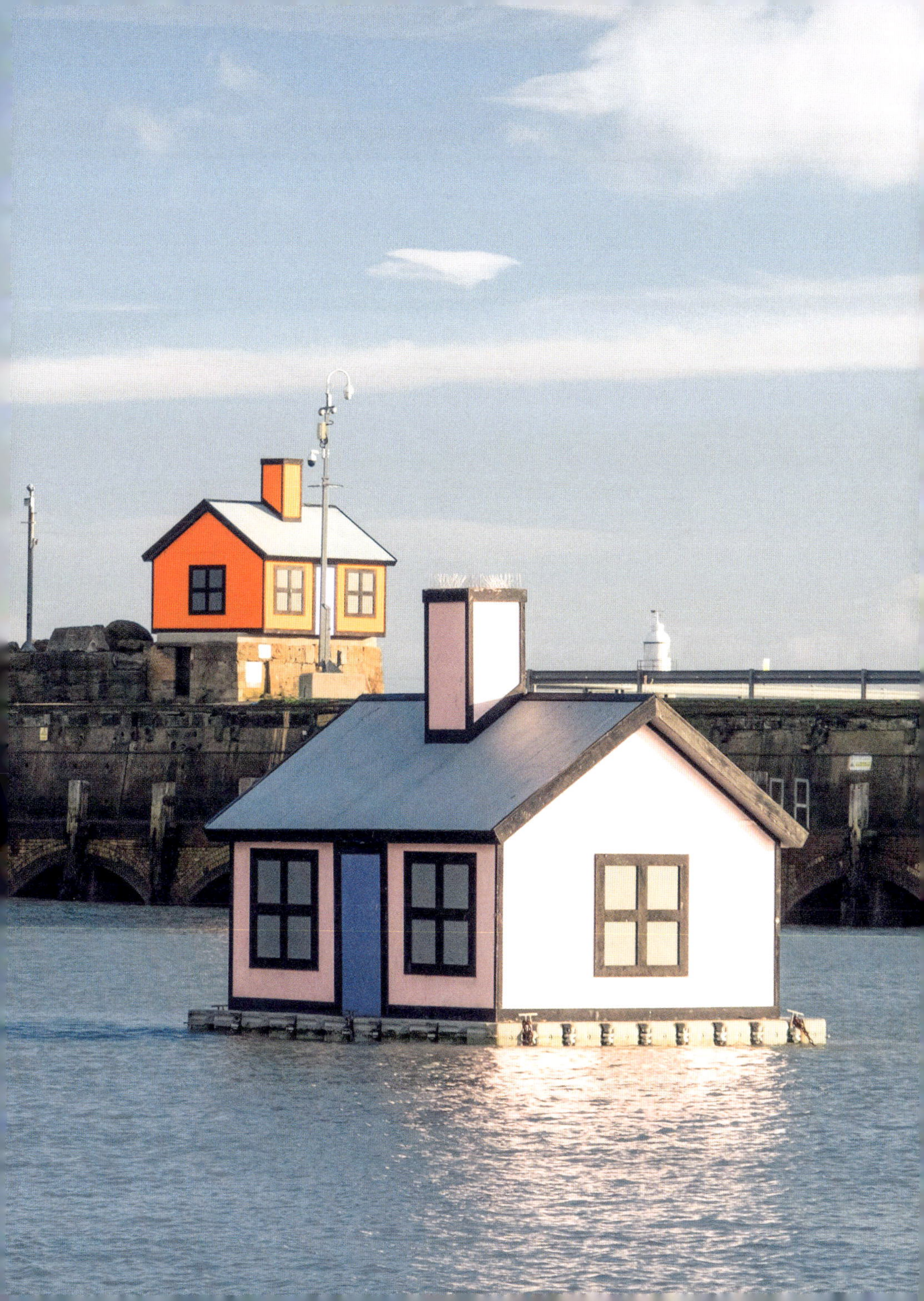

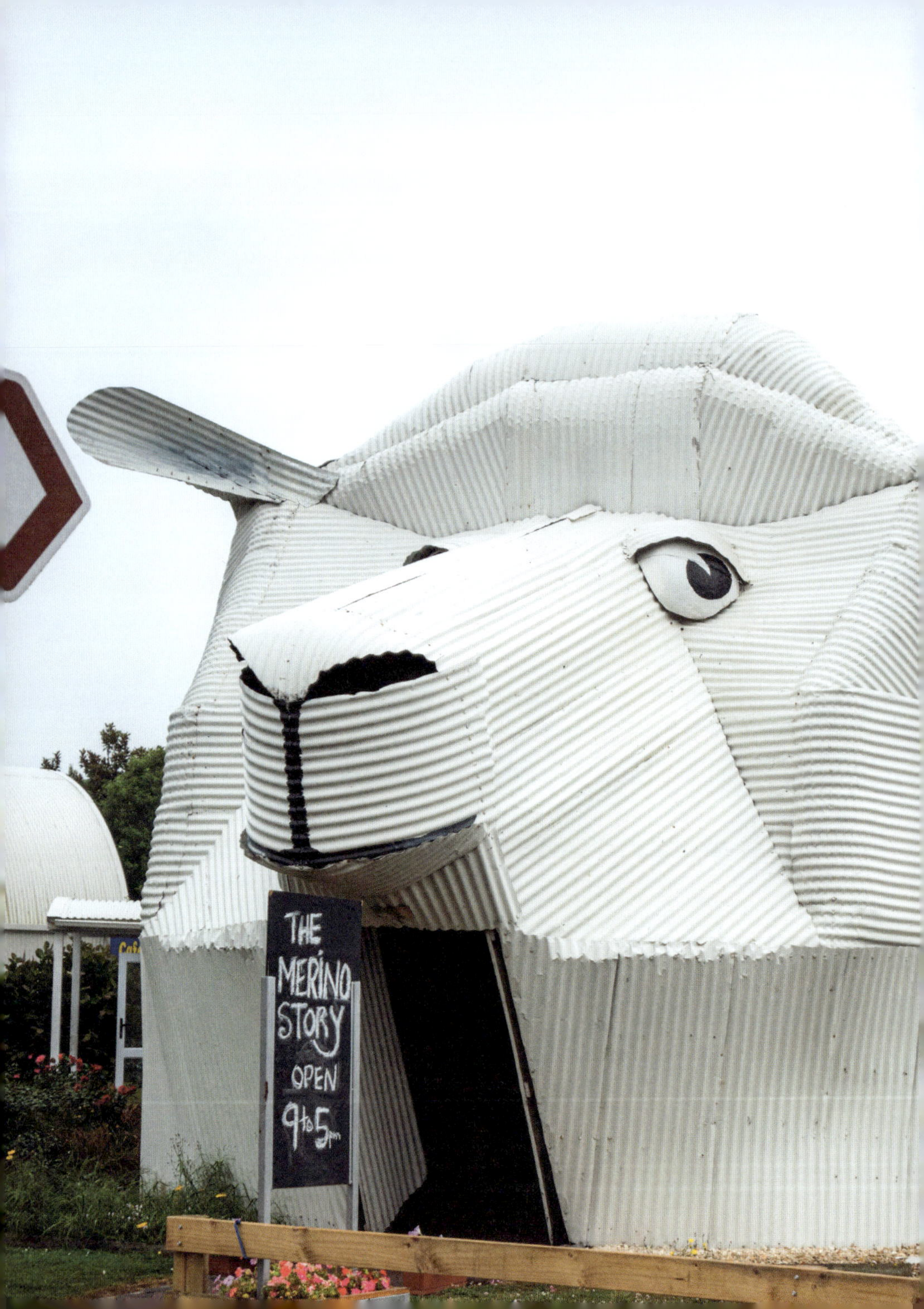
THE
MERINO
STORY
OPEN
9 to 5pm

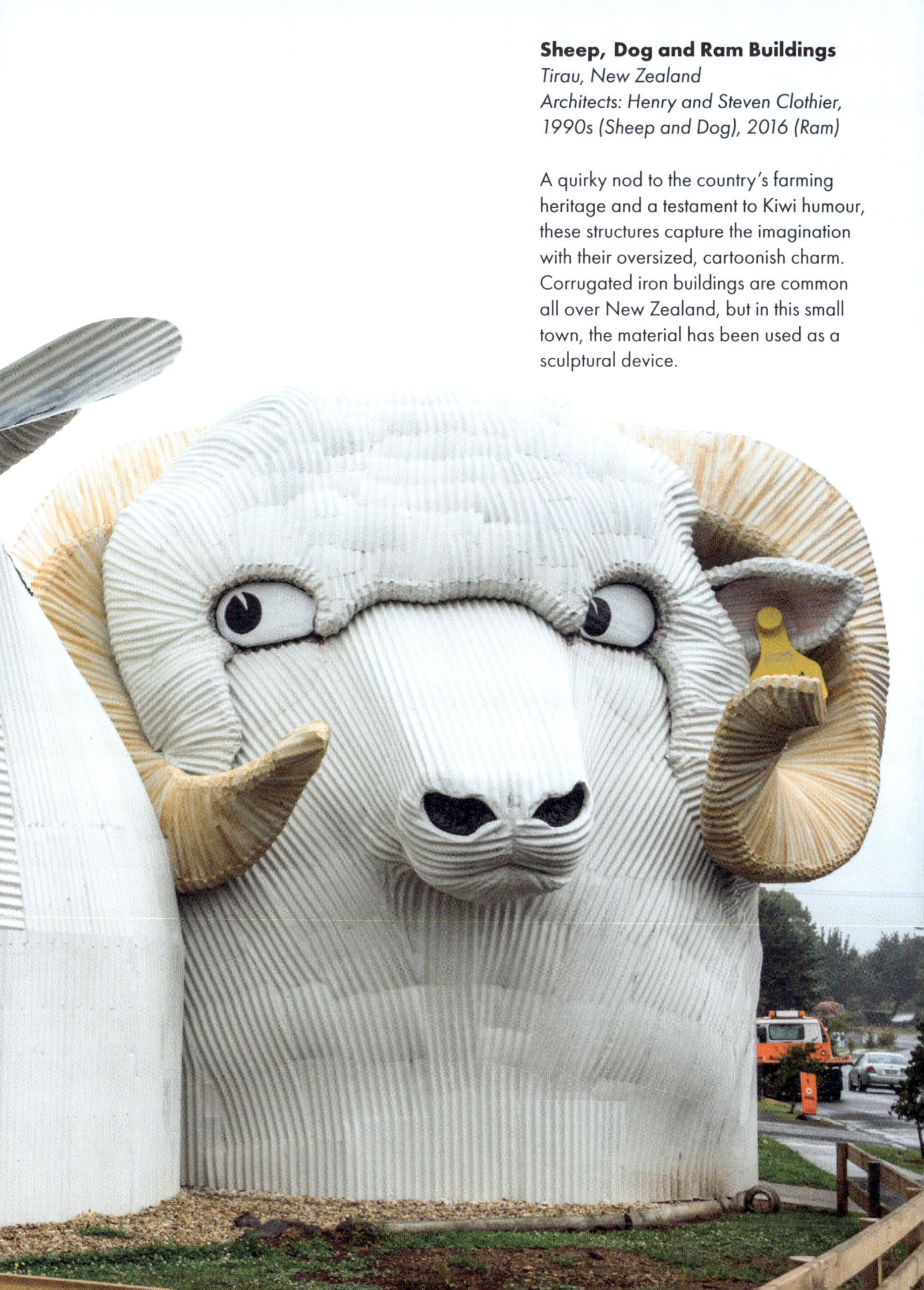

Sheep, Dog and Ram Buildings
Tirau, New Zealand
Architects: Henry and Steven Clothier, 1990s (Sheep and Dog), 2016 (Ram)

A quirky nod to the country's farming heritage and a testament to Kiwi humour, these structures capture the imagination with their oversized, cartoonish charm. Corrugated iron buildings are common all over New Zealand, but in this small town, the material has been used as a sculptural device.

Solar Egg

Kiruna, Sweden
Artists: Bigert & Bergström, 2017

This art installation-come-sauna provides a striking contrast to the frozen Arctic tundra, its golden mirrored panels reflecting the surrounding landscape. It was developed by the artists as a public sculpture to symbolise the rebirth of Sweden's northernmost city, which had been relocated to save it from subsidence.

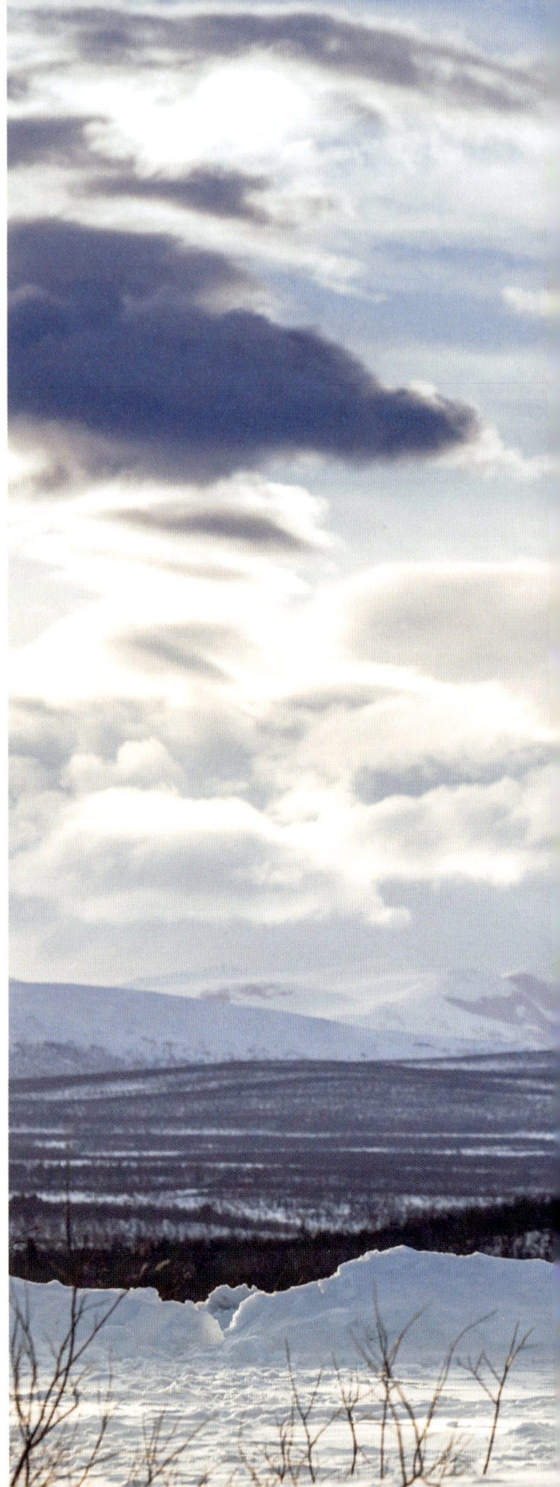

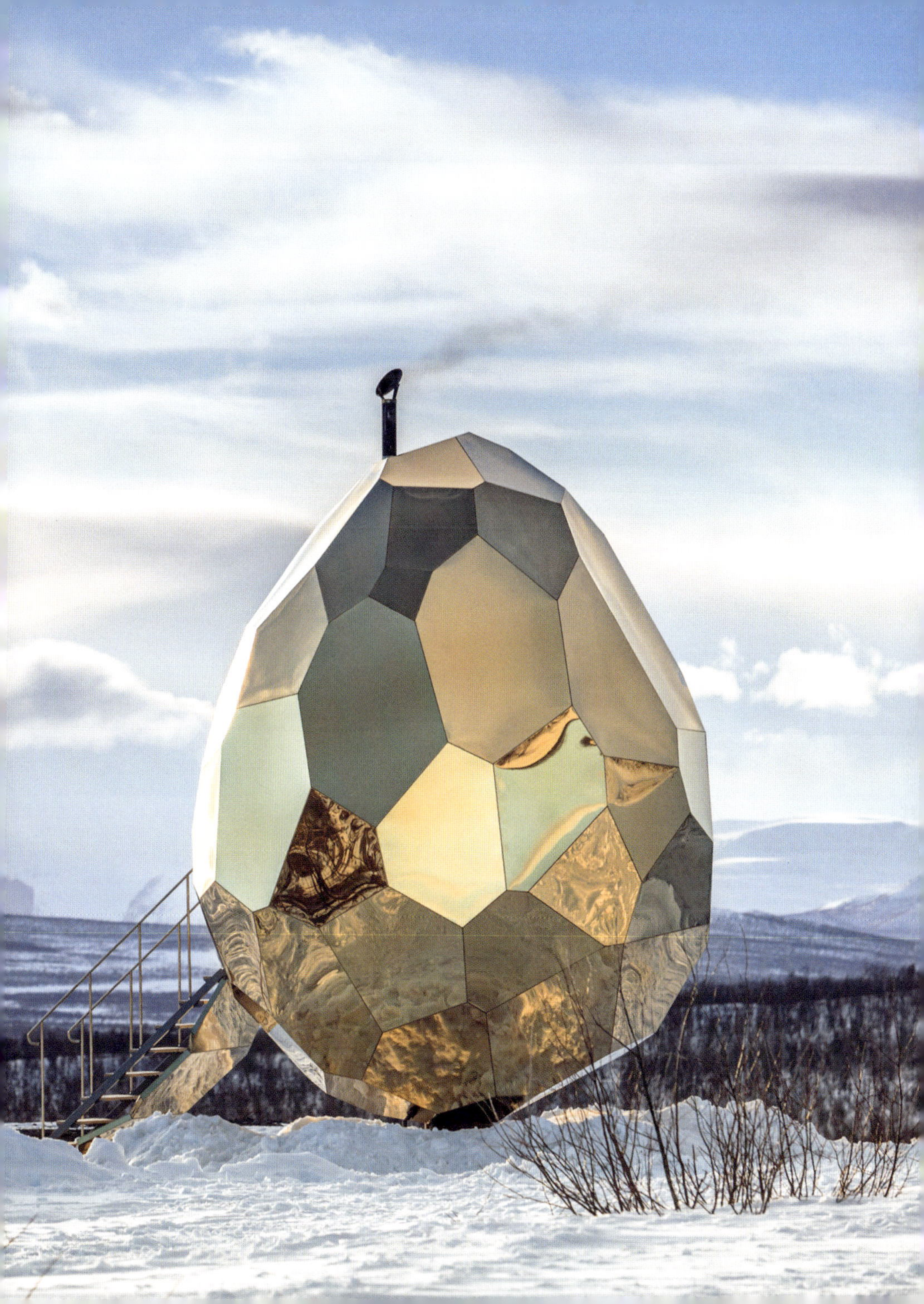

Presence in Hormuz 2
Hormuz, Iran
Architect: ZAV Architects, 2020

This historic port controls the shipment of oil from the Middle East, but despite this, the town struggles economically. You could be forgiven for thinking you'd stumbled upon a whimsical gnome village, but this cluster of brightly coloured domes was designed to attract tourists by providing an engaging alternative to high-rise holiday rentals. The rainbow topography mimics the landscape of the island.

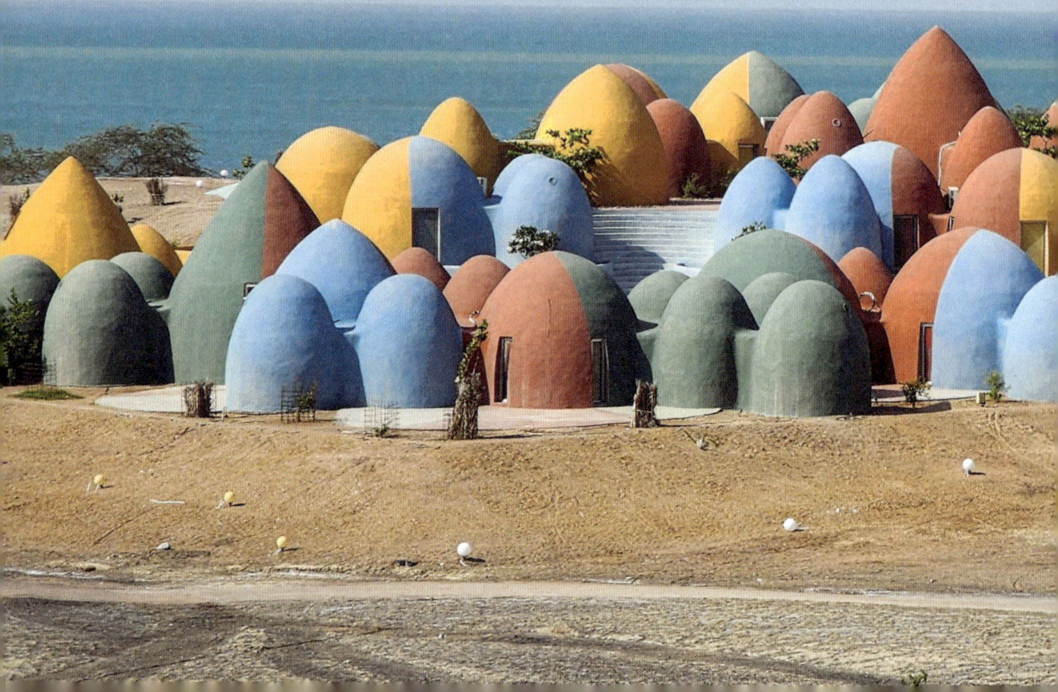

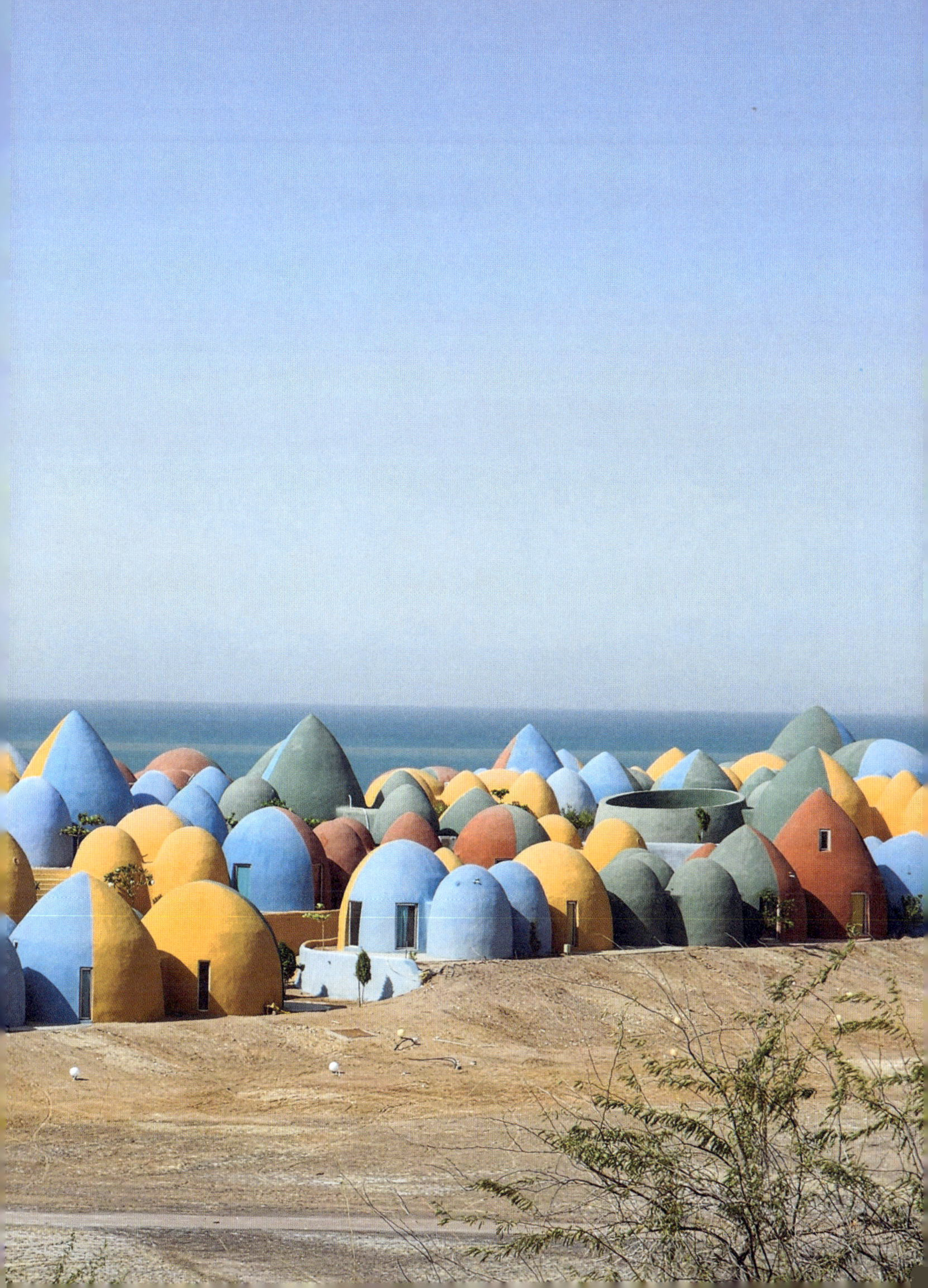

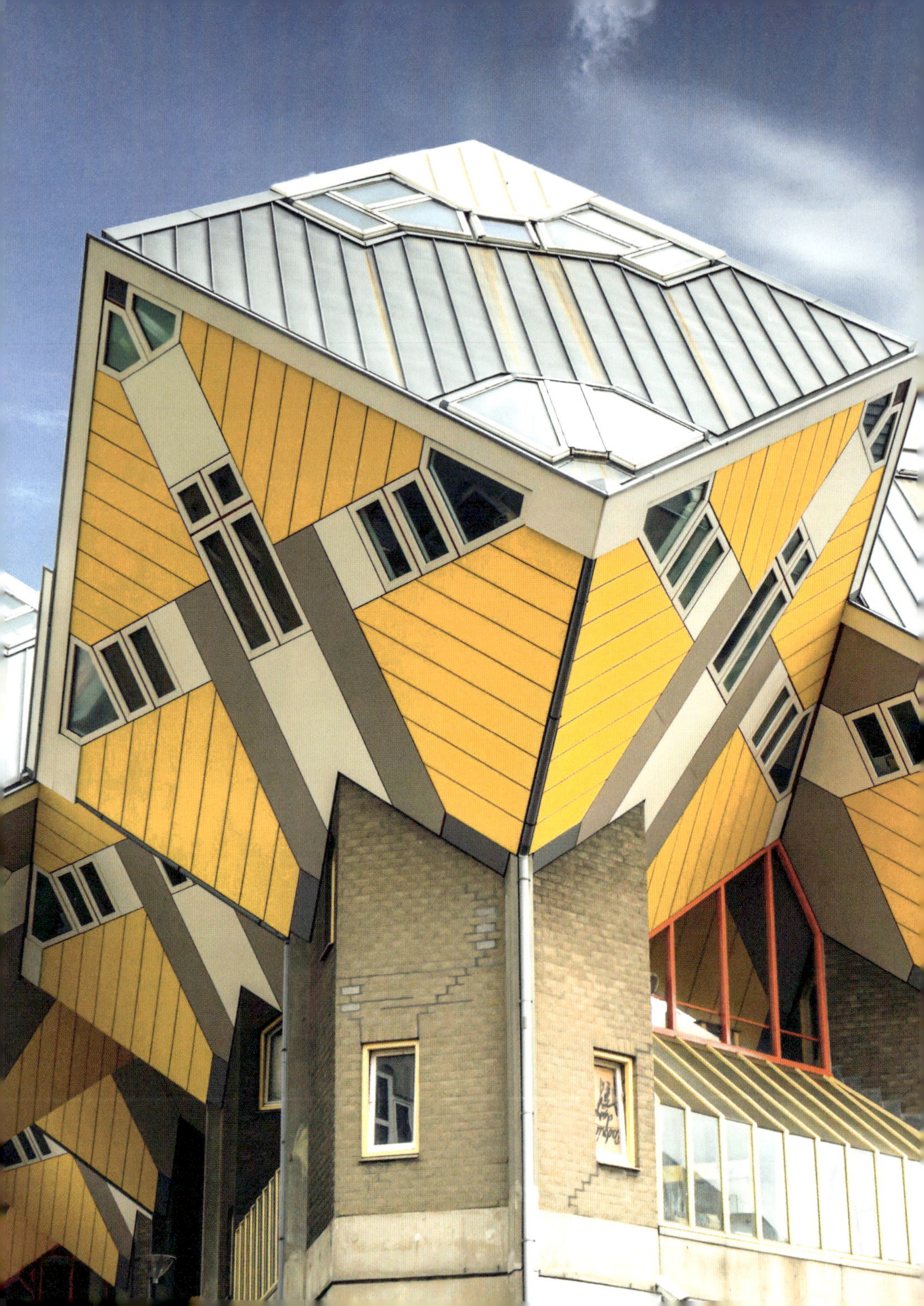

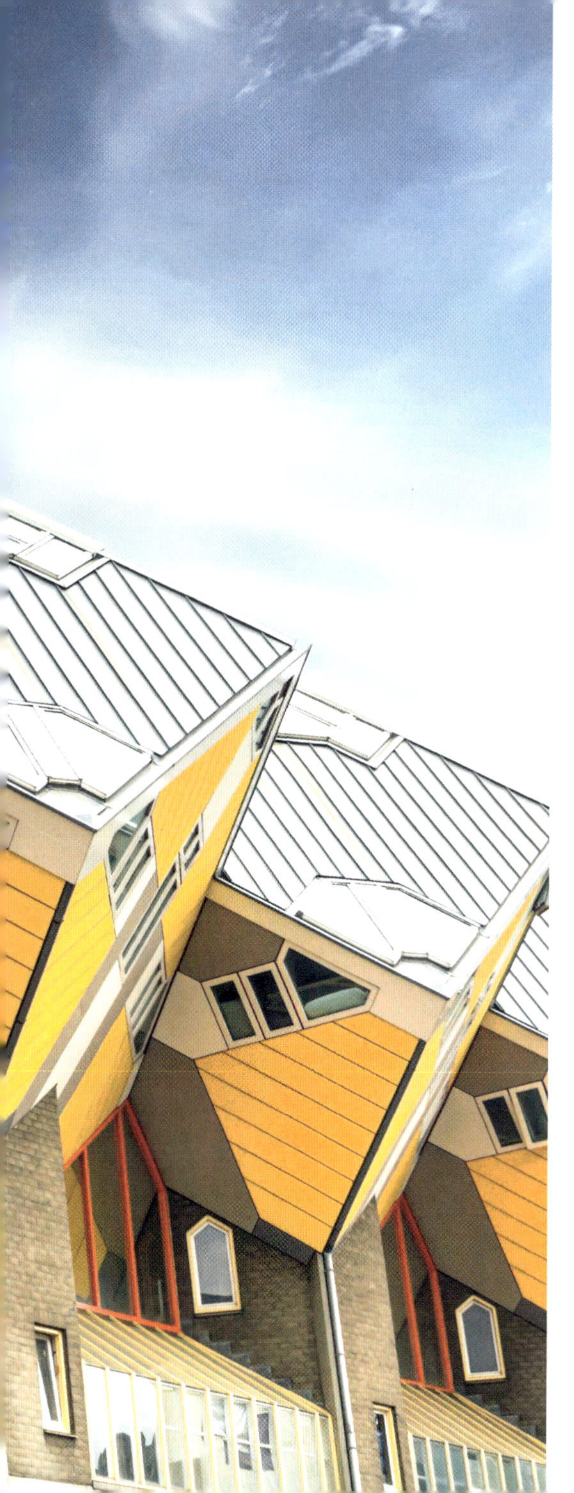

Kubuswoningen

Rotterdam, Netherlands
Architect: Piet Blom, 1984

Piet Blom was tasked with revitalising Rotterdam's historic Oude Haven neighbourhood, destroyed in World War II, with characterful architecture that included social housing. His Cube Houses (Kubuswoningen), representing trees supported by reinforced concrete 'trunks', were inspired by Le Corbusier and designed to elevate living spaces, maximising the recreational space below while creating views from above.

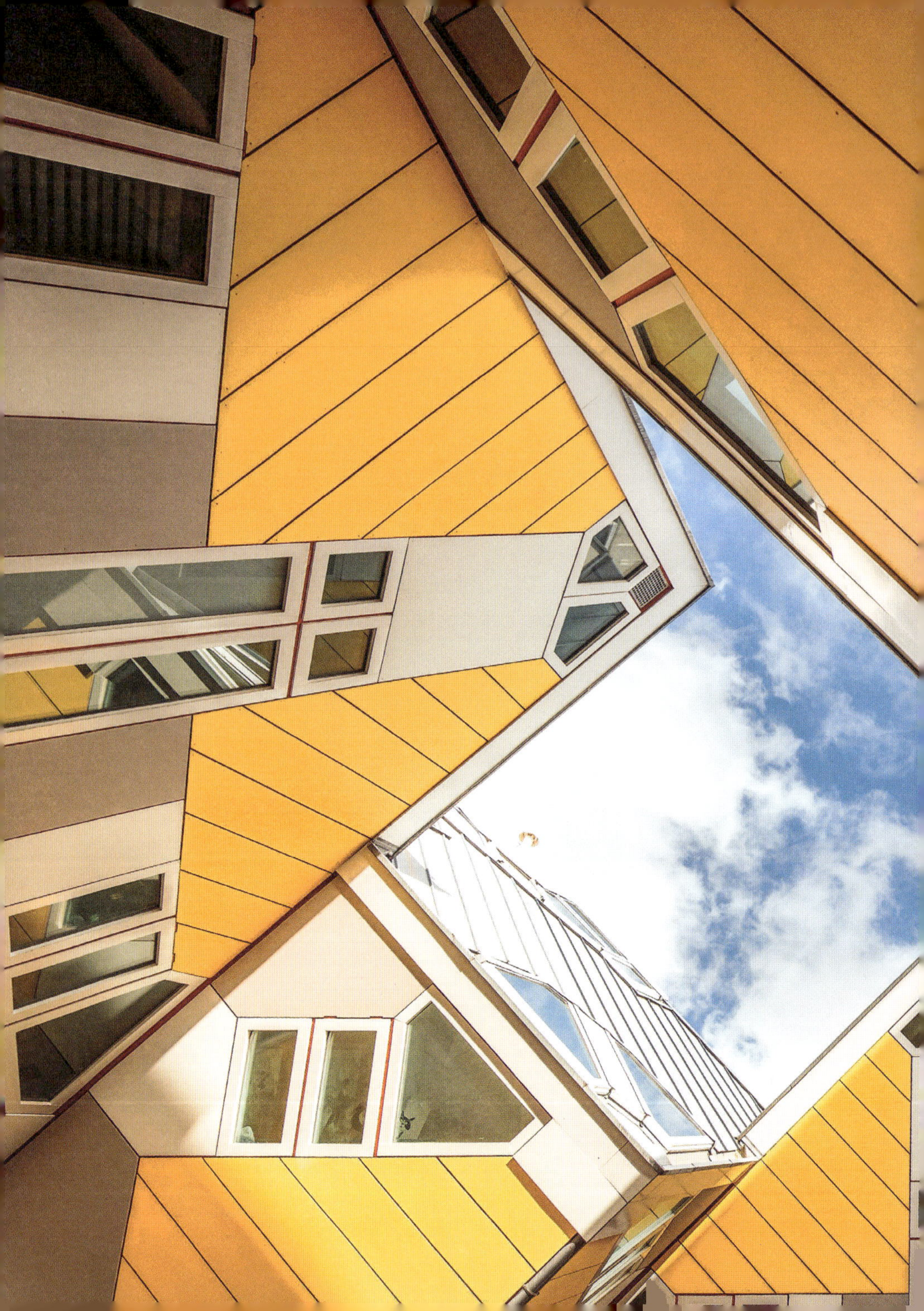

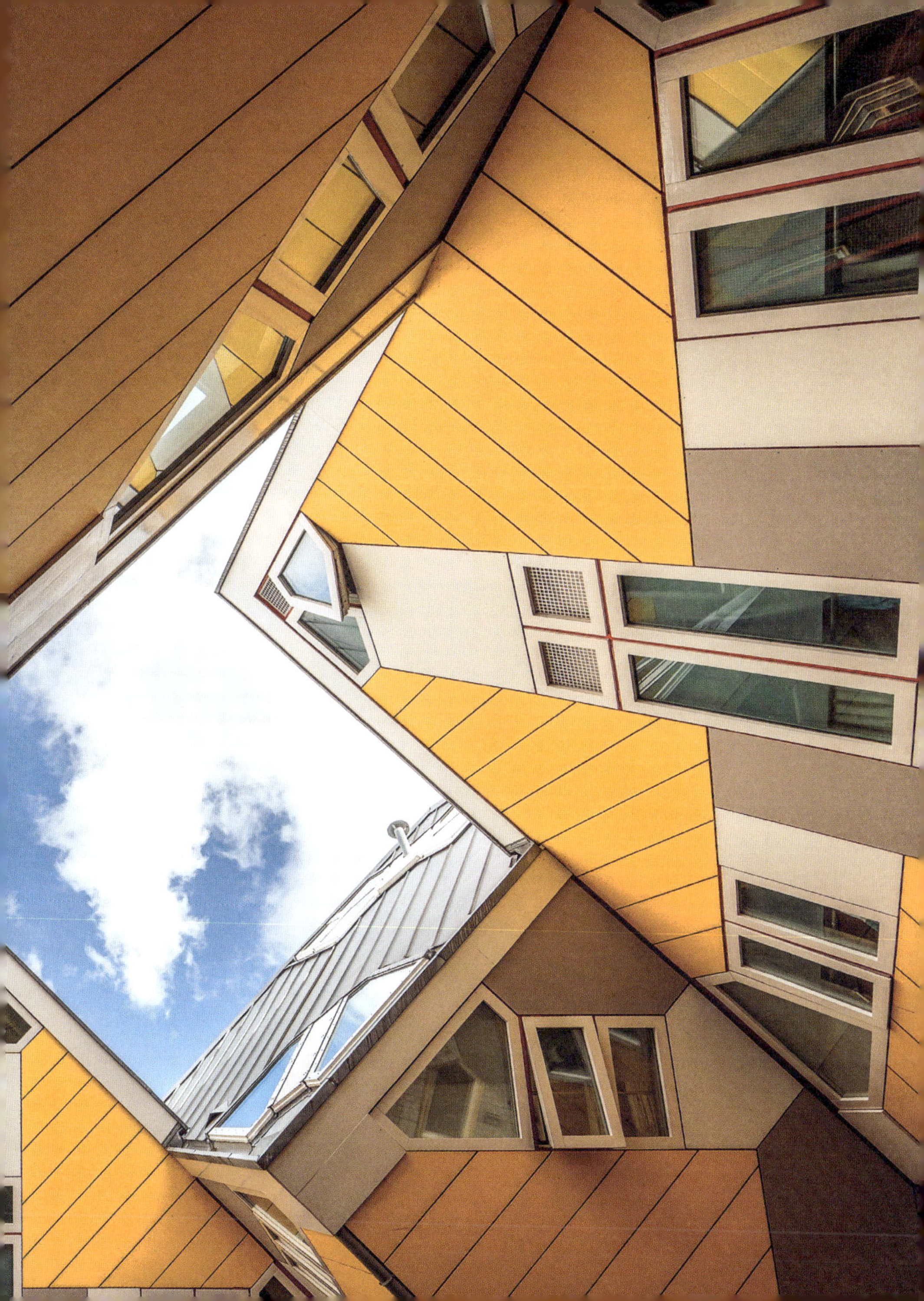

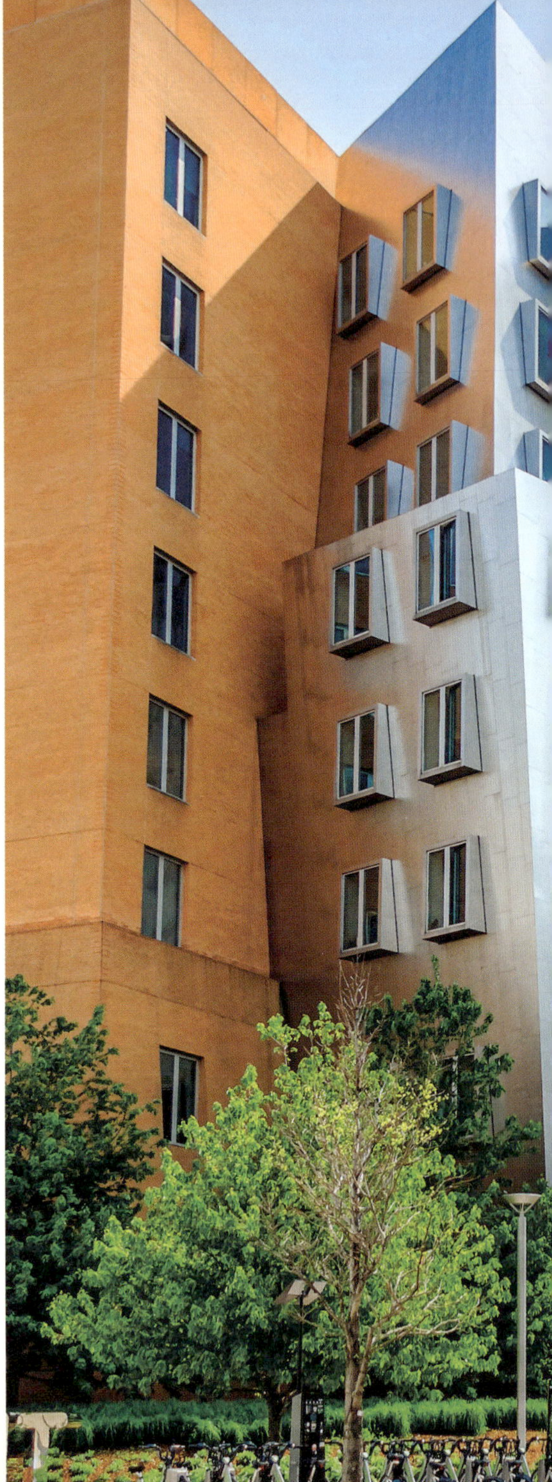

Stata Center at MIT

Cambridge, Massachusetts, USA
Architect: Frank Gehry, 2004

'A party of drunken robots that got together to celebrate' is how the architect described his design for the Computer, Information and Intelligence Sciences building. Some of the world's best-known architects have contributed buildings to Massachusetts' prestigious institute. Frank Gehry's features tilting towers, many-angled walls and whimsical shapes, and was designed to foster collaboration between different disciplines.

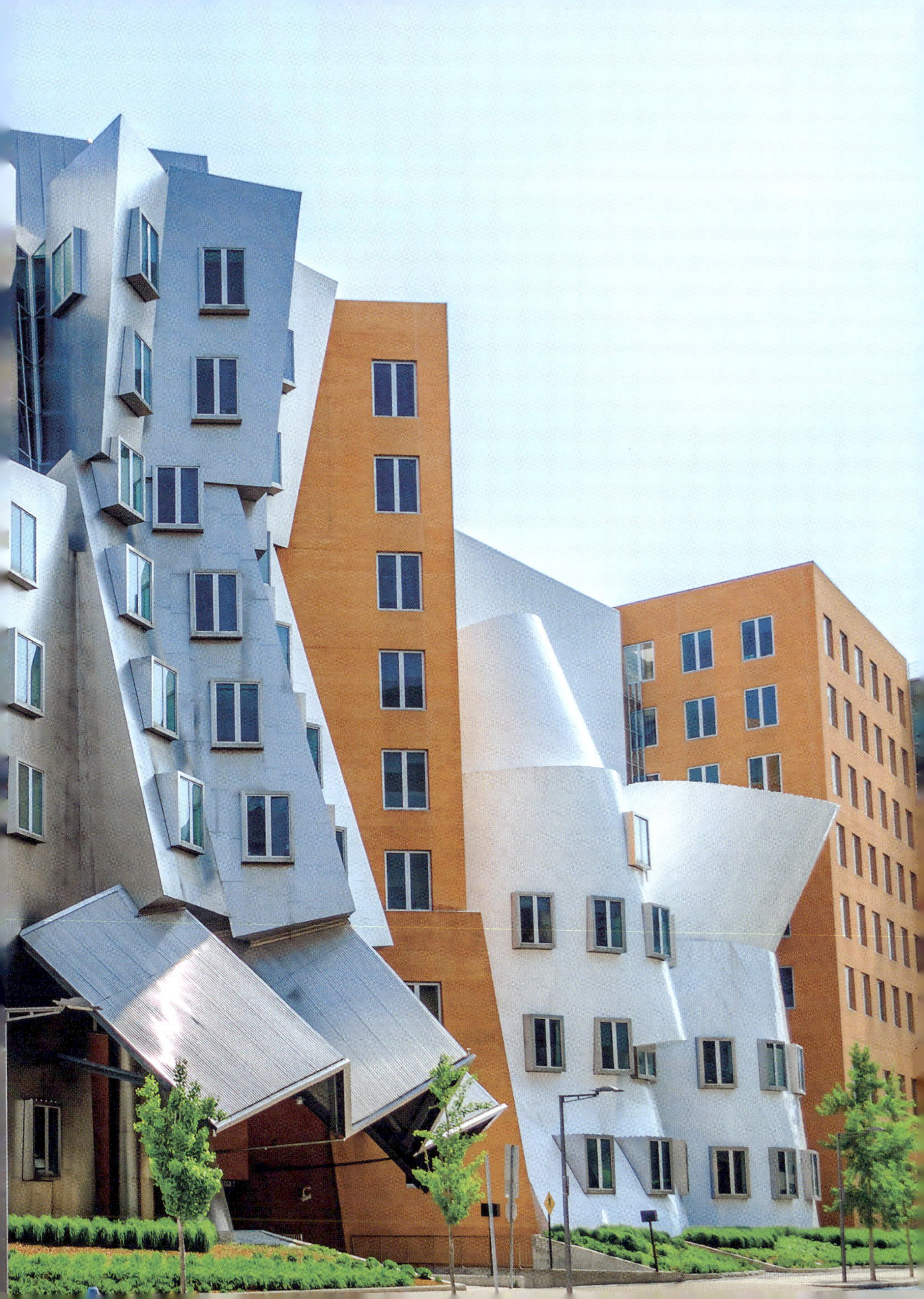

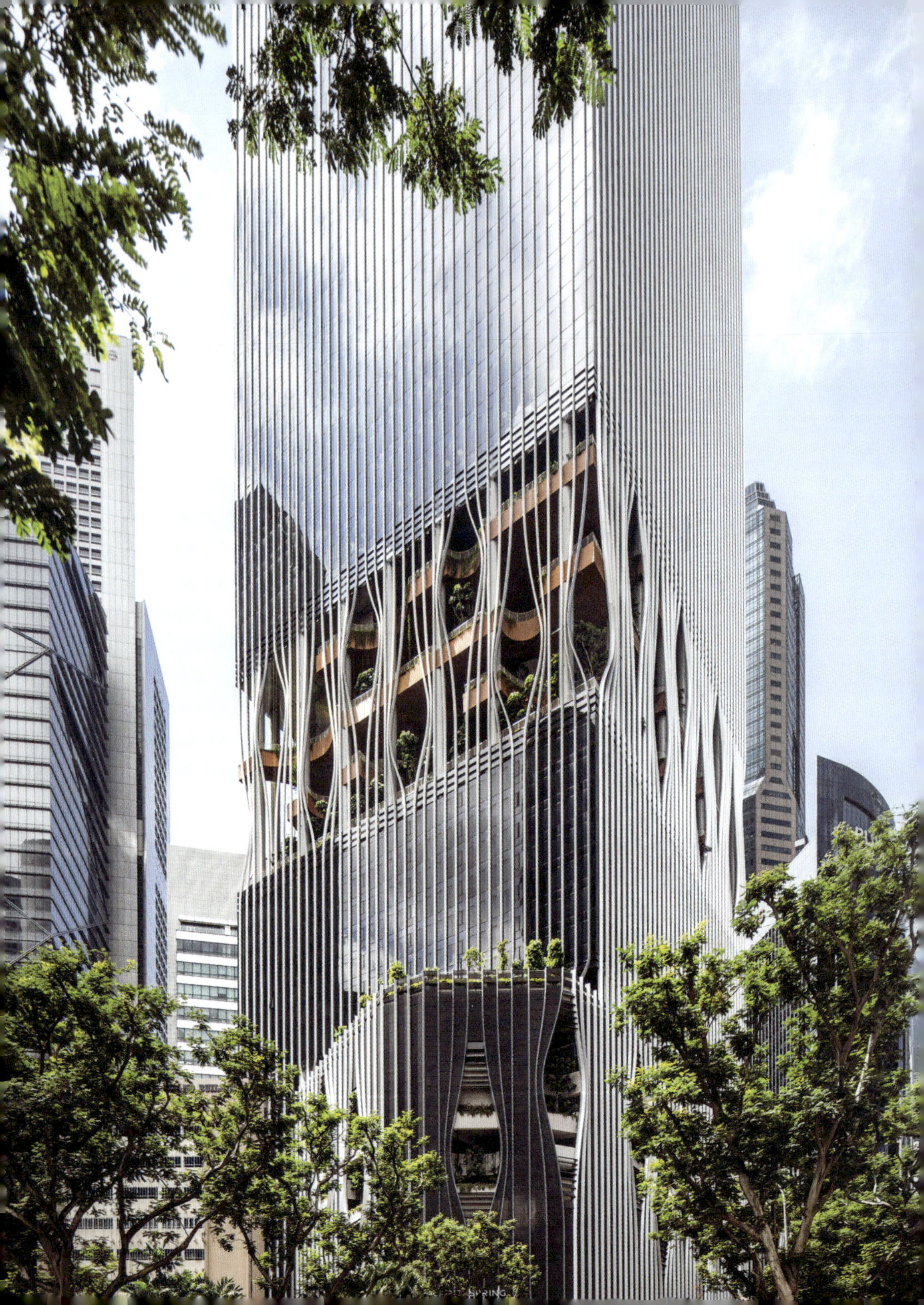

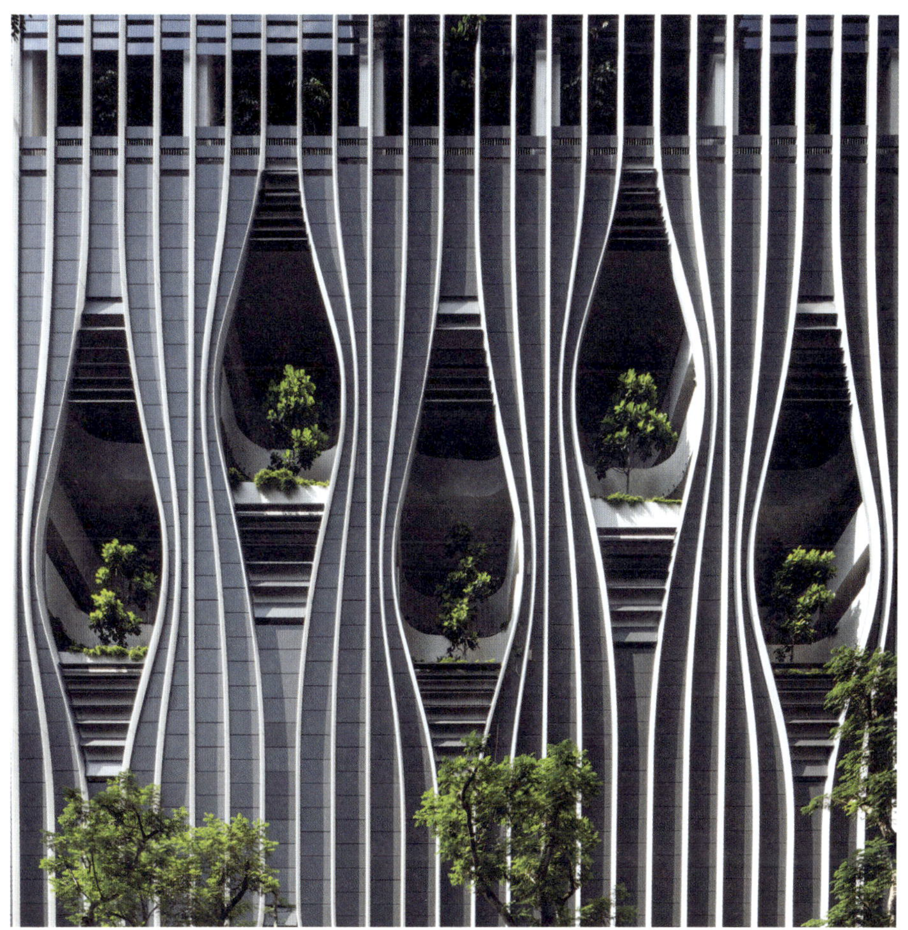

CapitaSpring
Singapore
Architects: Bjarke Ingels Group and Carlo Ratti Associati, 2022

Designed to bring nature to the heart of Singapore's financial district, CapitaSpring incorporates pockets of greenery and gardens in what appear to be openings stretched from the fabric of the building. This multi-purpose tower contains a four-storey vertical park filled with spiralling walkways and tropical terraces.

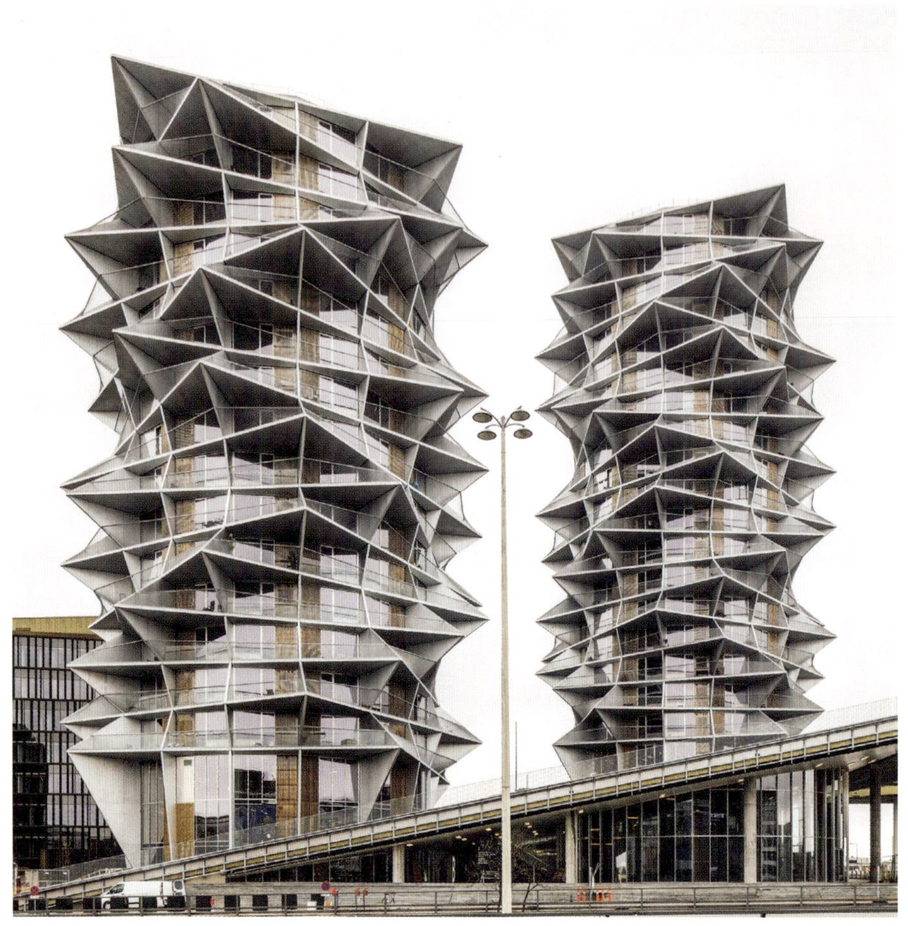

Kaktus Towers
Copenhagen, Denmark
Architect: Bjarke Ingels Group, 2024

Setting a spiky visual statement against the urban skyline are these two cactus-inspired residential towers. Linked by a raised public park, this modern complex has micro-apartments with jagged, angular balconies and communal spaces including an outdoor kitchen, fitness centres and party rooms, reinforcing the project's motto, 'sleep in the apartment – live in the building'.

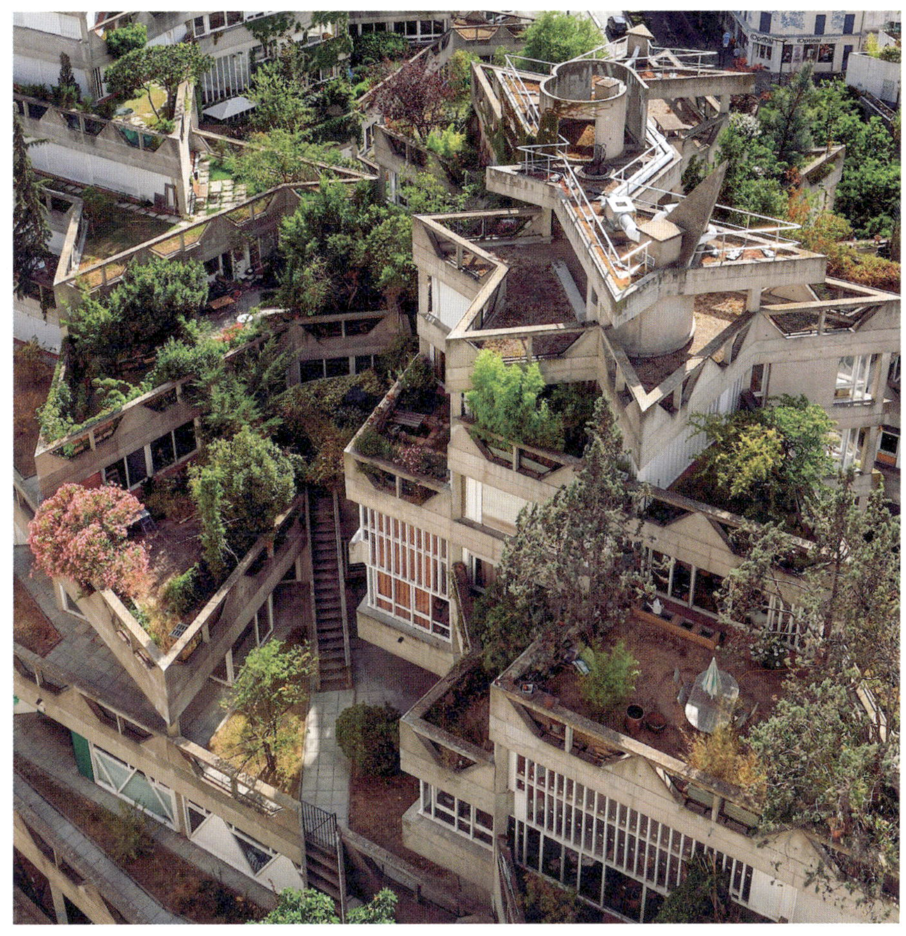

Les Étoiles d' Ivry

Paris, France

Architects: Jean Renaudie and Renée Gailhoustet, 1975

Resembling a Brutalist's crazed fever dream, this complex of social housing, offices and stores consists of a stack of sharply angled concrete stars with staggered terraces softened by wild greenery and urban gardens. It was designed to foster community as part of the post-war urban renewal programme in Paris's suburbs.

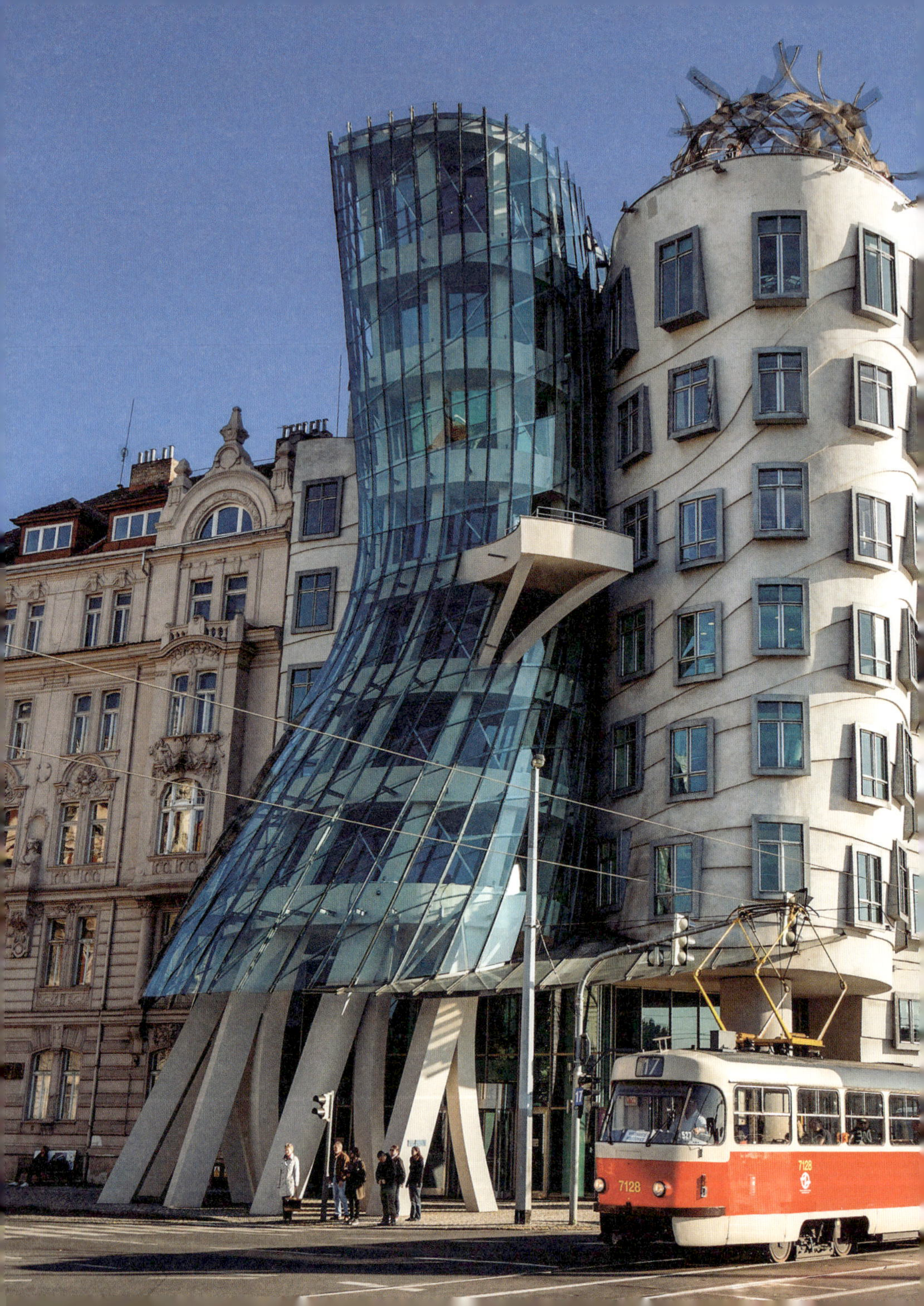
17
7128

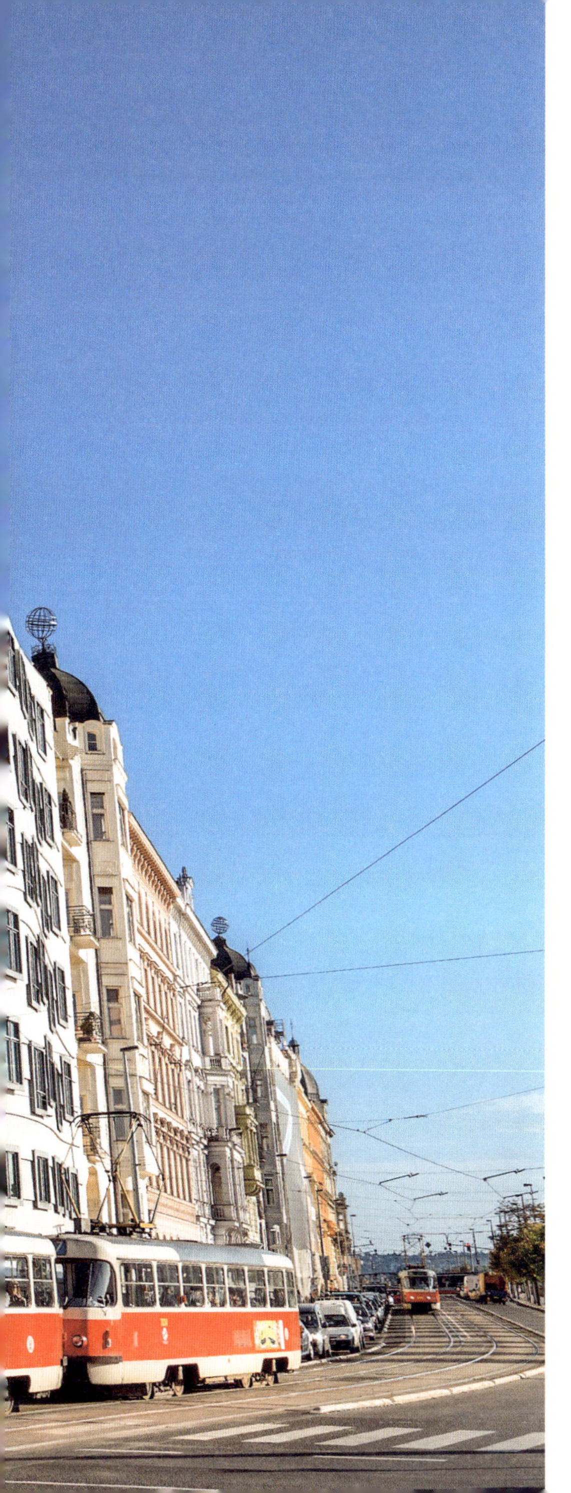

Dancing House
Prague, Czechia
Architects: Vlado Milunić and Frank Gehry, 1996

An unexpected and intriguing surprise amid a sea of harmonious Neoclassical buildings, this dynamic structure features a dynamic Deconstructivist design with two towers resembling a waltzing couple. Frank Gehry had wanted to name it 'Fred and Ginger' after the legendary Hollywood dancing duo, and this is a popular nickname for it among locals.

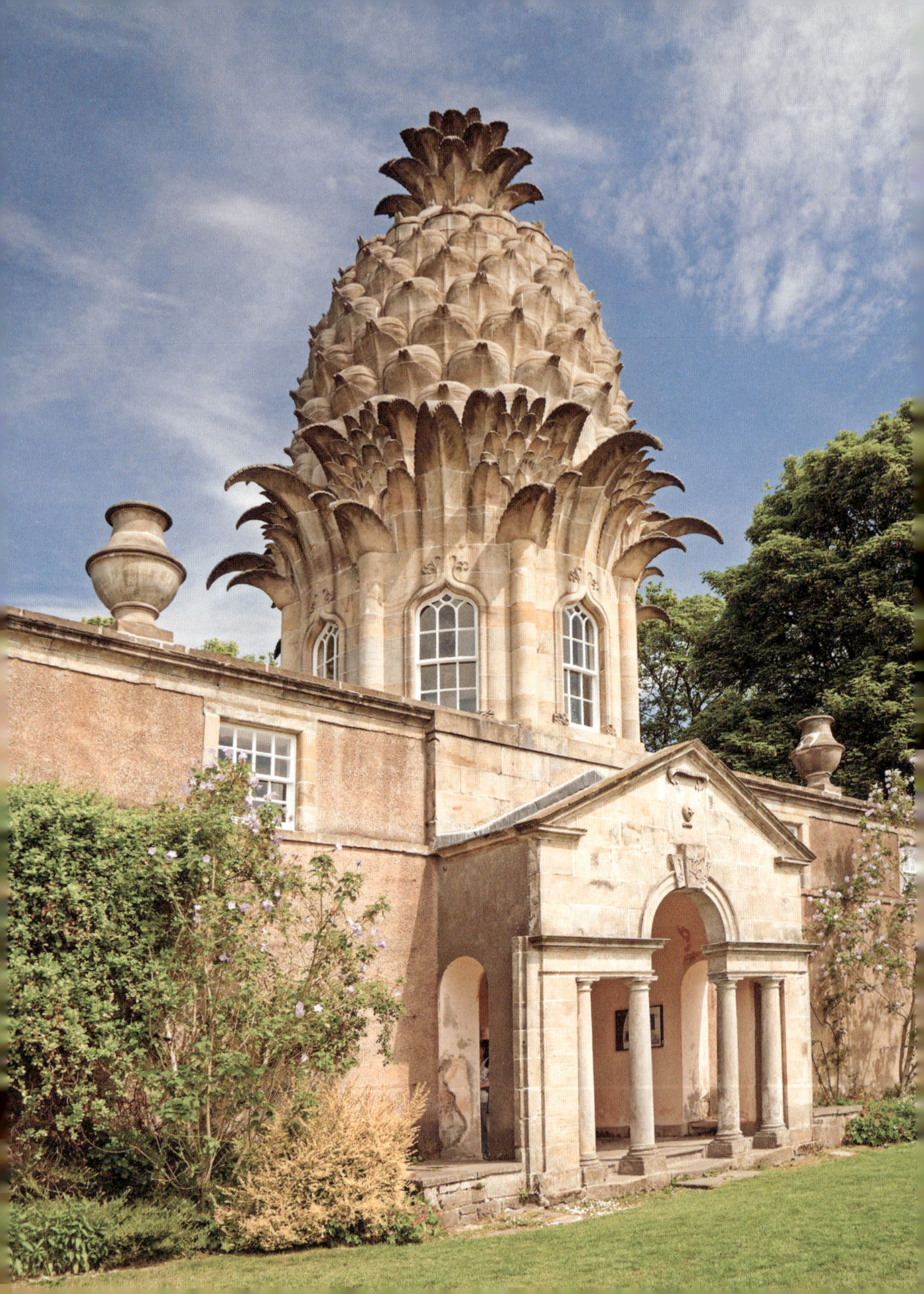

The Dunmore Pineapple

Falkirk, Scotland

1761

This fruity folly was built by John Murray, the fourth Earl of Dunmore, to enjoy the views over his family's estate. Pineapples were increasingly popular motifs in architecture in the late 18th century as symbols of wealth and hospitality. Some speculate Murray's was a display of the fortune he'd amassed during his time as Governor of the Bahamas.

The House in the Clouds
Suffolk, England
Architect: Frederick Forbes-Glennie, 1923

Appearing as though plucked from a fairy tale, this enchanting structure was once a cleverly disguised water tank, seamlessly blending in with the local architecture. It was built to provide the village of Thorpeness with water storage until it joined the mains supply in 1974 and was given its whimsical name by a local children's author.

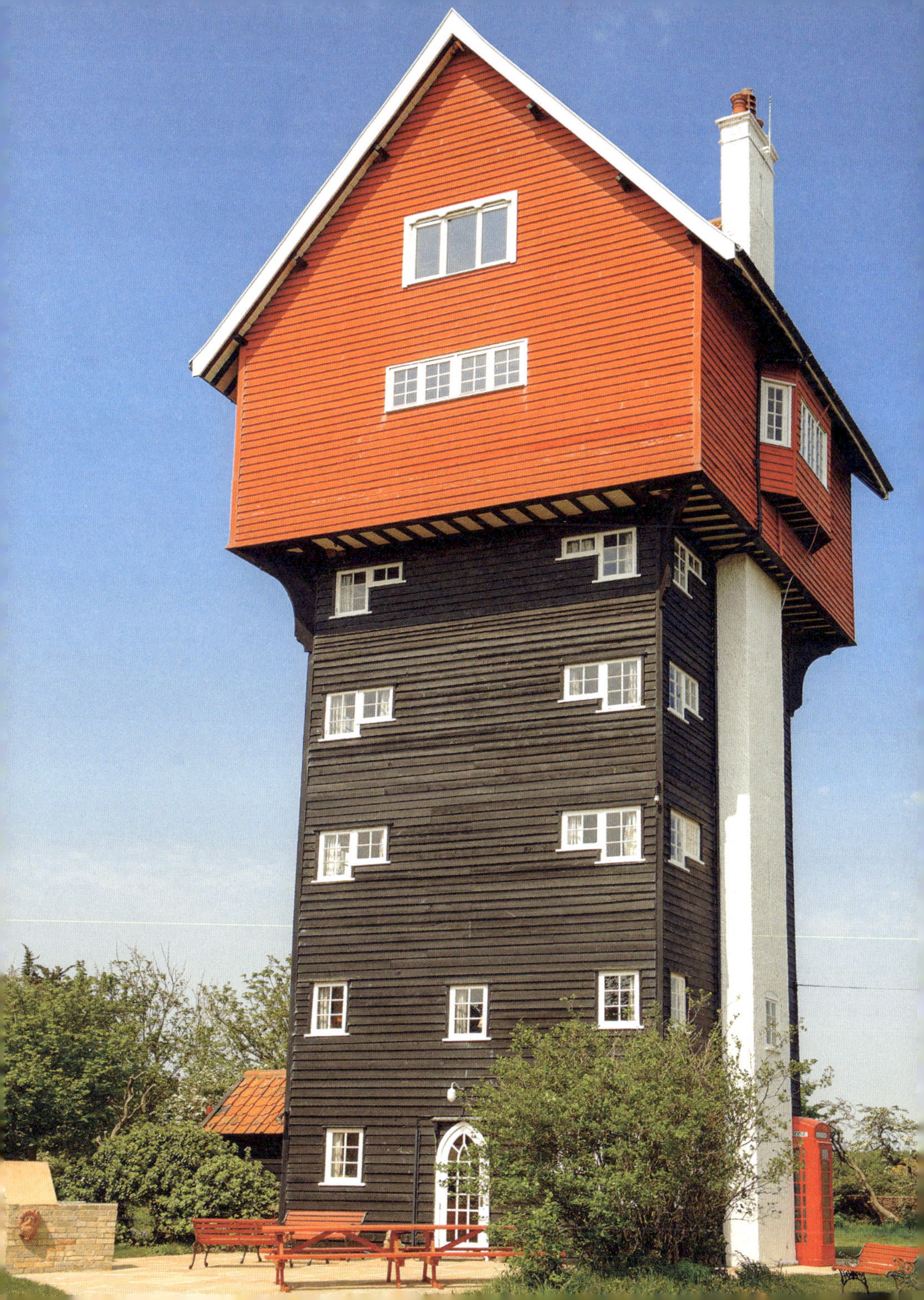

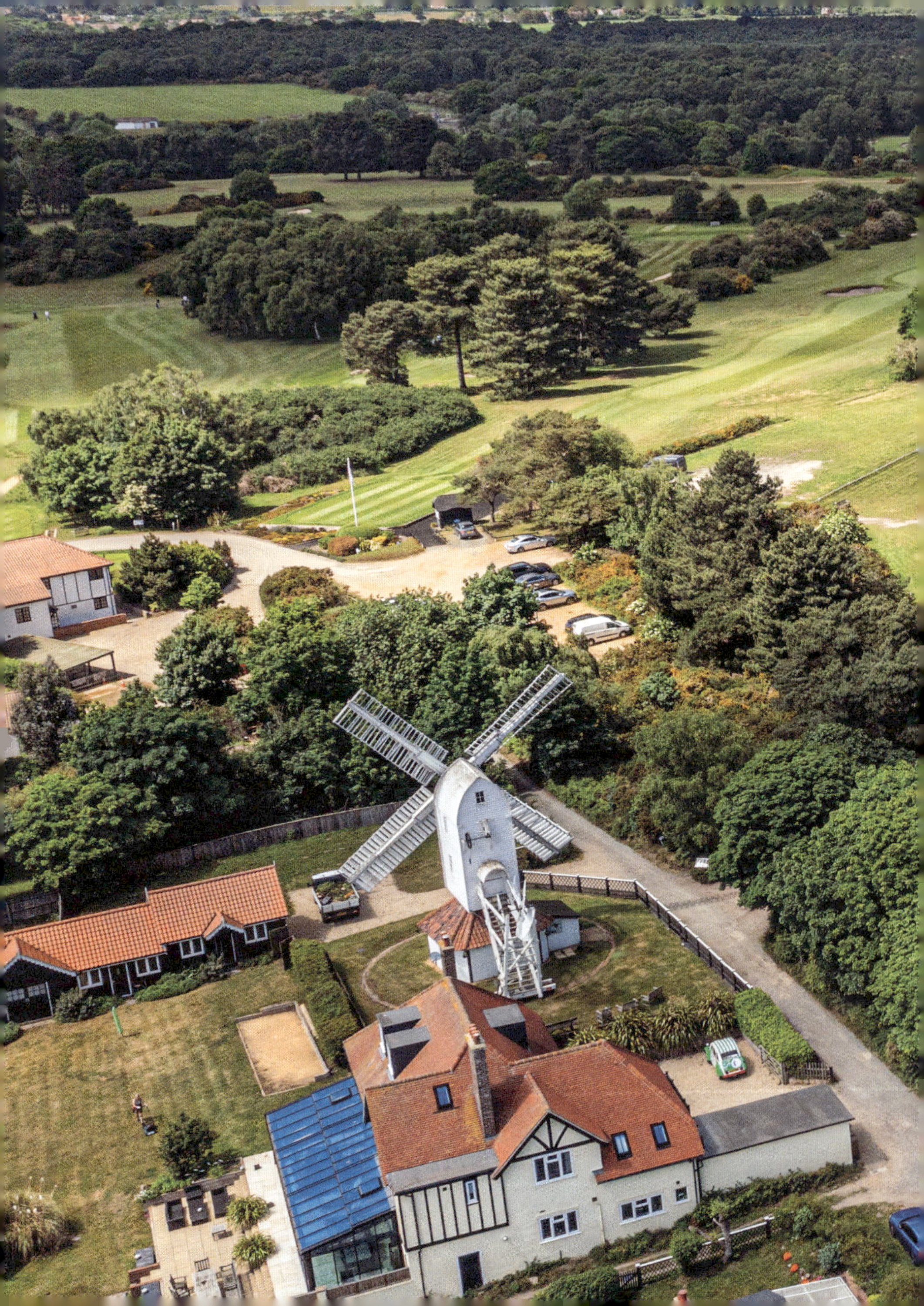

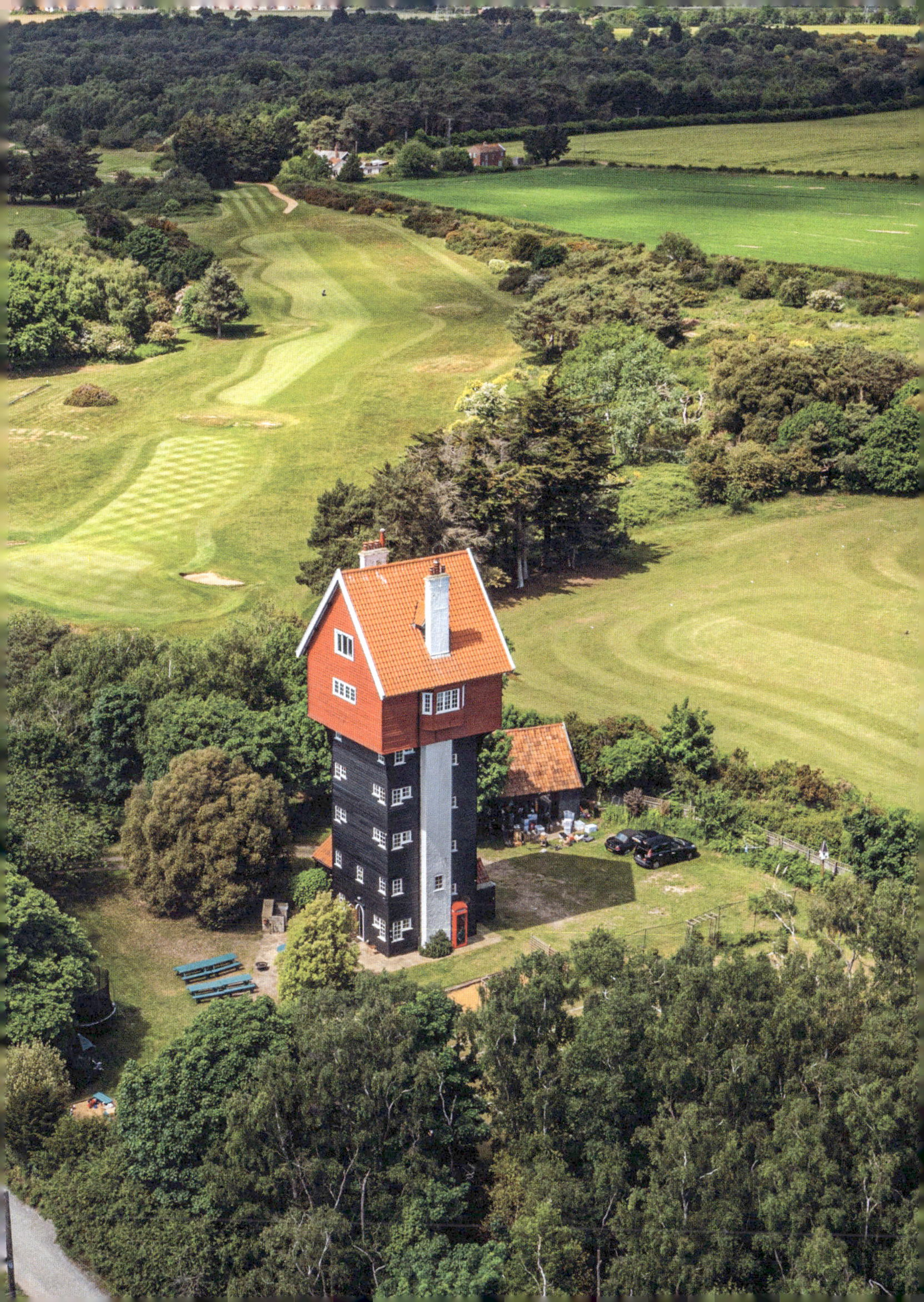

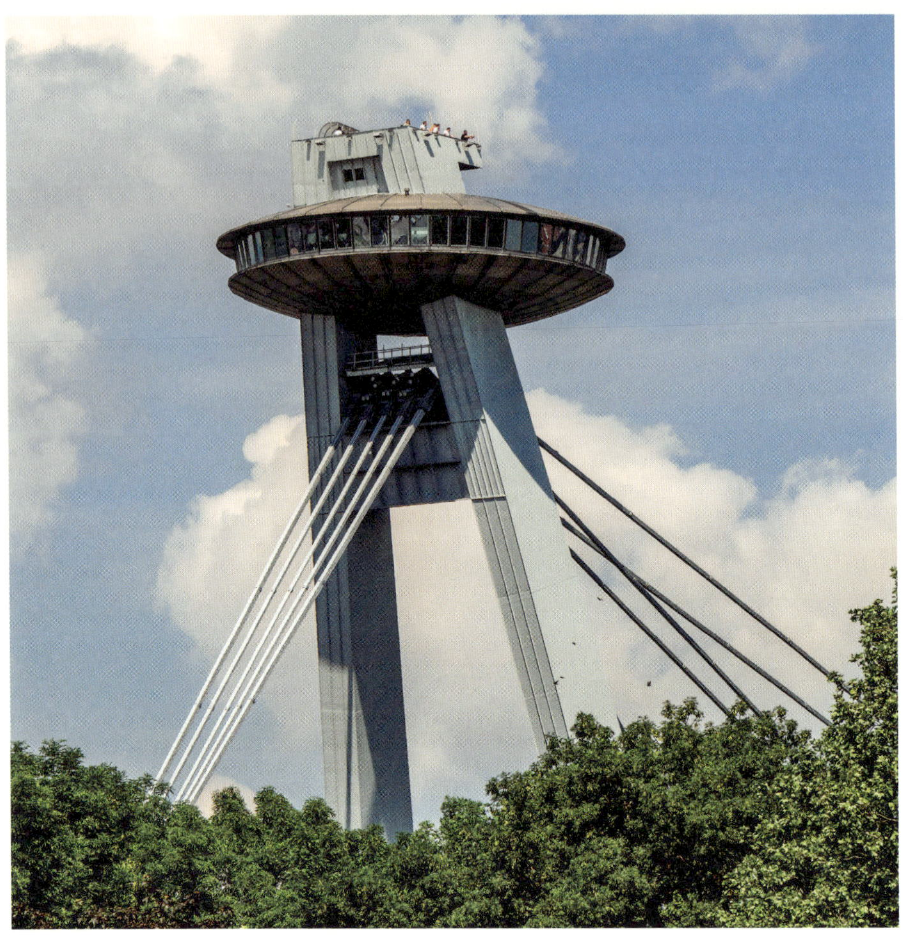

UFO Observation Deck
Bratislava, Slovakia
Architects: Jozef Lacko, Ladislav Kušnír and Ivan Slameň, 1972

Perched on the pylons of the SNP Bridge, this spaceship-like structure celebrates the futuristic style of this former Eastern bloc nation. Commissioned to connect the historic Old Town with the expanding Petržalka district across the Danube, nowadays it's an observation deck and a restaurant. The lift, located in one of the legs, takes just 45 seconds to reach the top.

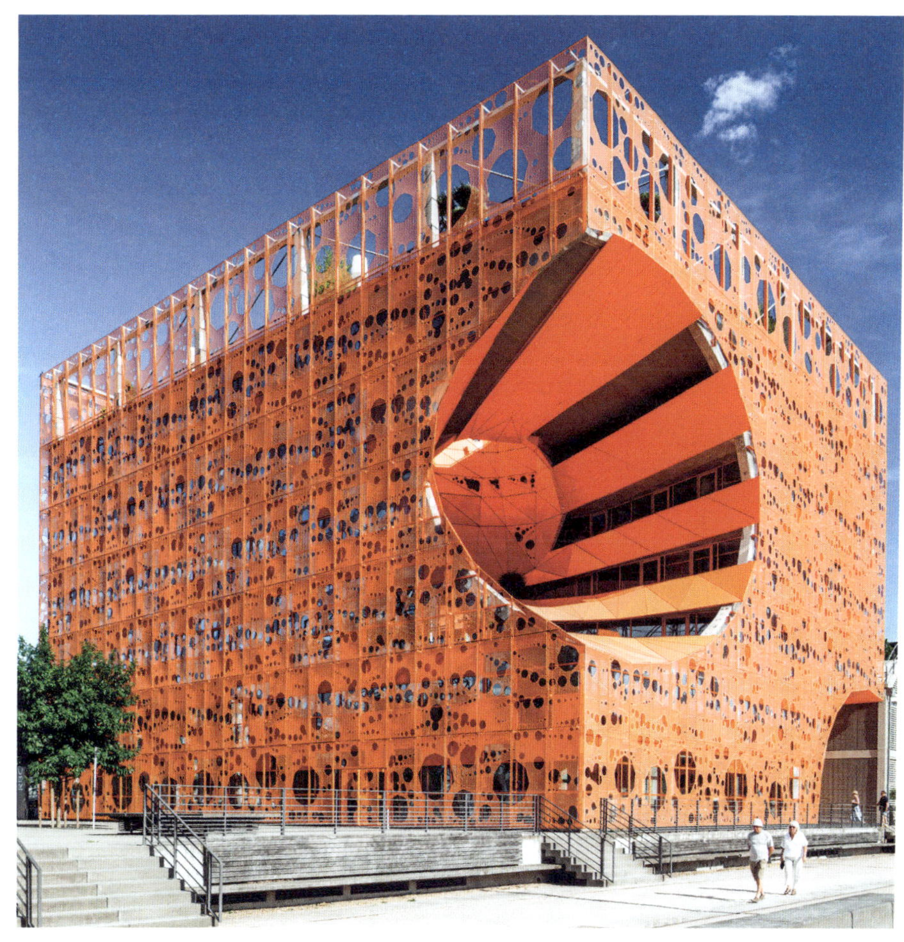

The Orange Cube
Lyon, France
Architect: Jakob + MacFarlane, 2011

The architects won a competition to design an eye-catching structure in a formerly derelict industrial zone. The bold colour references the site's history – orange is often used in industry to identify dangerous machinery or hazards. Striking architectural features include three large conical voids, enhancing light and ventilation and perhaps calling to mind a loud hailer safety system.

Panda Tower

Chengdu, China
Architect: UDG. Atelier Alpha, 2021

Built for the Chengdu Research Base of Giant Panda Breeding, there was, unsurprisingly, a panda theme to this structure's design: it's inspired by bamboo shoots, the giant panda's main food source. A mechanical system opens the top of the tower, designed to resemble a sprouting bamboo shoot, and is activated on special days, such as the birth of a giant panda cub.

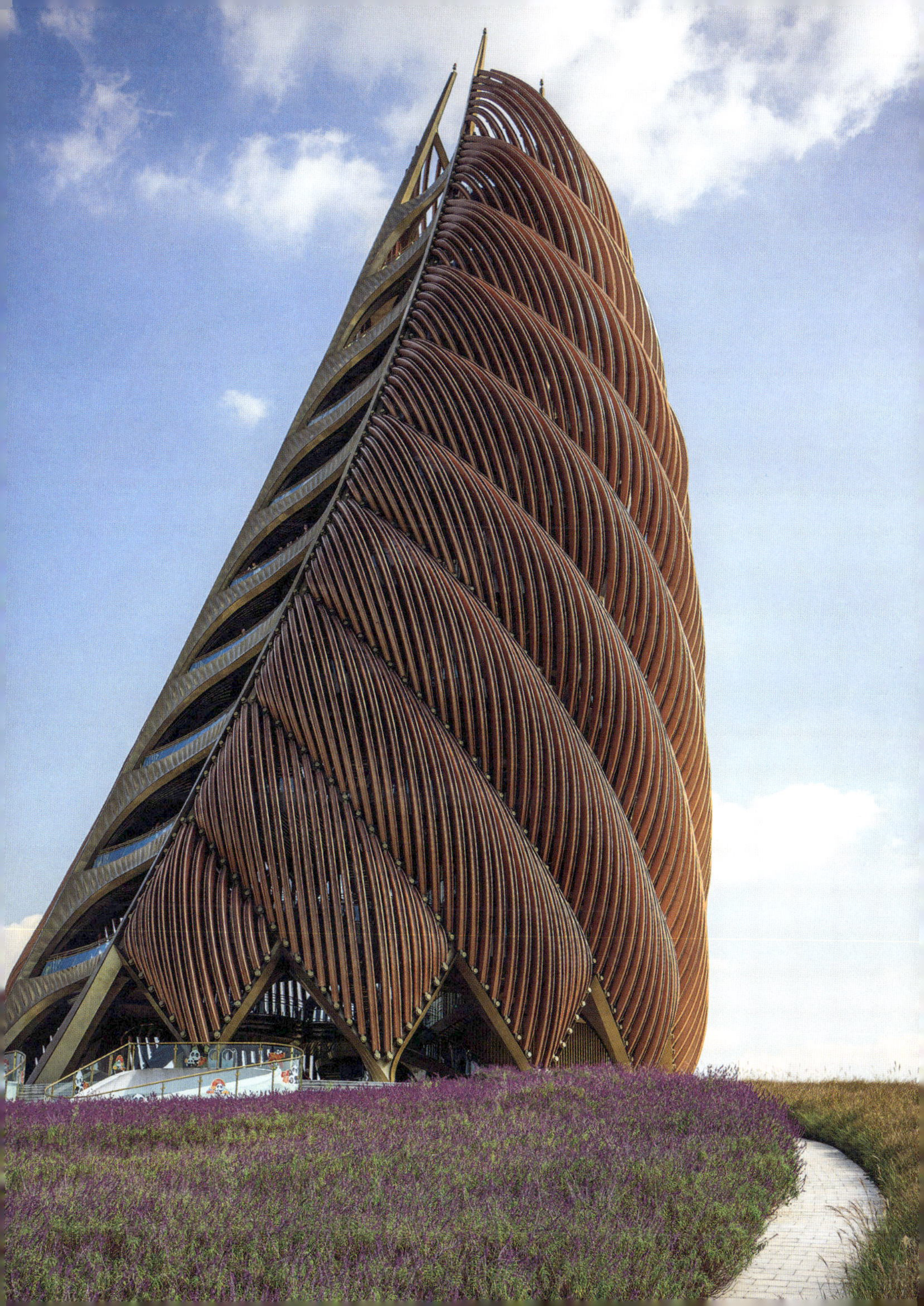

Vancouver House

Vancouver, Canada

Architect: Bjarke Ingels Group, 2020

The twisted form of this skyscraper, which widens as it climbs, is not due to architectural idiosyncrasy but necessity and consideration for local residents. The wedge-shaped site sits alongside the ramps leading to a bridge, and the structure's design ensures it is set back from the bridge at its base, avoiding overshadowing a local park.

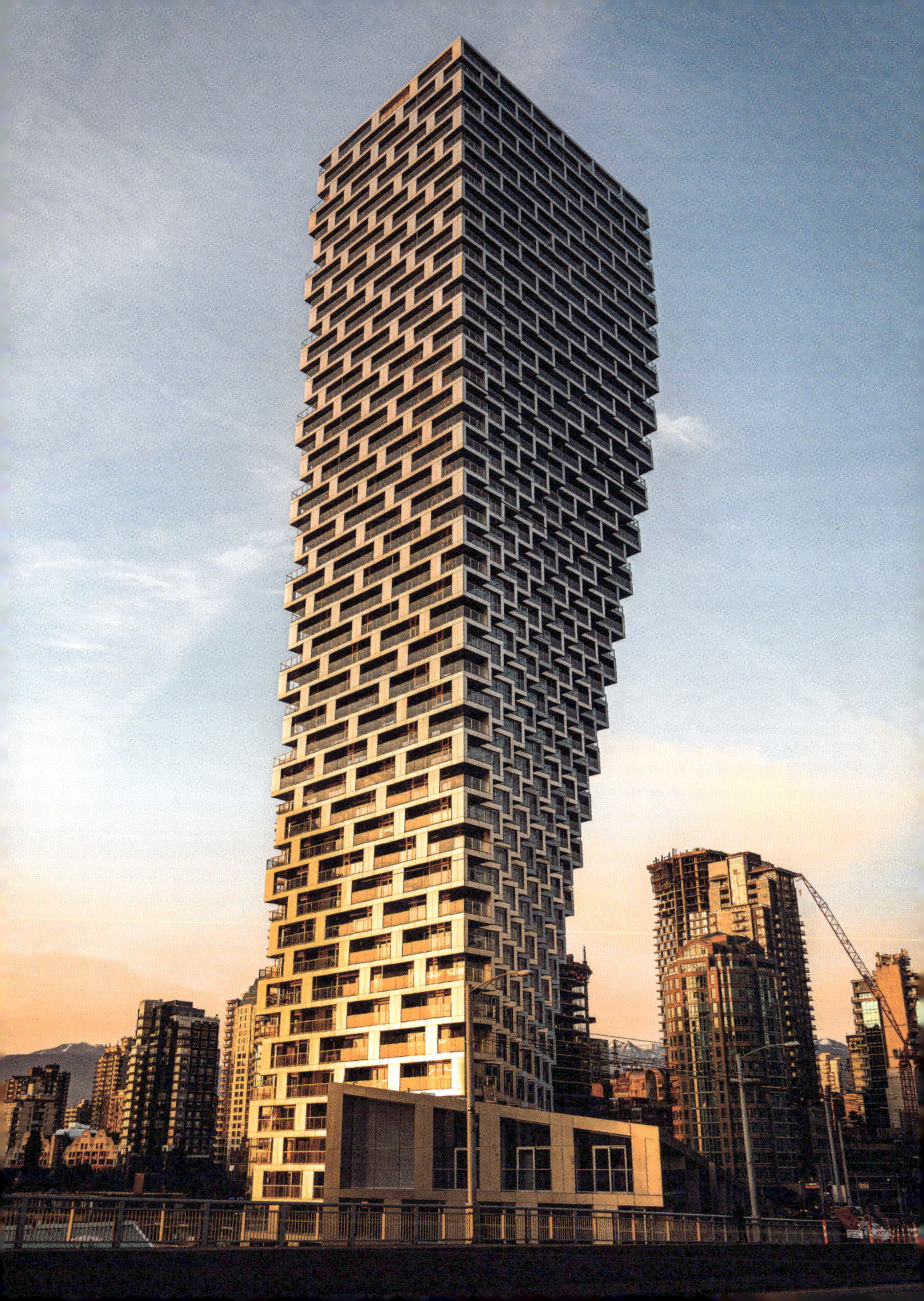

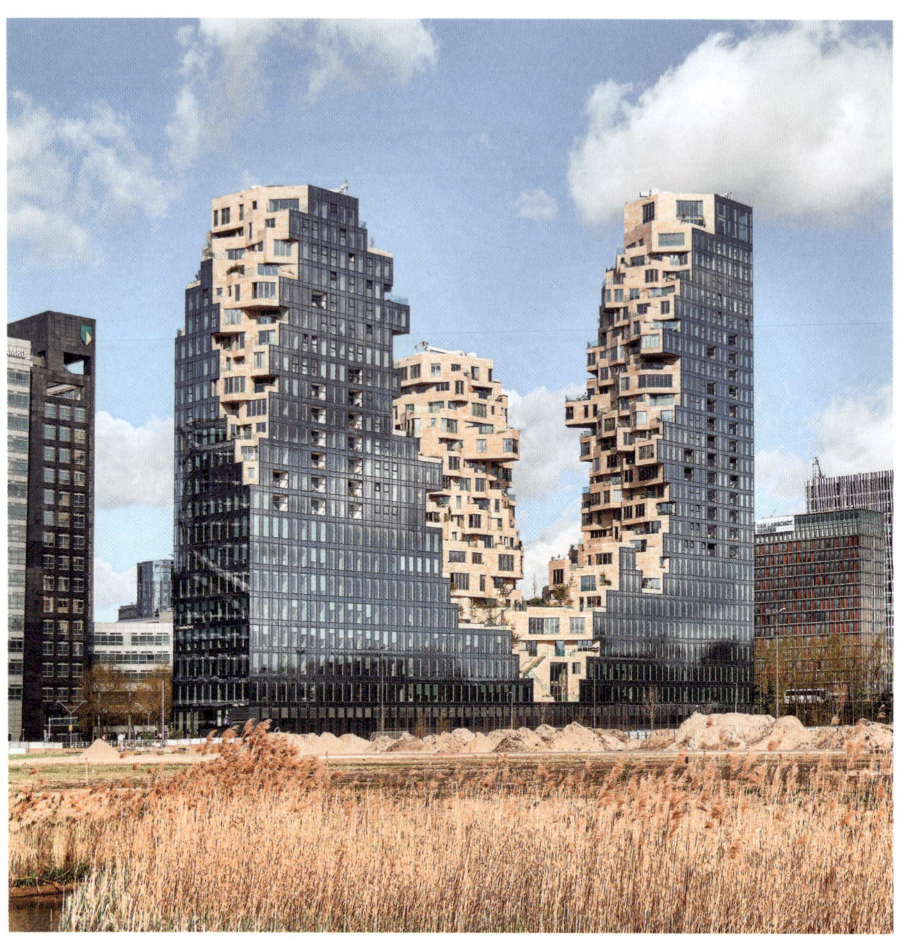

Valley

Amsterdam, Netherlands
Architect: MVRDV, 2022

Valley was conceived to introduce a green dimension to the austere office environment of Amsterdam's Zuidas neighbourhood. The multi-faceted building features smooth mirrored glass that blends with the shiny business district facades, while within the edges it has an organic appearance inspired by geology. It looks as if the glass shell has broken open to reveal a craggy rock face.

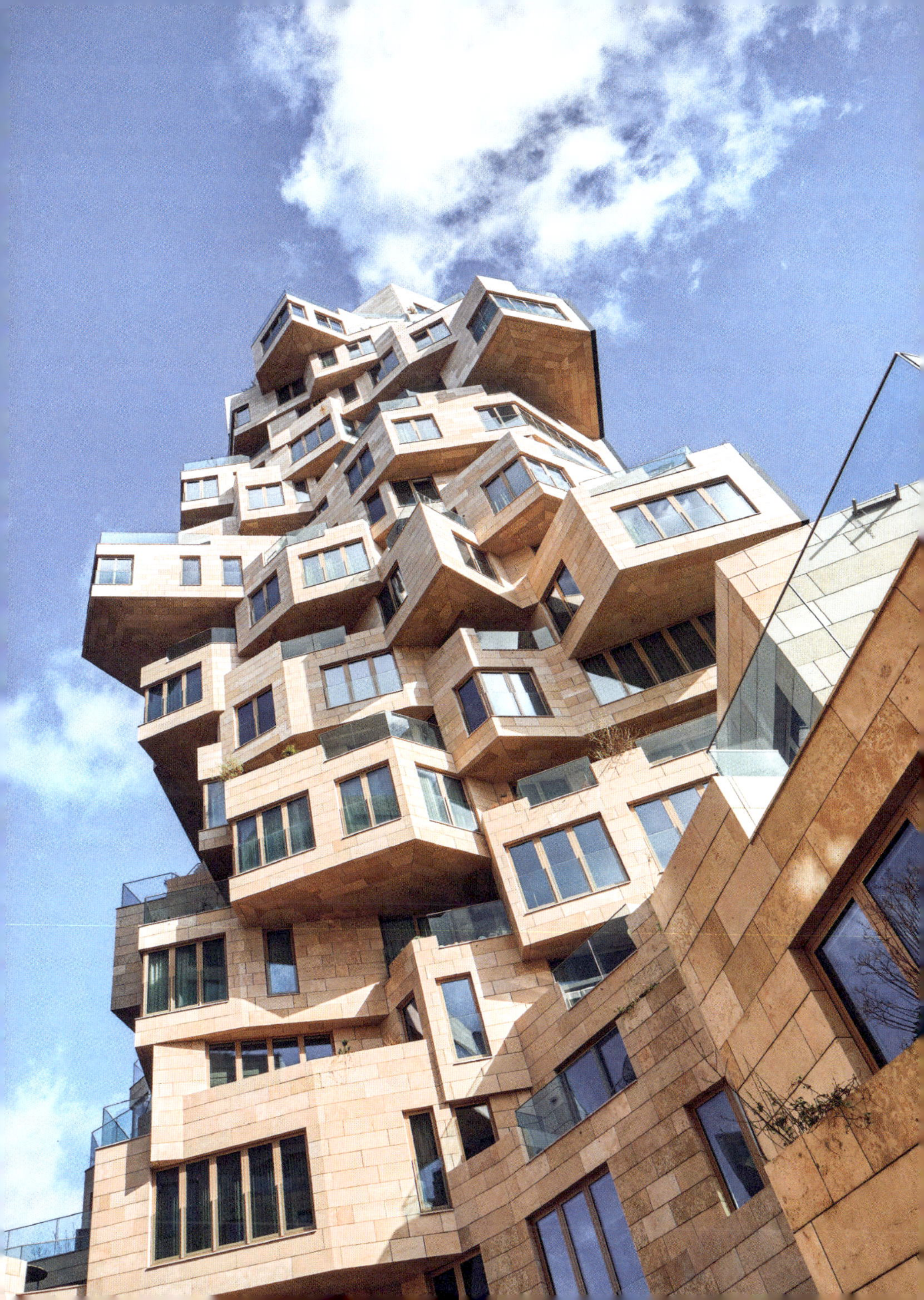

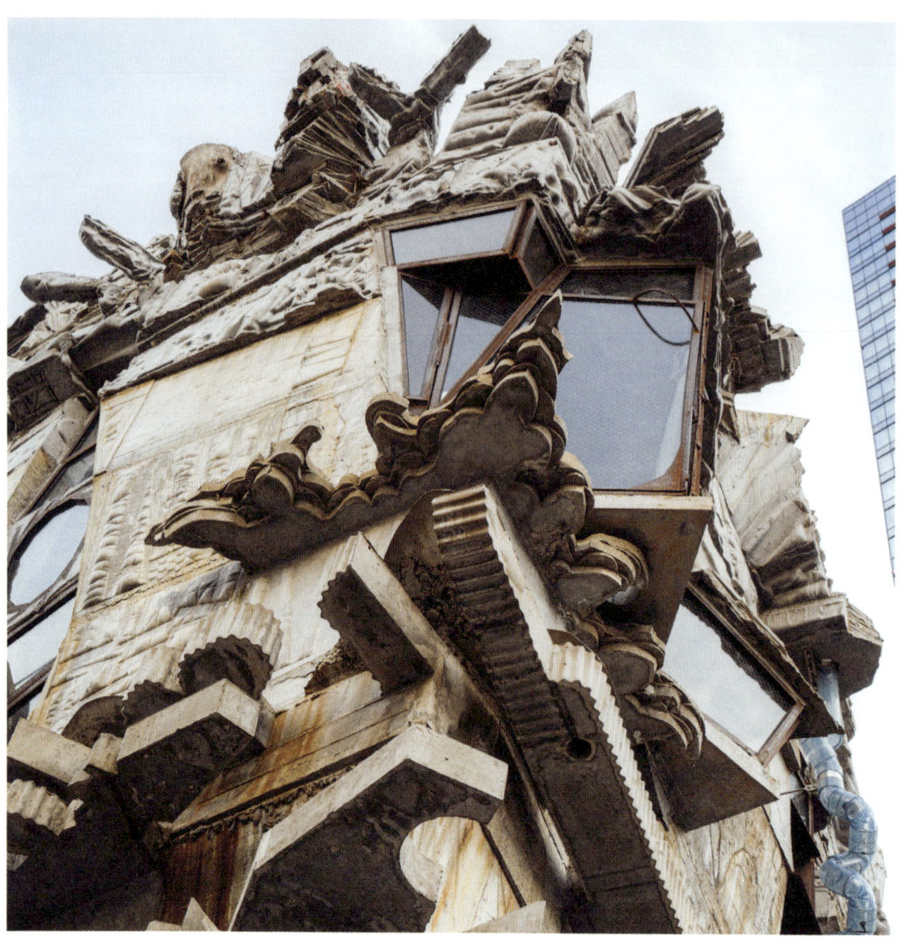

The Arimaston Building
Tokyo, Japan
Architect: Keisuke Oka, 2024

The architect began work on this building in 2005, constructing the concrete tower entirely by hand over 20 years. Its twisted, haphazard form is the result of his improvisational approach – he had no blueprints and made decisions as he poured the concrete, incorporating objects such as food trays and plants to create its textured form.

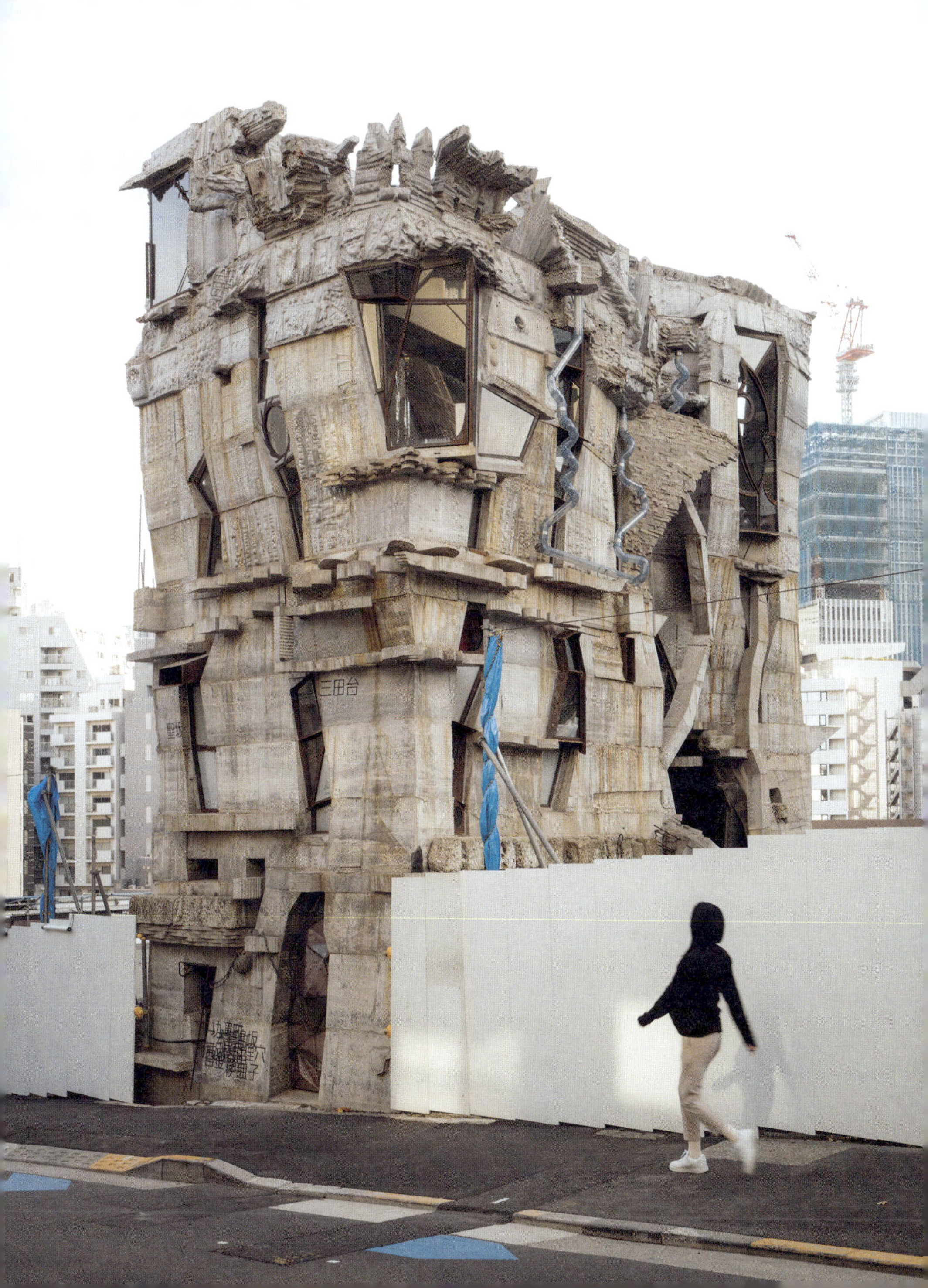
三田台

Nhow RAI Hotel
Amsterdam, Netherlands
Architect: OMA, 2019

With its off-kilter silhouette and super-shiny facade, this hotel has plenty of architectural swagger. Its triangular form of three stacked volumes jutting out in different directions means its 650 rooms enjoy different panoramic views across Amsterdam: the old city centre to the north, Schiphol Airport to the southwest and the city's sleek modern extensions in the southeast.

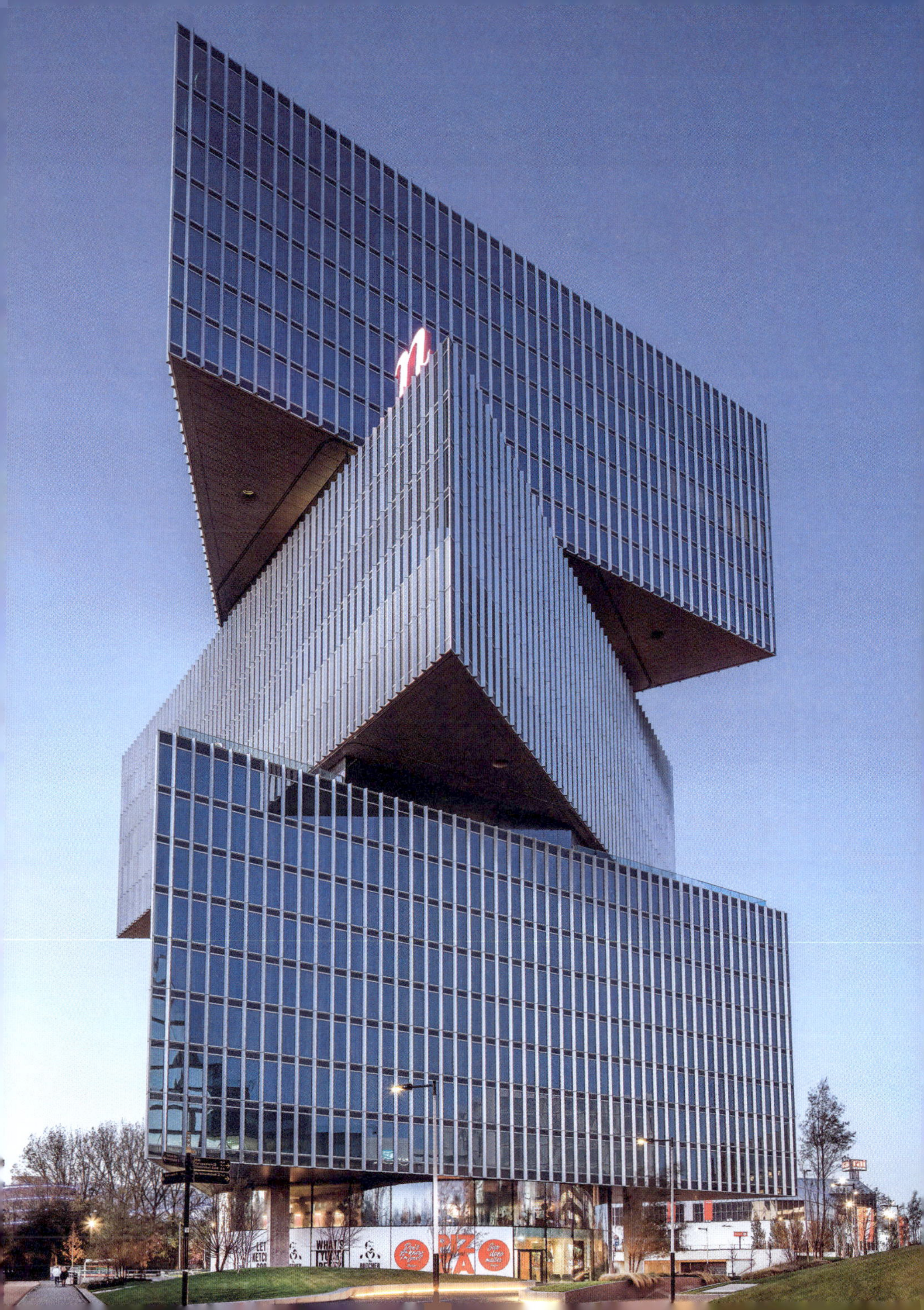
LET
WHAT'S
BUTCHER
PIZ
A

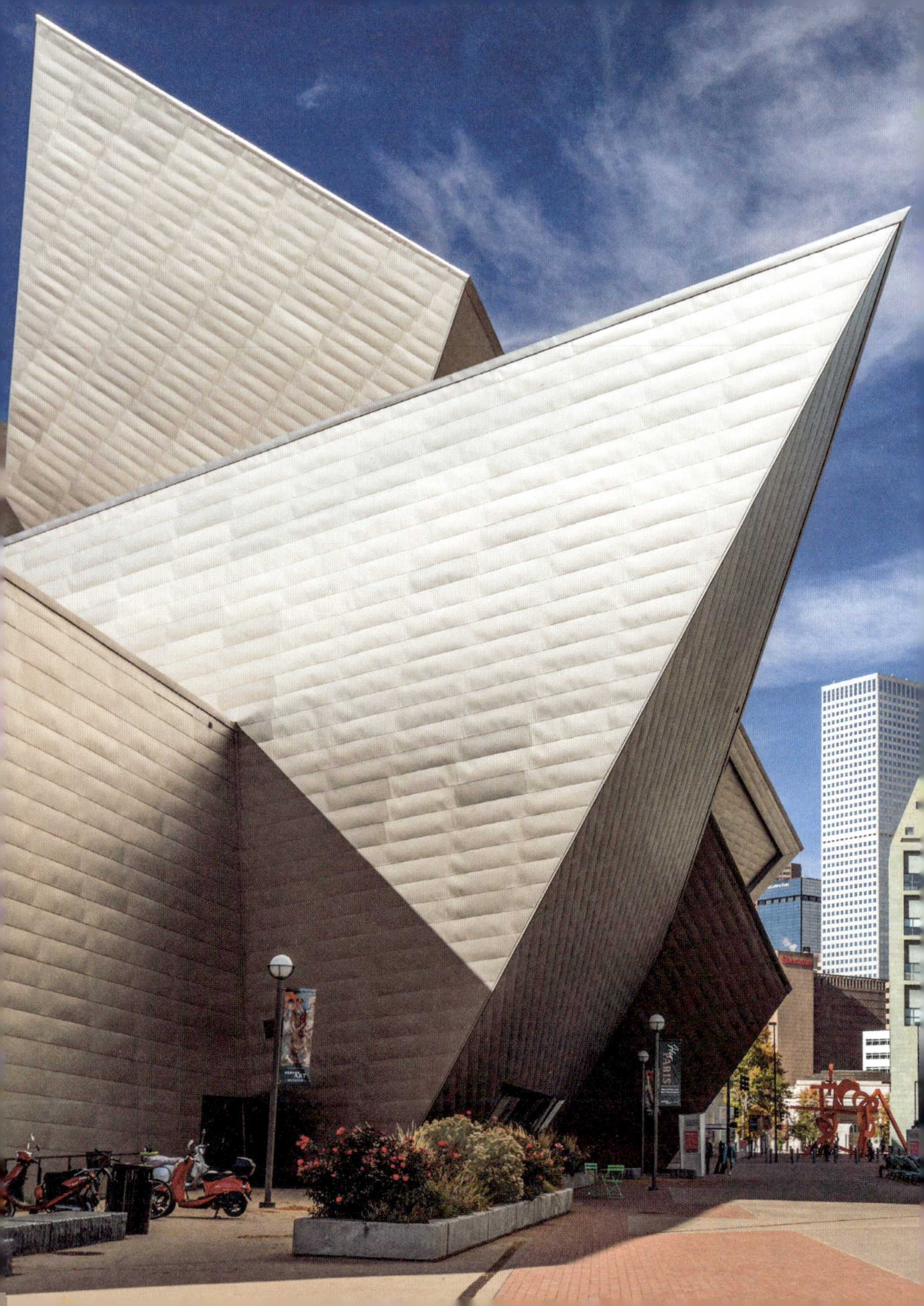

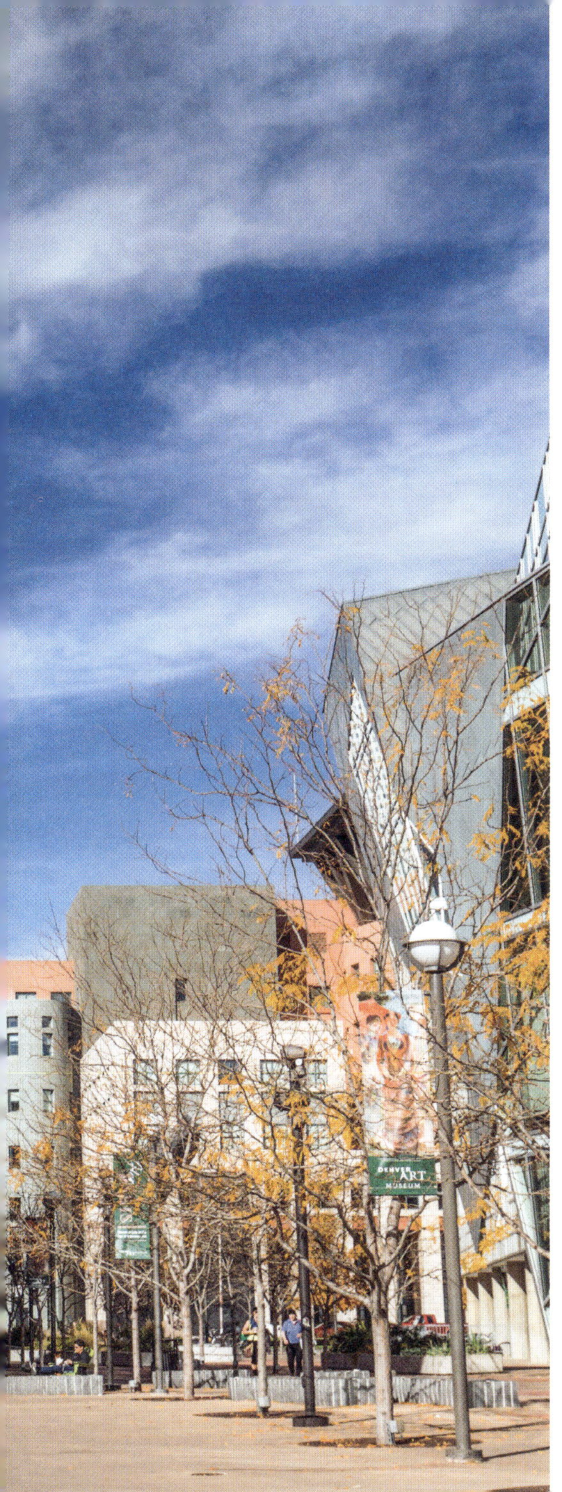

Denver Art Museum
Denver, Colorado, USA
Architect: Studio Libeskind, 2006

This titanium-clad extension to the Denver Art Museum slices through the city skyline, the angled cantilevered section pointing towards the original museum building across the street. Set against the dramatic backdrop of the Rocky Mountains, its edgy geometry is inspired by the peaks and valleys of the surrounding landscape.

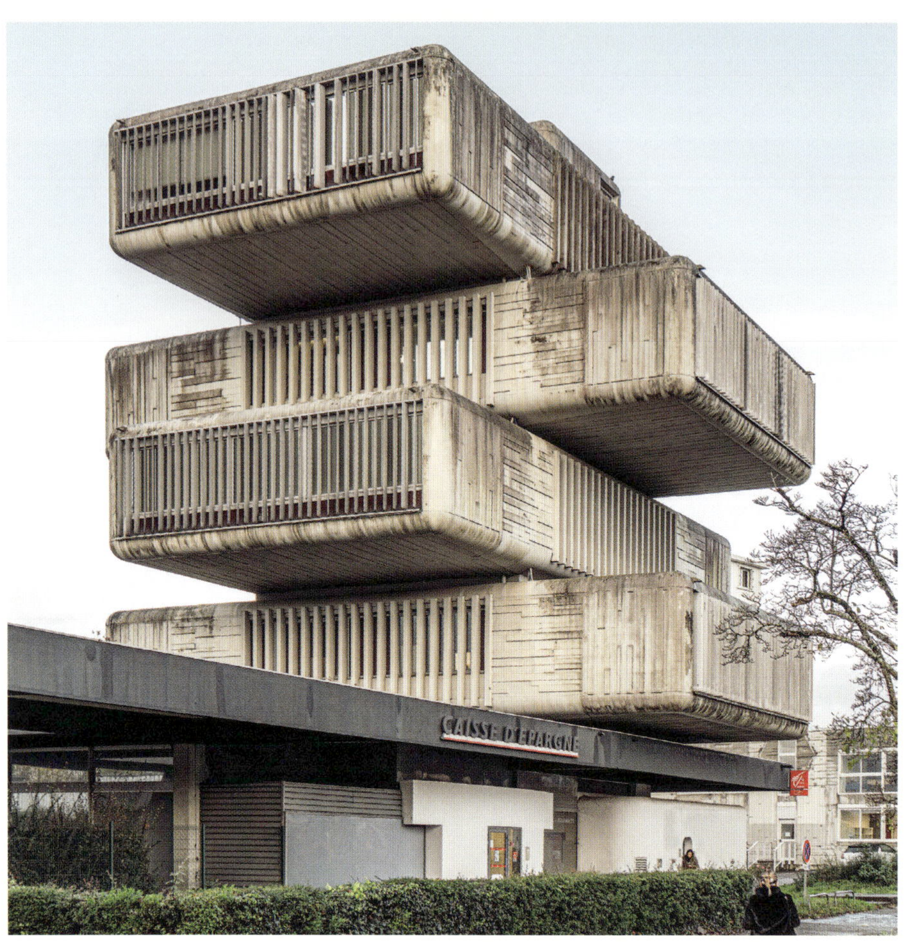

Caisse d' Epargne Bank
Pau, France
Architect: Jean-Pierre Boulin, 1975

This Jenga-like construction of stacked concrete boxes is a bold example of French Brutalism. The building's angular geometry and raw materiality reflects the movement's ethos, blending civic authority with sculptural form to give a powerful sense of solidity and functionality.

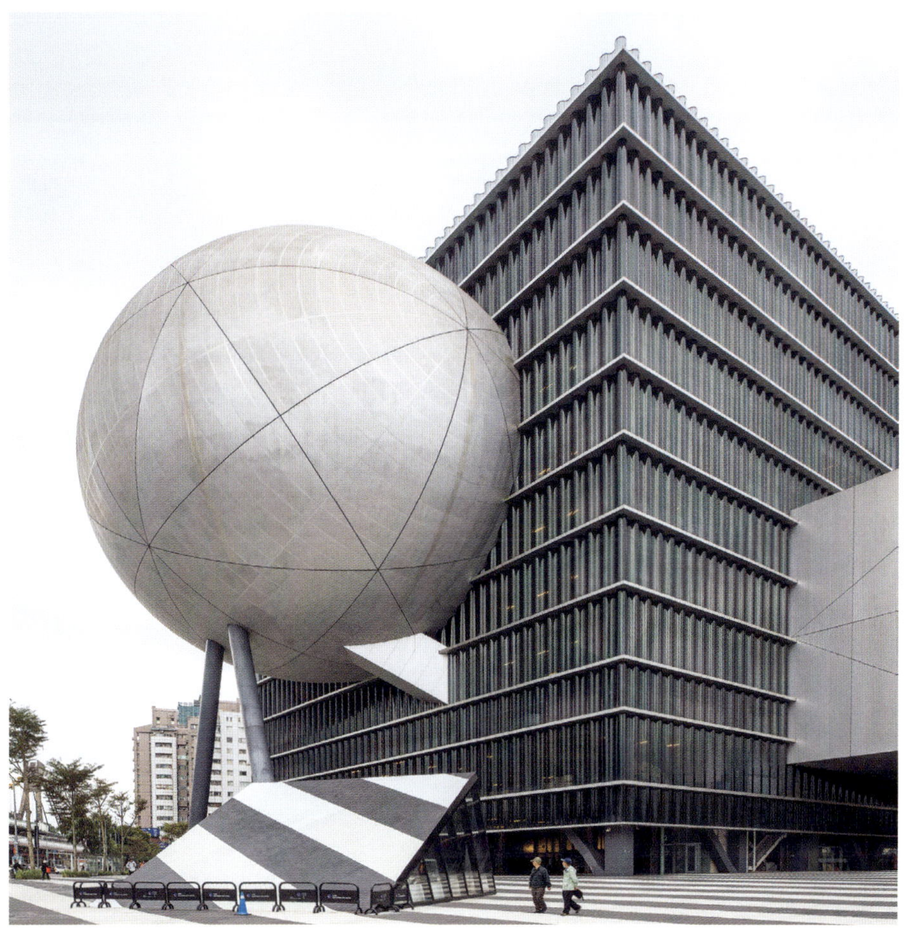

Taipei Performing Arts Centre
Taipei, Taiwan
Architects: David Gianotten and Rem Koolhaas, 2022

Three independent theatres are plugged into a central glass-clad cube in a multi-purpose design that was intended to reflect Taiwan's dynamic cultural expression. The back stages and technical support spaces are consolidated inside the silver cube, while the giant sphere, that looks as though it has crash-landed into the facade, contains the Globe Playhouse.

Konieczny's Ark

Brenna, Poland
Architect: Robert Konieczy,
KWK Promes, 2015

When designing his family home, the owner of this innovative architectural studio built a modern structure whose boat-like appearance is seemingly inspired by a very old one: Noah's Ark. Landslides are common in the Polish mountains, so to safeguard the house it was suspended on stilts, allowing water and mud to flow underneath, giving the impression that it is floating.

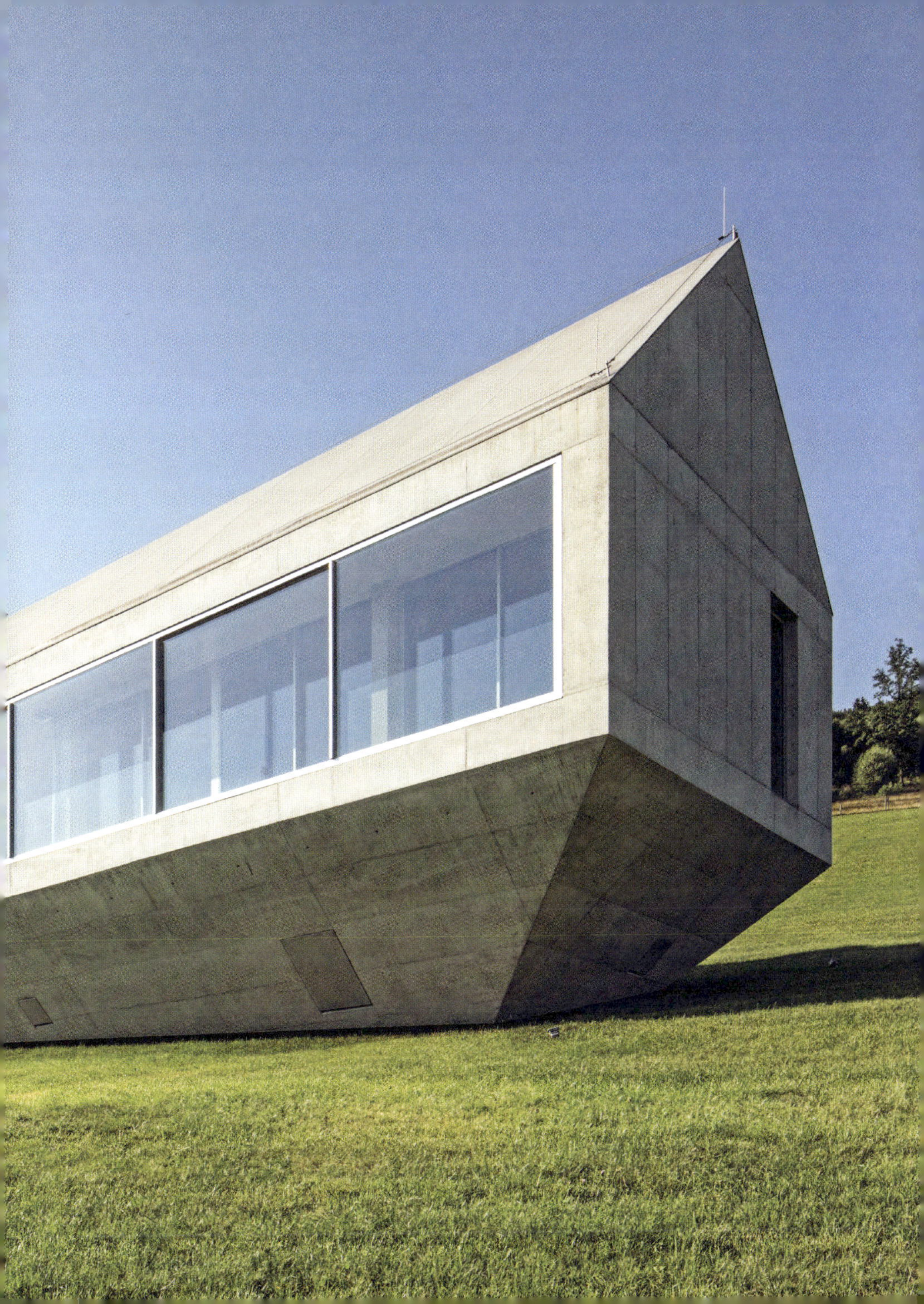

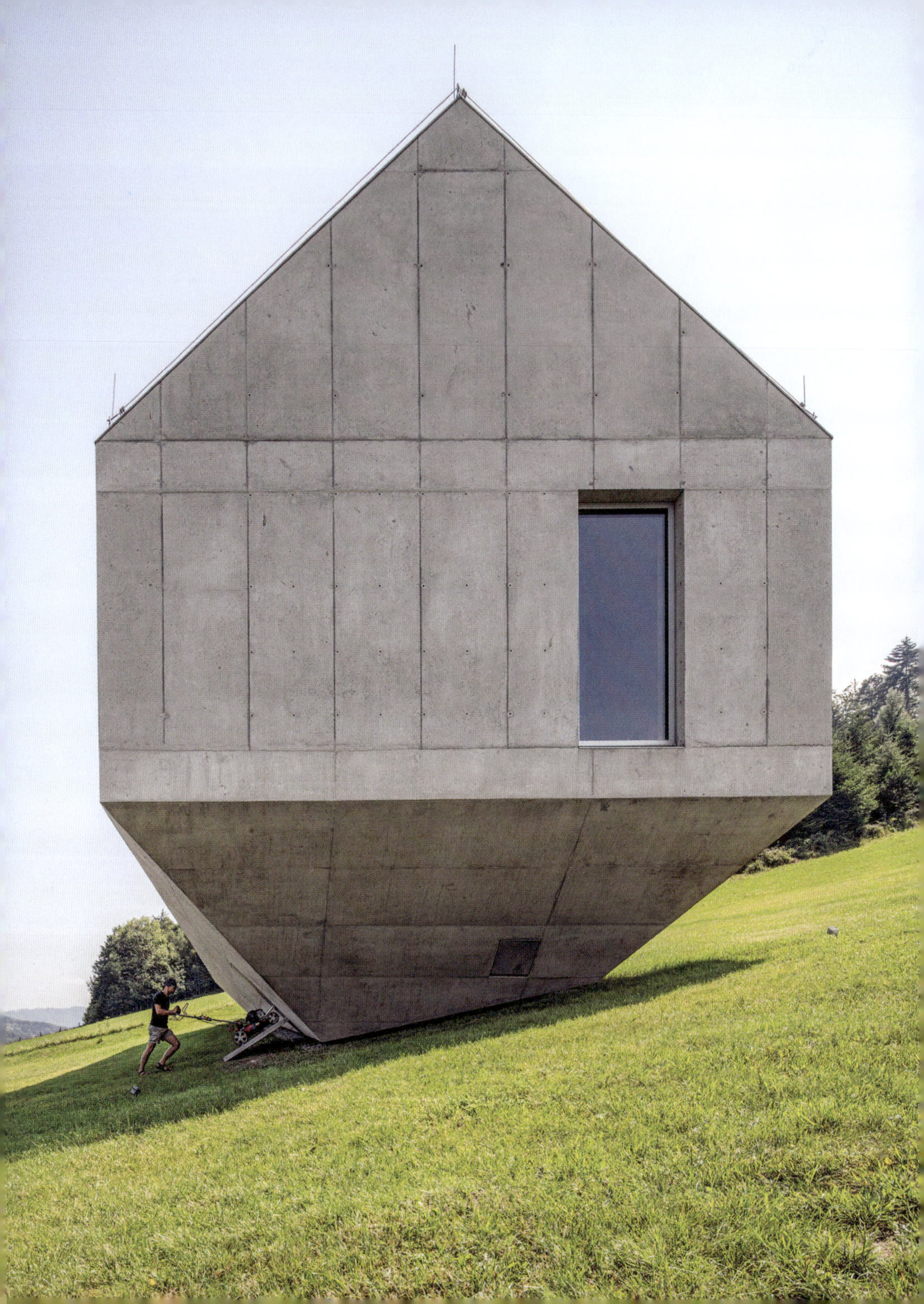

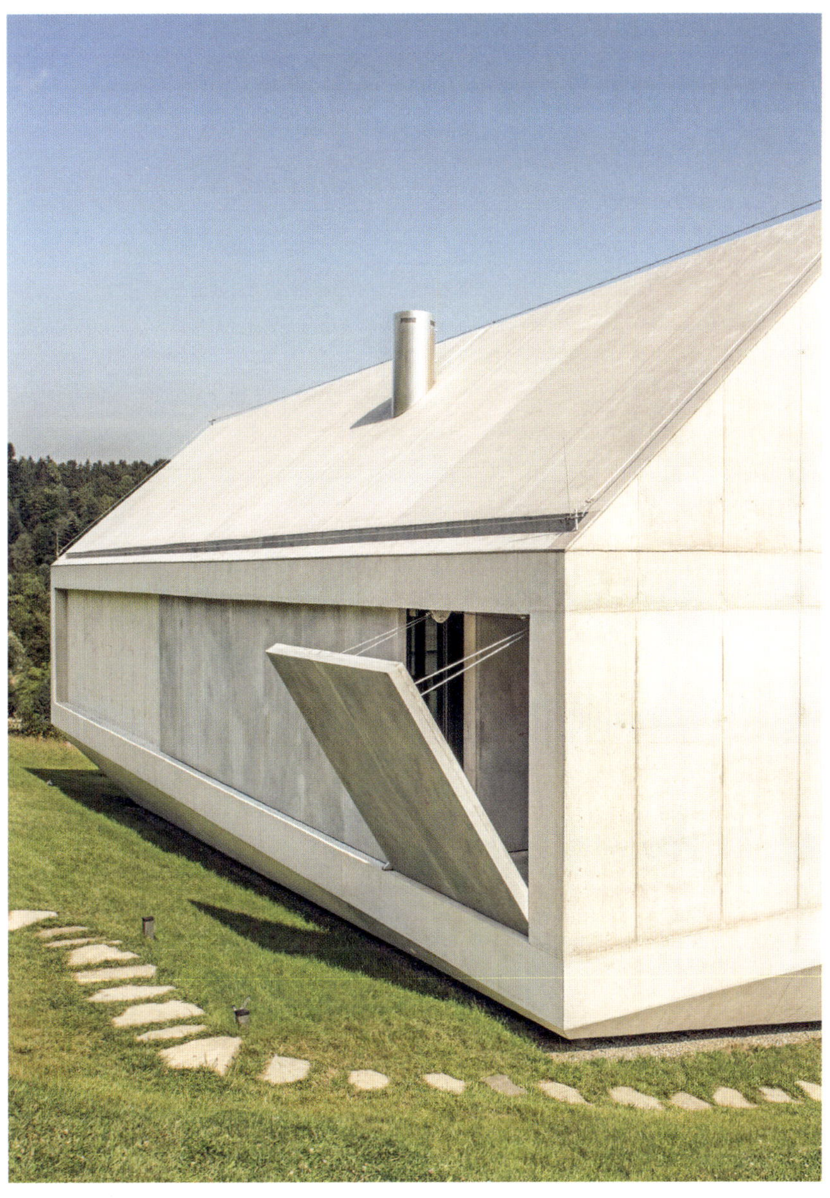

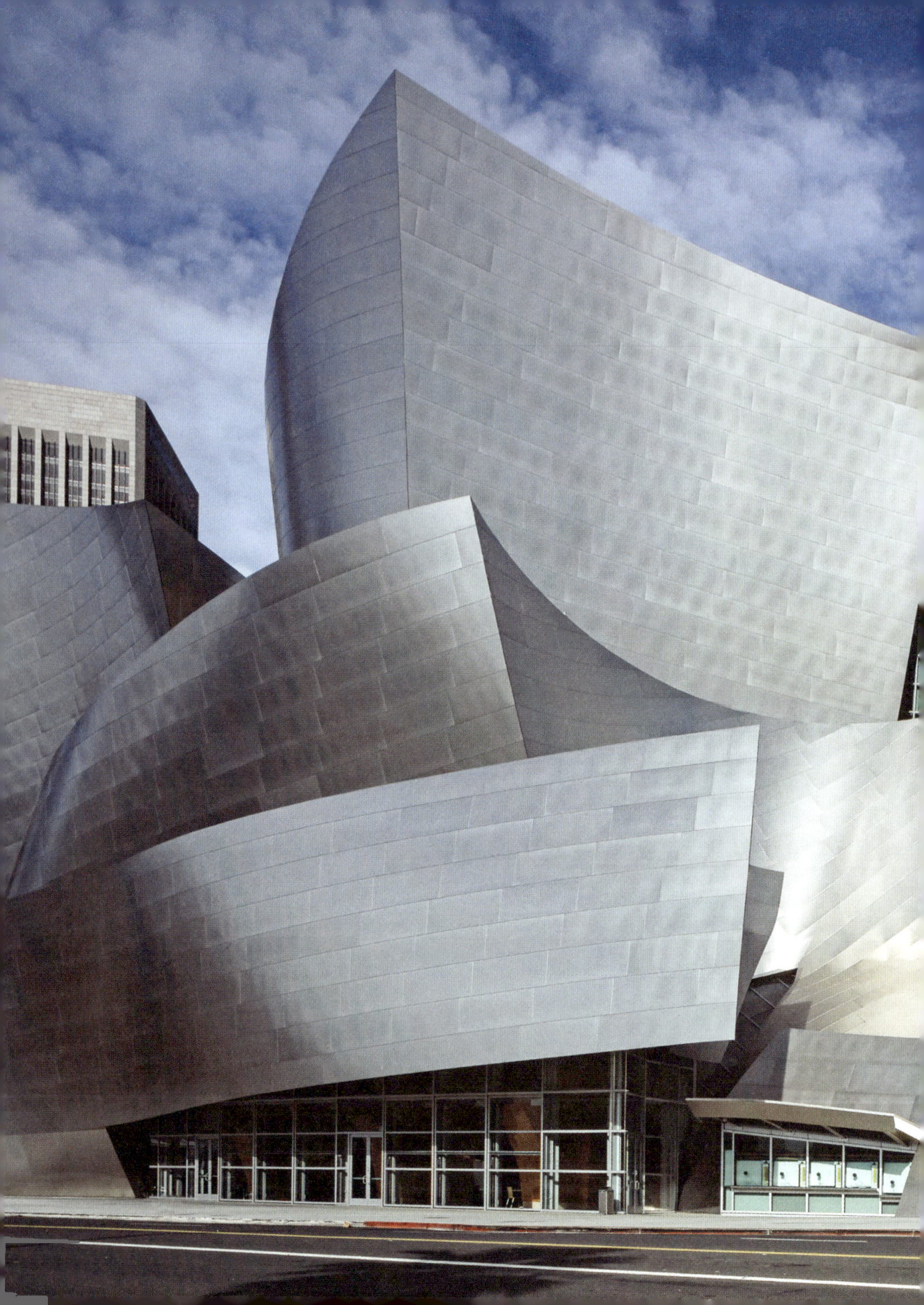

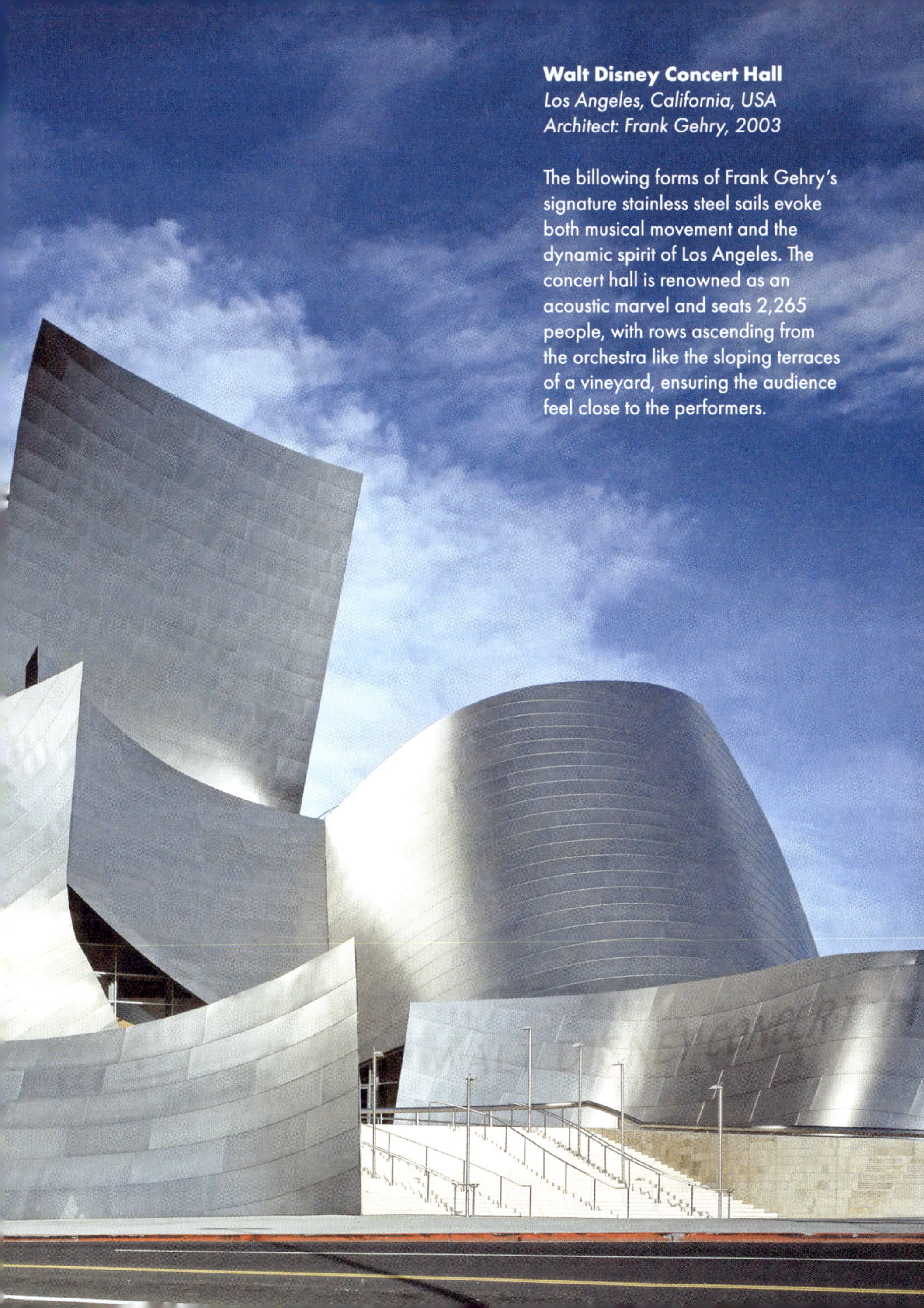

Walt Disney Concert Hall
Los Angeles, California, USA
Architect: Frank Gehry, 2003

The billowing forms of Frank Gehry's signature stainless steel sails evoke both musical movement and the dynamic spirit of Los Angeles. The concert hall is renowned as an acoustic marvel and seats 2,265 people, with rows ascending from the orchestra like the sloping terraces of a vineyard, ensuring the audience feel close to the performers.

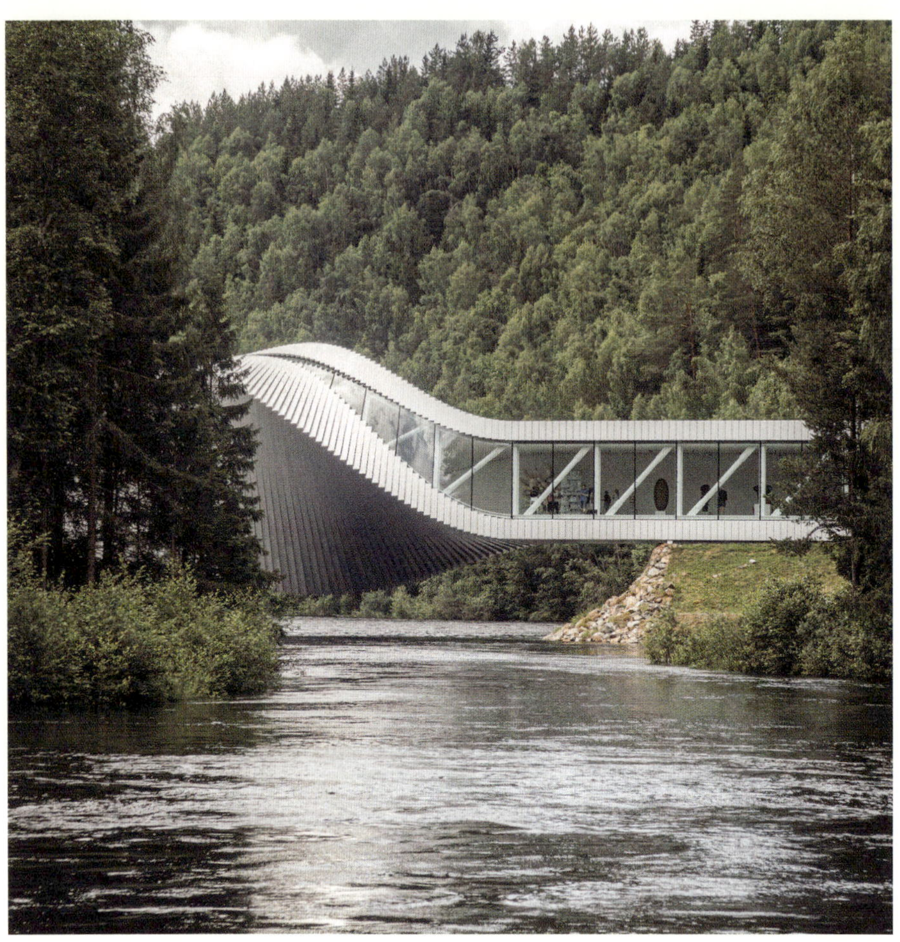

The Twist
Jevnaker, Norway
Architect: Bjarke Ingels Group, 2019

Corkscrewing through the trees in Norway's Kistefos Sculpture Park, this sleek structure serves as both a bridge and an art installation. The sculptural form of the warped beam connects the banks on either side of the Randselva River, enabling visitors to circulate around the park, and also provides additional exhibition space.

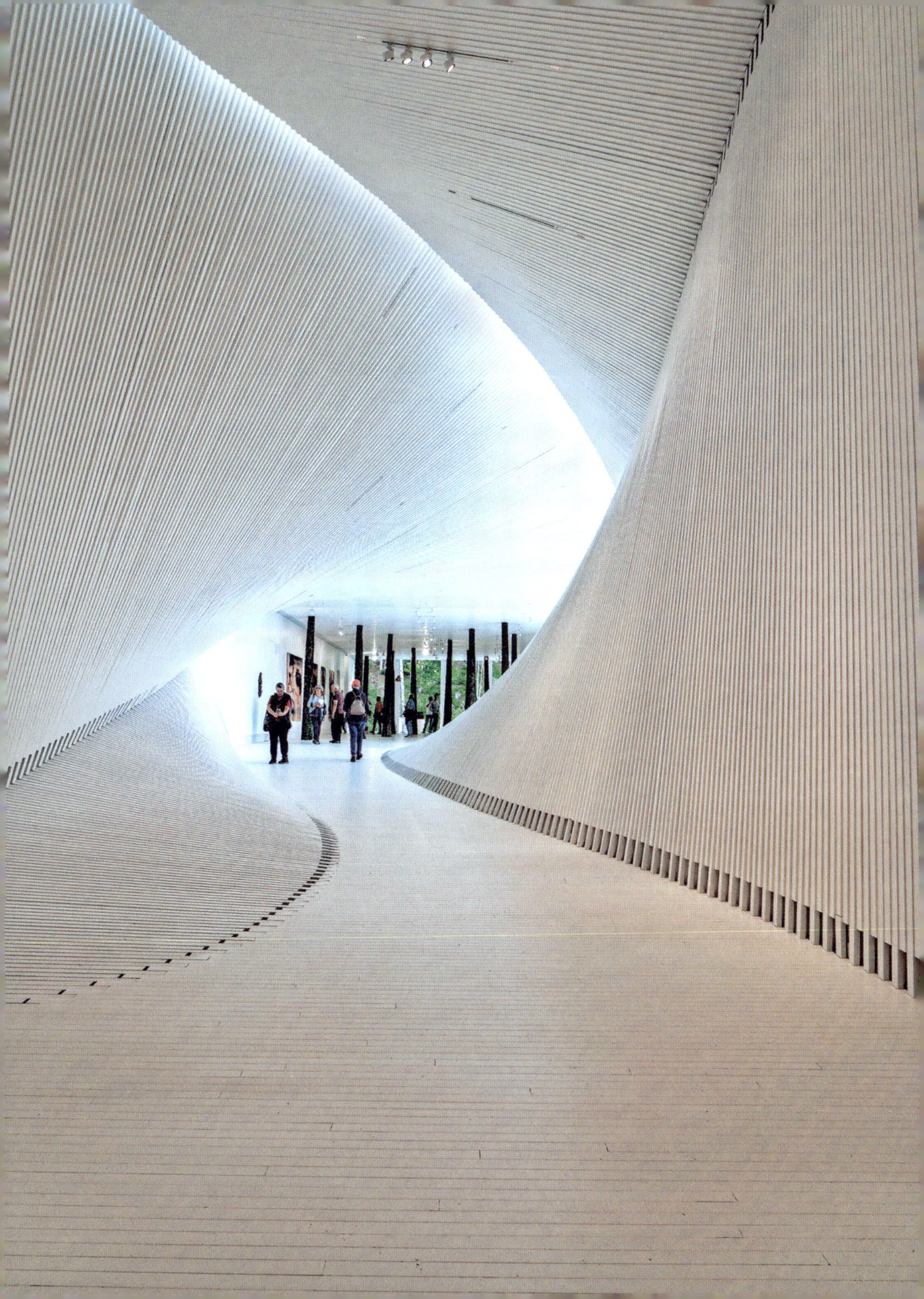

L'Hemisfèric
Valencia, Spain
Architect: Santiago Calatrava, 1998

This ocular structure houses an IMAX theatre, a planetarium and a laser light show. It was designed to represent the 'all-seeing' human eye: the 'pupil' is the hemispherical dome of the IMAX, and an 'eyelid' made of aluminium awnings can be opened and closed. A glass-bottomed pond surrounds the structure, and when the eyelid is closed, the reflection makes the eye look whole.

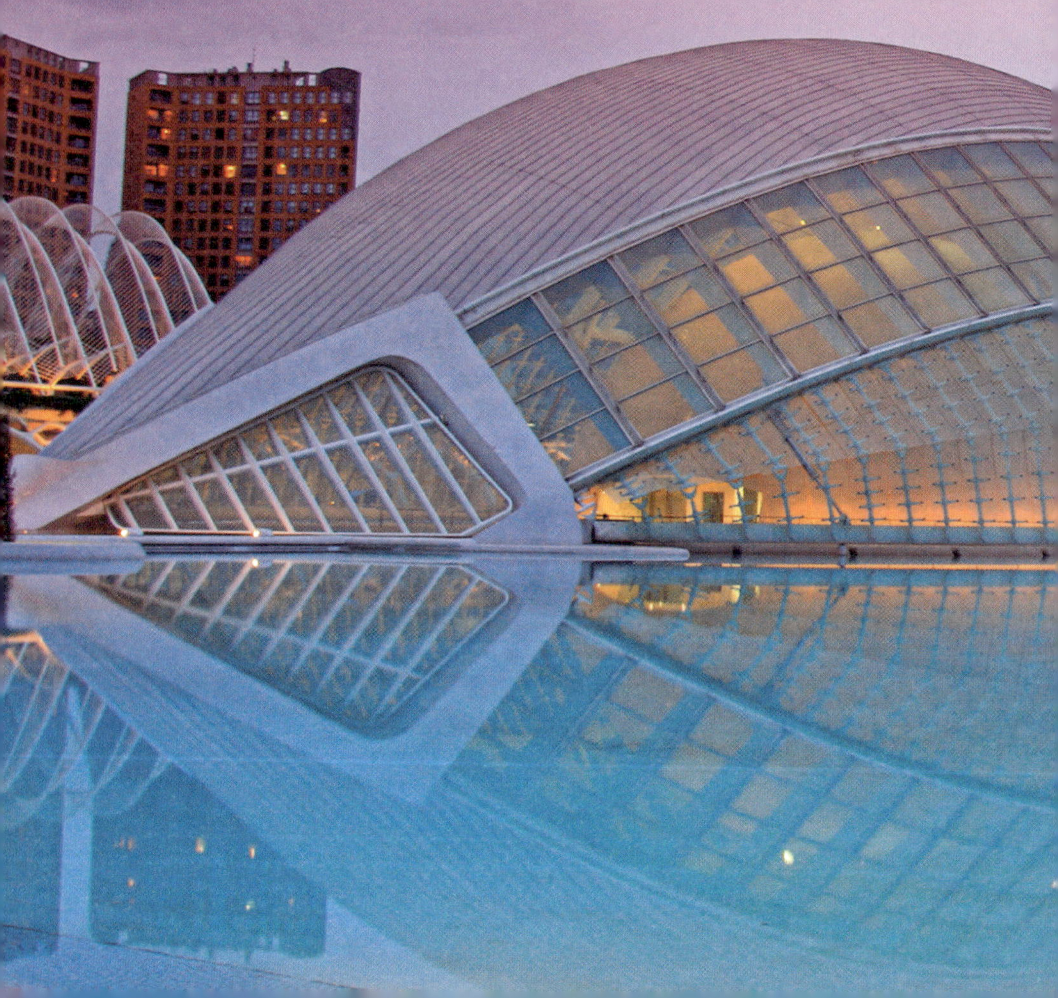

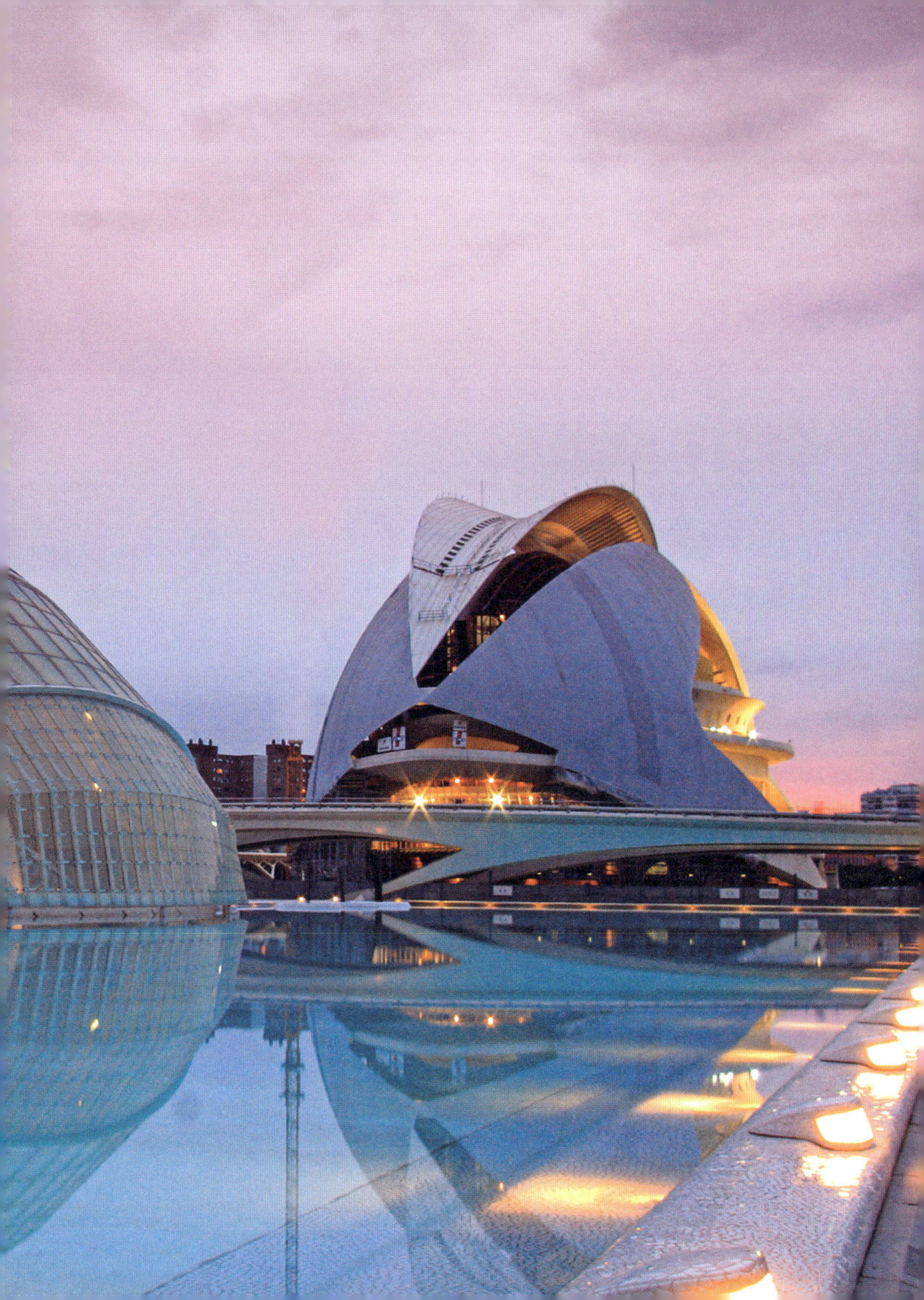

Guangzhou Circle
Guangzhou, China
Architect: Joseph di Pasquale, 2013

While similar in form to a Chinese coin, the Guangzhou Circle was inspired by the cultural significance of jade discs and the numerological principles of feng shui. Jade discs, which are emblematic of heaven, were historically used in ancient burial rituals. The building's reflection in the river below forms a figure eight, considered the luckiest number in Chinese culture.

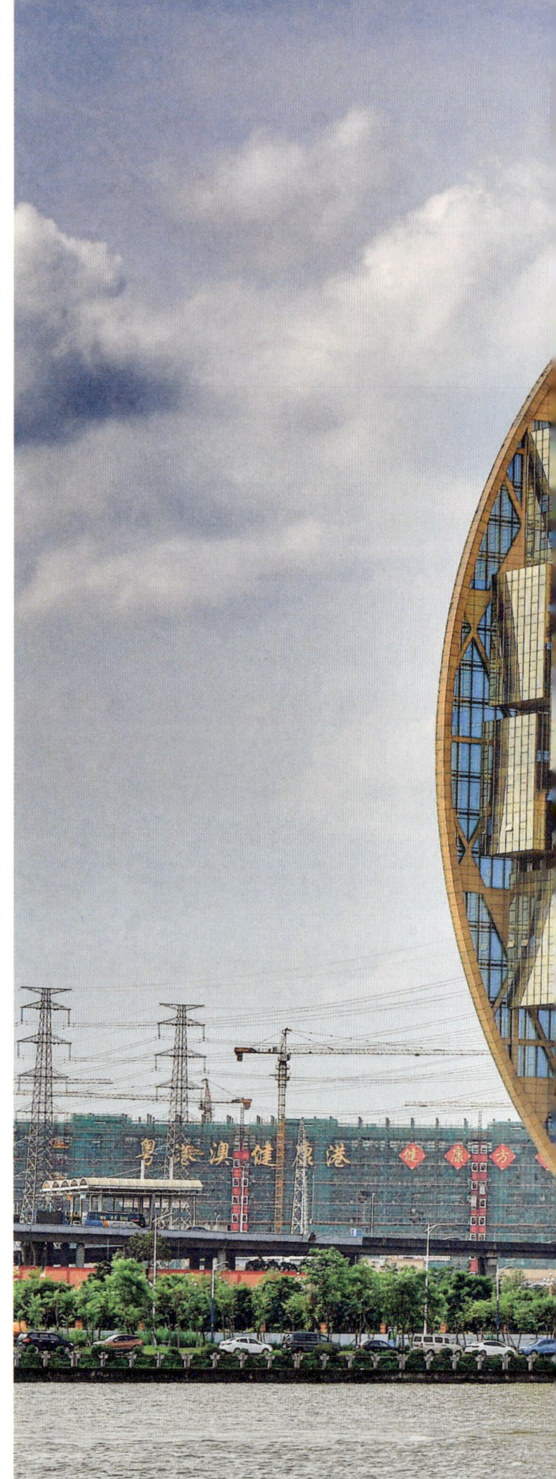

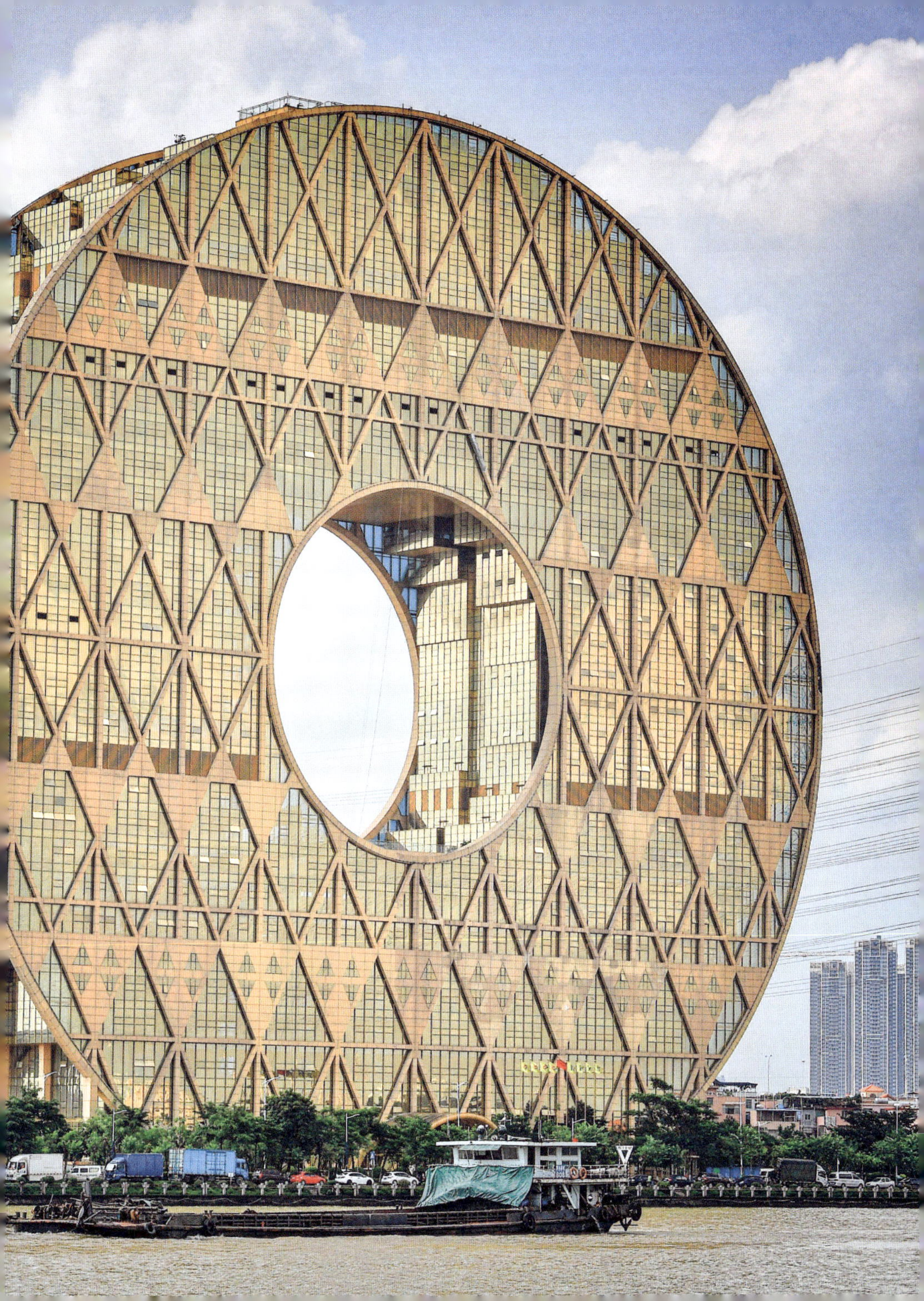

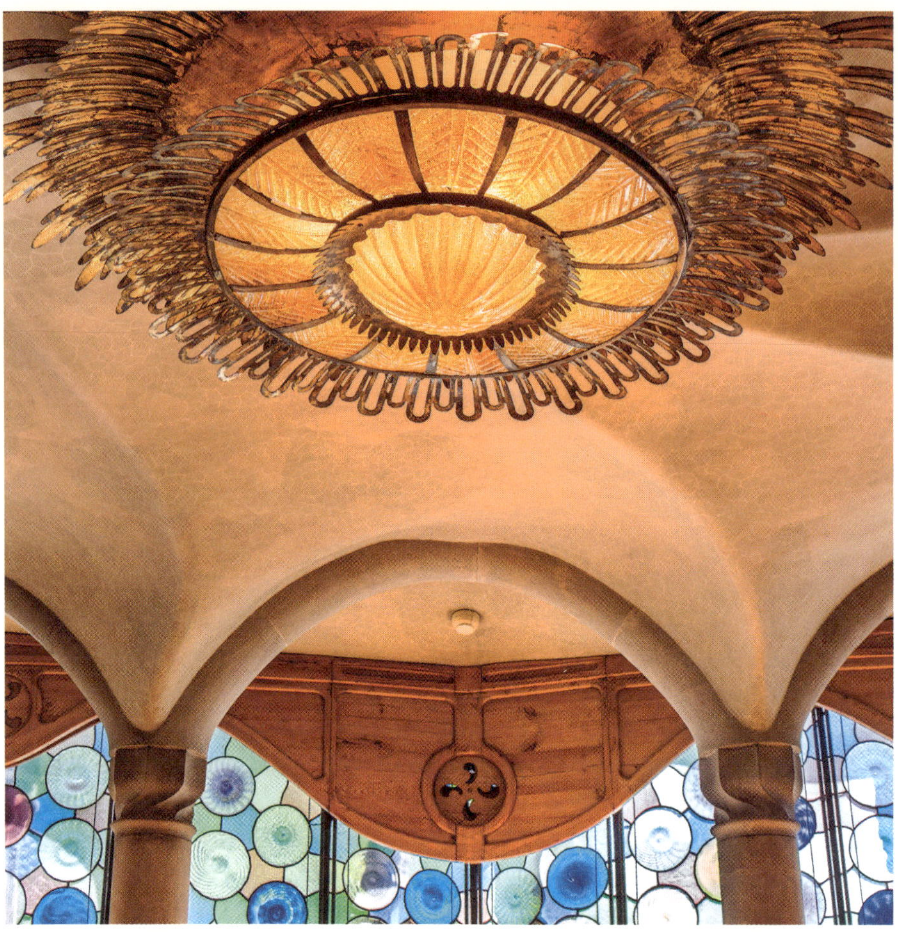

Casa Batlló
Barcelona, Spain
Architect: Antoni Gaudí, 1906

Gaudí's extraordinary imagination shines in this masterpiece of Catalan Modernism, featuring intricate, fantastical imagery and a medley of colours, materials and textures. The facade includes bone-like balconies, suggesting eyebrows or clavicles, supported by skeletal stone columns. The colourful mosaic of glazed ceramic and glass has marine-like characteristics, and a roof of diamond-shaped tiles has a reptilian quality.

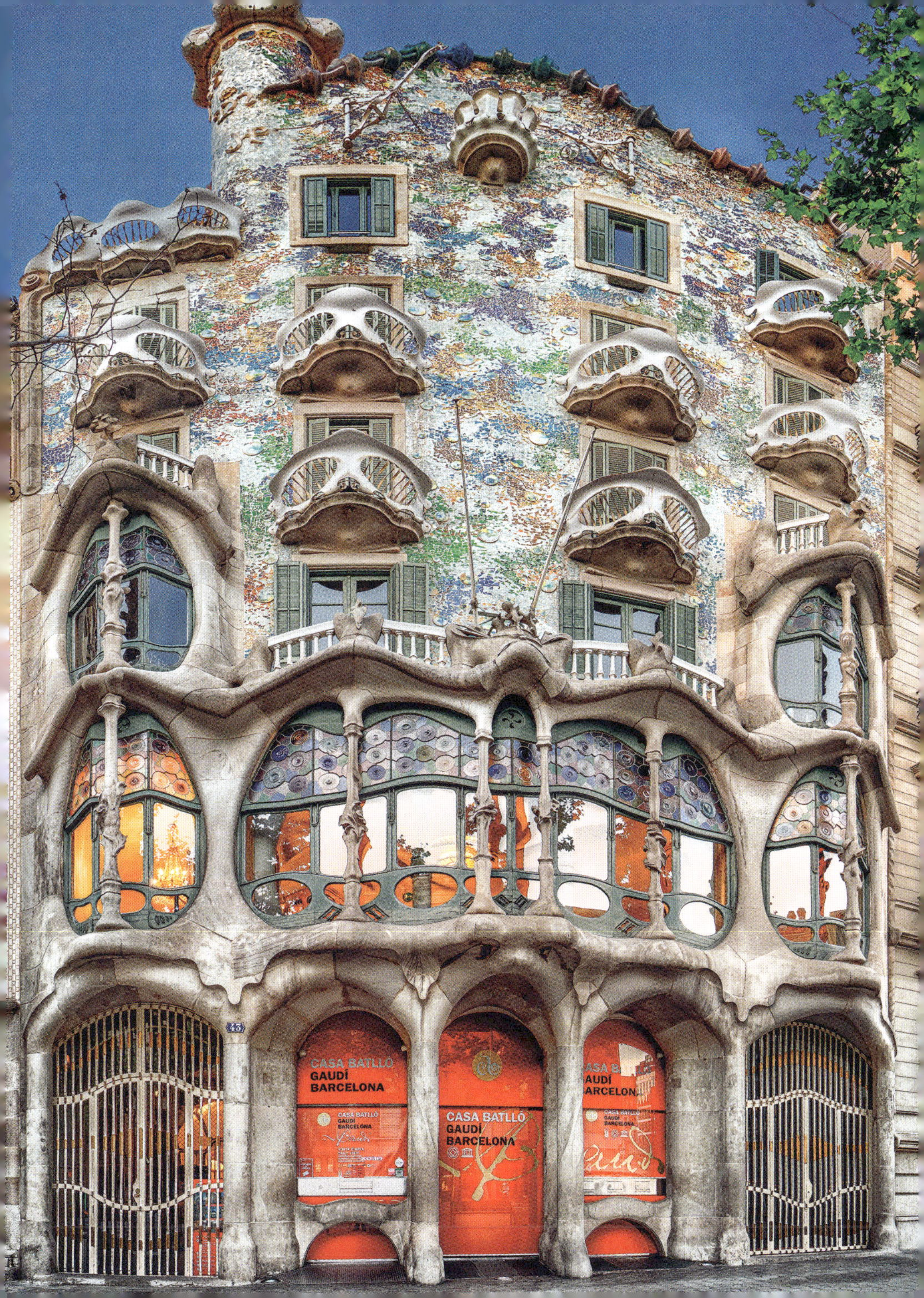
CASA BATLLÓ
GAUDÍ
BARCELONA
CASA BATLLÓ
GAUDÍ
BARCELONA

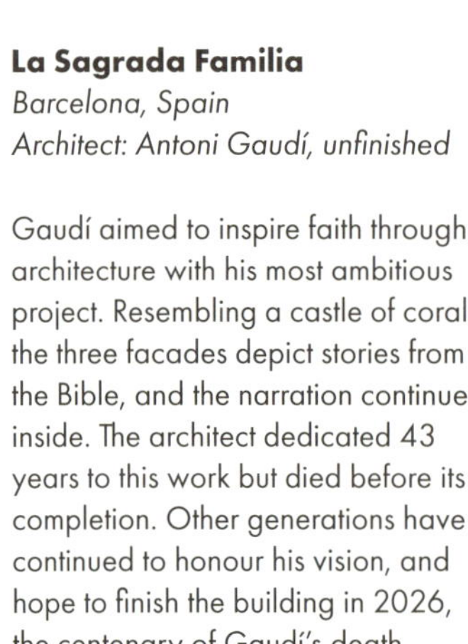

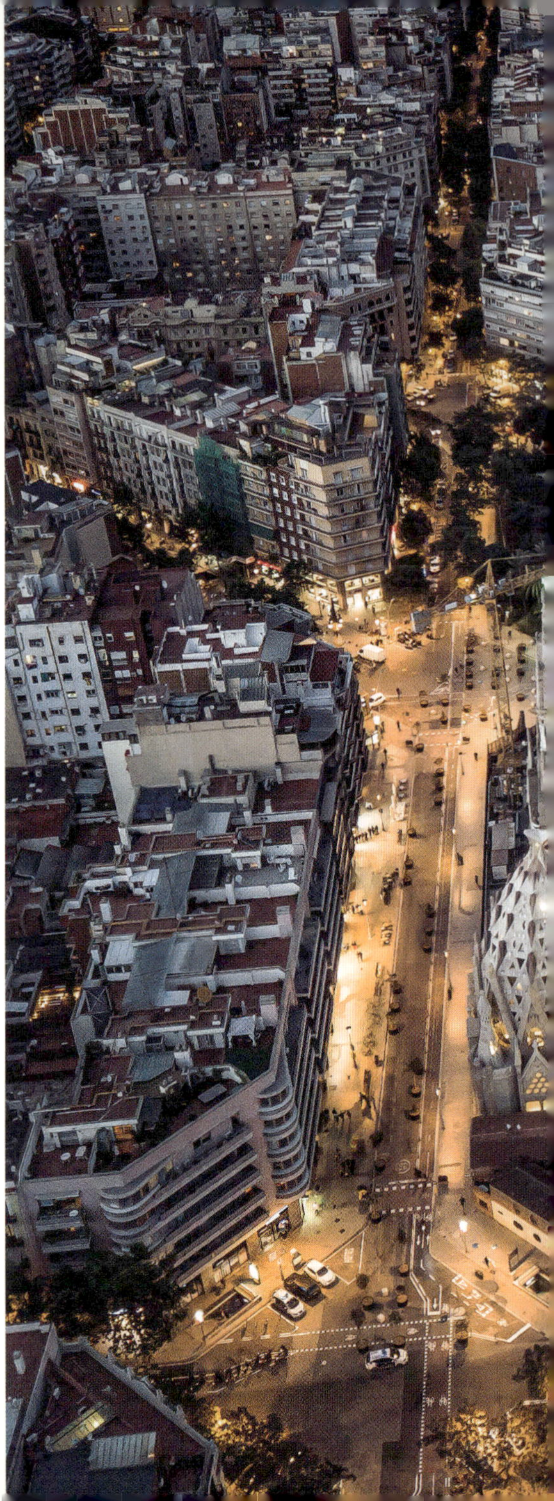

La Sagrada Familia
Barcelona, Spain
Architect: Antoni Gaudí, unfinished

Gaudí aimed to inspire faith through architecture with his most ambitious project. Resembling a castle of coral, the three facades depict stories from the Bible, and the narration continues inside. The architect dedicated 43 years to this work but died before its completion. Other generations have continued to honour his vision, and hope to finish the building in 2026, the centenary of Gaudí's death.

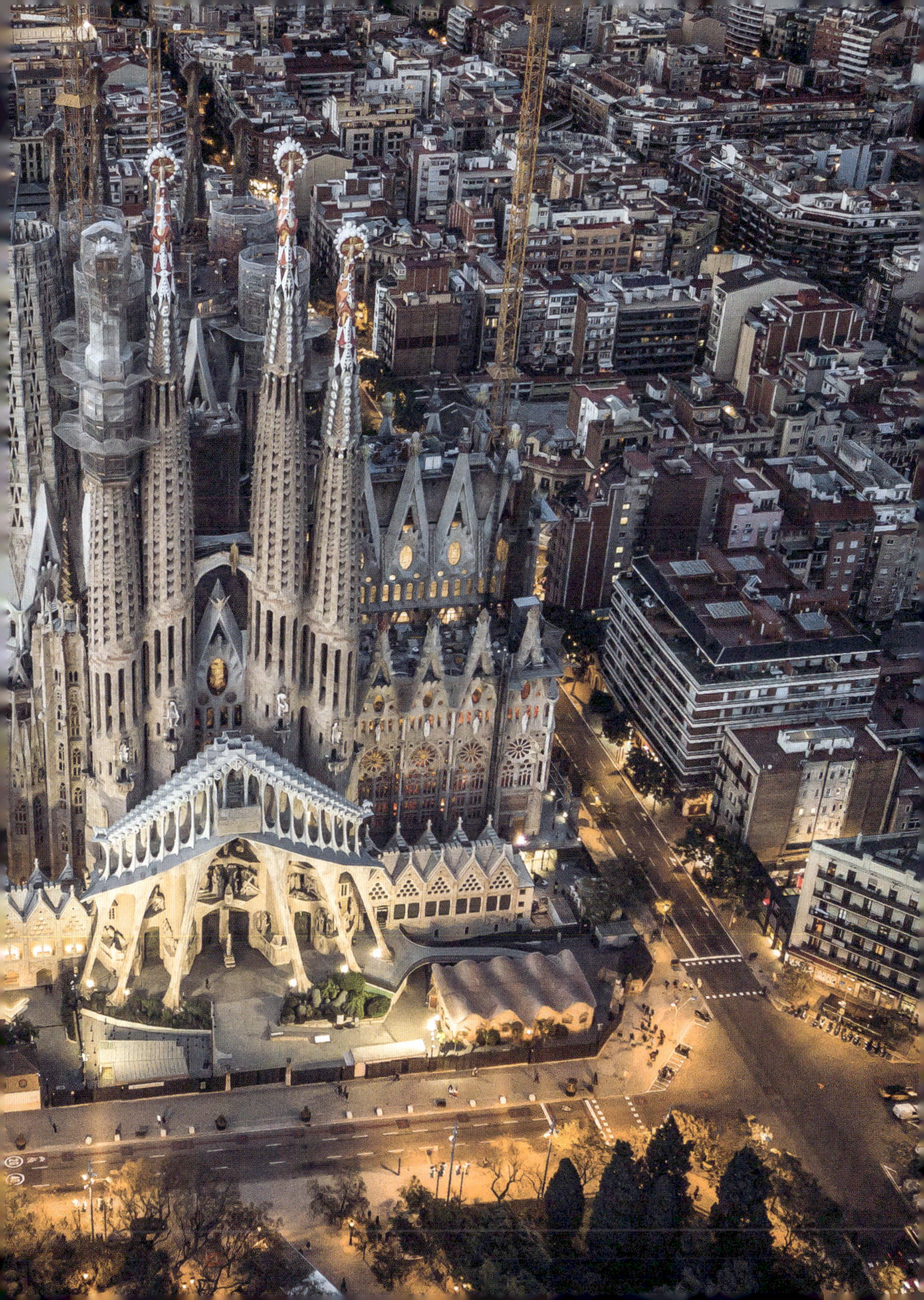

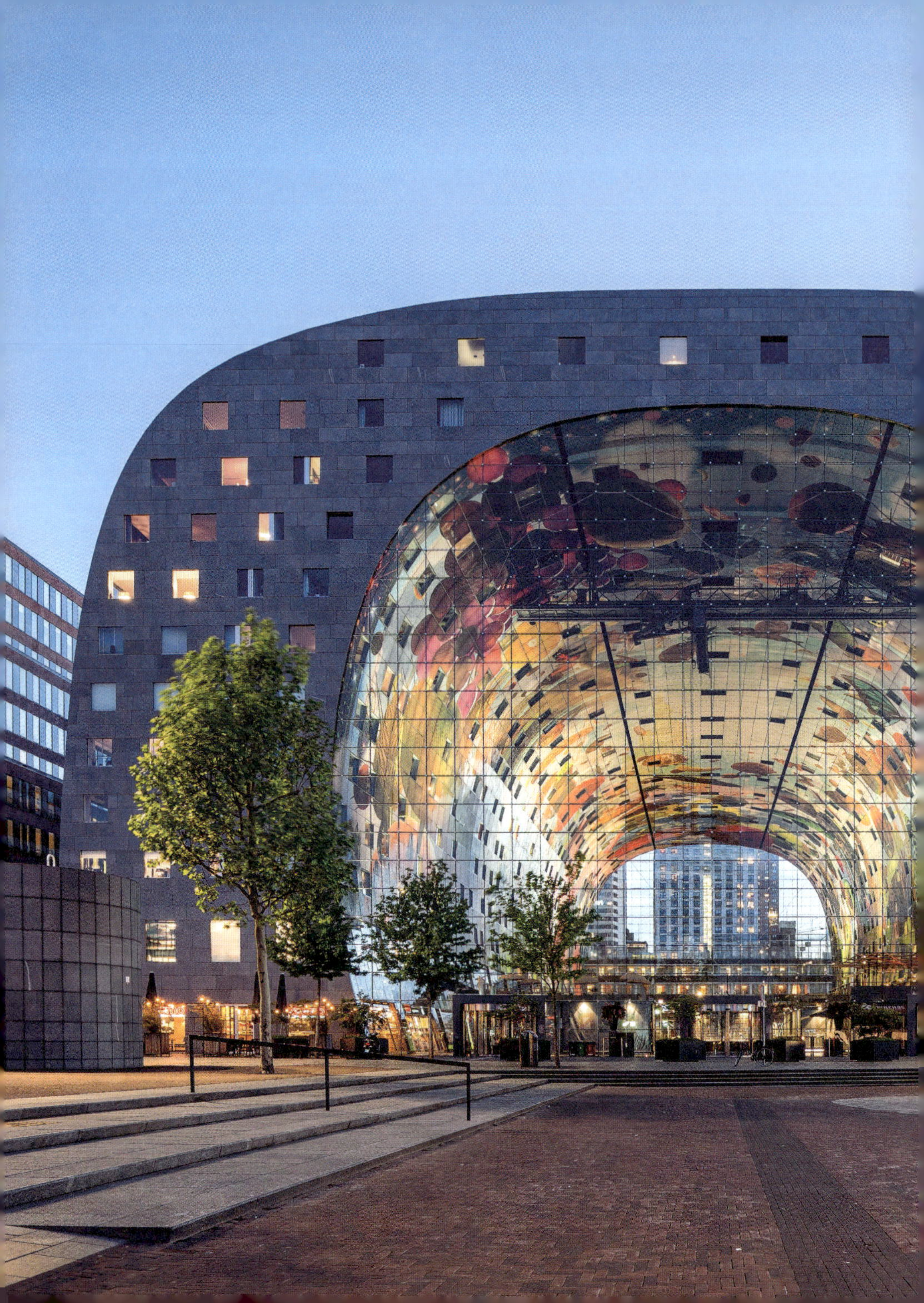

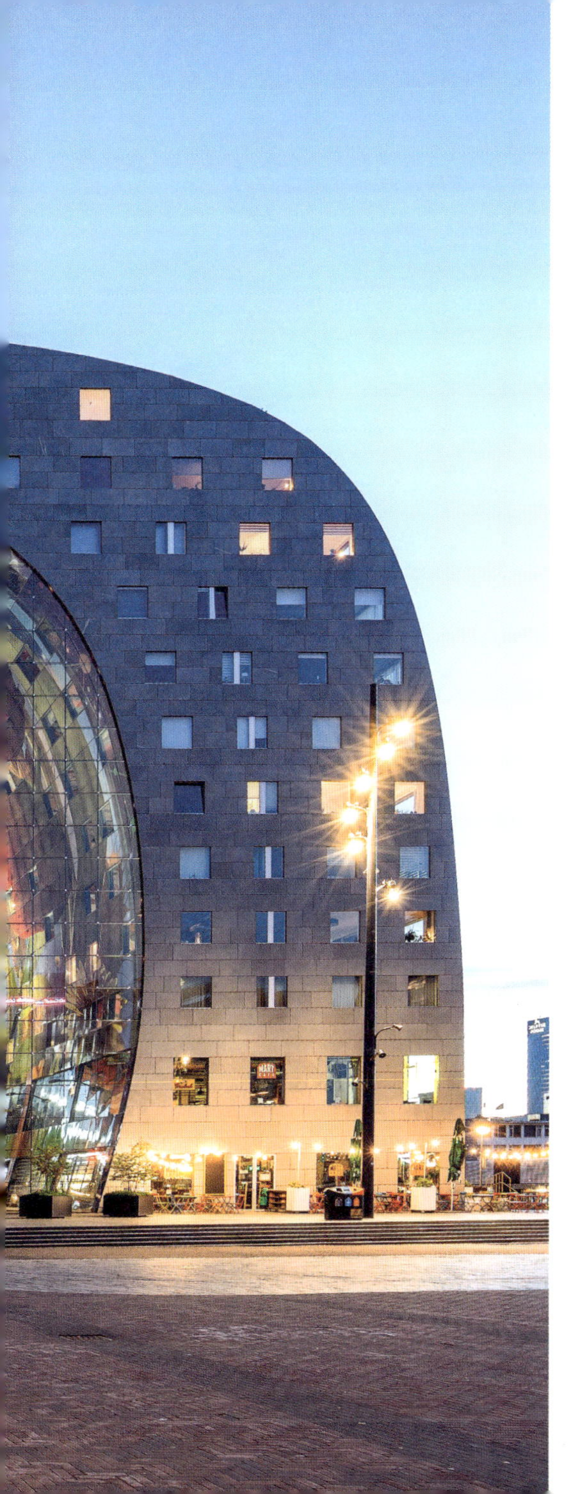

Markthal

Rotterdam, Netherlands
Architect: MVRDV, 2014

The first covered market in the Netherlands is notable for its shape and scope, combining a fresh food market, restaurants and underground parking beneath apartments. The inside of the arch features a colourful mural called *Cornucopia*, showcasing produce, flowers and insects, and the grey stone exterior contrasts with this vibrant centrepiece.

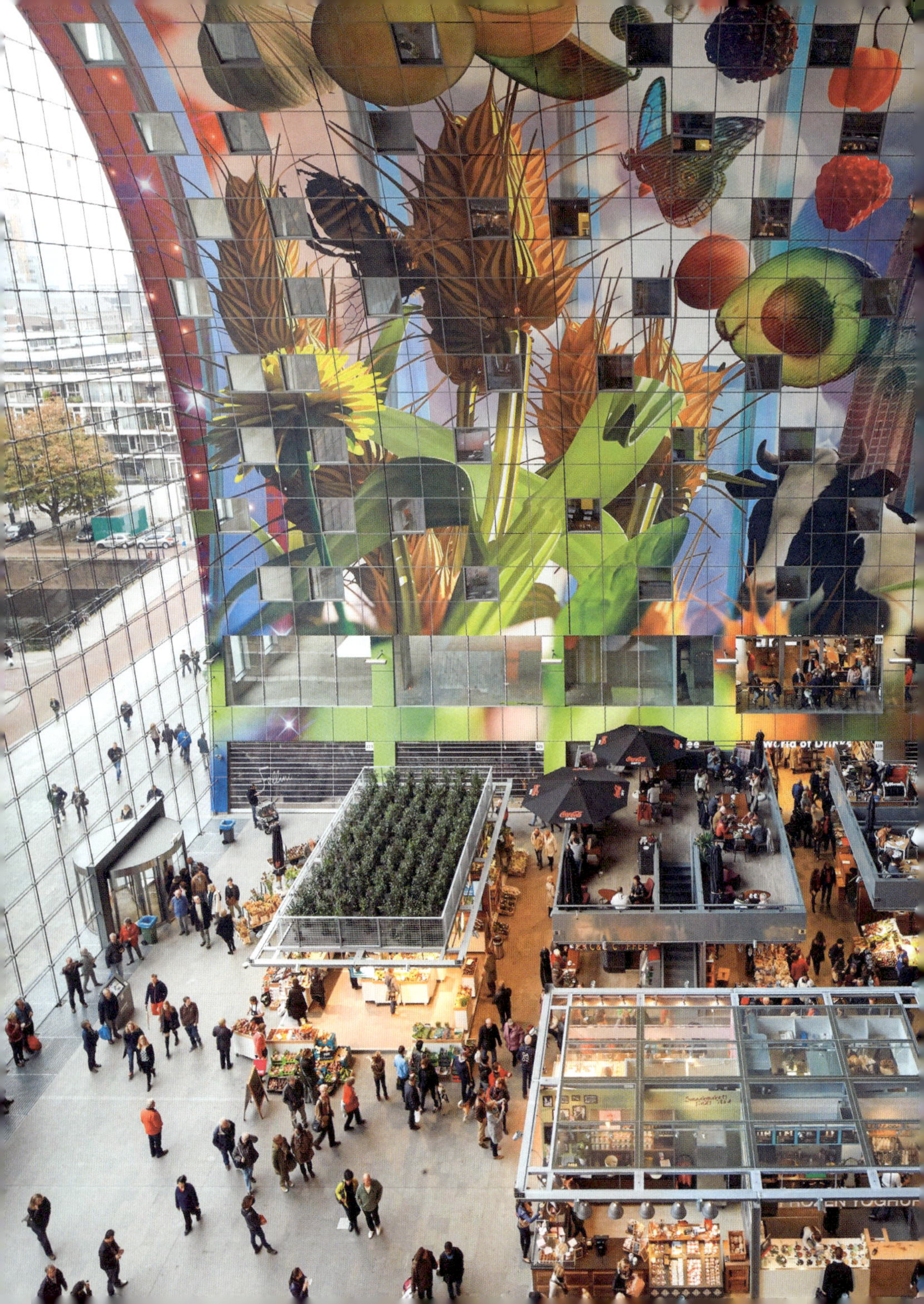

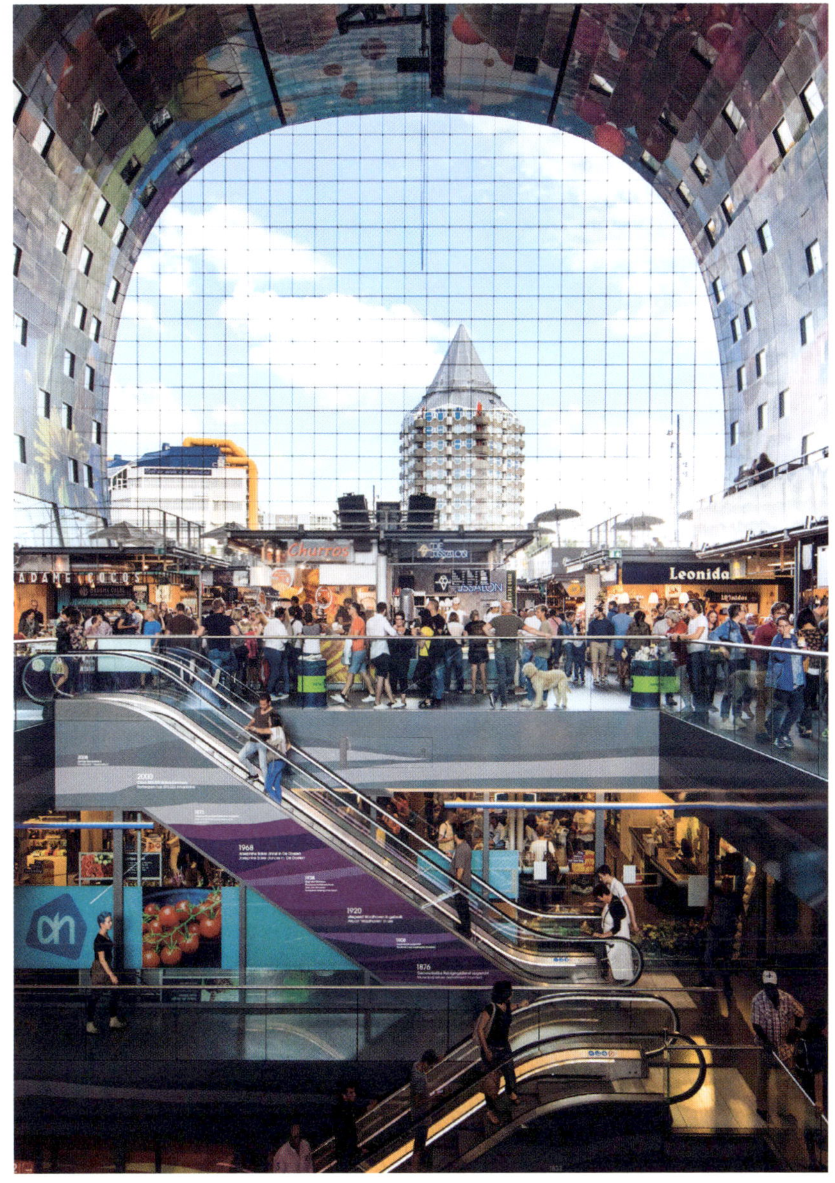
Churros

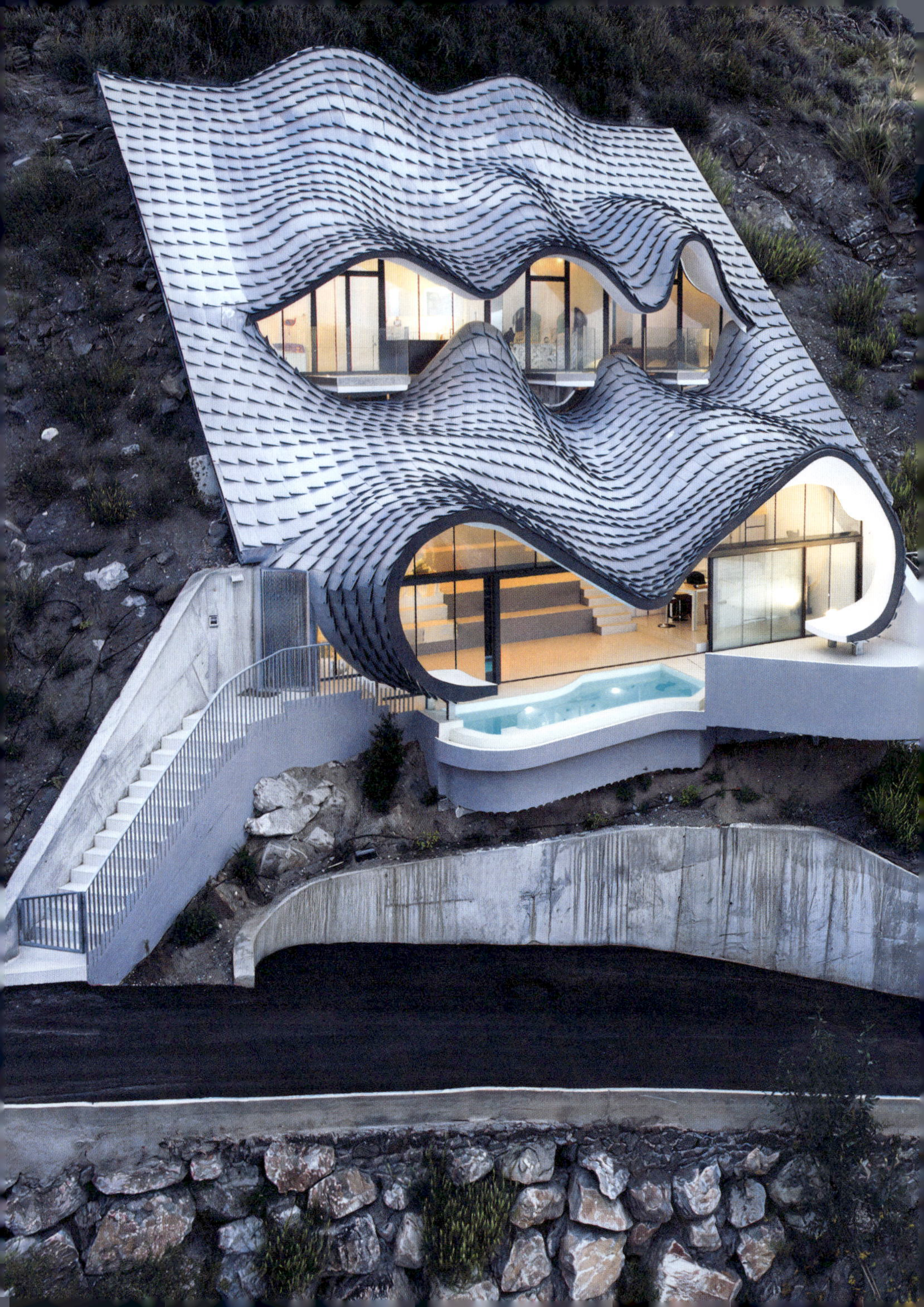

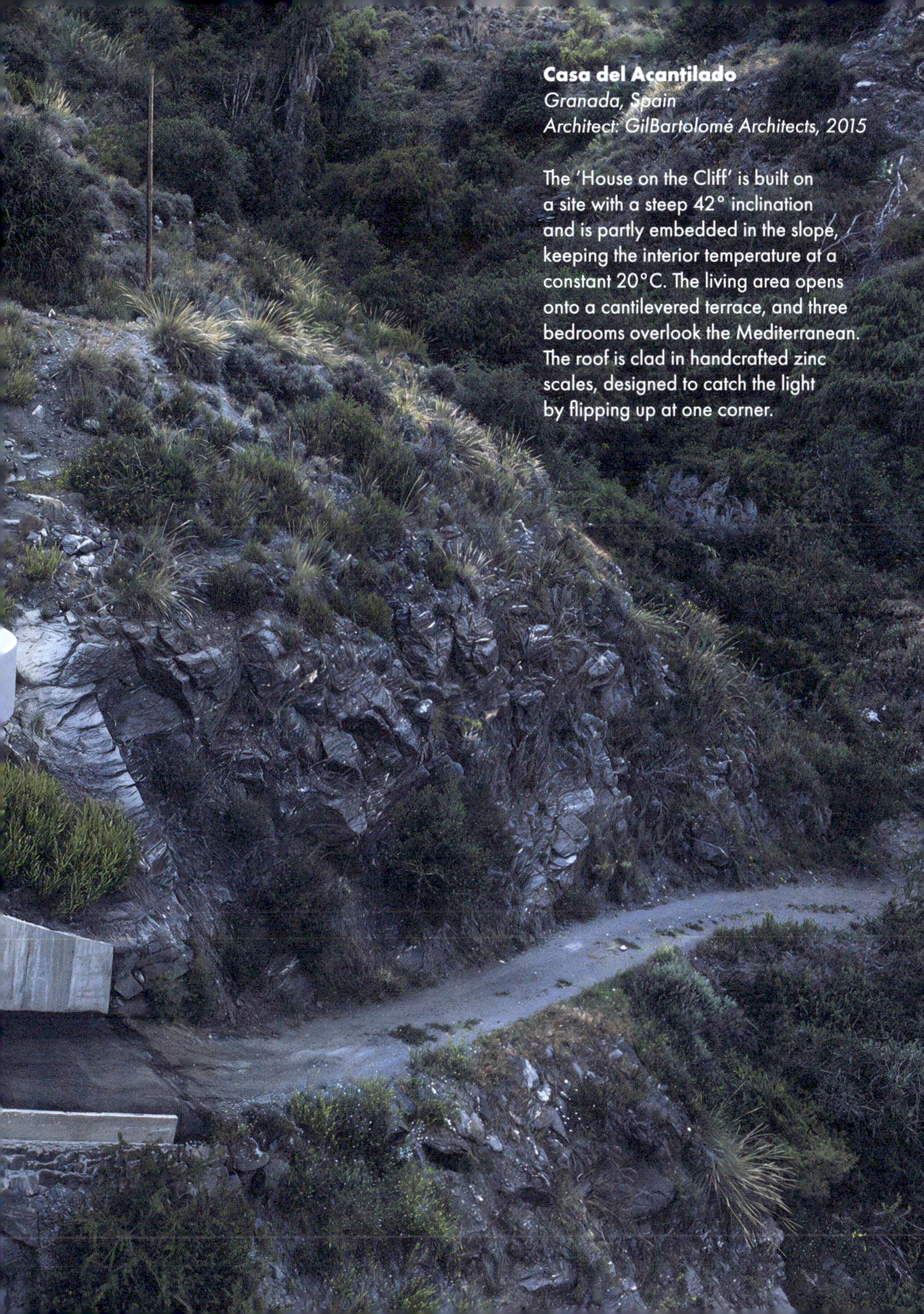

Casa del Acantilado
Granada, Spain
Architect: GilBartolomé Architects, 2015

The 'House on the Cliff' is built on a site with a steep 42° inclination and is partly embedded in the slope, keeping the interior temperature at a constant 20°C. The living area opens onto a cantilevered terrace, and three bedrooms overlook the Mediterranean. The roof is clad in handcrafted zinc scales, designed to catch the light by flipping up at one corner.

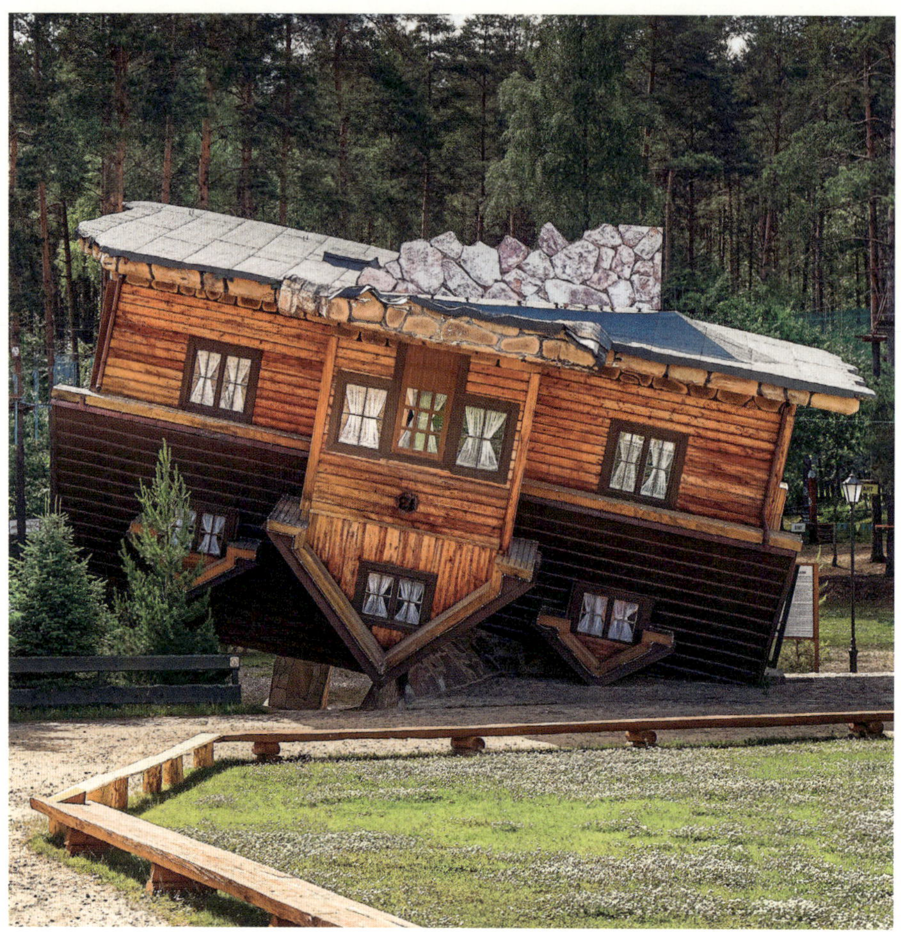

Upside Down House
Szymbark, Poland
Architect: Daniel Czapiewski, 2007

This topsy-turvy tourist attraction has a serious message. It was designed to teach visitors about the nation's tumultuous political history and the uncertainty of life after communism – an era the architect claims 'turned the country upside down'. The slanted orientation reinforces a sense of unease: entry is through an attic window, and visitors walk around on the ceilings.

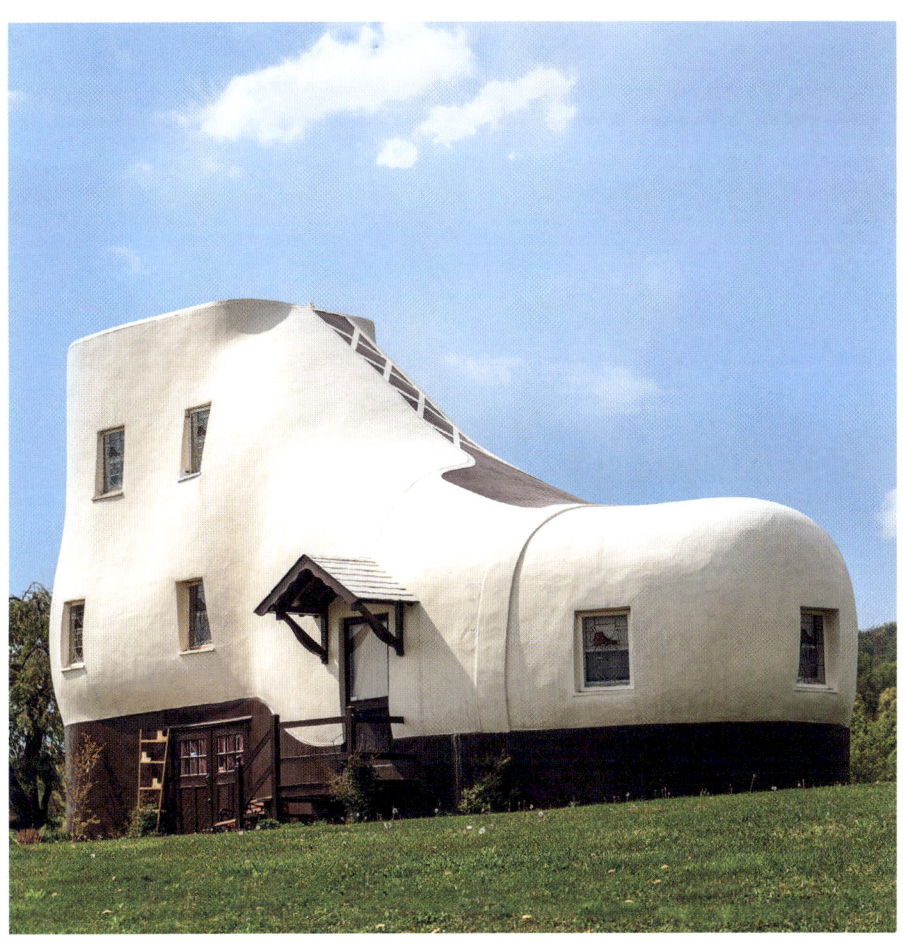

Haines Shoe House
Hellam, Philadelphia, USA
Architect: Mahlon Haines, 1948

This quirky boot-shaped building was designed by shoe salesman Mahlon Haines to advertise his business, but he also let it out to footloose road-trippers as a holiday home (he lived in a house opposite). The stucco-covered structure contains a living room in the toe, the heel houses the kitchen, and the ankle contains two bedrooms.

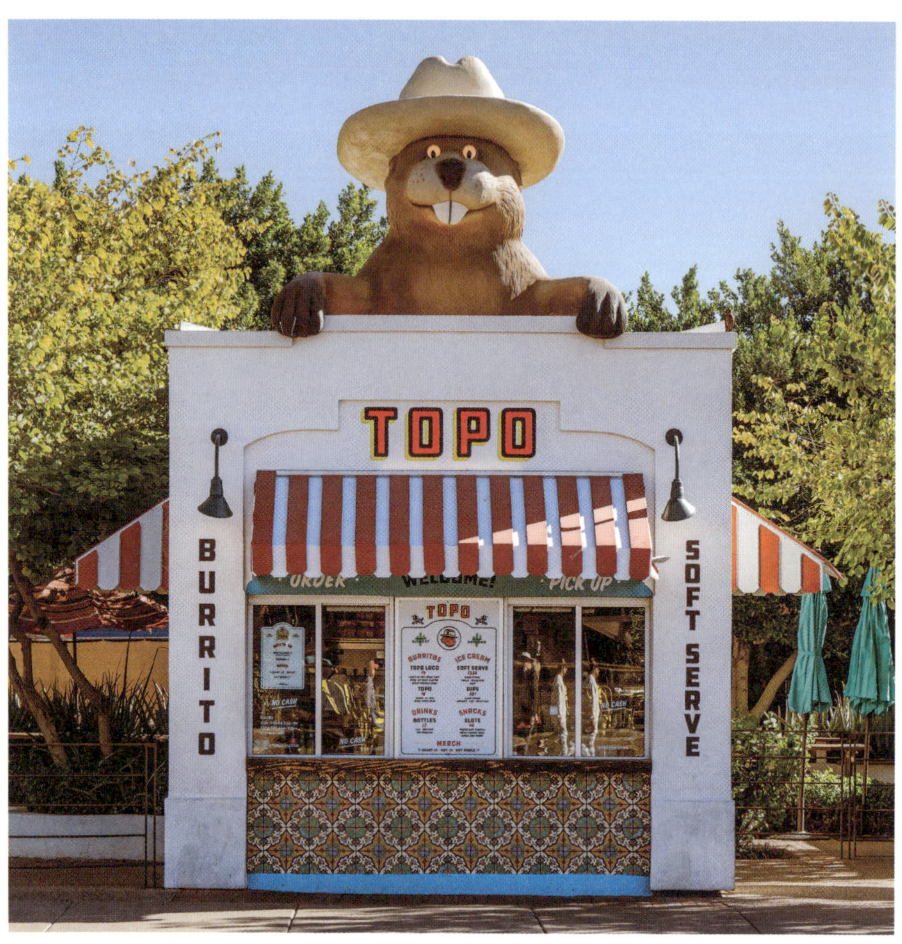

Topo Burrito Stand
Gilbert, Arizona, USA
Architect: Joe Johnston, 2019

A fascination with the golden age of roadside attractions inspired a local restauranteur to create this playful modern interpretation – a burrito stand in the shape of a giant gopher (*topo* being Spanish for gopher). Topo's creator wanted to reference his farming heritage, and memories of clashes with these rodents informed the building's design.

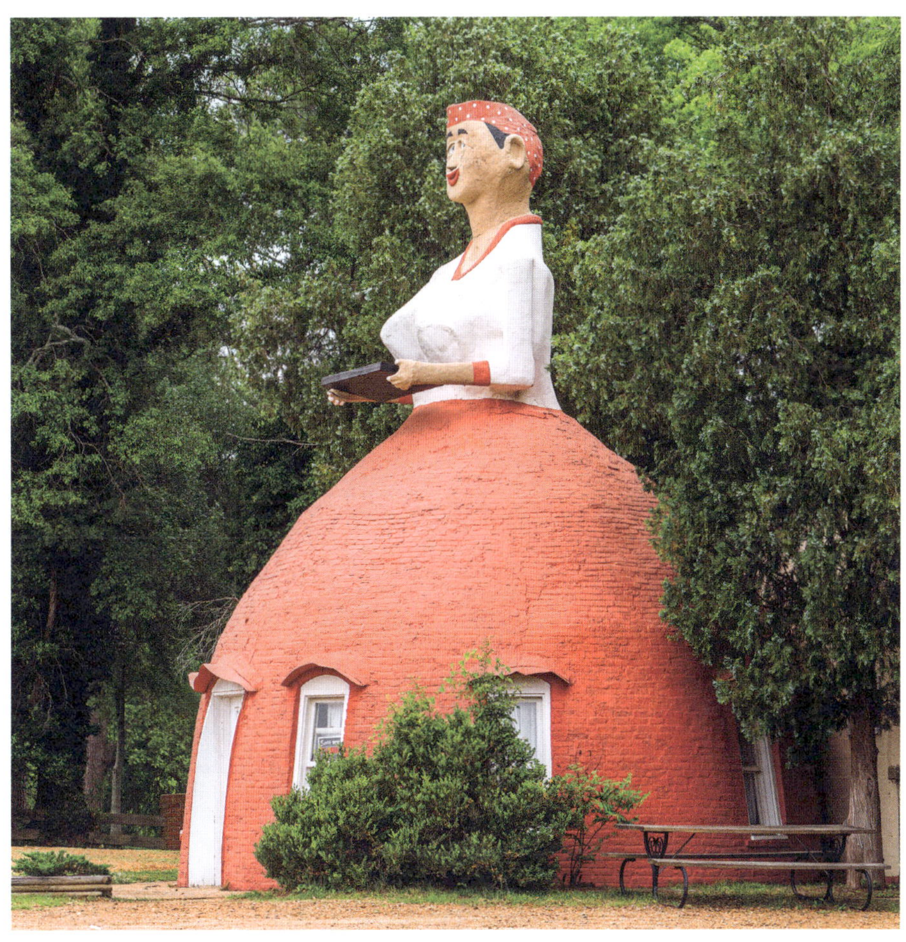

Mammy's Cupboard
Natchez, Mississippi, USA
Architect: Annie Davis Bost, 1940

This roadside diner embodies the 'mammy' caricature that reappeared in American cultural life via the film *Gone With the Wind.* During the Civil Rights Movement of the 1960s, the skin was painted a lighter shade and other modifications were made to try and downplay the problematic racial imagery, but it remains a reminder of the troubling stereotypes prevalent in American history.

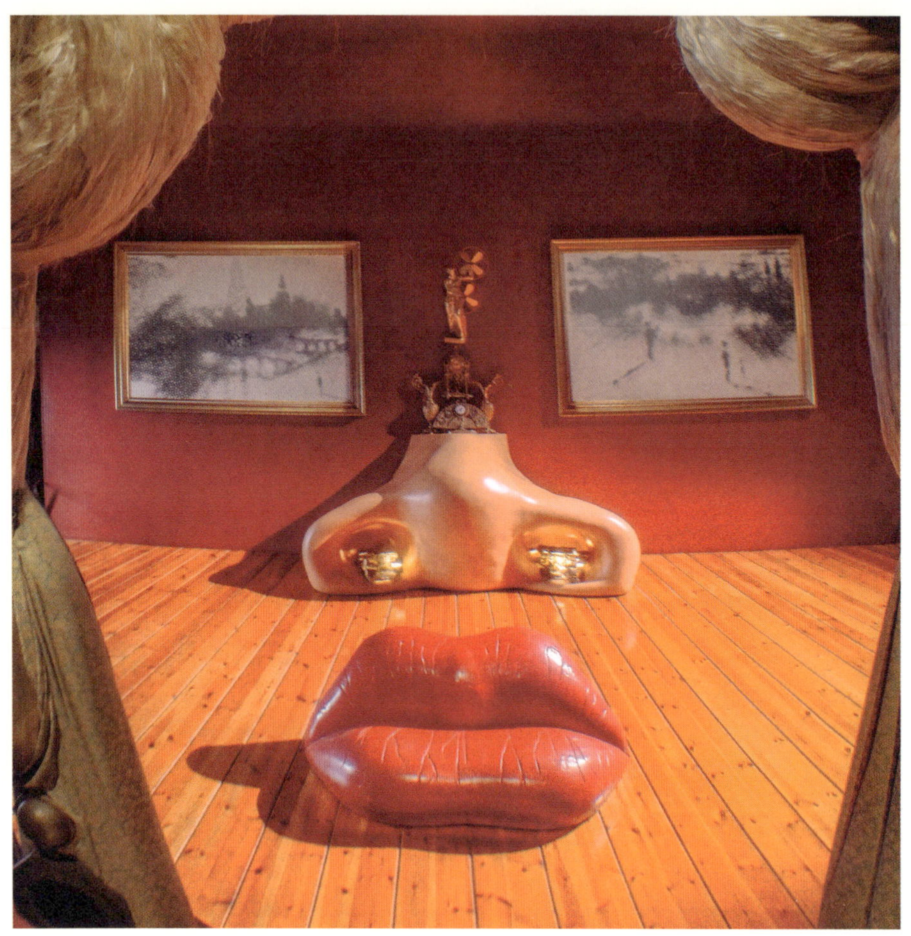

Torre Galatea at Dalí Theatre-Museum
Figueres, Spain
Architect: Emilio Pérez Piñero, 1974

Salvador Dalí wanted his museum to be as surreal and theatrical as his work, and this building perfectly captures his flamboyant artistic spirit. Giant egg sculptures are perched along the roof parapet, while the walls are decorated with imitation bread rolls. The tower was named after Dalí's wife, Gala, and Dalí lived in it until his death in 1989.

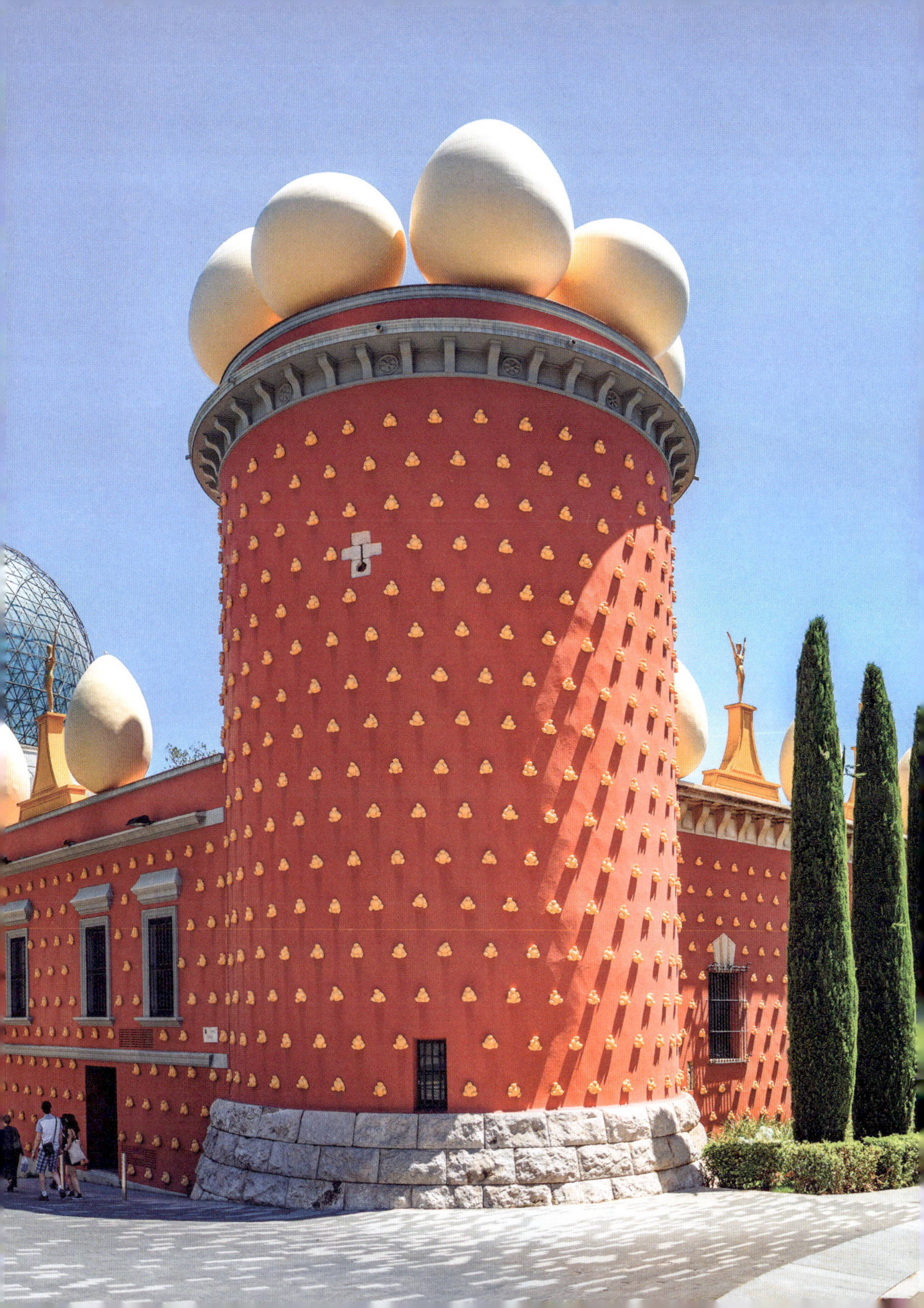

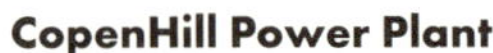

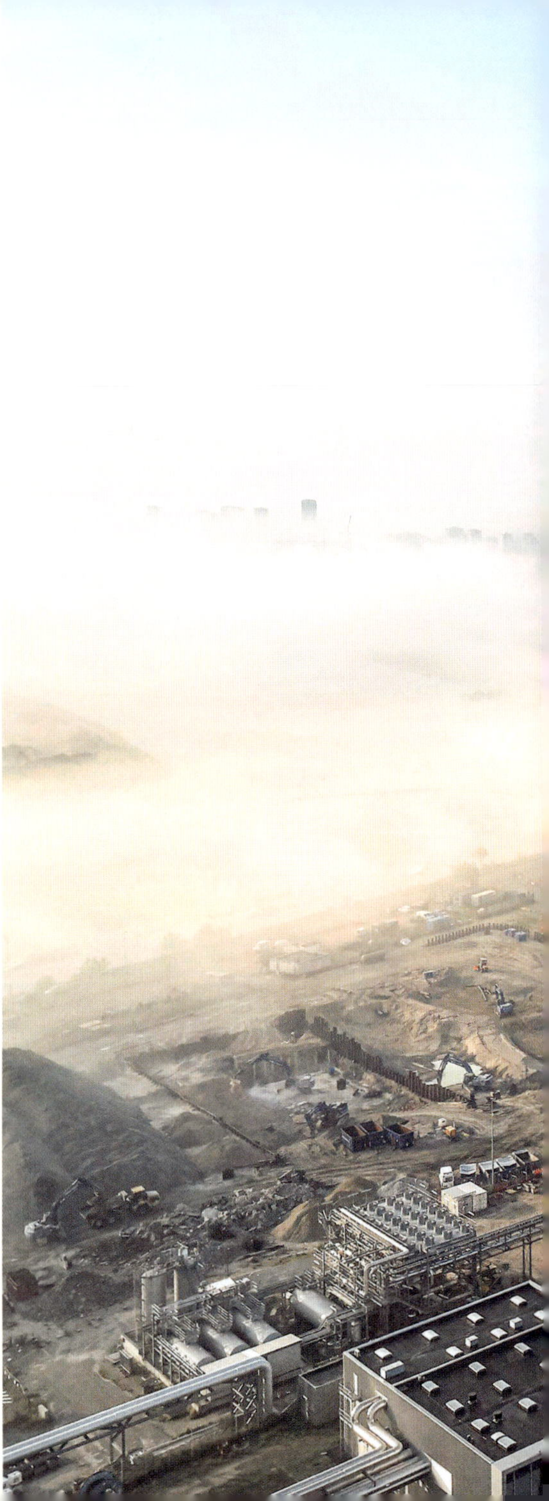

CopenHill Power Plant

Copenhagen, Denmark
Architect: Bjarke Ingels Group, 2017

This project transformed a waste-to-energy plant that provides clean energy for thousands of homes into a destination and architectural landmark. It is topped with a verdant ski slope, hiking trail, the world's tallest climbing wall, a recreation centre and an environmental education hub. This embodies the architects' philosophy of 'hedonistic sustainability' – prioritising fun and quality of life while pursuing sustainable practices.

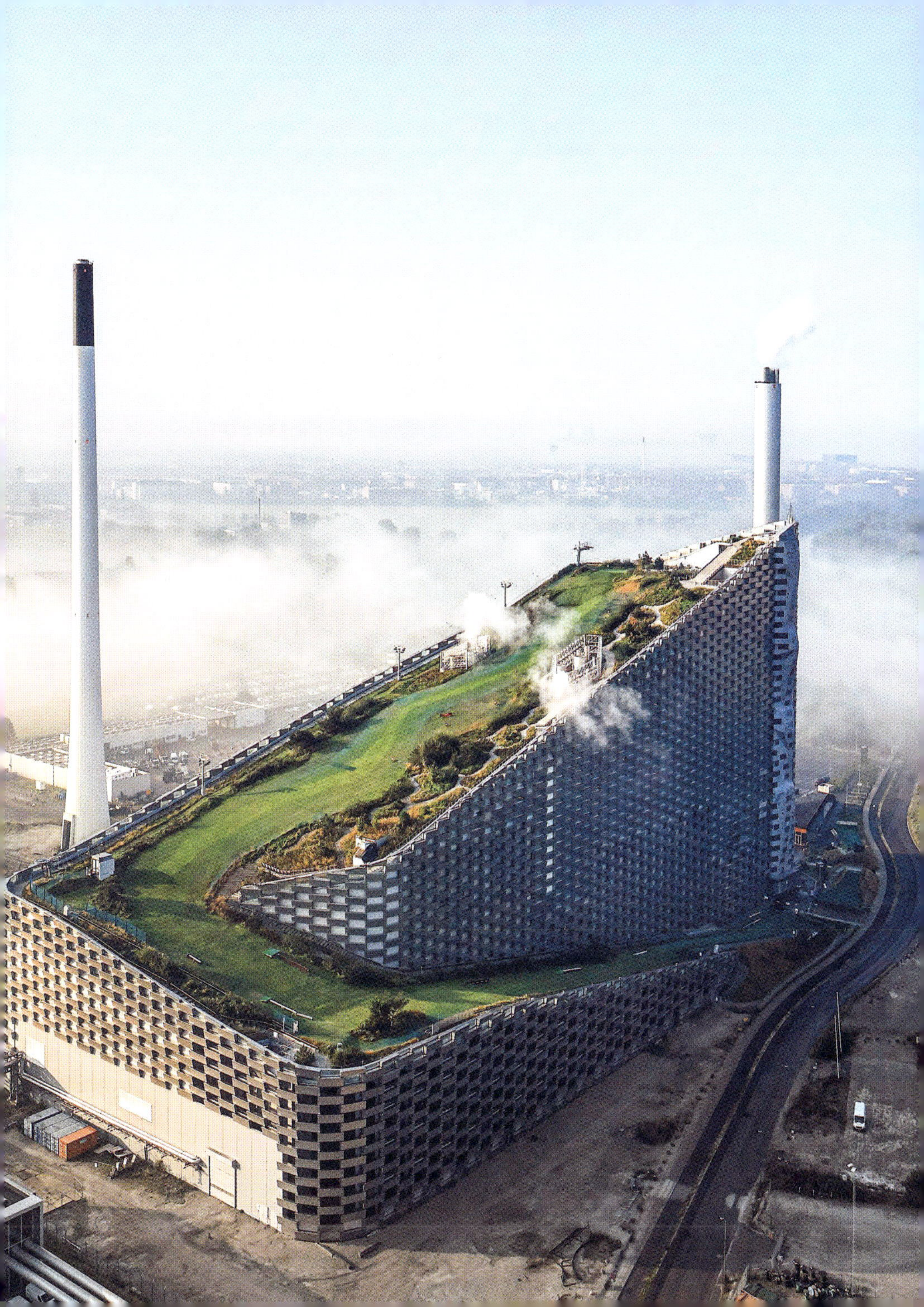

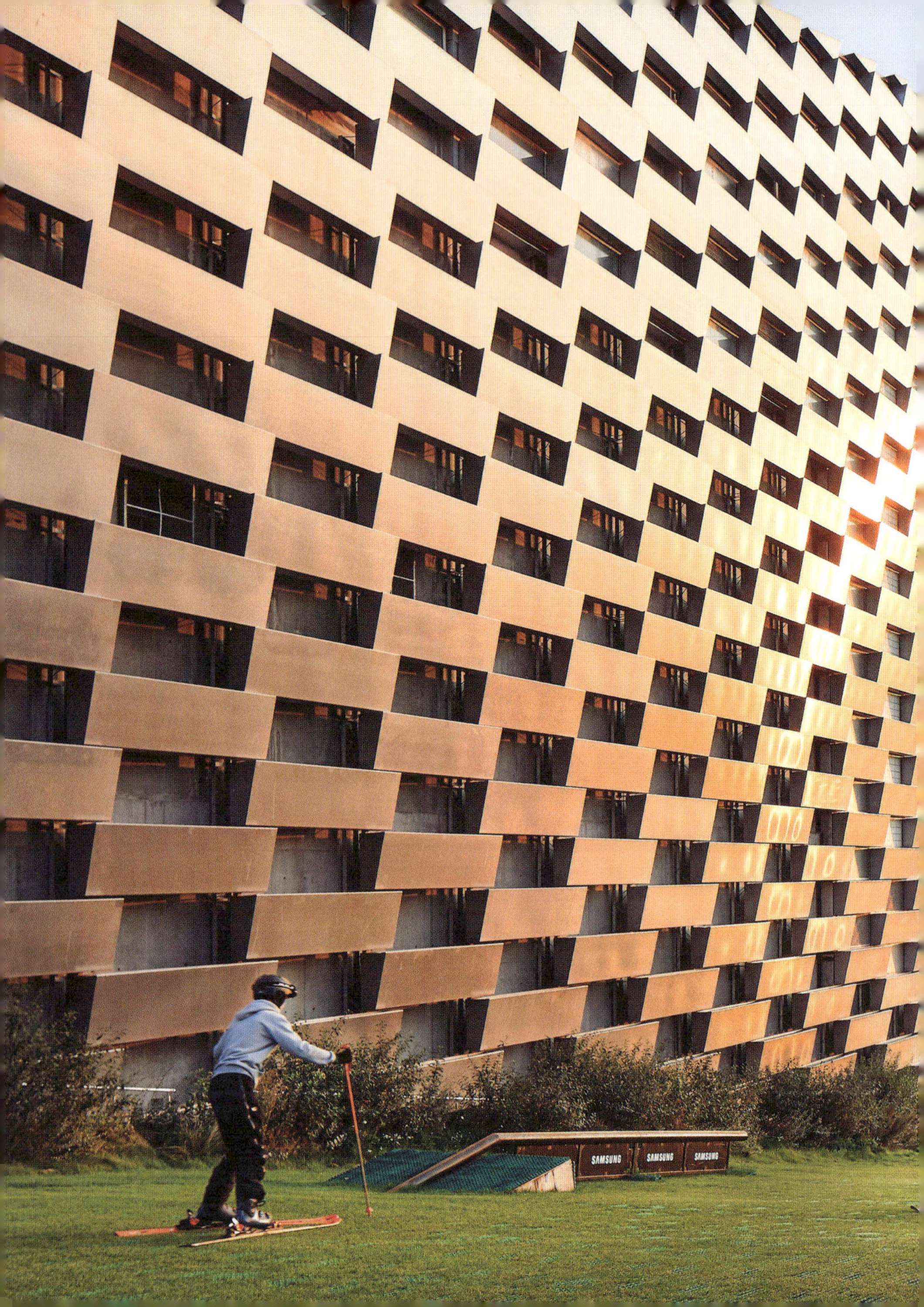
SAMSUNG
SAMSUNG
SAMSUNG

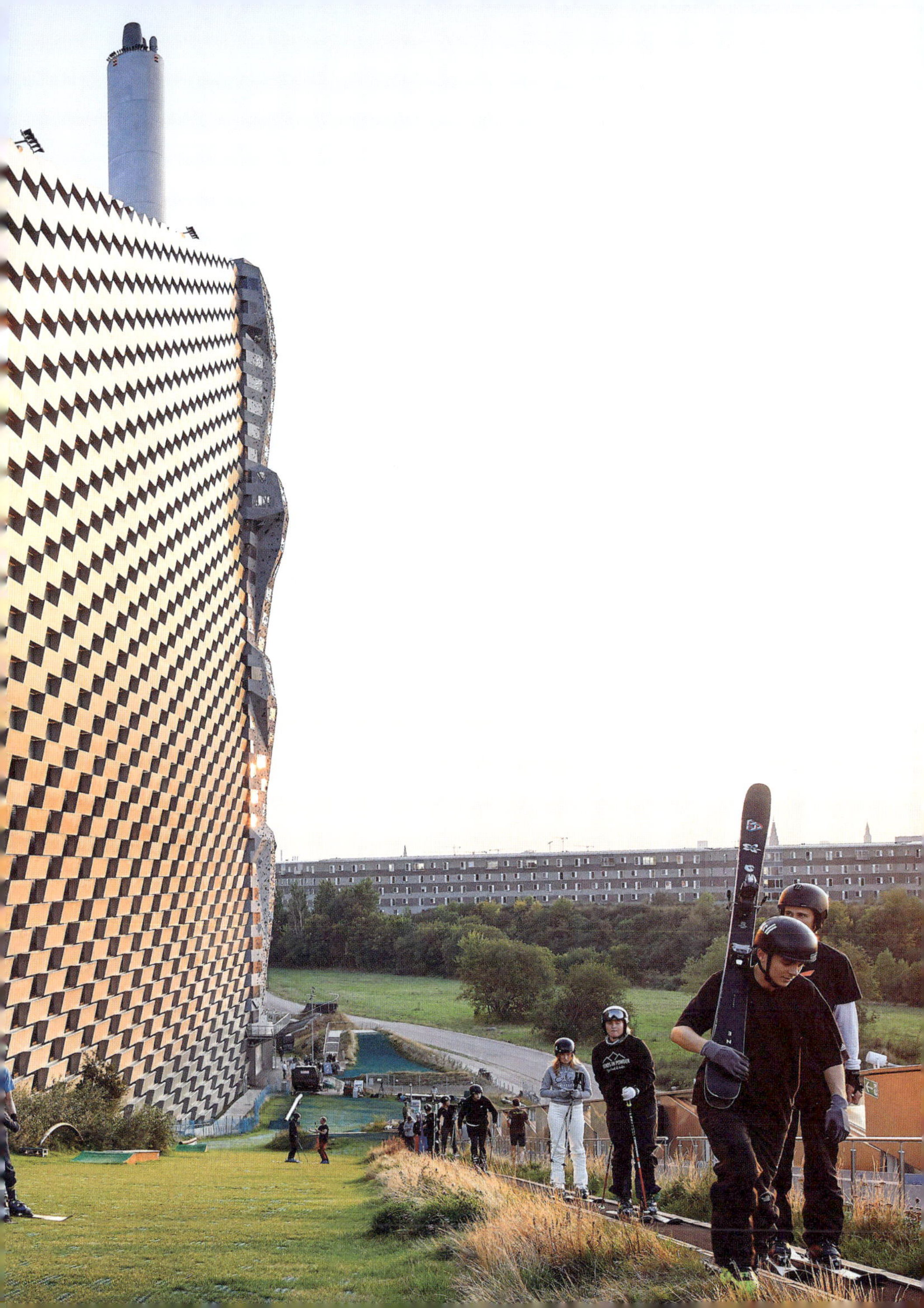

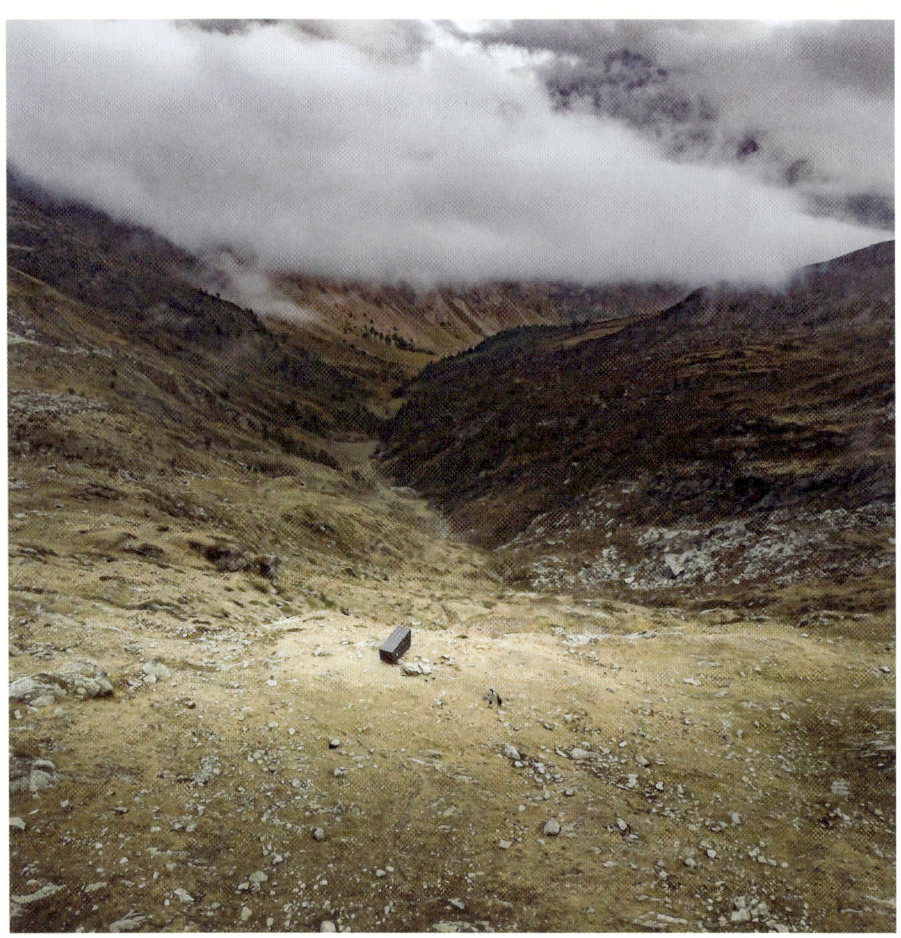

Bivacco Brédy
Aosta Valley, Italy
Architect: BCW Collective, 2021

This gravity-defying alpine shelter protrudes from the mountainside as if about to topple over. It was commissioned as a memorial to Claudio Brédy, a politician and climber who died during a mountain excursion, to provide refuge for mountaineers. Only accessible by foot, the dark aluminium-clad structure provides unrivalled panoramic views across the Aosta Valley.

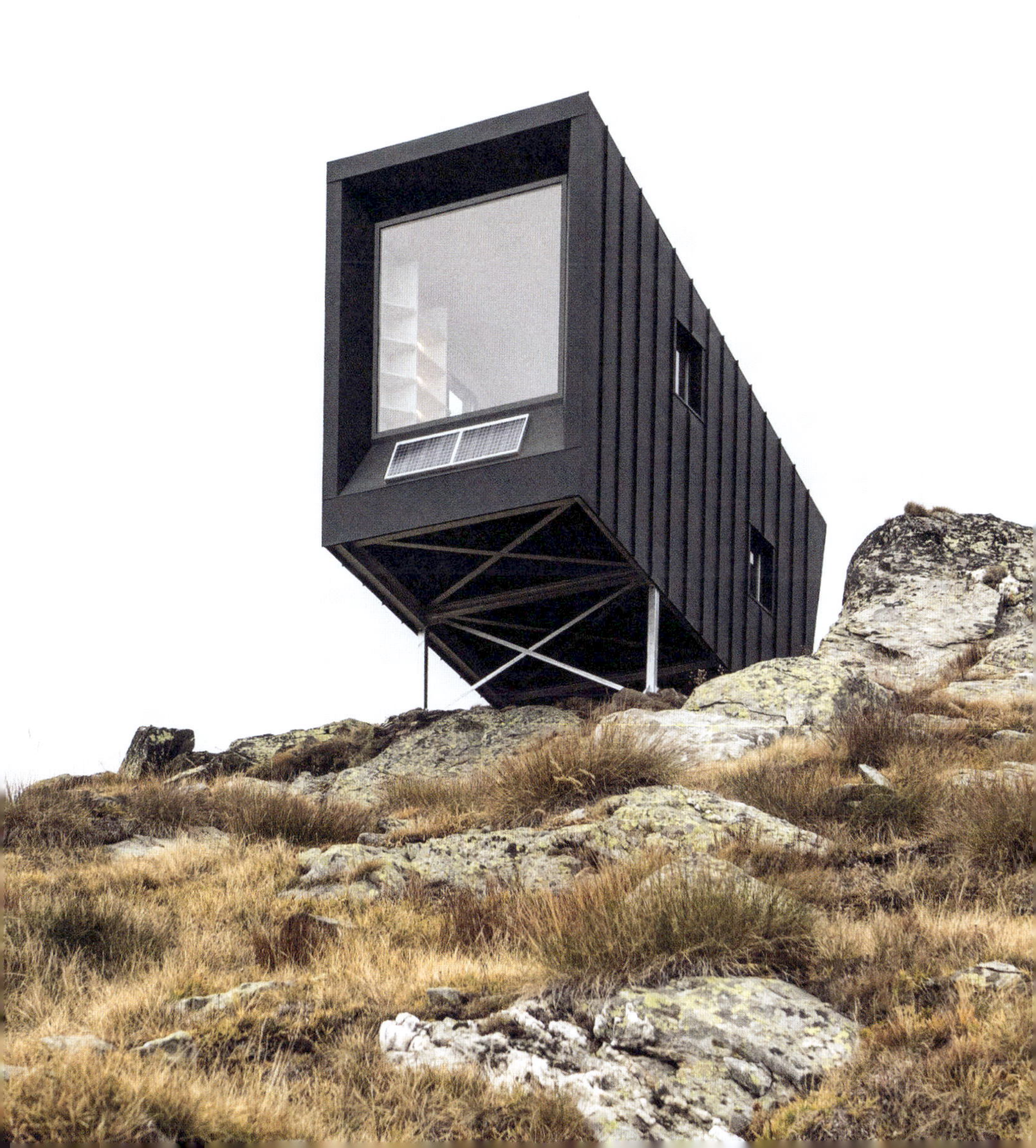

Mirrorcube Treehotel

Harads, Sweden

Architect: Tham & Videgärd, 2010

Vanishing into the landscape, this magical floating box is a tiny hotel in the far north of Sweden, close to the Arctic Circle. Cleverly suspended among the trees and accessed by rope bridge, the 4-metre-square lightweight aluminium cube is clad in mirrors to reflect the surrounding forest and sky so that the hideaway is perfectly camouflaged.

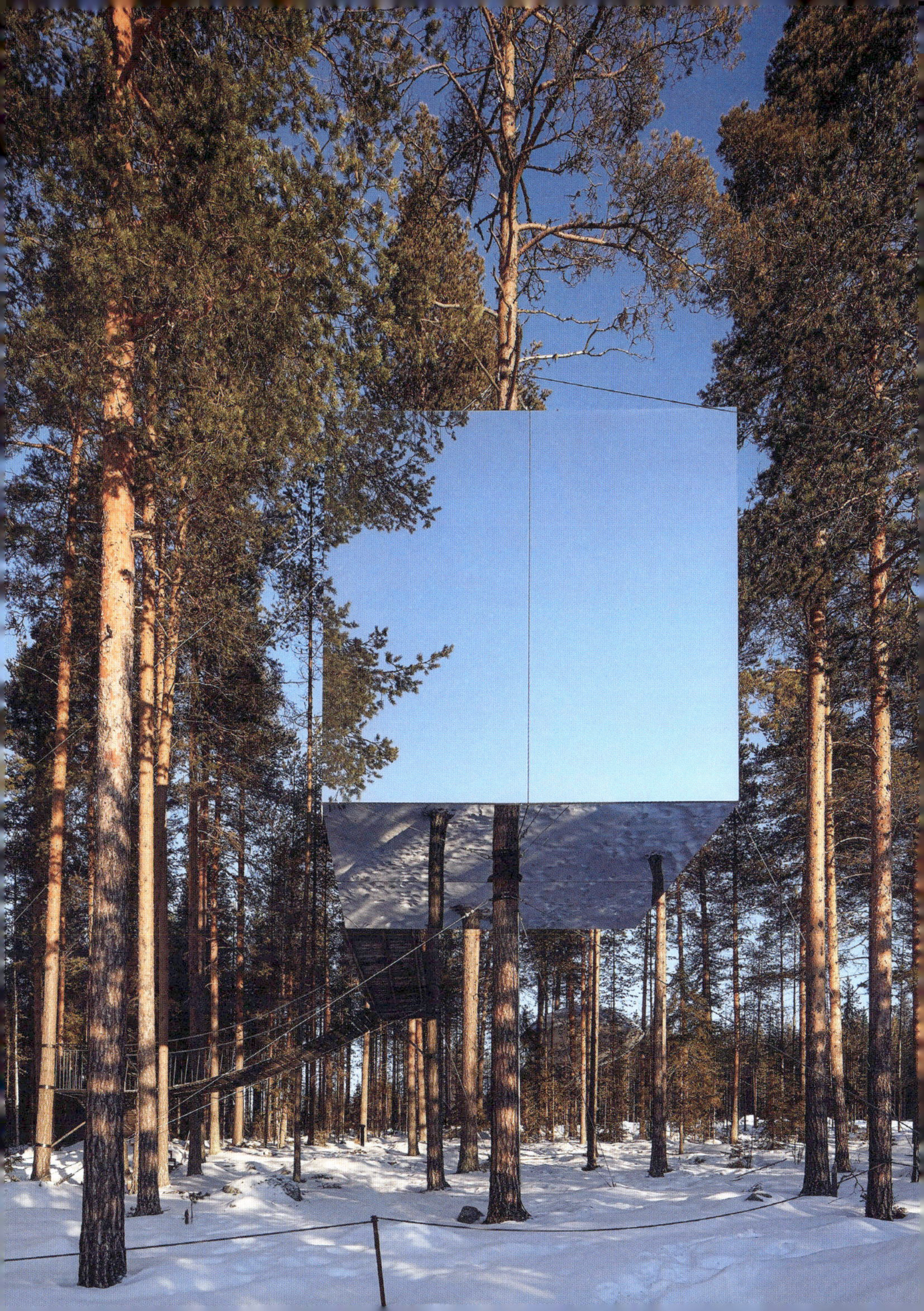

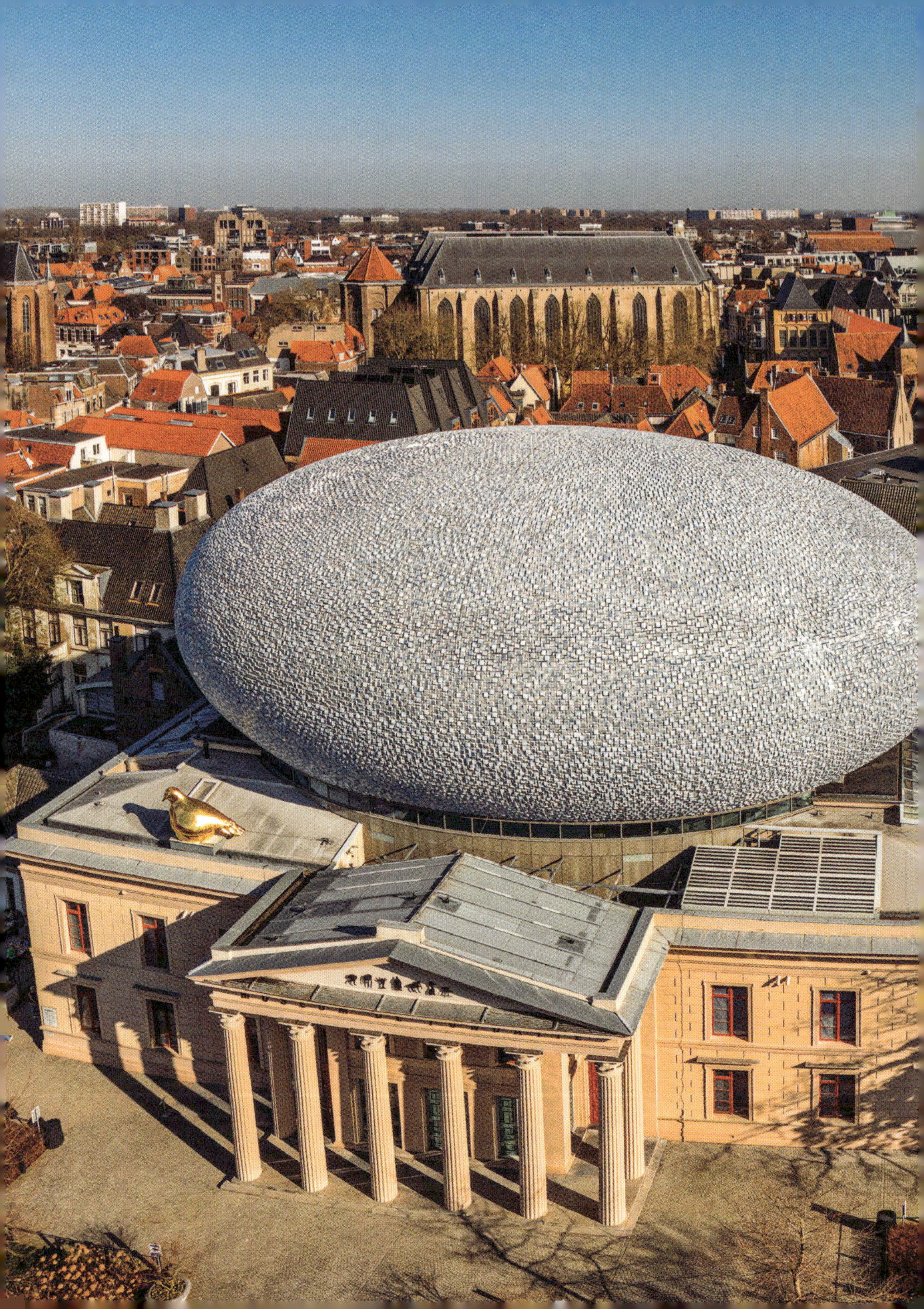

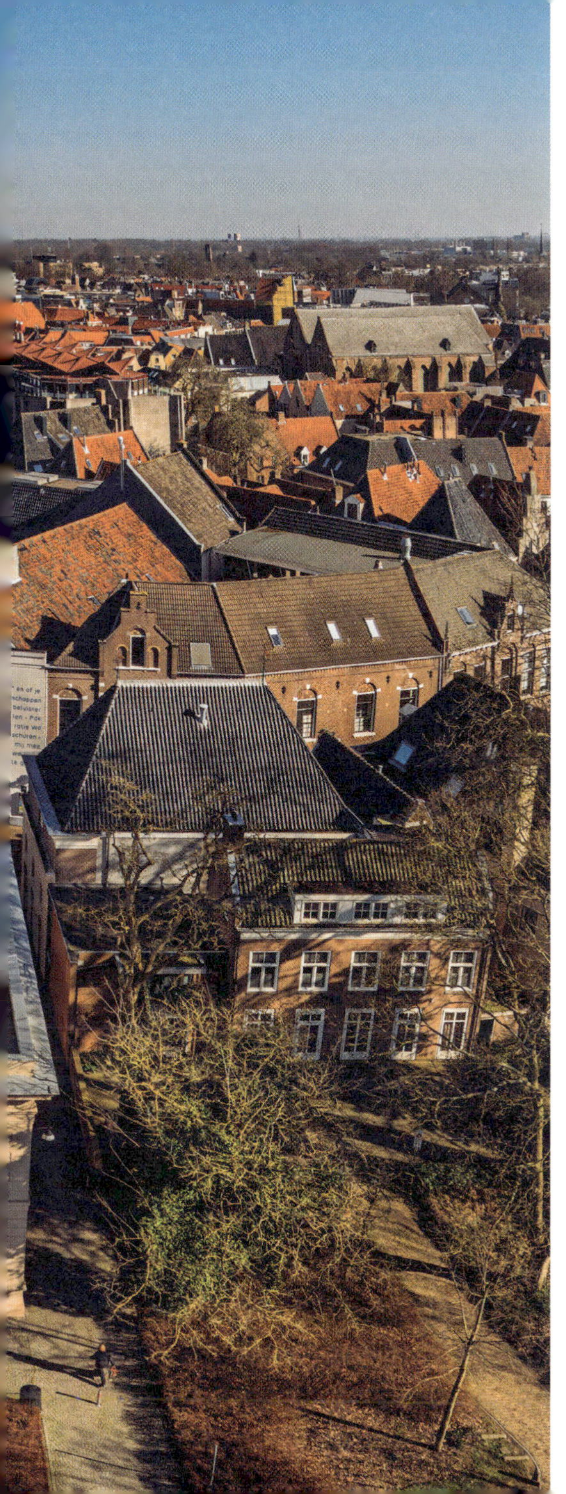

Museum De Fundatie
Zwolle, Netherlands
Architect: Bierman Henket, 2013

Old-school grandeur meets space-age design in this visual arts museum. Lack of room around the existing building and the technical difficulties of extending underground led the architects to place an extension on top of the 19th-century former courthouse. The elliptical pod is clad in three-dimensional ceramic tiles with a blue and white glaze, allowing it to blend with the sky.

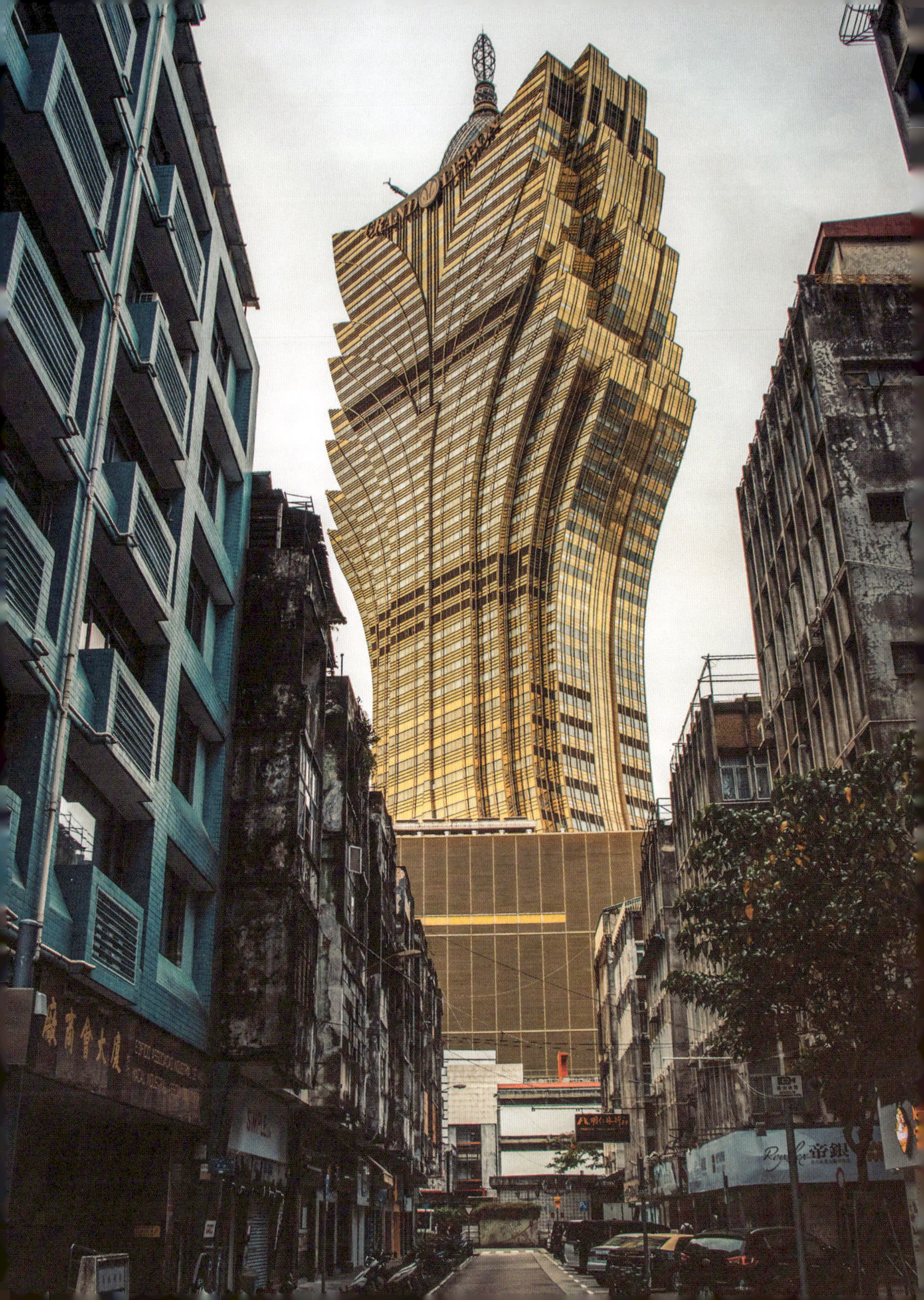
GRAND LISBOA
帝銀

Grand Lisboa

Macau, China

Architect: DLN, 2008

Resembling a showgirl's exotic headdress, the feathered form of this luxury casino hotel was inspired by the shape of a lotus flower, the official emblem of Macau. Rising to 228 metres, the building is one of the tallest in the region, and the glittering gold exterior combines traditional Chinese motifs with Las Vegas glamour.

Chaoyang Park Plaza
Beijing, China
Architect: MAD Architects, 2017

Set on the edge of the largest park in Beijing's central business district, these asymmetrical towers are unlike the typical box-like skyscrapers that carve out a sharp division between nature and the city. Designed with smooth, curved lines to blend with the park, they resemble mountain peaks rising from the neighbouring lake.

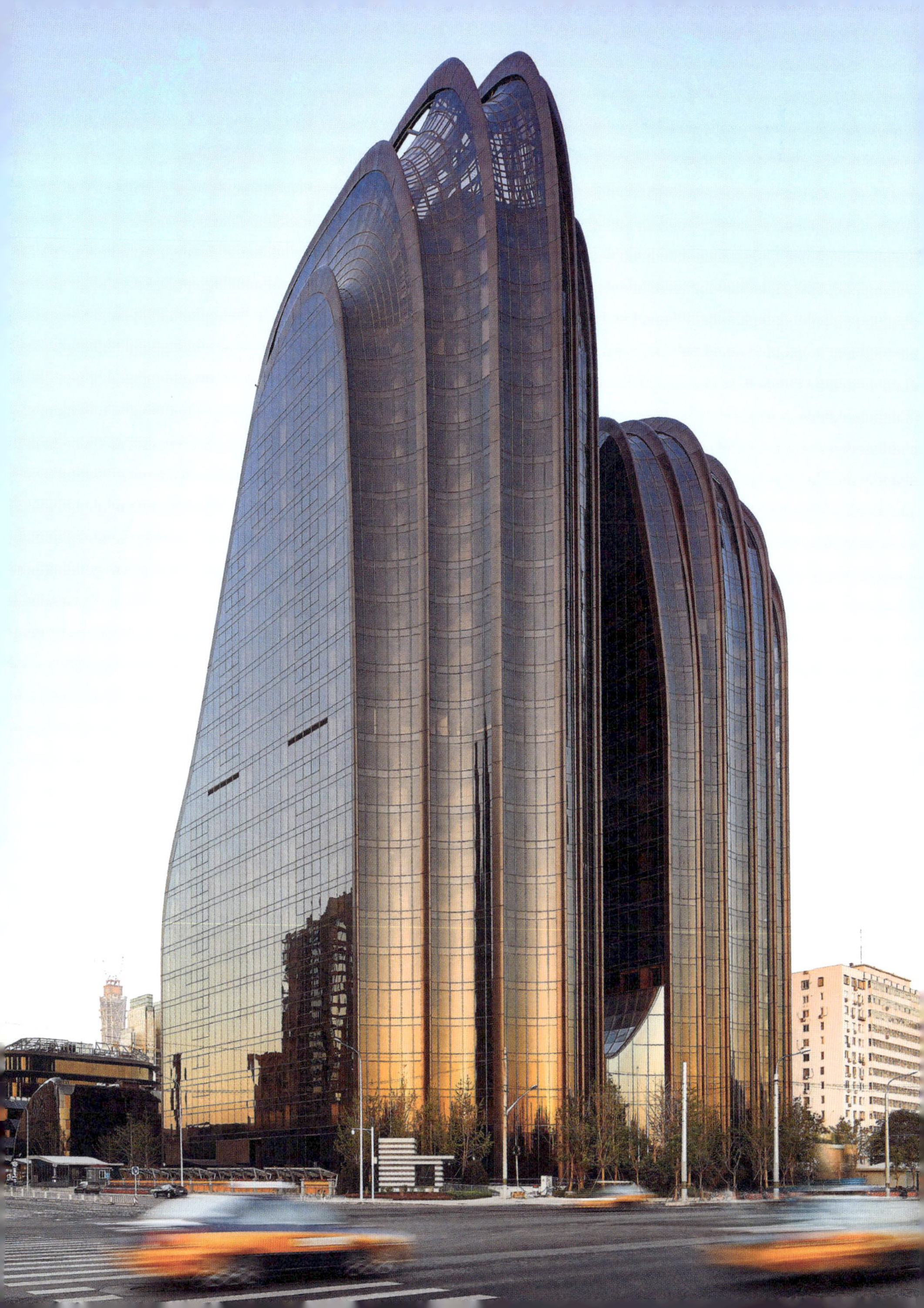

The Wave
Vejle, Denmark
Architect: Henning Larsen, 2018

The five towers of this housing complex ripple along the Vejle Fjord, mirroring the surrounding hills and the fjord's gentle waves. It has achieved several awards for its innovative approach to residential design and consists of 100 apartments divided between the five crests, with the top floor of each housing a double-height penthouse.

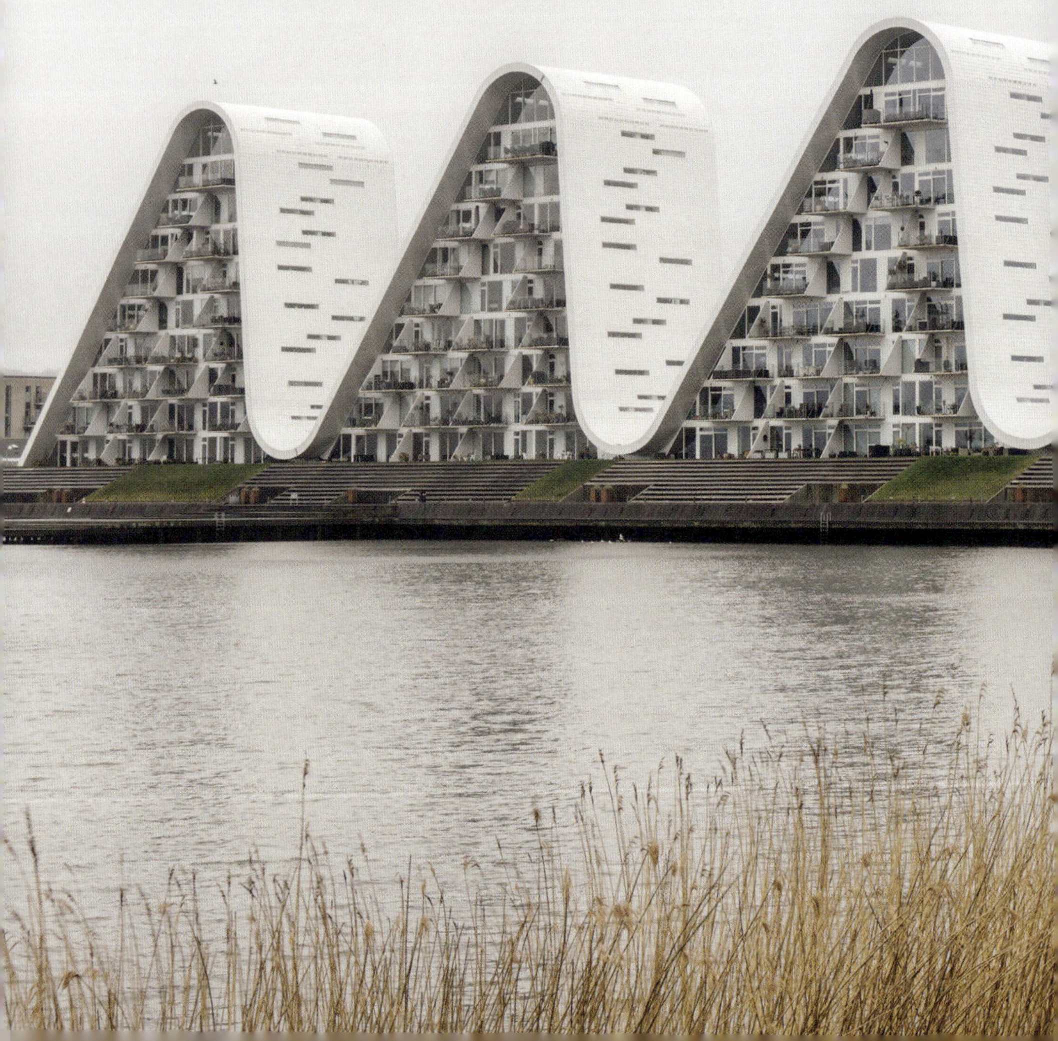

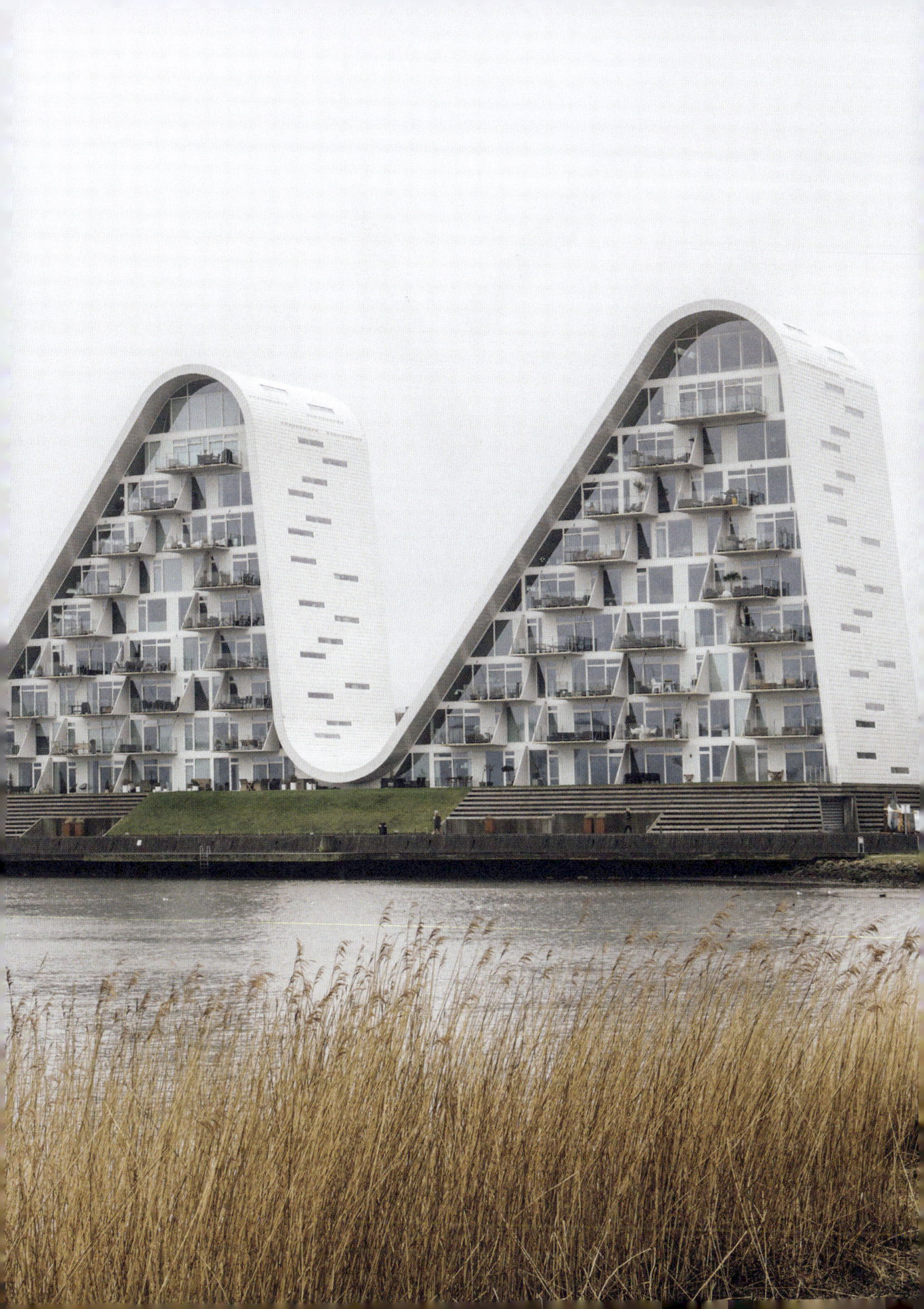

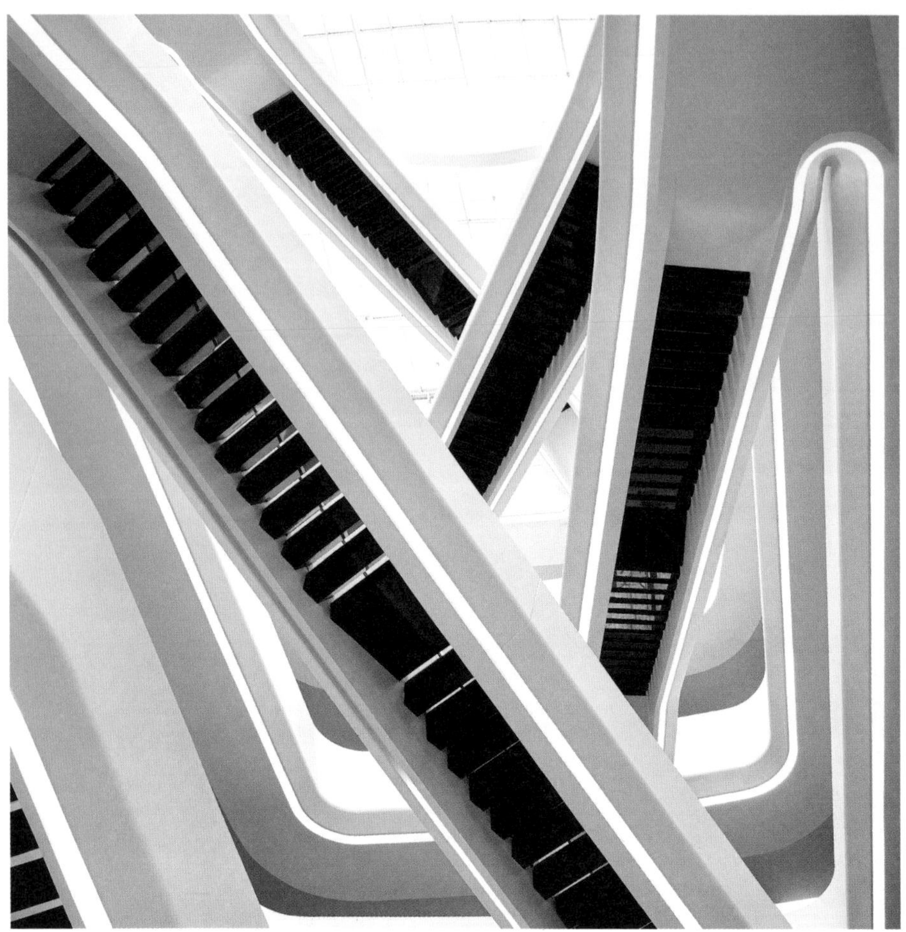

Dominion Office Building
Moscow, Russia
Architect: Zaha Hadid Architects, 2015

This stack of off-set white slabs jut and hover in what is at once an ordered yet seemingly precarious tower. This was one of the first projects in this industrial part of Moscow to be dedicated to the growing creative and IT sectors. The slabs are linked internally via interconnected staircases, designed to inspire connection and community.

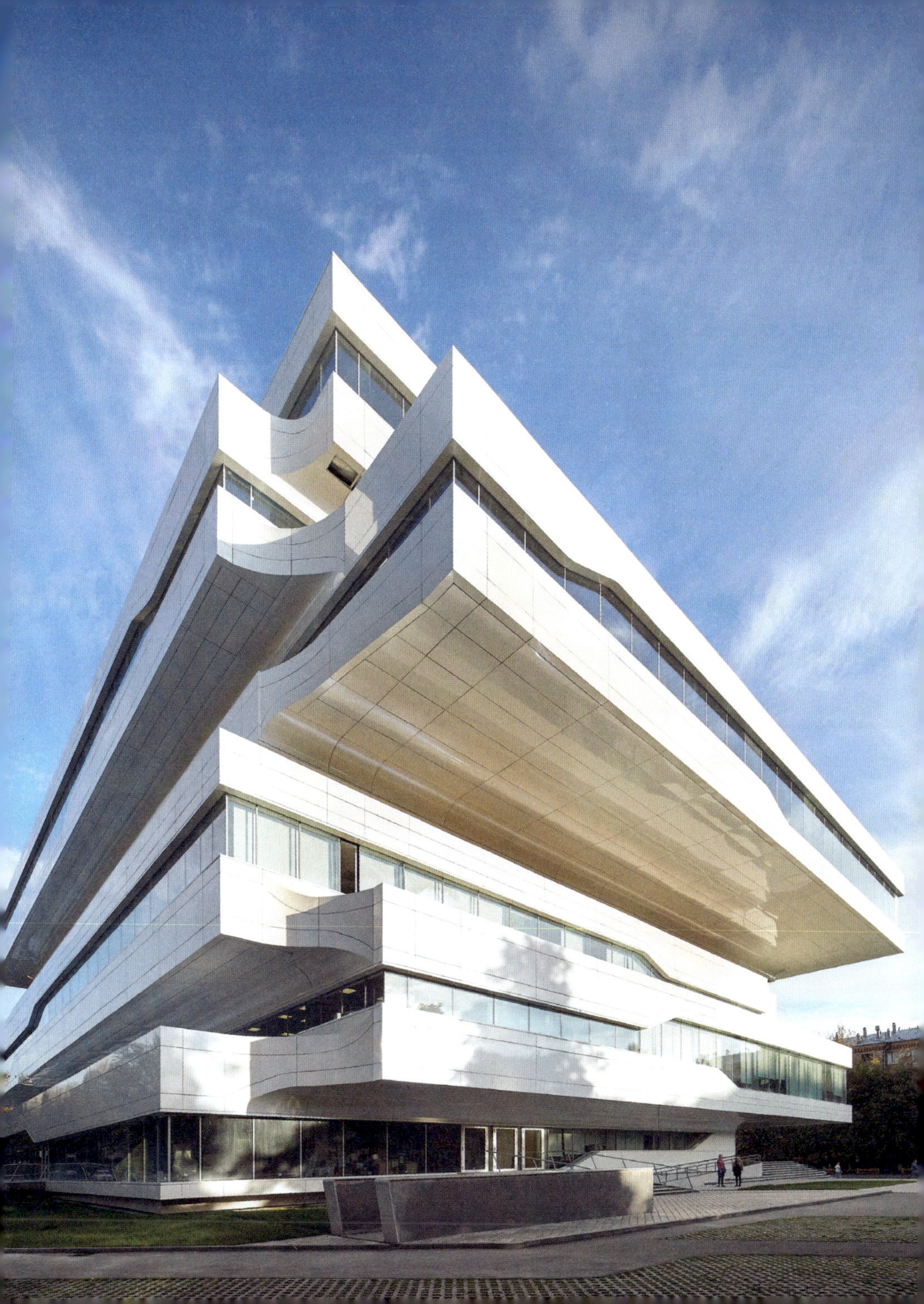

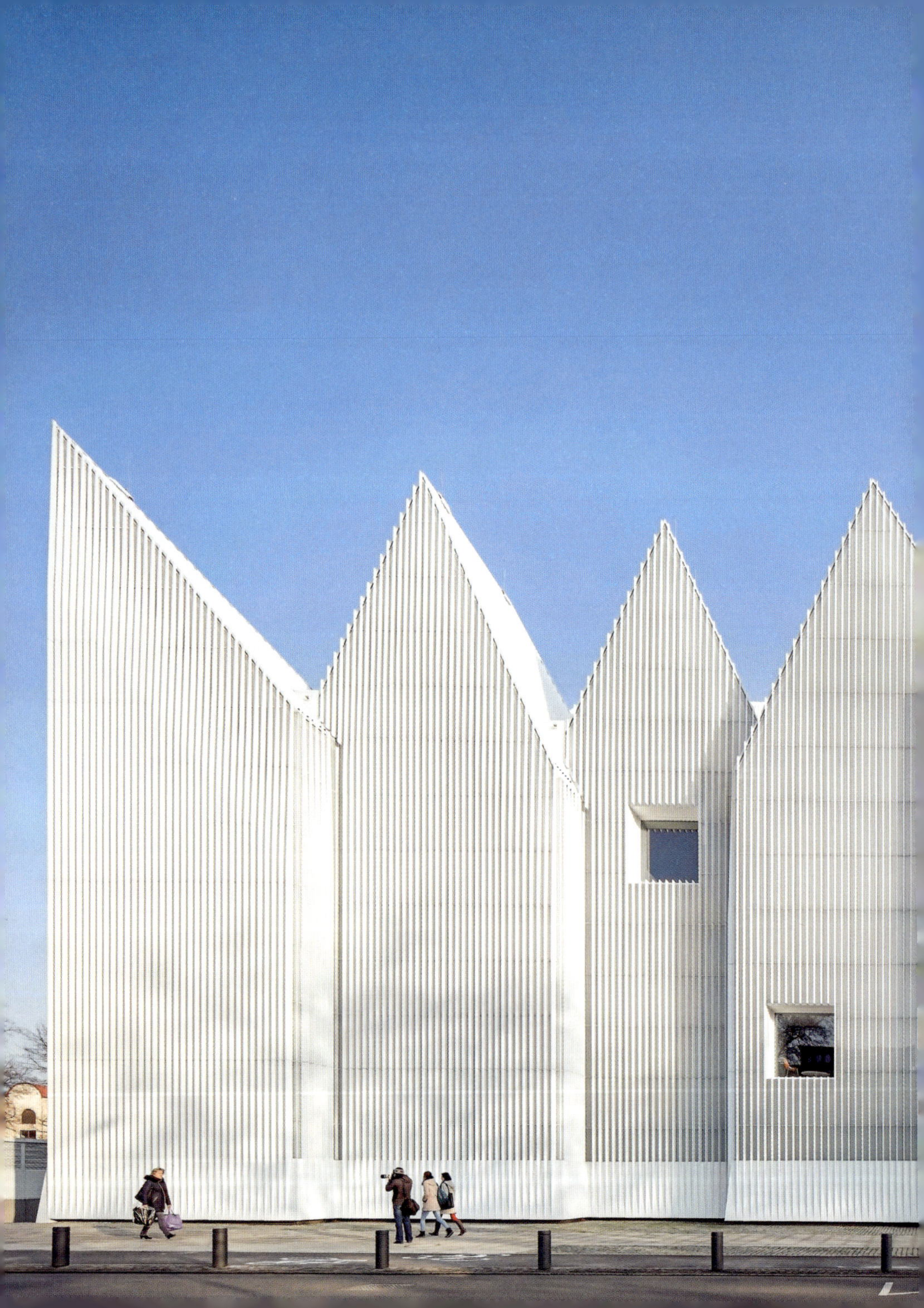

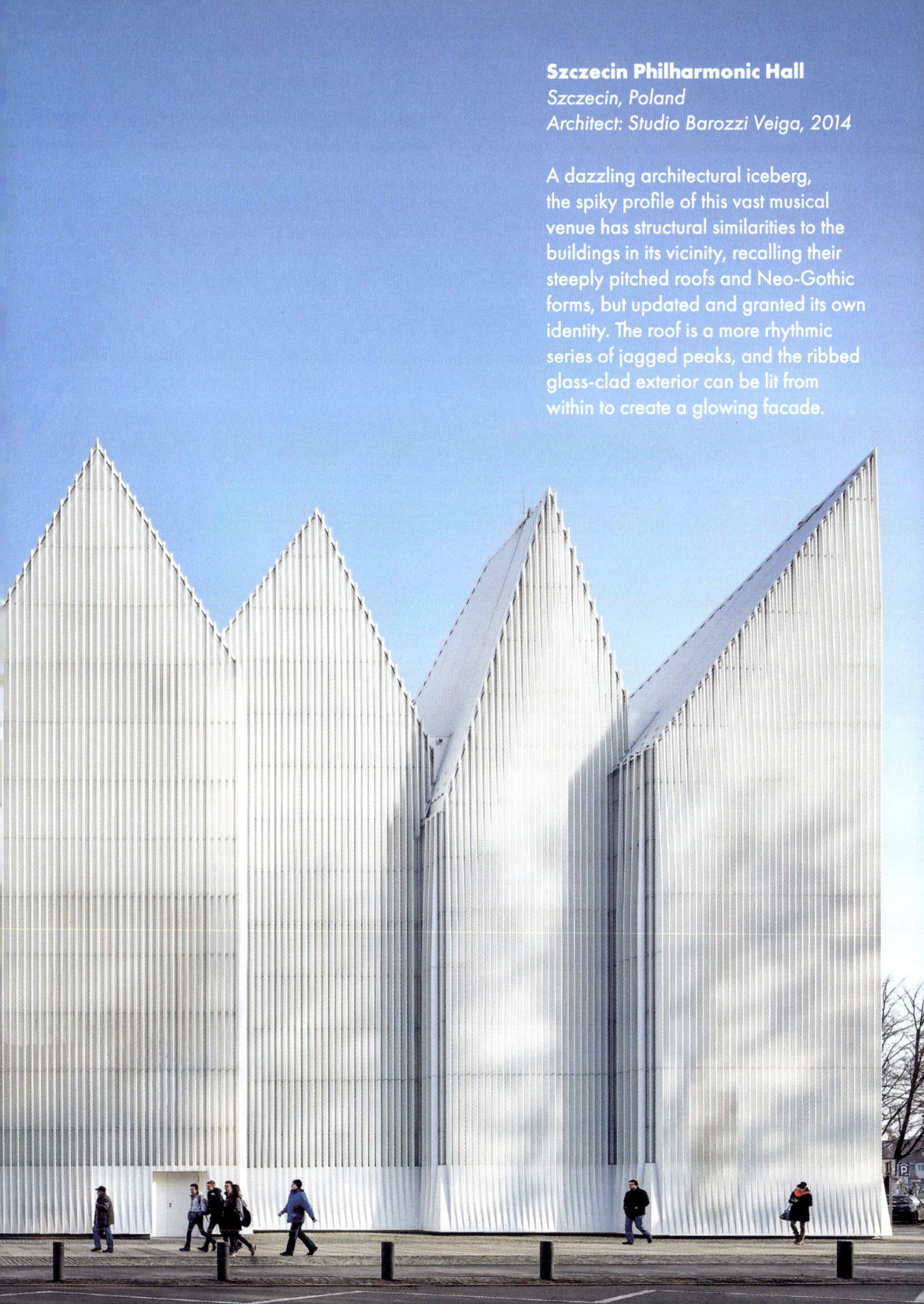

Szczecin Philharmonic Hall
Szczecin, Poland
Architect: Studio Barozzi Veiga, 2014

A dazzling architectural iceberg, the spiky profile of this vast musical venue has structural similarities to the buildings in its vicinity, recalling their steeply pitched roofs and Neo-Gothic forms, but updated and granted its own identity. The roof is a more rhythmic series of jagged peaks, and the ribbed glass-clad exterior can be lit from within to create a glowing facade.

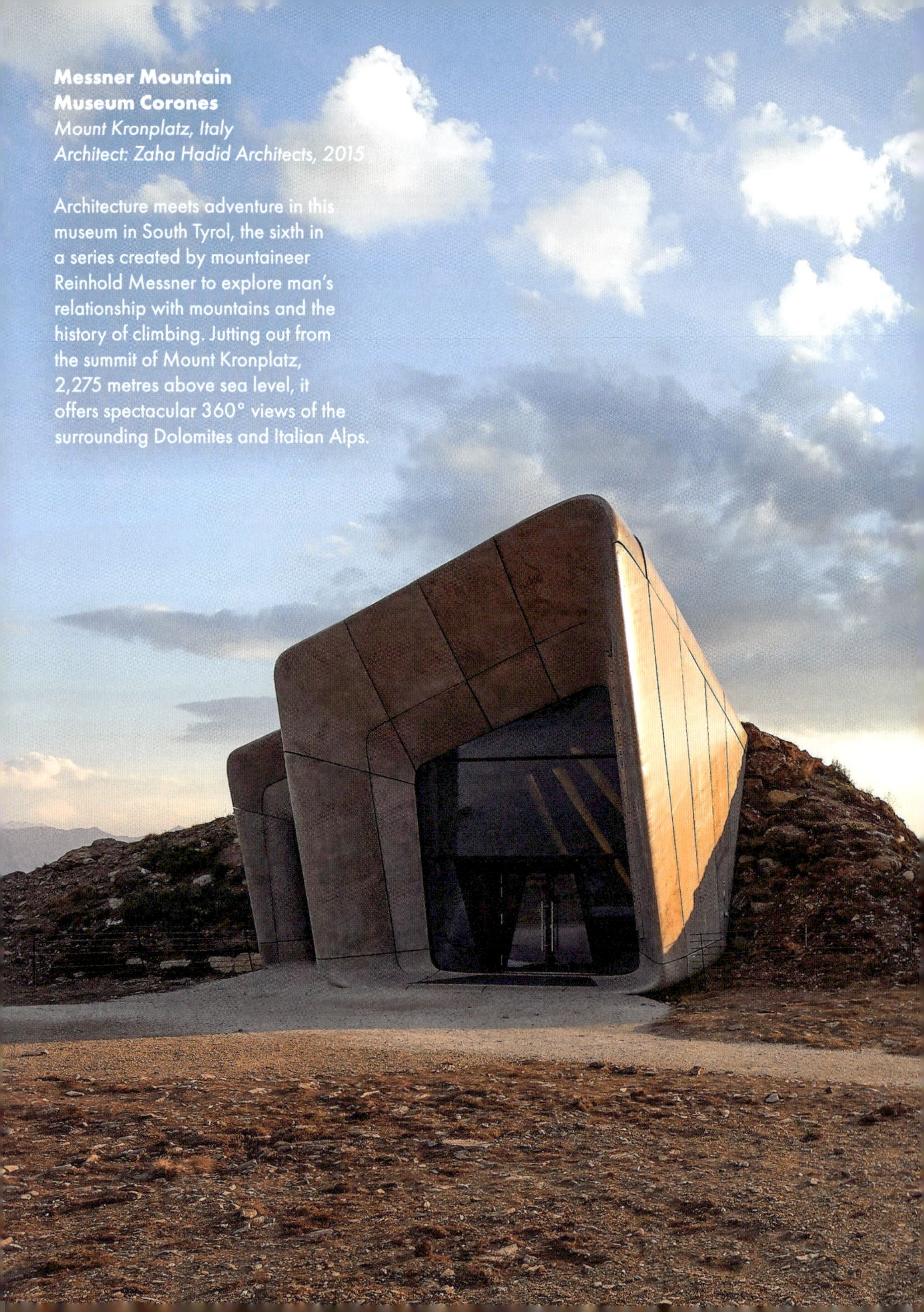

Messner Mountain Museum Corones
Mount Kronplatz, Italy
Architect: Zaha Hadid Architects, 2015

Architecture meets adventure in this museum in South Tyrol, the sixth in a series created by mountaineer Reinhold Messner to explore man's relationship with mountains and the history of climbing. Jutting out from the summit of Mount Kronplatz, 2,275 metres above sea level, it offers spectacular 360° views of the surrounding Dolomites and Italian Alps.

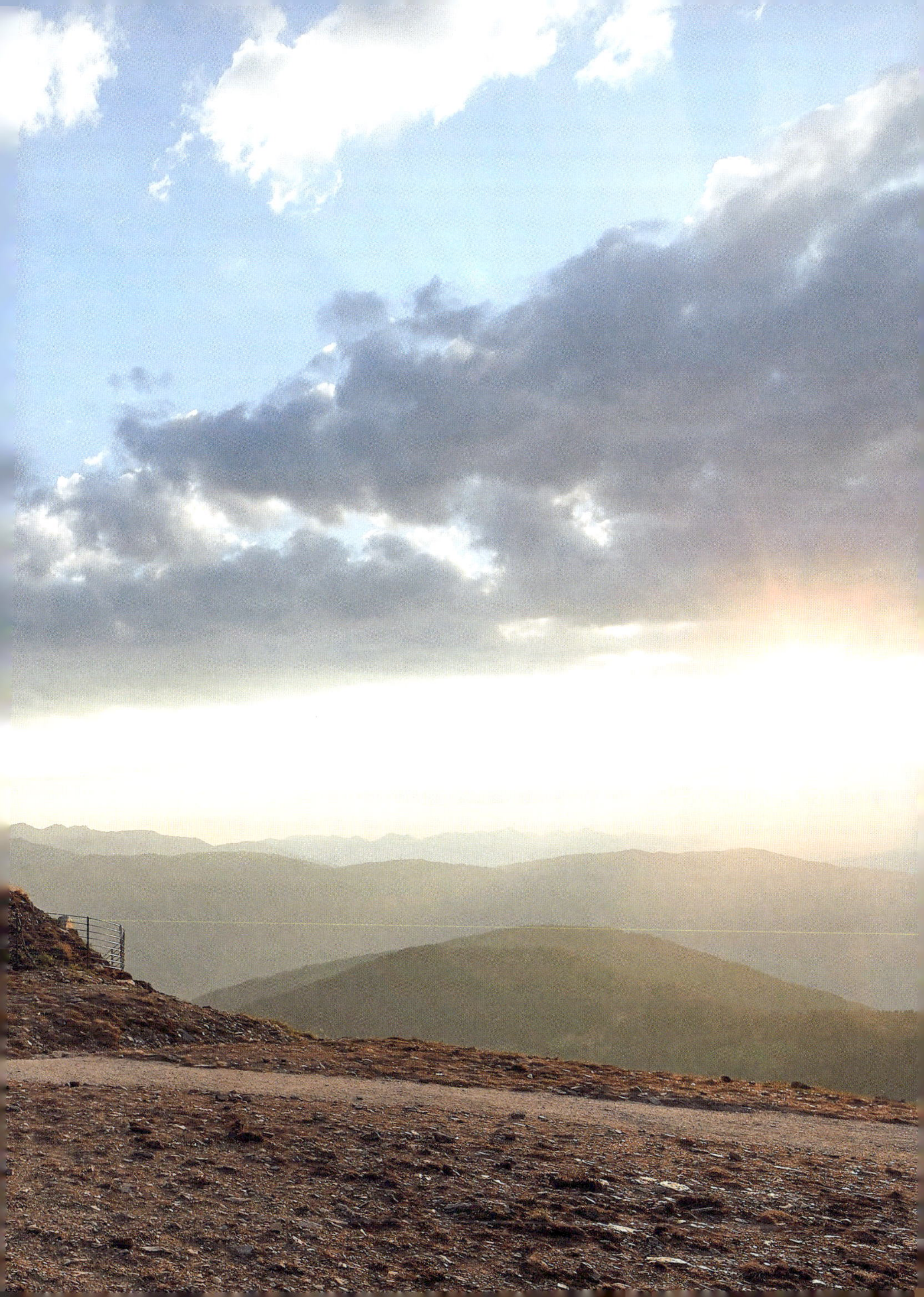

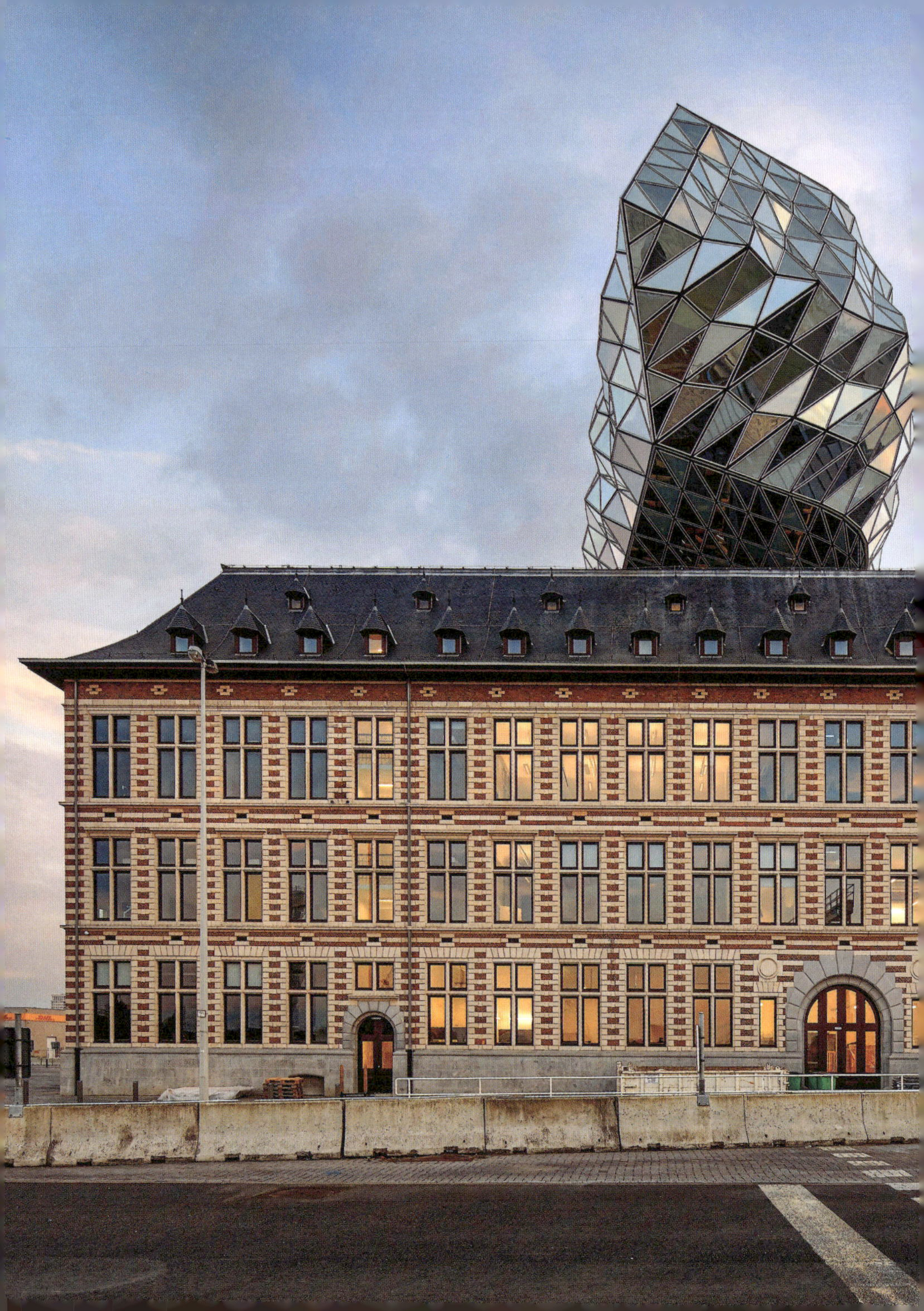

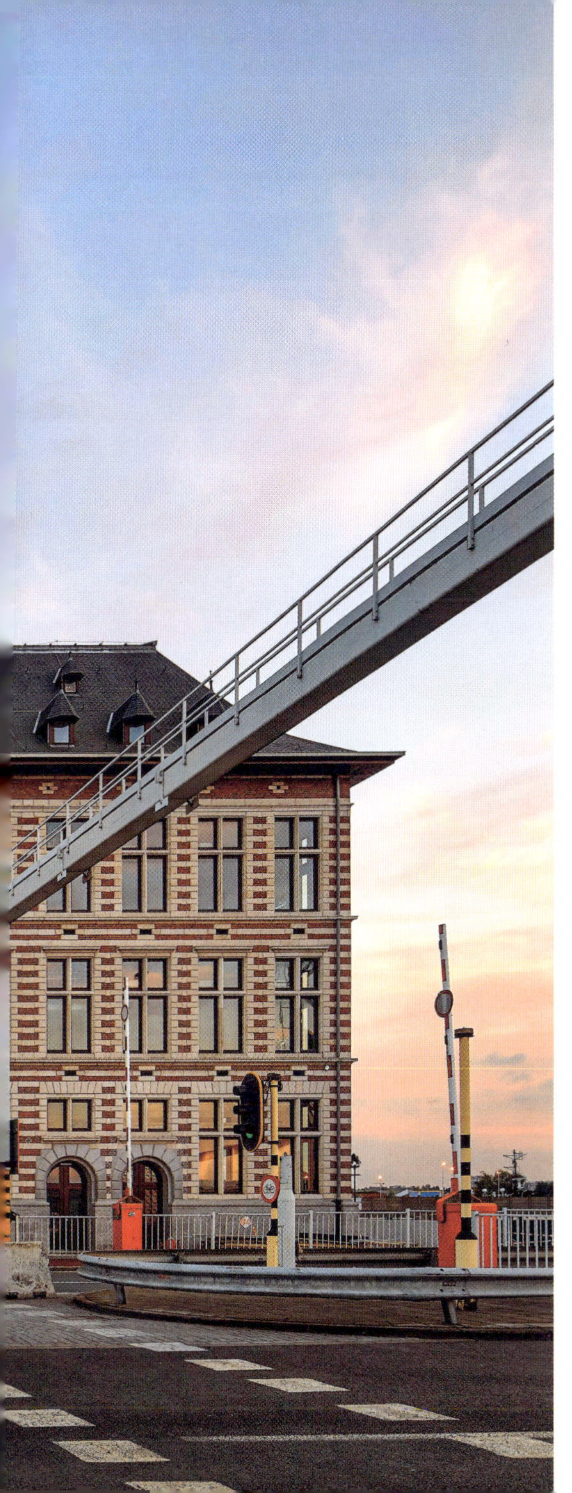

Port House

Antwerp, Belgium

Architect: Zaha Hadid Architects, 2016

Looking like a spaceship has docked on top of the old fire station, this ambitious design in Antwerp's docks placed a vast glass extension above the existing structure. Triangular glass panels – some transparent and some opaque to provide shade for the port staff within – have been arranged to create a flat surface at one end and a rippling wave-like texture at the other.

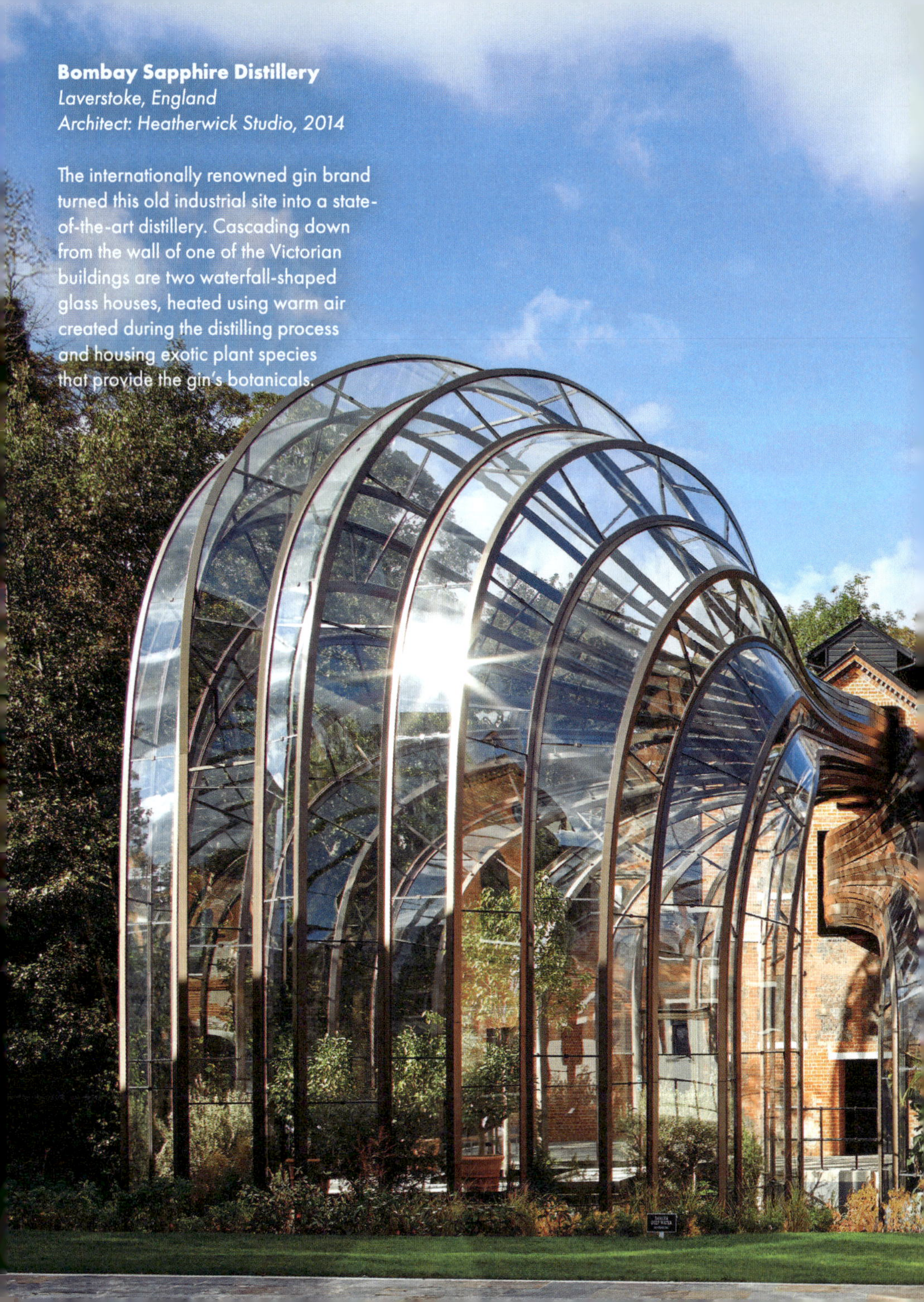

Bombay Sapphire Distillery
Laverstoke, England
Architect: Heatherwick Studio, 2014

The internationally renowned gin brand turned this old industrial site into a state-of-the-art distillery. Cascading down from the wall of one of the Victorian buildings are two waterfall-shaped glass houses, heated using warm air created during the distilling process and housing exotic plant species that provide the gin's botanicals.

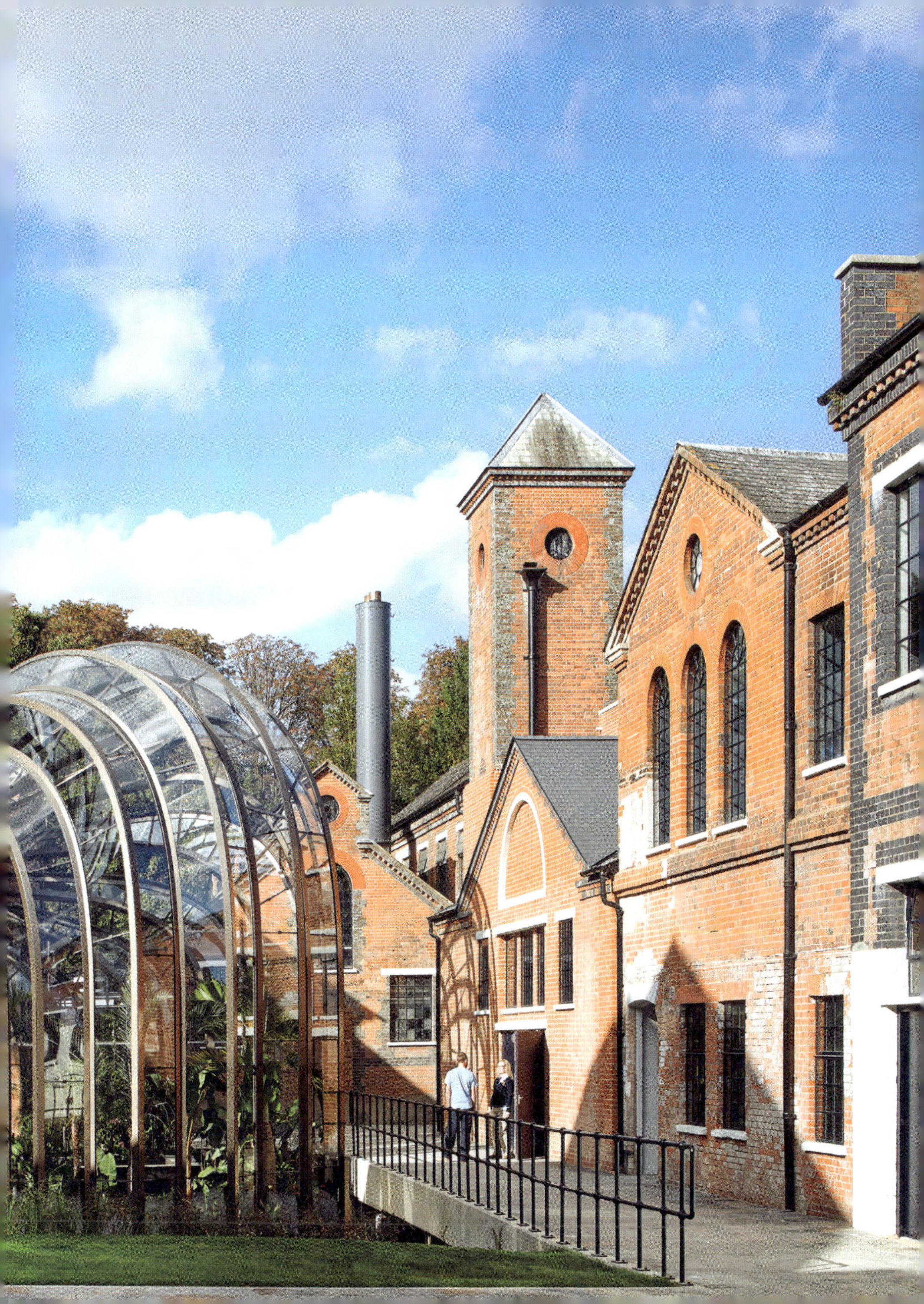

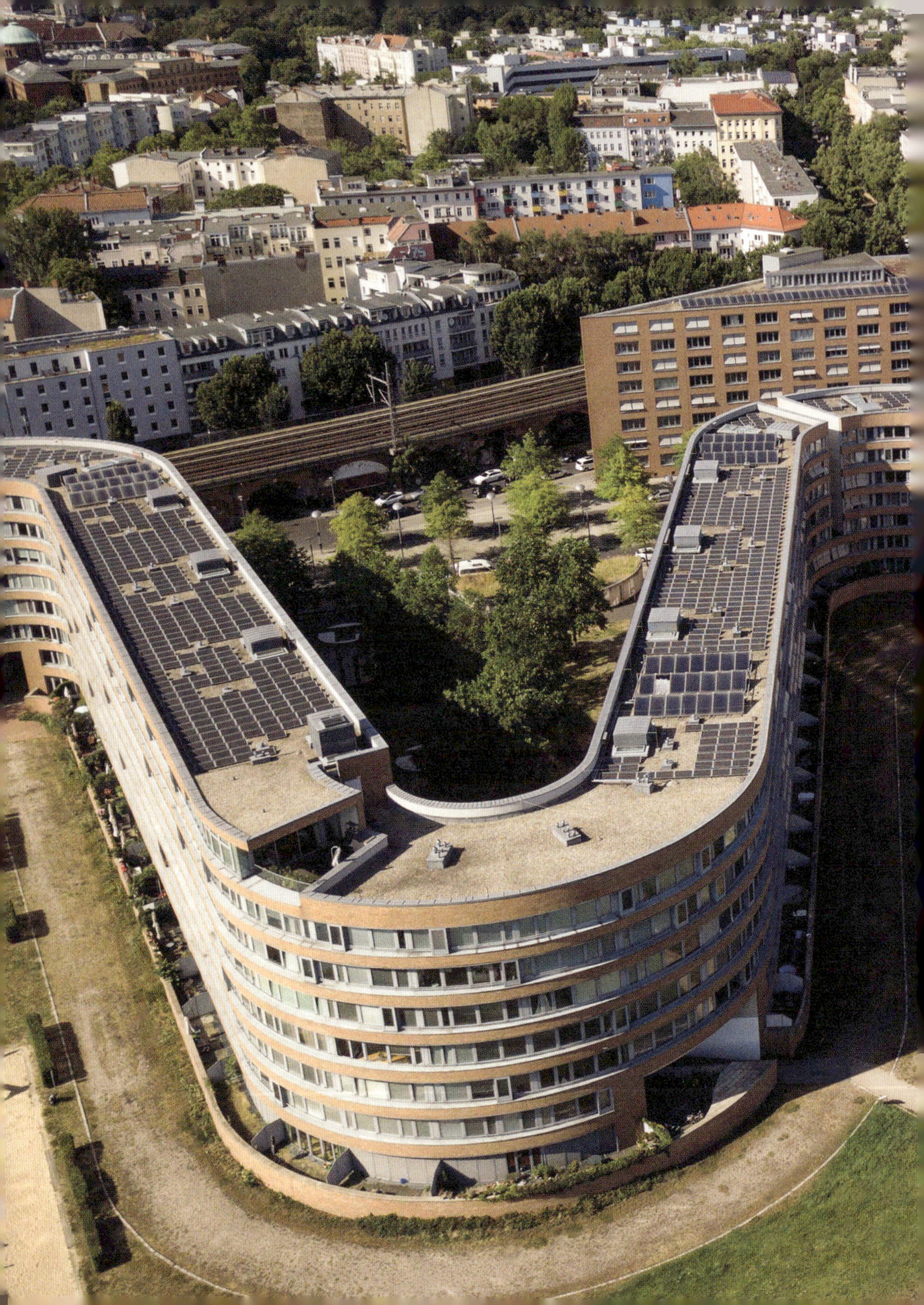

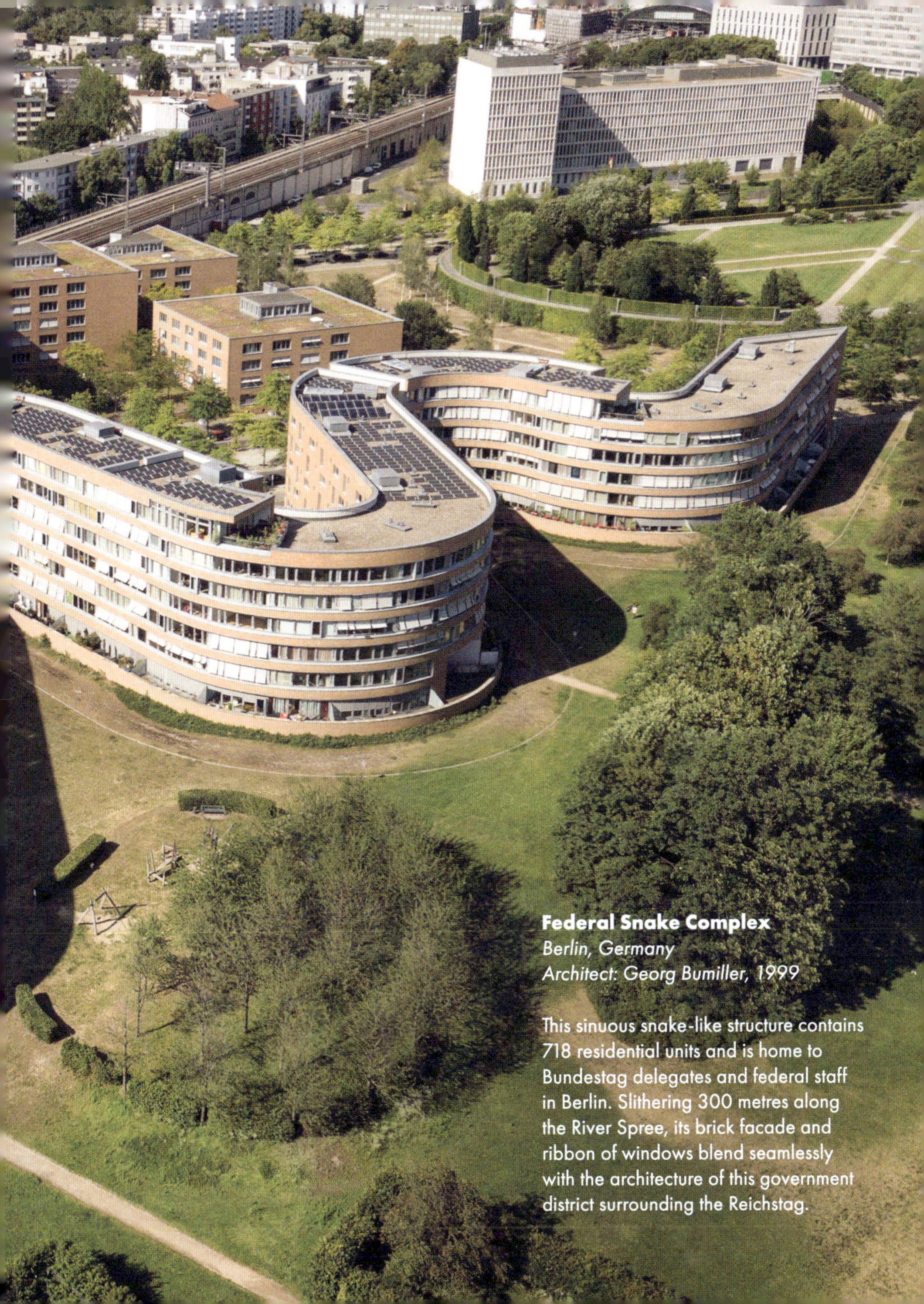

Federal Snake Complex
Berlin, Germany
Architect: Georg Bumiller, 1999

This sinuous snake-like structure contains 718 residential units and is home to Bundestag delegates and federal staff in Berlin. Slithering 300 metres along the River Spree, its brick facade and ribbon of windows blend seamlessly with the architecture of this government district surrounding the Reichstag.

Isle of Dogs Pumping Station
London, England
Architect: John Outram, 1988

Part of the regeneration of London Docklands, the most unusual thing about this building is its flamboyant design, given its mundane function of pumping run-off from rainwater around the city. The postmodern structure includes oversized columns resembling surreal trees and a central 'eye' that serves as an extractor fan.

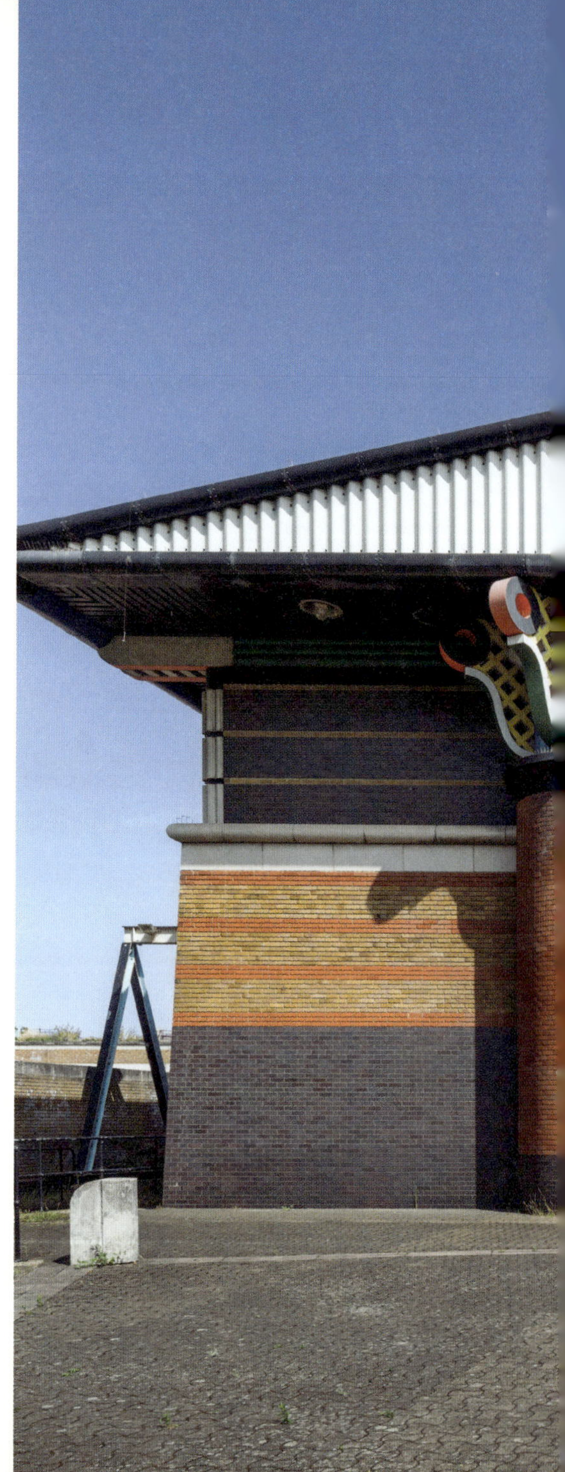

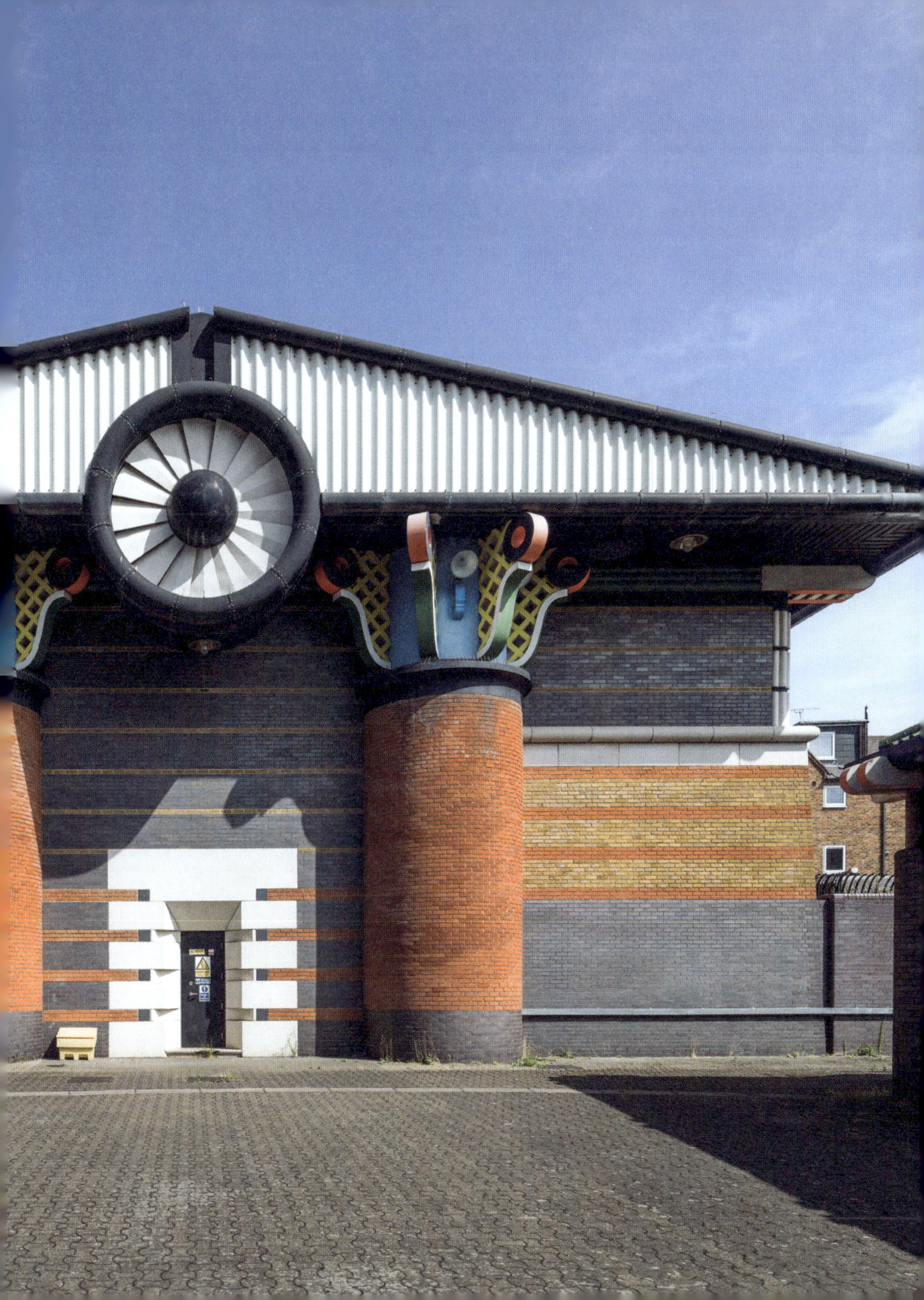

Image Credits

Front cover image: Gehry Las Vegas by Monster4711 (https://commons.wikimedia.org/wiki/File:Gehry_Las_Vegas.jpg), modified by Hoxton Mini Press (upscaled, colour-adjusted, cropped, and text overlaid), licensed under CC BY-SA 3.0 (https://creativecommons.org/licenses/by-sa/3.0/). Modified version also licensed under CC BY-SA 3.0. Back cover images: (Top left) Inntel Hotel, Zaandam, Netherlands © Alexey Komissarov (Top right) The Steel House, Lake Ransom Canyon, Texas, USA © Jerry Cotten (Bottom left) Guangzhou Circle, Guangzhou, China © Jason Yuen (Bottom right) The Imprint, Incheon, South Korea © Jet Dela Cruz. p.4 © Edmund Sumner – VIEW / alamy; p.5 © Ogulcan Ercal; p.6 © Hufton+Crow – VIEW / alamy; p.7 © frantic / alamy; p.8 © Jason Yuen; p.9 © Colin Sickler p.13 © Lynn Hilton; p.15 © Pixelbiss / Alamy; p.17 © Marc-Philipp Keller / Alamy; p.18 © Paul Brady / Alamy; p.19 © Jon Bilous / Alamy; p.20 © Scott Hargis; p.21 © Scott Hargis; p.22 © Jenny Lewis; p.24 © Edmund Sumner-VIEW / Alamy; p.26 © Eliane Haykal / Alamy; p.28 © Jerry Cotton; p.31 © architecture UK / Alamy; p.32 © Jean-Christophe Verhaegen; p.34 © John Dambik / Alamy; p.35 © Wirestock | Dreamstime.com; p.36 © Santi Rodriguez / Alamy; p.37 © Ben Morris; p.39 © Roger Garfield / Alamy; p.41 © Aleksandar Tomic / Alamy; p.42 © Jonathan Nelson / Alamy; p.45 © Lillian Tveit / Alamy; p.46 © dpa picture alliance / Alamy; p.49 © 2024 HornyHamster/Shutterstock; p.50 © Shawn.ccf / Alamy; p.52 © Scott Kemper / Alamy; p.53 © Zoonar GmbH / Alamy; p.54 © Mahabaleshwara L / Alamy; p.55 © Mahabaleshwara L / Alamy; p.57 © Arcaid Images / Alamy; p.58 © Ngbichhoan89 / Dreamstime; p.59 © Lex Lim / Alamy; p.60 © aerial-photos.com / Alamy; p.62 © Thomas De Wever; p.63 © Drew Buckley / Alamy; p.65 © Mike Fuchslocher / Alamy; p.67 © 2019 Nbeaw/Shutterstock; p.69 © Denys Nevozhai; p.70 © Hufton+Crow-VIEW / Alamy; p.71 © Hufton+Crow-VIEW / Alamy; p.73 © James Freeman / Alamy; p.75 © Prisma by Dukas Presseagentur GmbH / Alamy; p.76 © AndreaAstes; p.77 © Hufton+Crow-VIEW / Alamy; p.79 © Holger Woizick; p.81 © Jeremy Horner / Alamy; p.82 © Andre Jenny / Alamy; p.83 © Franck Fotos / Alamy; p.84 © Richard Cummins / Alamy; p.85 © Randy Duchaine / Alamy; p.86 © Maremagnum; p.88 © Image Professionals GmbH / Alamy; p.89 © Image Professionals GmbH / Alamy; p.91 © chuck / Alamy; p.92 © Hufton+Crow VIEW / Alamy; p.93 © Hufton+Crow-VIEW / Alamy; p.94 © Dudlajzov | Dreamstime.com; p.96 © Nicholas Klein / Alamy; p.99 © Robert Harding; p.100 © imageBROKER.com / Alamy; p.101 © Lucas Vallecillos / Alamy; p.102 © REDA; p.104-107 © Ossip van Duivenbode; p.109 © Jet Dela Cruz; p.110 © Ossip van Duivenbode; p.112 © David Clapp; p.113 © David Clapp; p.114 © Bardhok Ndoji / Alamy; p.116 © Yunus Tug; p.119 © Arcaid Images / Alamy; p.120 © Greg Balfour Evans / Alamy; p.122 © Mark Kiver / Alamy; p.123 © Ilene MacDonald / Alamy; p.125 © Marcelo Nacinovic; p.127 © Nathan Willock-VIEW / Alamy; p.128 © UniversalImagesGroup; p.130 © Sean Pavone / Alamy; p.133 © Taran Wilkhu; p.134 © Akimov Konstantin; p.137 © Sergey Dzyuba / Alamy; p.138 © ams images / Alamy; p.140 © Ambling Images / Alamy; p.143 © Jean-Baptiste Béranger, Solar Egg by Bigert & Bergström for Riksbyggen; p.144 © Mohammadreza Azali; p.146 © MDart / Alamy; p.148 © Geza Kurka / Alamy; p.151 © Panther Media GmbH / Alamy; p.152-154 © Finbarr Fallon; p.155 © Hemis / Alamy; p.156 © JOHN KELLERMAN / Alamy; p.158 © Phil Seale / Alamy; p.161 © Paul Williams; p.162 © Aerial Essex; p.164 © Zdenek Kajzr / Alamy; p.165 © Julian Castle / Alamy; p.167 © Jakub Tomasik; p.169 © Carlos Gilbert; p.170 © BERK OZDEMIR / Alamy; p.171 © BERK OZDEMIR / Alamy; p.172 © Finbarr Fallon; p.173 © Finbarr Fallon; p.175 © Tony Vingerhoets / Alamy; p.176 © Brian Overcast / Alamy; p.178 © Benoît Santiard; p.179 © Finbarr Fallon; p.181 © Olo Studio; p.182 © Olo Studio; p.183 © Olo Studio; p.184 © Carol Highsmith; p.186 © Patrik Bloudek; p.187 © Zoonar GmbH / Alamy; p.188 © travelstock44 / Alamy; p.190 © Sipa US / Alamy; p.192 © Steve Allen Travel Photography / Alamy; p.193 © dleiva / Alamy; p.195 © Pol Albarrán; p.196 © Nattee Chalermtiragool / Alamy; p.198 © Hufton+Crow-VIEW / Alamy; p.199 © Mickey Lee / Alamy; p.200 © Jesús Granada; p.202 © Filip Olejowski / Alamy; p.203 © Wiskerke / Alamy; p.204 © Rosemarie Mosteller / Alamy; p.205 © Wiskerke / Alamy; p.206 © Mark Green / Alamy; p.207 © Pavel Dudek / Alamy; p.209 © Hufton+Crow-VIEW / Alamy; p.210 © Hufton+Crow-VIEW / Alamy; p.212 © YAC srl; p.213 © YAC srl; p.215 © Hufton+Crow-VIEW / Alamy; p.216 © hans engbers / Alamy; p.218 © David Jamoner; p.221 © Hufton+Crow-VIEW / Alamy; p.222 © Finbarr Fallon; p.224-232 © Hufton+Crow-VIEW / Alamy; p.234 © Artur Voznenko; p.237 © Finbarr Fallon; p240 © Tahmineh Monzavi.

Weird Buildings
First edition, first printing

Published in 2025 by Hoxton Mini Press, London

Text by Imogen Fortes
Editing by Gaynor Sermon
Production design by Dom Grant
Production control by David Brimble
Proofreading by Kate Overy
Editorial support by Richard Enright and Flora MacKenzie

Thank you to all of the individuals and institutions who have provided images and arranged permissions. While every effort has been made to trace the present copyright holders we apologise in advance for any unintentional omission or error, and would be pleased to insert the appropriate acknowledgement in any subsequent edition.

A CIP catalogue record for this book is available from the British Library.

ISBN: 978-1-914314-89-6

Printed and bound by PNB, Latvia

Manufacturer: Hoxton Mini Press, 104 Northside Studios, 16-29 Andrews Road, London, E8 4QF, UK
www.hoxtonminipress.com

Represented by: Authorised Rep Compliance Ltd., Ground Floor, 71 Lower Baggot Street, Dublin, D02 P593, Ireland
www.arccompliance.com

Hoxton Mini Press is an environmentally conscious publisher, committed to offsetting our carbon footprint. This book is 100 per cent carbon compensated, with offset purchased from Stand For Trees.

Every time you order from our website, we plant a tree:
www.hoxtonminipress.com

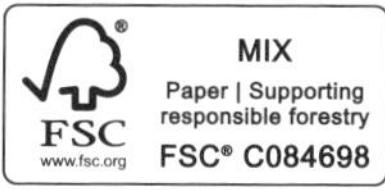

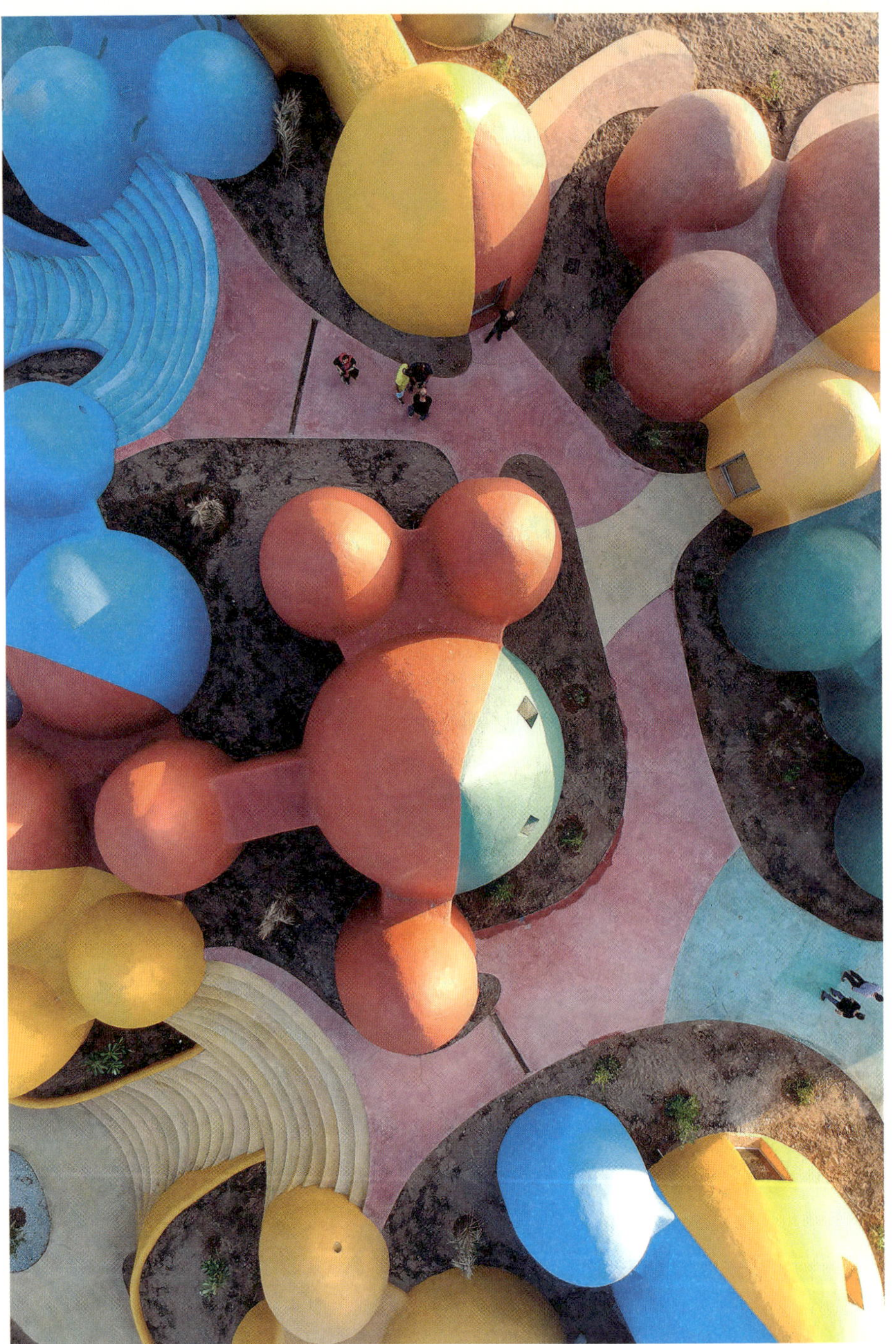